LIGHTNING OVER YEMEN

LIGHTNING OVER YEMEN

A HISTORY OF THE OTTOMAN CAMPAIGN (1569–71)

being a translation from the Arabic of Part III
of al-Barq al-Yamānī fī al-Fatḥ al-'Uthmānī
by
Quṭb al-Dīn al-Nahrawālī al-Makkī
as published by Ḥamad al-Jāsir
(Riyadh, 1967)

Translation, with
introduction and notes,
by *Clive K. Smith*

I.B.Tauris *Publishers*
LONDON · NEW YORK

Published in 2002 by I.B.Tauris & Co Ltd,
6 Salem Road, London W2 4BU
175 Fifth Avenue, New York NY 10010
www.ibtauris.com

In the United States of America and in Canada distributed by
St Martin's Press, 175 Fifth Avenue, New York NY 10010

The Library of Ottoman Studies: Volume 3

ISBN 1 86064 836 3

A full CIP record for this book is available from the British Library
A full CIP record for this book is available from the Library of Congress

Library of Congress catalog card: available

Set in Monotype Ehrhardt and Franklin Gothic Heavy by Ewan Smith, London
Printed and bound in Great Britain by MPG Books Ltd, Bodmin

CONTENTS

Illustrations viii
Acknowledgements ix
Glossary xi

Introduction 1

LIGHTNING OVER YEMEN 13

1 Sinān Pasha's appointment to lead the expeditionary force to Yemen, and his passage to Mecca 15
2 Sinān's journey from Mecca to Yemen 19
3 Sinān's arrival at and activity in Jīzān 20
4 Sinān's journey from Jīzān to Ta'izz 21
5 Sinān's directions concerning the battle at al-Aghbar, near Ta'izz, against Zaydī forces 23
6 The Zaydī defeat at al-Aghbar 24
7 The surrender of al-Qāhirah, citadel to Ta'izz 26
8 Turkish preparations for the assault on Aden 30
9 Sinān's consultations concerning the journey northwards 31
10 'Uthmān Pasha's refusal to attend Sinān for consultations 32
11 'Uthmān Pasha's dismissal and arrival at Mecca 34
12 Sinān Pasha's deliberations over the choice of route to Dhū Jiblah 39
13 The conquest of Aden 41
14 Sinān's appointment of his nephew as governor in Aden 44
15 The journey to Masjid al-Qā'ah, on the Maytam route 45
16 The journey to Wadi Maytam 48
17 The battle of Maytam, and the completion of the journey to Dhū Jiblah 50
18 The capture of the strongholds of al-Ta'kar and Baḥrānah 53
19 The Dā'ī 'Abdullāh's capture of the strongholds of Khadid and al-Ḥubaysh 55
20 Sinān Pasha's conquest of Ibb and Shamāḥī stronghold in Ba'dān; flight of the Zaydī commanders, Muḥammad b. Shams al-Dīn and 'Alī b. Shuway' 57

21 Rewards for the Turkish troops and reflections on the Yemeni budget and the Zaydī leader, Muṭahhar 61
22 Sinān's dispositions concerning Ḥabb castle in Ba'dān 63
23 Sinān's journey over the Samārah pass to Yarīm and Dhamār 64
24 Sinān's journey via Dhirā' al-Kalb to Ṣan'ā' 65
25 Engagement with Qaṭrān and capture of Khawlān stronghold 67
26 Ḥasan Pasha's raids into Wadi al-Sirr for plunder 69
27 Sinān's journey to Shibām; its capture and the release of prisoners from al-'Āriḍah 70
28 The transfer of Sinān's base to the plain below Kawkabān and Thulā, and the departure of the Dā'ī 'Abdullāh to collect reinforcements 72
29 The Dā'ī Ṣalāḥ's raids into Wadi Bawn 74
30 Skirmishes between Turkish and Zaydī forces 75
31 The massacre of Janissaries and the dispatch of Ḥasan Pasha to retrieve the Dā'ī 'Abdullāh 76
32 Sinān's reconnaissance of Kawkabān and attacks by Muṭahhar 78
33 Sinān's customary visits to Kawkabān escarpment and the defeat of a Zaydī attack on his camp 80
34 Muṭahhar's attack on Sinān's camp, with the death of his son, al-Hādī 82
35 Sinān's capture of Ḥabb al-'Arūs stronghold and a further unsuccessful attack on his base by Muṭahhar 84
36 Two unsuccessful attempts by Sinān to capture the stronghold of Bayt 'Izz, and news of success in Wadi Khubān 88
37 The Dā'ī 'Abdullāh's campaign in al-Ḥaymah, Ḥarāz and Sāri' 92
38 The submission of Mt Tays district and Ḥasan Pasha's movements 95
39 Ḥasan Pasha's engagement with Zaydī leaders in the ranges west of Kawkabān and the Dā'ī 'Abdullāh's capture of Mt Siwwān 97
40 Turkish success in climbing the Mt Ḍula' escarpment and capturing two key forts thereon; flight of Muḥammad b. Shams al-Dīn and other Zaydī leaders 102
41 Ḥasan Pasha's assignment to lay siege to Kawkabān; capture of Shamāt stronghold and the release of prisoners in Kawkabān 105
42 Move of the minister's camp next to Kawkabān and the surrender and destruction of various strongholds 108
43 Death of the Zaydī General Abū Dāwūd in an engagement near Thulā 113
44 Death of Muḥammad b. Shams al-Dīn's twin brother and other Zaydī leaders, and the submission to the sultan's authority of an important sharīf from the Jawf 115
45 Turkish criticism of Muṭahhar and his invitation to people in the Jawf and Ṣa'dah. Their failure to appear on the battle field 118

46 A comparison of numbers of Turkish and Zaydī forces in the field. Two unsuccessful Zaydī attacks 122
47 Battle near Ḥaḍūr al-Shaykh resulting in Zaydī defeat but with loss of senior officers on both sides 126
48 Muṭahhar's successful call to renewed rebellion after advice from the Prophet Muḥammad in a dream; the story of pre-Islamic Ṭasm and Jadīs 130
49 Widespread rebellion from tribesmen near Ṣan'ā' southwards to Ta'izz, in which Qaṭrān and 'Alī b. Nushayr were prominent 135
50 Near outbreak of revolt in Ṣan'ā' 139
51 Crisis over Turkish military funds; Turkish military numbers; deaths of Qaṭrān and 'Alī b. Nushayr in engagement at Mt al-Lawz 141
52 Change of governors in Ta'izz; deterioration of situation in Dhamār and catastrophic losses in Turkish besieging force at Ḥabb castle at the hands of 'Alī b. Sharaf al-Dīn, following the widespread, renewed rebellion 146
53 Sinān Pasha's attention to the widespread disorder through dispatch of key Turkish officers to Aden, Ta'izz and Samārah; appalling condition of Egyptian reinforcements in Zabīd, dispatched from Cairo; defeat of large Zaydī force at Samārah 151
54 The rebuilding of Shamāt stronghold for strategic reasons and the murder of its Turkish commander 155
55 Attempts to cross the ditch/chasm protecting Kawkabān; deliberations and correspondence leading to the request for peace terms over the siege of Kawkabān from Muḥammad b. Shams al-Dīn, and the arrival of the Zaydī delegation at Sinān's camp; details of the terms agreed 157
56 Muṭahhar's request for peace terms, and Sinān's agreement to them 167
57 Sinān Pasha's return to Ṣan'ā'; the arrival in Zabīd of the new governor-general, Behrām Pasha; inconclusive fighting between the latter and the Zaydī in the area of Naqīl Aḥmar 171
58 The assistance given to Behrām Pasha, and the defeat of the Zaydī and collection of hostages 174
59 Behrām Pasha's concentration on the siege of 'Alī b. Sharaf al-Dīn at Ḥabb castle; Sinān's move to Dhamār, and 'Alī b. Sharaf al-Dīn's death at Ḥabb; Sinān's settlement with Muṭahhar 176
60 Sinān Pasha's transfer of the government of Yemen to Behrām Pasha; Sinān's journey to Mecca; his reception there and his performance of the pilgrimage before leaving for Medina and Cairo 181

Notes 193
Bibliography 219
Index 222

ILLUSTRATIONS

Maps

1 Route followed by Sinān Pasha during the campaign against Muṭahhar b. Sharaf al-Dīn 5

2 Leading commanders and forts at time of the battle before Jabal al-Aghbar 7

3 Commanders, forts and features relevant to the siege of Kawkabān 8

Fort Plans

1 The stronghold of al-Taʿkar 49

2 The stronghold of al-ʿArūs 85

3 The stronghold of Ḥaḍūr al-Shaykh 127

ACKNOWLEDGEMENTS

§ A project of this nature could not have been undertaken without considerable help; and I am heavily indebted to a number of people.

Professor Rex Smith has encouraged me from the beginning and latterly has read through both translation and notes and made a number of helpful amendments and suggestions. Professor Osman Sid Ahmed Isma'il al Billi, whom I was fortunate to get to know in the Sudan in the early 1980s when he was Minister of Education, has undertaken the laborious task of studying the first draft of the translation and made a large number of corrections and suggestions; and I am also heavily indebted to Mohamed Nāṣir al-Maḥrūqī from Oman who, over a long period of time, while engaged on his PhD research, has helped me in the understanding of the Arabic for the first draft. And I am most grateful to John Evans, ODA Survey adviser in Yemen from 1981 to 1989, for his painstaking and imaginative creation of the three maps which illustrate the campaign.

Many others have generously given their time and help in a variety of ways for which I am deeply grateful: Peter Barber and staff of the British Library, Peter Colvin and staff of the School of Oriental and African Studies Library, Pierre Yves Crozet, Russell Fox of the Ordnance Survey, Southampton, Nicholas Hall of the Royal Armouries at Fort Nelson, Karen Hearn of Tate Britain, Charles Newton of the Victoria and Albert Museum, Dr Eric Olijdam, Carl Phillips, Alexandra Porter who computerised the fort plans, Thom Richardson of the Royal Armouries at Leeds, Dr Muḥammad Thunayyān, Dr 'Abdullāh al-Udharī and Ken Walton.

I must also express my debt to the late Sa'udi Arabian scholar, Ḥamad al-Jāsir, whose published text of *al-Baraq* I have used; to the publisher John Murray, for suggesting I contact Iradj Bagherzade of I.B.Tauris who then, with great patience, translated his initial interest in the project into a practical proposition; and to his editor, Turi Munthe, for his help and encouragement along the way.

Finally, there are two vital acknowledgements I should express, to Alistair Duncan for part sponsorship of the work through the Altajir World of Islam Trust, and to my wife Ann for allowing me the space to feed the mini-obsession that has consumed me over the last three years!

Note on Illustrations

Jacket illustration: A Janissary (hand-coloured woodcut by Jost Amman) and the first image of the colour plate-section reproduced by courtesy of the Victoria and Albert Museum, London. All other internal illustrations are photographs taken by the author except the following: numbers 1–14 of the black and white plate-section, number 2 of the colour plate-section and the illustrations at the beginning and the end of the translation which are reproduced by courtesy of the British Library, London.

GLOSSARY

Āghā	regimental commander
Aḥāmīs	those whose mothers come from the Prophet's tribe of Quraysh
'Āqil	headman
'Arabāt	(s. *'arabah*) wagons
Ashrāf	descendants of the Prophet
'Āshūrā'	voluntary fast day on 10 Muḥarram for Sunnī Muslims; and day of mourning for Shi'ites
'Atharah	favour
Būlukyāt	cavalry attached to the Janissaries
Burj	(pl. *abrāj*) tower or constellation
Chavūs	Turkish for *jāwīshiyyah*, the elite corps of pursuivants
Dā'ī	(pl. *du'āh*) missionary or propagandist, here used of the Ismā'īlī. The plural can be used to include members of the sect, and is not restricted to its leaders
Ḍarbuzān	culverin gun
Da'wah	mission, here used of the Ismā'īlī
Devshirme	periodic levy of Christian children for official and military Ottoman service
Dirham	(pl. *darāhim*) silver coin
Dīwān	office or council
Dizdār	captain of the guard, or constable
Faqīh	expert in *fiqh* or jurisprudence
Ḥadīth	tradition concerning the Prophet Muḥammad
Ḥamal	kid
Ḥawḍ	the Prophet's pool, for drinking on Judgment Day
'Īd al-Aḍḥā	feast of the Sacrifice
Iḥrām	ritual pilgrimage clothing
Īwān	recessed area, or arch-like enclosure
Jāwīsh	a member of the elite corps of pursuivants
Jāwīshiyyah	the elite corps of pursuivants
Jihād	holy war

Kāshif	(pl. *kushshāf*) tax collector
Kawrkajiyyah	galleys
Kawthar	river in Paradise
Kedkhudā	steward or senior officer
Kharaj	land tax
Khunkyār	sovereign khan or ruler
Khuṭbah	sermon delivered in the mosque on Fridays or important occasions
Lālā	tutor or nurse
Levend	privateer or mercenary sailor
Madhhab	one of the four schools of orthodox Islam
al-Madhhab al khāmis	the fifth school of orthodox Islam, referring to the Zaydī
Madrasah	teaching mosque
Maghrib	evening
Maḥmal	ceremonial, camel-borne Islamic litter for the pilgrimage
Muḥallaq	a unit of currency or bale
Mühimme	important document
Mutafarriqah	an elite military corps
Nafṭ	used here as form of Greek fire
Nāḥiyah	(pl. *nawāḥī*) administrative sub-district
Naqārah	Persian term for drum
Naqīl	pass
Qaḍā'	administrative district
Qā'id	high-ranking officer
Qanṭar	a varying weight of 100 *ratl* or pounds
Qarāwul	see note 27 to Chapters 39–44
Qaṣabah	fort or stronghold
Rakūb	mounted section
Rand	sweet bay, victor's laurel
Rumāh	(s. *rāmī*) shooters, of arrows or of shot
Rūmī	Turk from Anatolia
al-Sabā	the eastern wind
Saj'	rhymed prose
Sanjak	standard or flag, hence district and district governor
Sa'y	ritual course during pilgrimage, involving running
Serāser	silk tissue, popular with Ottomans in sixteenth century
Shaflūt	(pl. *shafālīt*) mountain tribesman enrolled with Turks
Shayb	probably new luxury material called *shahbenek*
Shīḥ	wormwood

Simāk	shoulders
Sinān	spear head
Sirdār	commander-in-chief
Sulṭānī	unit of currency equivalent to Venetian ducat
Taḥallul	sign or indication of completing the pilgrimage
Tashrīq	three days of celebration after ʻīd al-Aḍḥā
Ṭawāf	circumambulation of Kaʻba at Mecca
Tays	billy goat
Ṭughrā'	sultanic monogram incorporating signature and other symbols
ʻUmrah	lesser pilgrimage
ʻUthmānī	unit of currency
ʻUzlah	administrative district smaller than *nāḥiyah*
Waqfah	the religious stand at Mt ʻArafāt
Zand	device for kindling fire
Zarbāf	gold velvet
Zurdakhānah	weaponry or armoury

The culinary delights mentioned in Chapter 60 are not included in the glossary.

TO OSMAN AND REX,
without whom this translation would
not have emerged

Published with the kind assistance of
the Altajir World of Islam Trust

INTRODUCTION

§ The magnificent mountain scenery, stretching like a spine down the back of the country, never fails to impress visitors to the Yemen. In its southern section, south of the Samārah pass, the mountains enjoy the full force of the monsoon rains and are blessed with fertile and well-watered land for agriculture. Further north, the rainfall is more erratic and the tribesmen rely more heavily upon the methods of water conservation and terracing they established in early times.

A visitor also cannot fail to notice the castles and towers that seem to crown every mountain and form a complex pattern of defence throughout the country. As early as the tenth century of our era, a versatile and prolific Yemeni scholar, al Ḥasan al-Hamdānī, in a work called the Iklīl, produced an account of the ruins in Yemen which he had visited. One of its two surviving books has been translated into English by Nabih Faris and contains most interesting descriptions of some of these castles, many of which date from pre-Islamic times.

Other invaders had, of course, come to Yemen before the Turks, not least the Ayyubids, a dynasty from Syria to which the illustrious Saladin belonged; his elder brother was to conquer Yemen in the twelfth century. All such invaders were to find that, without the possession of such castles, they could not claim to occupy their territory, and that some at least were unconquerable by force alone; and the Turkish minister, Sinān Pasha, sent in 1569 to retrieve the province for the Turks, despite the awe-inspiring weaponry of the Ottoman state at his disposal, was to prove no exception.

Throughout its history, foreign powers had become involved in Yemen for reasons of strategy, riches, trade, religion and even *lebensraum*. In the case of the Ottoman Turks, such involvement had been inherited from the Mamluk state after Cairo fell to them in 1517. For they had two fundamental interests to safeguard: the Holy Cities of Mecca and Medina and the trade route with India in spices and textiles, both of which had been threatened and the latter virtually eclipsed by the arrival of the Portuguese in the

Indian Ocean and the Red Sea in the early part of the century. Such preoccupations were reinforced by reports from reliable sources of the potential riches of a country that had sustained such powerful earlier dynasties as the Rasulids and Tahirids.

For a brief period, the long effort and expense which even a degree of control over the country had cost the Turks may have seemed worthwhile; for, in the early 1560s, the country did pay its way and spices were being sold in Egypt at a profit to the Ottoman state. Indeed, one successful candidate for the governor-generalship of the country is said to have paid a vast sum in bribes for the post. But this happy period for the Turks had only followed a satisfactory truce with the Imam Sharaf al-Dīn's eldest son, Muṭahhar, who had by then been accepted as the Zaydī leader in Yemen. Otherwise, the province ran at a loss, and, as the author points out earlier in the work, no foundry like Yemen had been seen for Turkish troops who had melted away like salt in water, with casualties already exceeding 70,000!

Renewed rebellion under Muṭahhar had broken out, and in September 1567 a new governor-general, Murād Pasha, had been slaughtered, and his head dispatched to the Yemeni leader. By June 1568 Ottoman control had been reduced to an enclave around Zabīd in the Tihāmah.

The new Ottoman sultan, Selīm II, furious with developments in the rebellious province, had commissioned his former tutor, Muṣṭafā Lālā Pasha, to head a large expeditionary force to suppress the rebellion, but the latter was so delayed in Cairo making preparations for the expedition that the impatient sultan commissioned the new governor-general in Egypt, Sinān Pasha, to replace him. It would seem that Sinān, an Albanian born in about 1520, had himself coveted the leadership of the expedition and had intrigued with the veteran grand vizier in Istanbul, Sokollu Meḥmed Pasha, to that end.

Sinān was accused of delays over providing materiel and weaponry for Muṣṭafā Pasha and circulating rumours that Muṣṭafā wished to establish a state in Cairo independent of the sultan. Such behaviour would have been in character; for Sinān was to prove an ambitious figure who regularly rebounded from overseas campaigns to the high office of grand vizier until his death in 1596. He would have seen the political advantage of a speedy and efficient end to the rebellion but he misjudged both the risk and danger he was taking against an experienced and formidable adversary who would exploit every advantage the mountainous and well-defended terrain afforded him, as well as the deep dislike for Turkish rule its inhabitants had developed.

In any event, Sinān was elevated to the rank of vizier and instructed by the sultan 'to punish and eradicate the reprobate called Muṭahhar' and 'without delay, to go to all lengths to get shot of him, lock, stock and barrel'. It is worth bearing in mind that Sinān did not achieve such a neat solution; nor was he able to reciprocate the murder of the former governor-general by sending Muṭahhar's head to the sultan in Istanbul!

The Author, Quṭb al-Dīn al-Nahrawālī

It was near Mecca, on his way south to Yemen, that Sinān first met the author, Quṭb al-Dīn al-Nahrawālī (917–90/1511/1512–82). It would not be until his return from Yemen, however, when Sinān was carrying out the pilgrimage, that he commissioned him to write this account. Ḥamad al-Jāsir, the editor of *al-Baraq al-yamānī* (translated for our purpose as *Lightning over Yemen*), in the introductory sections to his work, explains how Sinān, in commissioning the author, discussed his campaign in Yemen and handed to him an epic poem in Turkish by one of his senior officers there named Muṣṭafā Bey al-Rumūzī. This poem was published later with 104 illustrations and is housed in the manuscripts library of the University of Istanbul, now closed to the public. Quṭb al-Dīn made a number of additions to the description of the campaign which forms the main section of *al-Baraq al-yamānī* which is preceded by a history of earlier campaigning by Mamluk and Turk in Yemen; and it is the main section which forms the subject of this translation.

Quṭb al-Dīn was well suited to the task. By the time of Sinān's campaign he was some fifty-eight years old and an established figure in Mecca. He was recognised as Mufti of Mecca and had been awarded the first Ḥanafī professorship in Sultan Sulaymān's recently completed college for the four orthodox rites. An early acquired knowledge of Turkish enabled him to cultivate acquaintance with Ottoman officials posted in the region, including, of course, successive governors-general and senior officials from Yemen on their way through Mecca. He became the most sought-after guide for visitors to Mecca, who would often reward him with great generosity.

He would have gleaned further information about conditions in Yemen from a close relative who was a Hanafite qadi in Jiblah, from which the rebellion forced him to flee, in 1567, 'without shoes or clothing, from village to village to Zabīd'. All the qadi's possessions were stolen, including some valuable books belonging to Quṭb al-Dīn himself!

Earlier members of his family had for some time acted in Mecca on behalf of the Sultan of Gujerat, and by the middle of 932/1526 his father had brought his son from Gujerat to live there permanently at a time of great disturbance in Gujerat during the machinations of Mogul and Portuguese. He had been born in Lahore in 917/1511/12 into a scholarly family which originally hailed from Aden, and gained his early education from his father, a mufti and *ḥadīth* scholar. Later he had studied in Mecca under eminent scholars and teachers, including the Yemen chronicler, al-Dayba', and had continued his studies in Cairo. He composed works on religion, literature and history, the most famous of which was a much-quoted chronicle of Mecca which the explorer John Lewis Burckhardt used as a primary source during his visit to Mecca and Medina in 1814–15.

Quṭb al-Dīn had visited Istanbul twice, first in 943/1536, in a ministerial delegation from Gujerat seeking help from the sultan against the Portuguese, and second in 965/1557/8, on behalf of the Grand Sharīf of Mecca whose confidence he enjoyed.

His treatment in Istanbul on the latter occasion left something to be desired and the visit did not achieve its object. The account by Ḥamad al-Jāsir throws some light on the small-mindedness and envy his high favour with the Grand Sharīf had provoked. The aim had been to obtain the sultan's agreement to the removal of the Ottoman governor of Medina who had been rough in handling the Ḥijāzī sharifs and less than respectful in his treatment of the Grand Sharīf himself; and the delegation was laden with expensive gifts and armed with a personal letter from the Grand Sharīf.

Unfortunately, discord broke out within the delegation between Quṭb al-Dīn and other members, apparently over allegations against the qadi of Medina; and he was jostled and insulted by some of the Hijazis in the presence of ministers to the extent that one of the latter, in seeking clarification from the Hijazis as to Quṭb al-Dīn's exact position, was told that he was merely a servant with a knowledge of Turkish and completely unknown personally to the Grand Sharīf. Quṭb al-Dīn produced a detailed account of the insulting treatment and slanderous statements levelled at him during his time in Istanbul. The situation may have been clarified in due course but the atmosphere appears to have been far from congenial, and the curtain is raised on the intrigue pervading the Sharīf's court! Elsewhere in Ḥamad al-Jāsir's introductory sections there are indications that Quṭb al-Dīn was not averse to involvement in the political and other intrigues with which his environment was charged. He was far from being the detached scholar and clearly played the courtier in the service of both Turk and Sharīf.

The Account of the Campaign

The author covers Sinān's campaign framed by his passages through the Ḥijāz in sixty chapters. The account reflects his informant's soldierly concern for the details of the route and strategy employed by the Turks.

Map 1 gives details of the relentless thrust via Jīzān and Zabīd up into the highlands at Ta'izz and northwards over the mountainous spine via Ṣan'ā' to the heartlands of the Zaydī leader controlled from the ancient strongholds of Thulā and Kawkabān. Within seven weeks the powerful citadel of al-Qāhirah

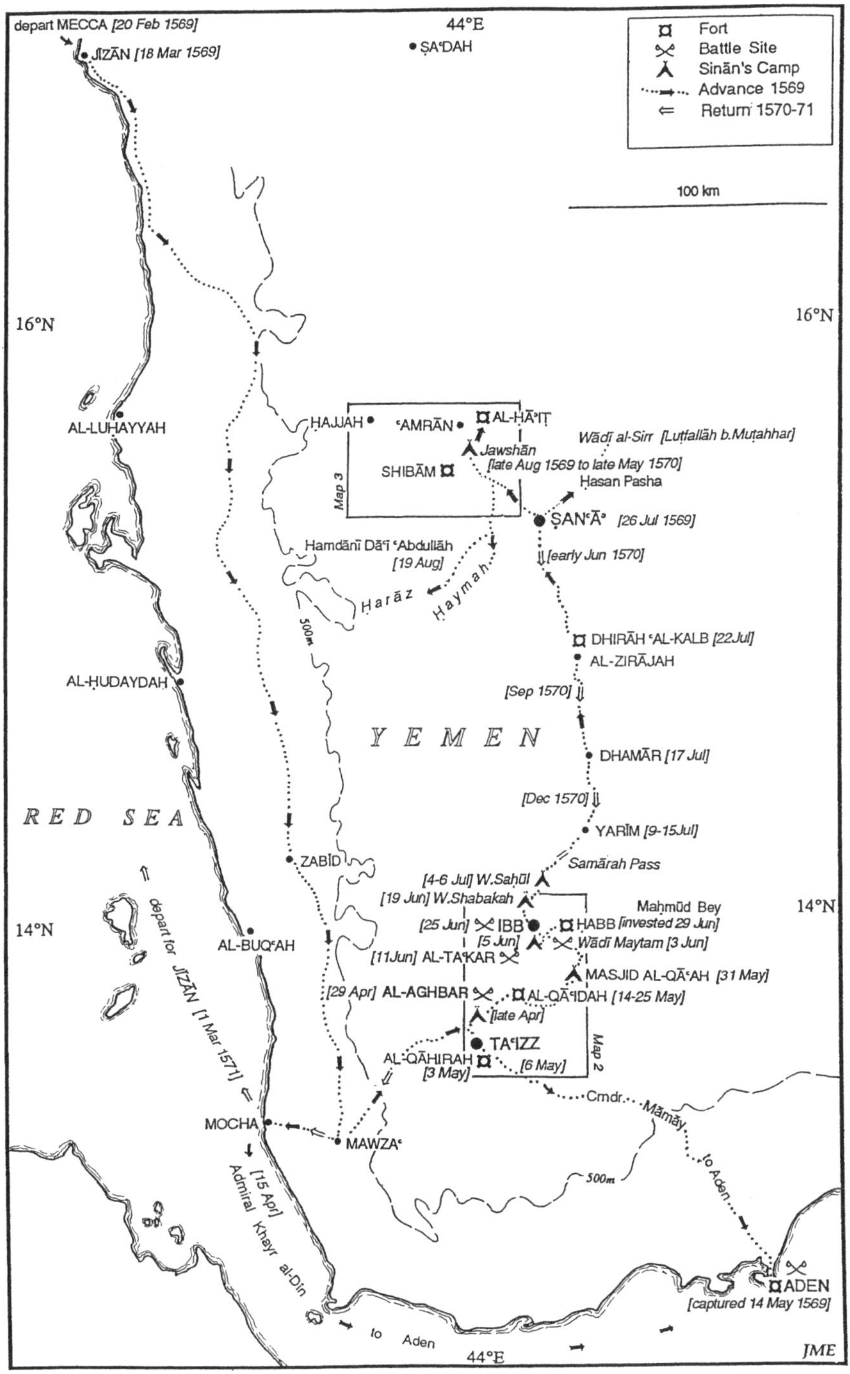

MAP I Approximate route followed by Sinān Pasha during the campaign against Muṭahhar b. Sharaf al-Dīn in Yemen from Jīzān at the end of Ramaḍān 976 (18 March 1569) to Mocha on 4 Shawwāl 978 (1 March 1571). The map includes some actions by his commanders.

above Taʿizz had surrendered; within sixteen, Sinān was over the Samārah pass leading to the transmontane plains; within five months he had taken the capital; and a few days later, on 22 August 1569, he had reached Shibām, the ancient town at the foot of the mountain where the fortress town of Kawkabān was situated. But there the momentum stopped.

Kawkabān was the base of Muṭahhar's nephew, Muḥammad b. Shams al-Dīn, who had commanded Muṭahhar's forces retreating from the south. Shams al-Dīn had been a former *sanjak* and protégé of the Turks who had taken their part in battles against Muṭahhar; and Sinān decided to concentrate his forces on putting Kawkabān under siege in the expectation of prising the son, Muḥammad b. Shams al-Dīn, from his uncle's control.

It was an expectation that was to be rewarded but only after a seven-month siege at great expense to the Turkish forces in men and weaponry. The truce, reached with Muḥammad, and later Muṭahhar, was urgently required by the Turks because of widespread renewed rebellion elsewhere in the country, but its terms returned to the Zaydī leaders most of their former territory and authority and certainly fell far short of the sultan's commission. Map 2 illustrates the military dispositions at the time of the first major engagement between the two forces in the south before Mt al-Aghbar, while Map 3 gives the leading commanders, forts, towns and features relevant to the long siege of Kawkabān which was raised in late May 1570.

The remainder of the account is largely devoted to the deteriorating Turkish position in the south before the newly arrived governor-general, Behrām Pasha, was able, with Sinān's military help, to quell the renewed rebellion, allowing Sinān to hand over his responsibilities and make his return in triumph through Mecca.

The account is informed at intervals by details of the increasingly parlous situation facing the Turks over troops, funding and supplies; for the governor-general in Egypt had failed to help with required funds and troops and the new governor-general for Yemen had arrived in Zabīd with 600 troops in complete disarray, 'naked, hungry and poor'.

The author is at pains to stress the difficulties of terrain and climate which the Turks had to face in this inhospitable land. Mountain tops were defended by myriads of armed tribesmen; rivers were diverted to turn roads into swamps; mountain passes were blocked and rocks hurled down on to troops attempting to climb the narrow mountain defiles. However, the Yemeni unwillingness to engage in the pitched battles favoured by the Turks is interpreted as cowardice; and successful Yemeni guerrilla attacks are regarded as defeats since the Yemenis retreated after their ambush was complete. The Turks could do little but cry 'Foul' at these engagements of 'hit and run'.

If the conclusion of peace terms with Muḥammad b. Shams al-Dīn over

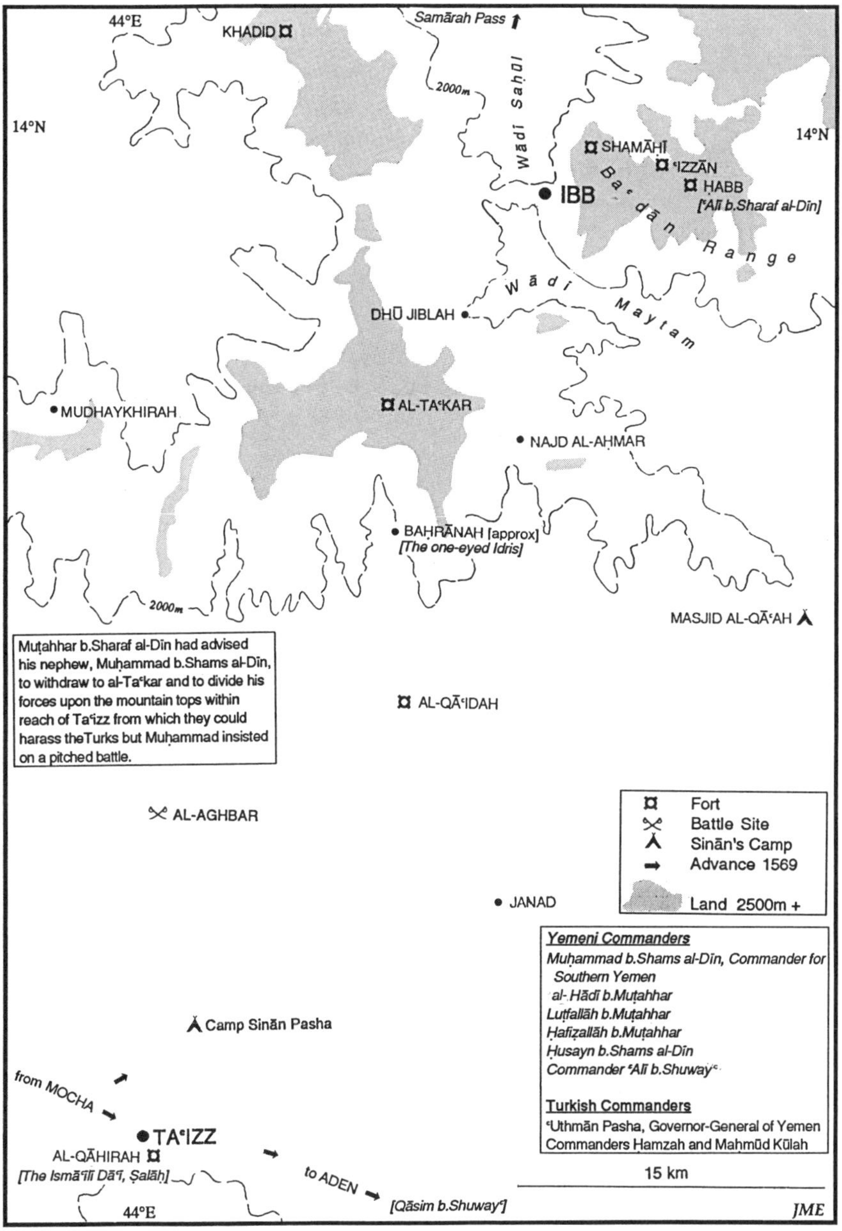

MAP 2 Leading commanders and forts in southern Yemen relevant to Sinān Pasha's campaign at the time of the battle before Jabal al-Aghbar on 13 Dhū al-Qaʿdah 976 (29 April 1569).

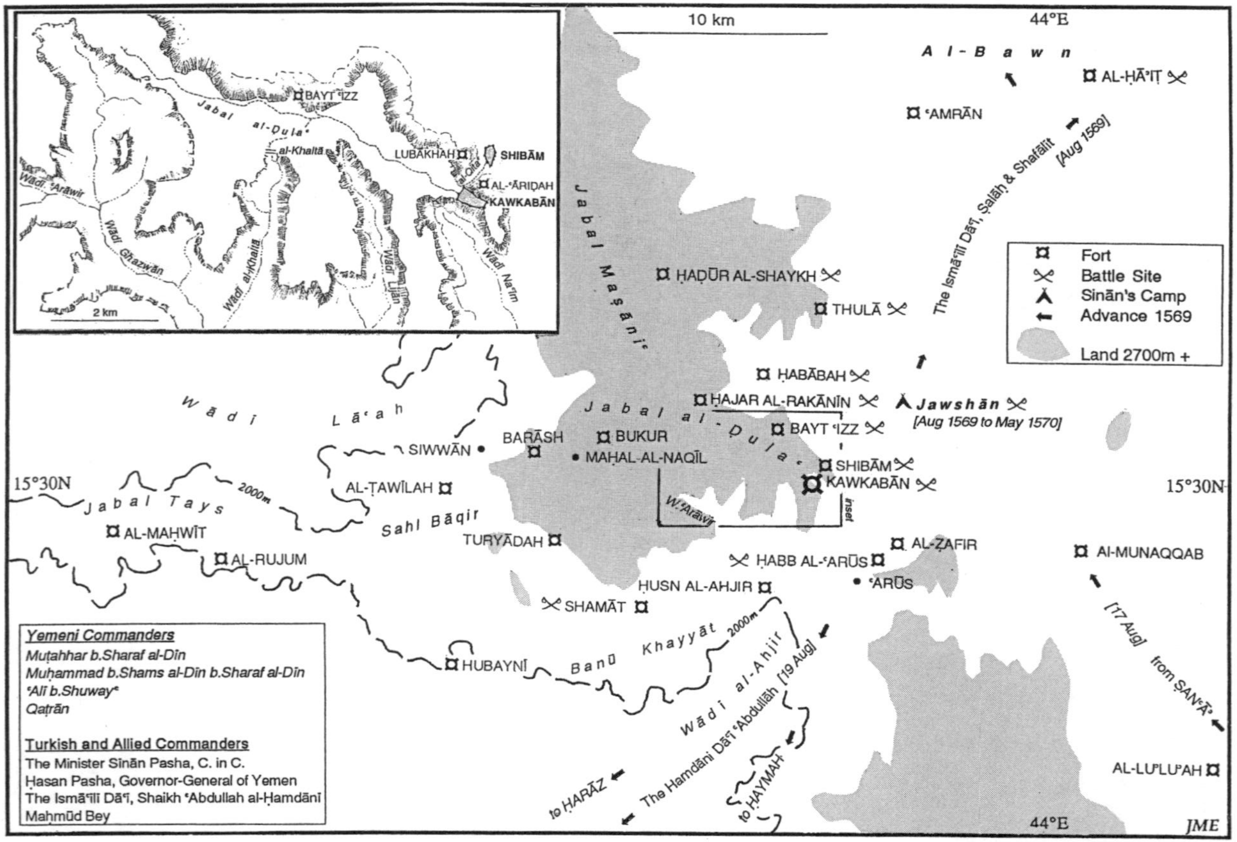

MAP 3 Leading commanders, forts, towns and features relevant to Sinān Pasha's siege of Kawkabān while based at his camp in Jawshān, facing Thulā and Kawkabān in mid-Rabī' al-Awwal 977 (late August 1569) until mid-Dhū al-Ḥijjah 977 (late May 1570).

Kawkabān – soon neutralising Muṭahhar's forces to allow Turkish troops to be used elsewhere – can be regarded as the key to the campaign, the role of the Ismāʿīlī leaders in Yemen was crucial, as the author indicates time and again.

The Ṭayyibī Ismaʿilis, scions of the Fatimid Sulayhids, had been in Yemen, independent of Fatimid and Sulayhid control, for four hundred years under the leadership of their Chief Dāʿī or Missionary, and had usually maintained good relations with successive rulers in Yemen, with the conspicuous exception of the Imam Sharaf al-Dīn and his son, Muṭahhar, who had persecuted them. In these circumstances they had become allies and supporters of the Turks but had, for the most part, joined Muṭahhar's rebellion because of the recent extortionate behaviour of the Turks.

As our author explains, for the Ismāʿīlī commander at the citadel above Taʿizz who had been induced to surrender to the Turks by his fellow Ismāʿīlī, the Dāʿī Shaikh ʿAbdullāh, his reason for deserting the Turks had been their 'governorate's rough treatment of Yemen, its ambitions there, its impossible requests and their (Yemeni) inability to satisfy its financial demands'. An interesting admission from an author prejudiced in favour of the Turks!

From his early meeting with Sinān in Zabīd, Shaikh ʿAbdullāh was fervent in his support for the Turks. As the expedition moved northwards he conquered the important fort of Khadid, west of the Samārah pass, and, once arrived before Shibām, in response to the obvious need for reinforcements and supplies, he went off to campaign on Sinān's behalf. Indeed, a large force under the nominal governor-general, Ḥasan Pasha, had to be dispatched to bring him back since the Turks proved incapable of climbing the escarpment of the Ḍulaʿ massif to get to grips with their siege of Kawkabān. It was he who found the defile that was not blocked by Zaydī forces and up which the combined Turkish force was able to climb; and it was he, we are told by the Yemeni chronicler, Yaḥyā b. Ḥusayn, who advised Sinān to seek terms with Muḥammad b. Shams al-Dīn over Kawkabān. From first to last he was a vital force and adviser on whom Sinān could rely.

The widespread renewed rebellion had been provoked by Muṭahhar in what appears to be a brilliant propaganda campaign in which he wrote far and wide proclaiming the Prophet Muḥammad's support in a dream for his cause, to be signalled by the moon's eclipse, and accusing the Turks of immoral and unlawful behaviour. 'So where is the fury? Where has the passion gone? While these men (the Turks) degrade women of high status, taking them off to evil haunts where they can take their pleasure … while you eat, drink, dance and play music.' Quṭb al-Dīn may have relished these accusations against such men!

The Fragrance of Sweet Bay and Wormwood

There is much to distract the modern reader in this account. The douceur of the well-watered and fertile lands south of the Samārah pass is conveyed. A wadi is redolent of sweet-smelling shrubs. Another is full of anemones. Paths curve like snakes and hide vipers in their dangerous crannies. An Adeni saint appears in a dream to show a Turkish sea captain the way to a mountain fortress, while another is high enough to converse with the stars. Imagery shines on every page.

Glimpses of local life appear. Hard-worked women of Ḥabb al-ʻArūs, opposite Kawkabān, carry loads of wood strapped to their brows like their traditional Kikuyu sisters in Kenya or Berber women today. The coffee houses of Ibb and Jiblah are full of soldiery, despite instructions to the contrary from Sinān to their commander, in itself an important early reference to such clearly long-established institutions in Yemen! A poisoned quince is served to an allegedly drunken commander in the castle of Ḥabb and a cat with a fused explosive attached to its tail is used to blow up the castle gunpowder store (a device said to have been employed in the 1960s against the British in Aden).

Some vivid military scenes spring into focus. Fifteen Janissaries with their *aghas* or commanders from Egypt and Istanbul, in an adventurous attempt to climb up the escarpment to Kawkabān, are slaughtered by Zaydī forces. (The Janissaries were an elite military corps formed from young Christian lads who had been seized during periodic levies in countries, often in the Balkans, under Ottoman rule; and those slaughtered here would have been dressed and armed like their colleague in the cover illustration.)

Sinān's army dazzles the inhabitants of Mecca with its 'sheer display, its great pavilions, pedigree horses dressed in gold, bridles of gold and silver, weapons, armour and helmets' and the cavalcade of horse and camel was 'an astonishing sight, filling the eyes and spirits; dazzling and overwhelming, it captivated the eye and regard'.

Sinān rides with his troops 'with his mighty band playing the drum and pipe, intoxicating the troops with the sight, as if they had drunk wine'. As a pasha of ministerial rank, Sinān would have in his personal entourage a great drum, some three feet high and carried on horseback into battle, as well as two pairs of kettledrums and seven pipes.

Quṭb al-Dīn was unusual for a writer of his time in Arabic in adopting a thematic approach to his work, with each chapter being devoted to a different aspect of the evolving story. He was not unusual, however, in his frequent use of *sajʻ* or rhymed prose, especially in describing battle scenes. It is not possible to do justice to the alliteration and imagery, the puns and double-meanings, and to the sheer pace of such passages.

Sir Richard Burton, in the Terminal Essay to his *Arabian Nights,* discusses the pros and cons of translating *al-saj‘* into rhymed prose in English. He points out that the Quran and many famous Arabic masterpieces are written in it but that the weight of opinion of English scholars was against the attempt to do so. However, with typical contempt for convention, he undertakes the task in his translation and quotes a favourable reviewer's comment: 'These melodious fragments, these little eddies of song set like gems in the prose, have a charming effect on the ear.'

Ḥamad al-Jāsir points out that such passages allowed the author to show off his linguistic skill and ability in Arabic, and that they would ring in the ears of the Turks for whom they were intended, many of whom would have only a slight knowledge of the language. In the same way, the author frequently introduces snatches of poetry from pre-Islamic and classical poets to illustrate his narrative as he quotes religious maxims and pieties to confirm his religious credentials.

Ointment Hiding Sores and Poison in the Fat

There can be no doubt that the account is marred by the religious and political prejudice of the author in favour of Turk and Meccan sharīf and against Muṭahhar and his Zaydī supporters. This prejudice grates and his incessant denigration of the 'cripple' Muṭahhar sticks in the throat but, as Ḥamad al-Jāsir points out, should not blind us to the value within his account. Moreover, as we have seen, despite his prejudice in favour of the Turks, he does not shrink from criticising Turkish actions in Yemen; and often in his biographical summaries of Turkish leaders, he dwells on their brutality, incompetence and other failings.

Moreover, despite his dislike of Muṭahhar, he displays a grudging respect for his defence against the Turks and allows the development of the campaign and the necessity to conclude peace over Kawkabān to release troops to fight the renewed rebellion to speak for themselves. Indeed, his long account of the oppression by the pre-Islamic tribe of Ṭasm against a weak Jadīs could indicate a degree of sympathy for its relevance as an allegory of Turk against Yemeni.

There are, however, failings of a factual nature. The author clearly misunderstands what he has been told about the ancient city of Shibām, nestling below the escarpment above which Kawkabān is situated, when he describes it as 'a strong castle at the summit of an impregnable mountain'. 'Shibām' may have replaced 'Kawkabān' in somebody's notes. There are inconsistencies over dates and the names of fortresses and towns, but not on a scale to affect the momentum or thrust of the account. And, at times, pre-Islamic information inserted into the description of places can appear to the modern reader as both whimsical and contrived.

In Mecca we pause before the adulation in which the Grand Sharīf and his family are held but remain fascinated by the detail of the pilgrimage, the comings and goings of those involved and the description of the delicacies produced for the minister by the Shaikh al-Islam in his gardens at Abṭaḥ. And Sinān's prickly nature and tendency to take quick offence can be seen in the initial welcome banquet at Mecca and in his later behaviour towards the superintendent of the well at 'Arafāt. Indeed, as we shall see in the Notes, we are told elsewhere that, in a fit of pique, he apparently had his horses trample over some rare and costly Chinese porcelain presented to him in the name of the Grand Sharīf. It appears that, throughout the period Sinān was in the area, Muḥammad Abū Numayy, who had ruled as Grand Sharīf since 1524, had already handed over his duties to his son, Ḥasan; and the author always refers to him as the revered Grand Sharīf. Abū Numayy died in 1584 in Nejd at the age of eighty.

Later Perspective

Sinān, true to character, was determined to wrest all he could from this campaign for which he was granted the title 'Conqueror of the Yemen'. He more or less forced the Grand Sharīf in Mecca to write to Istanbul about his success, and, great self-publicist that he was, commissioned at least two accounts of the campaign. From this account it is clear that he only just managed to get the Zaydī leader back in his box, so to speak; and that the province was regained for the Turks only at a terrible cost in manpower, weapons and funds. Sinān returned to the governor-generalship of Egypt for two years, after which his career continued to alternate between overseas campaign, high office and disgrace. He held the highest office of grand vizier on five occasions, dying as such in 1596.

Meanwhile, Muṭahhar was to die two years later with blood in his urine, and left to others the fight against the Turks which led to their expulsion in 1635.

Notes, attempting to throw light on unfamiliar subjects, have been divided into eight sections at the end of the translation. As indicated above, there are three maps to illustrate the campaign. In addition there are fort plans and a number of images. The latter come in two forms: first, those of contemporary, or at least old, prints and engravings to illustrate dress, transport, weaponry and equipment as well as plant and place; and, second, photographs taken by the translator during the 1970s.

· LIGHTNING OVER YEMEN ·

Sixty pearls of thought, set in a necklace, intent
(the return of the Yemeni provinces to Ottoman
sovereign control)

§ The accoutrements of war, from L. F. Marsigli's *Stato Militare dell' Imperio Ottomanno* (The Hague, 1732), II, frontispiece. The central turban is that worn by a sultan. It would be made of white muslin and adorned with black heron feathers. On the left is the ceremonial headpiece of an *Āghā* of the Janissaries, and on the right the headpiece of a Janisssary, heavily influenced, in its shape and the sleeve flowing from its crest, by the headgear of the Bektashi dervishes. Rings of gold encircle its base and a strip of gold adorns its front from the top to the bottom.

The headgear is surrounded by weapons, including an axe, mace, shield, bow and quiver with arrows, sword and horsetail. The musket strongly resembles the snap matchlock guns made at Brescia near Venice in the mid-sixteenth century.

Count Marsigli was imprisoned and enslaved during the Turkish siege of Vienna in 1683. He had arrived in Istanbul in 1679 and had witnessed a number of Turkish campaigns. He became an authority on the Ottoman army, especially the Janissaries.

CHAPTER I

[210] Muṣṭafā Pasha's dismissal, His Excellency[1] Sinān Pasha's commission; the issue of the imperial decree for him to go personally to Yemen; his appointment as minister; and his arrival in Mecca with the victorious army

§ As soon as the Ottoman sovereign learnt of Muṣṭafā Pasha's[2] delay in Egypt, together with some of the commanders, in departing for Yemen, he dismissed Muṣṭafā Pasha, and appointed Sinān Pasha as minister. Almighty God preserve the caliphate and support the sultanate for mankind.

The sultan directed that Sinān Pasha be *sirdār* (commander-in-chief) of the armed forces in Yemen and gave orders for the execution of Muṣṭafā Bey, one of the *sanjak*[3] commanders in Egypt, and Najmī Muḥammad Bey, a brigade commander there. He then gave instructions for the entire Egyptian army to proceed to Yemen, the royal edict containing such orders to be dispatched to Egypt by hand of the chamberlain from the Sublime Porte.

All of a sudden people were aware of their arrival in Egypt; and the country became agitated. The chamberlain's party went up to Sinān Pasha's *dīwān* (office) in Cairo and delivered to him the sultan's edict; and his reaction was to hear and obey. He would devote himself and his wealth to serving the sultan, without hint of reserve, in order to carry out the sovereign command. He summoned the two bey commanders and handed them over to the chamberlain who discharged the sultan's orders regarding them both, throttling them with a bowstring and passing their bodies to their families for burial. Their belongings were then registered in the *dīwān*.

[211] Fearful of what was in store for him, Muṣṭafā Pasha travelled at once all the way to the Sublime Porte and invoked the sultan's compassion, pleading his former service in the sovereign's cause. His ministerial rank was restored and, after a lengthy explanation of the circumstances, he was granted a pardon.

As for His Excellency the Minister, Sinān Pasha, he bared his upper arm and unsheathed his resolute sword. Immediately, he set out to submit and obey while the Egyptian army also hastened to do so once it had understood the gravity of the situation. Everyone who had not been able to contemplate leaving Egypt competed in their demand to travel; and all hastened to present themselves in the imperial *dīwān*, present and ready, until the major part of the Egyptian army had enrolled, the strong and the wealthy, the *kushshāf* [tax collectors], and the *mutafarriqah* and *būlukyāt* [two of the elite regiments].[4]

None remained in Egypt save the useless, such as a very old shaikh or child or the like. They left Egypt with the army by land, mounted on horses, camels and mules, sending the heavy baggage by sea and taking only necessary provisions and supplies. Placing their trust in Almighty, All-powerful God, they began their journey and set out on their march. The minister's departure from the Egyptian capital took place on 17 Rajab 976/5 January 1569.

The minister's cavalcade reached Yanbuʿ on 12 Shaʿban/30 January of the same year. At his service, and that of the mighty army, was Sayyid Nūr al-Dīn ʿAlī b. Durrāj b. Hujjār al-Ḥasanī, who transferred the cargo and heavy baggage from the beach at Yanbuʿ to the town. The shaikh of the noble Ḥaram at Mecca, our lord Shaikh al-Islam, leader of the ulema and learned men, the best of the noble sayyids and chief qadi in God's holy land, was our lord Sayyid Ḥusayn al-Mālikī who had earlier set out and travelled to Medina to meet Sinān Pasha. I was with him when the news came of the minister's arrival and we went out to meet him but failed to catch him at the stopover at Badr;[5] for he had gone on, but we called by and, following him, [212] caught up with him at Khabt Kulayyah after the evening prayer on 17 Shaʿbān 976/3 February 1569.

He gave our lord Shaikh al-Islam a splendid welcome, treating him kindly and chatting to him; and the minister continued with him until we had reached Rābigh. The minister had a splendid large banquet laid out and, summoning our lord guardian of the noble Ḥaram, awarded him a magnificent large honorary cloak. The Shaikh al-Islam accompanied him as far as Mecca. Then our noble lord, light of the world and religion, al-Ḥasan b. Abī Numayy,[6] long live his rule, sent to meet H.E. the Minister his eldest son, our lord Ḥusayn, with a suite of horses and men. He reached him as he emerged from ʿUsfān and was awarded the customary honorary cloak. On arriving for the *ʿumrah* [lesser pilgrimage],[7] he entered Mecca during the night of Tuesday 21 Shaʿbān/7 February; he performed the *ṭawāf* and *saʿy*,[8] to be met at the *ṭawāf* by the Efendī of Mecca, then returned for the *ʿumrah* and entered Mecca on the Wednesday morning.

On his arrival at Sabīl al-Jawkhī, the Qadi of Mecca, at the time Efendī ʿAbd al-Raḥmān b. Sayyidī ʿAlī, formerly military qadi for Rūmelī [the Balkans], arrived to meet him and he gave instructions for his camp to be pitched at the pool of Mājin. The population of Mecca came out as a whole to look and beheld the Ottoman army, the like of which they had neither seen nor heard before in those noble parts in the way of sheer display, great pavilions, pedigree horses dressed in gold with bridles of gold and silver, weapons, armour and helmets.[9]

I was told by one who had counted that there were between three and four thousand horsemen in the procession and nearly ten thousand camels.[10] The procession was an astonishing sight, filling the eyes and spirits; dazzling and overwhelming, it captivated the eye and regard.

Before the minister's arrival, Almighty God grant him victory, Mecca was gripped by rumour and evil. There was dread in the land and business was in confusion, with everybody burying their valuables for fear of plunder and attack. All were saved from such a fate by Almighty God through the minister's excellent arrangements and by his control and care for the great army; and many were [213] his good deeds for the poor and great was his generosity to the dignitaries and the great. He remained by the pool of Mājin in his splendid camp which the huge army, known for its good deeds, entered. The most senior of the commanders was Commander Ḥamzah, next to him Commander Māmāy, followed by the rest of the *sanjak* commanders, namely Kūlah Maḥmūd Bey, 'Alī Bey, and Kurd Maḥmūd Bey, the Egyptian Arab commander, Commander Salāmah b. al-Khabīr, and the *aghas*, *kushshāf*, *mutafarriqah*, and many of the *būlukyāt* and the *jāwīshiyyah*.[11]

In brief, it was as if the Egyptian administration with its entire army had transferred to Mecca, to which had to be added troops from Damascus, Aleppo, Karamān, Āmid, Mar'ash[12] and other Ottoman possessions to an extent unheard of in former years. Praise Almighty God, ruler of kings and kingdoms, in His glory, majesty and might.

Then His Highness the Sharīf Ḥasan, Almighty God preserve his glory, went in noble person to Jiddah to give orders for the transfer to Mecca of all the baggage belonging to the minister that had arrived by sea, and to be of general service to the noble sultan. He did not rely upon his own attendants and servants for the purpose since he anticipated them being inadequate, but ordered a generous banquet, of a standard fitting the occasion, to be spread for the minister in Mecca; and they spread it out in front of him. However, the minister had expected Sharīf Ḥasan to appear in person and, at his failure to do so, with all sorts of stories being bruited abroad by people at large, his mood changed markedly, and he intended to decline Sharīf Ḥasan's banquet placed in front of him.

So our lord Shaikh al-Islam, Qadi Sayyid Ḥusayn, apologised on his behalf, on the grounds that Sharīf Ḥasan, realising the minister's need for the early arrival of the sea cargo, had anticipated that, if he entrusted the task to his servants, they would not be able to discharge it quickly. He had therefore himself gone to expedite the matter since its discharge, in view of the minister's urgent need, was more important than his presence by his side. The country did not have adequate facilities for such a large army and famine might strike, causing worse hardship for the army and population; and he gave other such reasons. The minister accepted the apology and himself partook of the meal [214], full of kindness and courtesy and giving orders for it to be divided among the troops. Then he gave an honorary cloak to Khwājā Kamāl al-Dīn Abū al-Faḍl b. Abī 'Alī for having undertaken to provide the banquet on behalf of the Grand Sharīf, thus achieving, God be thanked, a high degree of harmony and affection.

Sharīf Ḥasan sent to him about a hundred horses and a thousand camels, apart from other valuables and appropriate presents; and real affection flowed between them which delighted the people. The land was reassured and the population calmed. For that, God be thanked and praised.

In short, all H.E. the Minister's doings were happy and his actions praiseworthy and commendable. His judgment was correct, his opinion sound, and his arrangements extremely efficient and methodical. His intelligence was marked in every reversal or confirmation of sentence. God increase his glory and majesty, double his happiness and good fortune and raise him to the ranks of glory until his friends say, 'Thus, thus ad infinitum!'

During this period the minister travelled to al-Mafjar to inspect the work at the well of 'Arafāt which was to serve Mecca. Its intendant at the time was Qāsim Bey, *sanjak* of Jiddah, whom the late vizier 'Alī Pasha[13] had selected as commander. He set out in a magnificent cavalcade of commanders and cavalry riding before and around him, in his coming and goings, presenting people with a display of perfect horsemanship.

In al-Mafjar Commander Qāsim had laid out a magnificent banquet, without thought of expense or effort, and presented to him three race horses, complete with gilded harness, with sword, mace, armour, helmet, saddle, bridle and stirrups of silver.[14] The minister presented Commander Qāsim with an honorary cloak of *serāser*[15] and gave the masons an increase of two to five ottoman pieces.[16] He then returned with his suite to his encampment in full glory and majesty. The entire matter went off, thanks be to God, without a hitch.

Then the month of Ramaḍān came upon him with much blessing and good-will while he was in his magnificent encampment with his splendid soldiers and victorious and efficient army, under his excellent command and administration. Nobody was able to pilfer a grain of mustard or take anything from [215] outside without his wish and agreement.

He spent four nights of Ramaḍān in full observance of its rules. He laid out its sustenance and arranged its fare, with full observances and good deeds for the ulema, arrangements for the officials, and prayers for the *faqihs*[17] and the poor. He made provision from the sultan's funds for the numerous *faqihs* in the vicinity who required help; something that had not been done before by any other visiting minister. In this way he evoked sincere prayers from the population of the Holy Places in support of the Sultan of Islam in east and west, and achieved more from those who fight with prayers than from those who do so in war; and more from those who wage war through supplication and miracles in the name of the Noble and the Supreme than from troops in battle and contest.

Indeed, the arrows of prayer from such people really hit their mark and the effect of their weapons is very clear both in their presence and their absence. And then he departed with his troops, vigorous and true, accompanied, God willing, by help and victory.

CHAPTER 2

[216] The minister's progress by land from Mecca to blessed Yemen

§ With the arrival of the fourth day of Ramaḍān, the minister decided to set out and gave orders for the troops to march without delay. Great was the dust and the commotion, and the clamour and din increased as the troops raced to collect their belongings and break their camp and quarters, raising their voices in calls to each other. The summons to march was like a bugle call and, as the troops spread out, in all the coming and going, the Day of Judgment could be seen.

With his fine intelligence the minister realised that sections of the army might lose their way during the journey and follow their own inclination. He therefore went himself to the head of the convoy and cautioned them against getting out of hand and breaking ranks. He travelled with the army, its contrast in colour, its plumes and its chain mail, its standards and its shields, its flashing swords and its scabbards, its spears and its sabres, and its brave hearts and pedigree horses. Nights of battle were adorned with stars struck through the clash of sword blades. Herds of horses stemmed the flow of blood. Clouds of arrows from both earth and sky showered upon the people of Thulā and Kawkabān.[18]

The minister directed Commander Ḥamzah, one of the leading commanders and a man of courage, resource and strength, to stay behind in Mecca and keep the troops from horseplay and dissipation, and, in the event of their persistent delay and procrastination, to drive them forward. In this he was absolutely right and correct for, without such foresight, the riff-raff who remained would have caused tremendous damage. Almighty God prevented [217] such disorder and, after such trouble and exertion, each one was able to take his ease. They went their way, appreciated, triumphant, with God's good-will, supported and victorious.

His blessed departure took place on Monday 4 Ramaḍān, 976/20 February 1569. The packs had been tied up and the loads carried out; and after the riding animals had been driven out and the horses led out, there had been some delay over the army's remaining slaves as there was over searching for those who had fled the expedition and avoided contact. But the Grand Sharīf's agent in Mecca, Qā'id[19] Muḥammad b. 'Aqabah, rounded them up and sent them after the minister so that they could catch him up at the first stopover. They accordingly did so at al-Sa'diyyah, where the minister had stopped to allow the troops to break ranks and rest. He was grateful for the *qā'id*'s effort and clothed his messenger in a caftan when he handed over some of the slaves who had accompanied the army from Mecca. After retrieving them the minister directed the messenger to restore them to their owners, treating him kindly and courteously and returning him to his post.

The population thanked the minister for acting in the way he had, conveying their prayers of gratitude, whereupon he struck camp and moved forwards. He continued to humour the bedu at the stopping and watering places, treating them kindly and giving them clothes at every stage. He covered all the stopovers and went right across the desert and savannah, all the time accompanying his troops, travelling by their side over some of the roads, and sustaining them through hardship and danger with his sound judgment and kind behaviour. In such a way they crossed plains and sands, climbed passes and mountains, wearing out the backs of their horses and camels, goading their horses and mules, and ploughing up the remains of the animal tracks throughout their journey. And they consumed all they came across throughout the countryside in the way of straw and pasture.

CHAPTER 3

[218] The minister's arrival, with his mighty army, at Jīzān;[20] its capture and its reorganisation

§ As the esteemed minister approached Jīzān, those within the town who had called for rebellion fled, leaving it completely devastated and devoid of livestock and valuables; for al-Sarrāj, a headman supporting Muṭahhar,[21] who had occupied it in the past, in fear of his life, had made his own escape to the open country. The minister arrived at Jīzān at the end of Ramaḍān, at the same time as the feast of al-Fiṭr, and pitched his large tent there. This struck a propitious note as people were celebrating the feast. He proclaimed for them peace and security, increasing their pleasure and sense of security. Indeed, this was his first conquest without fighting and intimidation; and the mighty army took it as a good omen for conquest and approaching victory.

During the minister's stay there, the tribesmen approached him from all sides asking permission to submit and offering their loyalty. Among them were the people of Ṣabyā[22] who came forward and presented themselves to him. They offered their fealty and submission, whereupon he welcomed them, handing them gifts and clothes and treating them with courtesy. They went off full of appreciation for the meeting with him and praising his kindness for such personal contact. Tribesmen from Yemen thronged to him in large numbers, offering submission and seeking peace, surrendering and capitulating without prevarication or [219] hesitation. The mountains and strongholds of Yemen waited in dread for news of his arrival: its castles, hills and centres trembled; and its regions shook at the approach of this expedition.

On his arrival in Zabīd, 'Uthmān Pasha[23] had observed Ḥasan Pasha's[24] treatment of the population. For he had impounded their property and put them in prison. 'Uthmān gave orders for Ḥasan Pasha to be searched and he was able to recover much that had been taken which he returned to the owners, to the great delight of the townsfolk. Ḥasan Pasha was much put out by the search and the recovery of the property and began in vain to look for assistance. He then decided to return to Egypt and took a boat for Kamarān[25] but, at news of the minister's arrival in Jīzān, he immediately appealed to him, throwing himself on his mercy. The minister gave him a friendly reception and pardoned him for his crimes during the period of unrest. The pasha began to devote himself to duty and the minister was most responsive. He treated him with generosity and honour and began to entrust him with important business and to give him special commissions.

In truth, a great man's vision does what the elixir cannot do; although, if Ḥasan Pasha had not done that, he would not have escaped such dangers. God will be the judge.

CHAPTER 4

[220] The minister's journey from Jīzān to Ta'izz to counter difficulties faced by 'Uthmān Pasha

§ Having finished organising Jīzān and strengthening its commanders, the minister hastened to travel to Ta'izz with the army where he was told that 'Uthmān Pasha and the garrison remaining with him in Ta'izz were in dire straits; for the mountain tribesmen had disrupted their supplies from every direction. Famine had set in. They lacked forage and provender for their livestock and were greatly perplexed since they could neither return to Zabīd nor complete their seizure of the area surrounding Ta'izz. The citadel of al-Qāhirah[26] was hard to capture and covered Ta'izz and its gate, allowing none of the Turks to enter or leave the town without being hit by the guns from the citadel heights. Many of the brave Ottoman troops were killed, including

Ḥusayn Āghā, head of the Kawkaliyyah (light cavalry) in Egypt, and a number of its brave men.

This situation had discouraged them as they waited for speedy relief from God in His might and glory until they heard of the minister's arrival. Their spirits returned to their bodies and, after such depression and despair, they felt the pulse of life within them. But the seditious tribesmen were terrified and, seizing their meagre possessions, they all fled. Then, the minister, with tremendous speed, cut across the stages of his way like a book scroll, avoiding camp and spring, till his banners waved in victory and his marvels were clear to the eye as dawn broke [221] in the depths of a dark night. The light of his face shone forth and the features of that desperate period relaxed in smiles as the faithful delighted in God's victory his blessed arrival had brought; and, after such terror, fear and anxiety began to leave them.

As the minister pitched his camp in the district with his armies, God with utmost favour kept a watch over him. The mighty army tramped the mountains of Ta'izz and its environs; the conscripted troops filled its valleys and plateaux. Their numbers cast a dark curtain over the light of day; their white banners threw flashes of radiant light. The noble tents were erected; and the vast and splendid encampment fixed in the scorching desert of that broad landscape as if the seven tiers were one of its domes,[27] and the rays from the sun and the moon were among the ropes that held its tents; indeed, the sky's constellations were within the angle vaults of its pavilions and the cloud covering was one of its marquee ceilings.

At sight of this tremendous army, as they looked towards the clash of waves within this enormous sea, the Zaydī sought a mountain refuge to protect them from the water and began for their safety to strengthen their positions on Mt al-Aghbar.[28] They did not realise that flight to Mt al-Aghbar would not protect them; for today virtue is the only defence against God's command.[29]

Their reason for gathering at Mt al-Aghbar, without fleeing in a mass to the open country, arose from their desire to encourage the people of al-Qāhirah who would see their steadfastness in face of the Ottoman troops and would thus refuse to hand over the citadel as a demonstration of assistance and a gesture of numerical support. It is the practice of the Arabs of these parts to light fires so that they can be seen by the people in the castles; and, likewise, the castle occupants light fires for the bedu and hillmen to let them know they have received such a signal. Both sides therefore kindled their fire to encourage each other by showing they were standing firm rather than fleeing; so they, for so long anticipating hell, now set to with the utmost urgency and continued their efforts until day broke. Meanwhile, they shouted at each other from a distance, using the language of people in hell-fire and the misery of the hereafter.

CHAPTER 5

[222] The minister's instructions for his commanders to muster and make war on the population of Mt al-Aghbar; and his orders for 'Uthmān Pasha to go with them as their leader

§ Once his camp had been pitched in the area between Ta'izz and Mt al-Aghbar, and Zaydī sections had withdrawn to that mountain, the minister decided to leave his force where it was but to take a section of hand-picked troops to launch an attack on the Zaydī on Mt al-Aghbar which would take them completely by surprise; and to that end he formulated his tactics and began to make his plans. Now it occurred to him to hold a council with his commanders so that he could take their opinion and advice on the subject in a practical manner, as the Almighty states 'and consult with them upon the conduct of affairs'.[30]

One said:

Judgment comes before the courage of the courageous; the former is first, and the latter the second place.
So when they are combined in a haughty spirit, that spirit reaches every place of elevation.
But for reason, the meanest lion would be nearer to nobility than man.

And another said:

I add another view to yours and I advise. Right must appear from two opinions.
Man is a mirror which shows him his face. To see his back, he requires two mirrors.

[223] And again a third:

Seek advice from another, when one day misfortune befalls you, even if you are a man of good counsel. The eye sees far and near but cannot see itself save through a mirror.

He summoned the commanders and the *aghas* and all upon whom he relied for sound and firm judgment and, explaining to them what he had in mind, described the debate that had taken place in his head as he recalled it. They discussed and argued the question till they reached agreement that the minister would remain at his post and continue to look after his forces in camp, and assign the task to his bravest commanders, with a group upon whose courage and bravery he could rely. They approved this excellent proposal, basing their decision thereon, and chose for the task Commander Ḥamzah, formerly a *kāshif* in Egypt, and Commander Maḥmūd known as

Kūlah,[31] both at the time among the bravest of horsemen and fully expert in military strategy and battle. The two of them set out with about five hundred horsemen, complete with weapons and mounts in armour. They thundered over the hills and pounded the ground as they rode without time for rest or thought of sword and fire.

He sent for ʿUthmān Pasha to become their *sirdār*; for he was governor-general of Yemen and the chief commander in the area, and he and his father had previously fought with these impudent Zaydī. It is essential that the troops have a leader to refer to and a chief to rally round and fight before, and the minister realised that ʿUthmān Pasha deserved such advancement before anybody else, seeing in it a lucky omen and fair augury for him.

So ʿUthmān Pasha accepted the minister's orders, mounted his resolute charger, and set out together with his companions; and the two commanders, with their party, advanced to Mt al-Aghbar, 'with snorting coursers'.[32] They launched dawn raids upon the Zaydī, firing shot at them from their muskets and causing great agitation in the haze cast by gunpowder and horse hoof. They infused the day with the darkness of night. The Zaydī military commanders were al-Hādī and Luṭfallāh, both sons of Muṭahhar, ʿAlī b. Shuwayʿ [224] and Ḥusayn b. Shams al-Dīn,[33] those pillars of sedition and evil and the source of revolt, wrongdoing and resistance.

With them were about 50,000 fighting men comprising horsemen, infantry, musketeers and archers. The darkness of their numbers equalled that of their evil. However, the sultan's troops, the Ottoman army, some one thousand strong, shattered with their resolution the most obdurate mass. They were sincere in their determination and firm in their resolve. How often, with God's permission, has a small force overcome a mighty one! Right excels and is not exceeded; and wrong sheds its power.

CHAPTER 6

[225] The Zaydī defeat and victory for the unitarian Sunnī forces

§ The Zaydī appreciated their superiority in numbers and equipment, the strength afforded them by Mt al-Aghbar, and the reliability of their supplies, as against the small number of Ottoman troops attacking them. Comparing them to the white spot on a black bull, they descended to the foot of the mountain ready for battle and armed for the fight. Each of their horsemen was accompanied by a number of musketeers on foot to protect him at the front and behind; and these men on foot would always discharge their weapons when the horseman was attacked. No horseman could reach them before he was shot dead by these muskets. None approached them even if he had the fastest of steeds. Such was their custom in battle and their way of fighting champion warriors.

Once the sultan's victorious troops saw their foe had come down from the mountain, to complete their tactics and strategy, they paused to let them finish their descent. However, some of them had no sooner reached its foot than they gave free rein to their horses so as to catch the fresh breeze. Each plunged in and, charging with a will, attacked with élan. They controlled those horses that tried to bolt and, with whinnies, to toss the loads from their backs as they scattered dove-like foam from their throats, the blazes on their faces lighting up with stars the pitch of the fray, and the white of their armour mingling with the black of their flanks.

Flights of arrows, with true aim, seek their targets and bowstrings demand revenge from the insolent sect: iron allows no scope for arrow and sword breaks against sword as if against a hedgehog. [226] Armour has been breached and spears have shattered; rivers of blood have flowed and souls and spirits have passed away.

The veil of night dropped between the Ottoman troops and their enemy who were put to flight on the bare backs of their horses, calling, after the fighting, in anger and distress. They climbed the mountain and took to their heels, abandoning their camp and fleeing for their lives. The heads of their dead rolled about like balls in a field. The victorious troops seized their goods in triumph and, grasping every baggage and load, removed all clothing and attire they could find. After the scarcity and hardship of their existence, they made themselves comfortable with such booty and returned to the minister, safe and sound and full of thanks to God. They filled the place with the gunpowder, arms, swords, spears, armour and coats of mail they had seized; and the minister showed general favour to all the sultan's troops in the camp. He rewarded each one individually in a suitable and befitting manner and gave everybody at least one Ottoman piece, together with generous praise. All obtained what they wished.

The minister awarded 'Uthmān Pasha two excellent cloaks made of the finest *serāser* lined with sable. There was absolute joy and delight, complete euphoria, in the Ottoman camp, whereas the enemy went off in distress and anguish. The good news rang out; flags were hoisted; curtains were raised; the country was *en fête*; slaves were happy; and passions were stilled. This blessed victory took place on Saturday 13 Dhū al-Qa'dah, 976/29 April 1569.

CHAPTER 7

[227] The conquest of the citadel of al-Qāhirah by the noble methods of Āṣāf;[34] and, at sight of death, its population's request for peace

§ The citadel at al-Qāhirah is one of the most strategic strongholds, the highest in size and altitude, of precise and meticulous construction, and with excellent fortifications. No bird save the eagle soars above it, and no arrow reaches it, even if served by the strongest flight. Within it are guns and cannon – none can approach – as well as archers who are true of aim, not to be deflected by coats of mail.

The minister, having settled the troops on Mt al-Aghbar, went alone at night, away from his servants, suite and soldiers, and circled al-Qāhirah, studying it and reflecting upon it. He was looking for a place from which it could be captured and was hoping to find a path or passage there when he noticed a spot from which the houses and parts of the citadel out of view would be within artillery range; and the cannon would also be able to hit anyone visible on the exposed areas and attack the sides and highest parts of the citadel.

He therefore gave orders for the large cannons to be carried on the shoulders of free men and placed in the new positions by night as it was not possible by day; for the artillery from al-Qāhirah had them within range and stone bullets from its riflemen could reach them. So the guns were transferred there by night and a screen of rocks was erected to prevent the Zaydī [228] from destroying them.

He prepared the men there to home in with the guns and hit people in the citadel with the result that none of them was to be seen on the heights. The people there realised that the Zaydī troops had lost and that their fire had been doused by Indian sword. Frustrated and dejected, they were frightened and at a loss. From such positions the Ottoman artillery caused their defences to shake and their homes to be destroyed. They blasted the positions of the al-Qāhirah population whose houses became their graves, while the Ottoman troops, after the fall of Mt al-Aghbar, advanced to take al-Qāhirah, encircling it with a number of military posts, each one larger than a village.

The commandant of al-Qāhirah was a man belonging to the Hamdānī *du'āh*[35] called Ṣalāḥ whose allegiance to Muṭahhar had lost him the meaning of al-Ṣalāḥ and al-Falāḥ [Goodness and Bravery], leaving him without a proper name, a dead term without meaning. His fellow tribesmen of the Hamdānī *du'āh* are among the greatest enemies of the Zaydī sect and among the staunchest of the sultan's supporters such as the Ja'farites.[36] Only hostility to his people and tribal jealousy had placed him in Muṭahhar's camp. He was at variance with his people and then withdrew, out of loss of judgment and discernment. Muṭahhar was delighted by his allegiance, placing him in the bosom of his following and trusting him with important tasks. He then appointed him commandant of al-Qāhirah. One of Ṣalāḥ's main reasons for coming to Muṭahhar was his opinion of the governorate's rough treatment of Yemen, its ambitions there, its impossible requests and their inability to satisfy its financial demands.

Thus he was coerced into Muṭahhar's service, appearing to be intimate with him, and friendly with him because necessity had forced him to it; for out of necessity one is forced to what one does not wish. As is said:

> For shelter, one is obliged to face difficulties: without them, it would not be on offer.

And is also said:

> Without it being necessary, we wouldn't have come of our own free will to faces intimate with infidelity.

The upright commander, the Dā'ī 'Abdullāh al-Hamdānī,[37] was one of the most important *du'āh* commanders, with an Ottoman district and the noble title of *sanjak*. [229] Shaikh 'Abdullāh the Dā'ī was a great friend to the Ottoman forces, only at the time Muṭahhar took Ṣan'ā' under truce, he was one of a number of commanders to whom Muṭahhar gave protection after concluding terms and then offering pardon. They were imprisoned and deceived but, because of his high standing with his people, the Dā'ī 'Abdullāh was not imprisoned but was offered pardon in the hope that he would become Muṭahhar's friend and one of his intimate commanders. However, the *dā'ī* turned up his nose at the offer. He did not trust him and began to contrive an opportunity to escape from him, albeit feigning affection for him and appearing to be among those devoted to him. Muṭahhar was happy with the situation and keen to humour him but he arranged for a guard to keep an eye on him and watch him from a discreet distance.

'Abdullāh was aware of the watch as he prepared a ruse to escape from Muṭahhar. Beneath the town wall, he would get ready a good fast horse, quick to respond and race like lightning, driven to frenzy with youth and fervour and in complete harmony with his will.

> Lo he chargeth, turneth, – gone is he – all in one,
> like to a rock stream – trundled, hurled from its eminence.[38]

He tethered the horse in a special place he knew and at night hung suspended by rope from the citadel till he reached the ground and mounted his horse. Then fleeing throughout the night, he covered a great distance unobserved by the guard. However, they realised that he had escaped and reported the fact to Muṭahhar who, seeing that he had got away and that none could catch him, regretted not having imprisoned him, with the words, 'We've begrudged using ten weights of iron on the Dā'ī 'Abdullāh. I mean we've left him without fetters.' And the tyrant began to bite his hands, full of regret over him. Then he bore down hard on the rest of the commanders in prison, separating them among different strongholds and increasing the weight of their fetters which for each commander now weighed half a *qanṭar*[39] of iron. He kept away from them their servants and those who would meet them, increasing his oppression and tyranny over them. 'Those who do wrong will come to know by what a [great] reverse they will be overturned!'[40]

The Dā'ī Shaikh 'Abdullāh continued his furtive flight from village to village, changing his identity and appearance until he reached the country of the Ja'farites, a large tribe loyal to the sultan and without tie to Muṭahhar or any disloyal role, throughout the evil and terrible days of [230] the rebellion.

The Ja'farites[41] are Sunnī of the Shāfi'ī school, without hint of heresy or inclination to evil and corruption. Their commander at the time was Shaikh Abū Bakr al-Ja'farī whose brother and son had fallen into the hands of Muṭahhar;[42] and Muṭahhar had said to them, 'Write to Abū Bakr to show allegiance to me, and I will raise his standing and status. I shall assign him part of the country and make him extremely happy.' They promised him that they would write in such terms and indeed did send a message to the shaikh. 'Make sure your castle is well fortified. Don't obey Muṭahhar. Let him kill and flay us. We have offered ourselves to Almighty God.' Muṭahhar had failed in his attempt to influence them and win them over.

Shaikh Abū Bakr al-Ja'farī gave hospitality to the Dā'ī Shaikh 'Abdullāh when he arrived, doing what was necessary for him and sending him to Ḥasan Pasha in Zabīd where the people and all the remaining Ottoman troops were delighted by the shaikh's arrival and came out to meet him. They brought him into Ḥasan Pasha who entertained him and gave him an official Ottoman honorary robe. The people of Zabīd drew strength from him till the arrival of the minister, may Almighty God help him, under whose authority and in whose service the shaikh now fell.

The minister sought their advice in matters of importance and was attentive to their views when the unhappy problems of the rebellion were disclosed. He consulted with them over the capture of al-Qāhirah, and the shaikh and Ḥasan Pasha sought his permission to go to Ṣalāḥ with plans for his removal. He gave such permission; so, with his authority, they went up to the citadel with advice for Ṣalāḥ, that either he had to give up and surrender, and seek terms of peace with the minister, or he would be quickly taken by force. Its fortifications would be of no avail for him; nor would his castle and fortress protect him. For all that are under siege are taken. Indeed Muṭahhar is now unable to protect himself; so how could he protect his supporters? This is the only sort of talk of use to such people. Ṣalāḥ realised that this was correct and that there was no point in such arrogance and resistance. He was inclined to their view; so, confident that he would seek peace from the minister, they obtained assurances for his safety from him; and the minister obliged.

One of the minister's best characteristics was his fulfilment of promises made and his standing by his word and commitment.

They brought Ṣalāḥ down to the minister whose feet he kissed, displaying his submission and surrender; and Ṣalāḥ handed over to him the keys of al-Qāhirah, expressing his innocence over what had happened. The minister then reproved him for [231] his resistance, for his conduct during the rebellion, for the loss of people and property on both sides, and for his stubborn persistence in wrongdoing over which he had been very pig-headed.

Ṣalāḥ responded with some splendid excuses. The oppression of the governorate and its party, their extreme greed and their unbearable demands on him of which he gave numerous examples. It was they who had driven him to beg off his neighbours and to come out in rebellion against the power which was a force for good. But he now expressed both his loyalty, for what he had heard of the minister's kindness and justice, and his return to government and authority. He had great affection for him and was seized with love and devotion for him. And, of course, he had, in the citadel of al-Qāhirah, weapons, machinery and lots of equipment, together with food and men to last a long time, as well as the fortifications and defences of the stronghold and its tremendous height in the sky. He now offered all that out of affection for the minister, preferring submission to him to conflict and trouble.

Observant of his good promises and compelled by his sincere commitment, the minister accepted his excuses, receiving him with generosity and pardon, and offering his protection to him and all those in the citadel. He awarded robes of honour to all who deserved them. There were some fifty persons, all of whom he summoned, treating them kindly and giving them clothes. He awarded Ṣalāḥ a magnificent robe and assigned him and the others suitable remuneration. He began to treat them kindly and chat to them, enrolling them in the ranks of the Ottoman army.[43]

The mass of the Ottoman army mustered and took over the positions containing cannon, war apparatus, food, gunpowder – double what was expected – and Ta'izz was then delivered, with all its outlying districts, strongholds, fortresses, mountains, highways and byways, and returned to the Ottoman possessions, to be restored to its customary Ottoman rule. Muslims were delighted by the magnificent victory and the general population looked forward to enjoying the justice of the magnificent sultan, through the good judgment of this great and generous minister. This blessed conquest took place on Wednesday morning, 17 Dhū al-Qaʻdah, 976/3 May 1569.

CHAPTER 8

[232] The minister's dispatch of Commander Khayr al-Dīn the admiral by sea and Commander Ḥusayn by land to capture Aden from Qāsim b. Shuwayʻ and the Zaydī there

§ It has been told how ʻAlī b. Shuwayʻ captured Aden during the days of unrest and established there Zaydī forms of worship, and how his brother, Qāsim b. Shuwayʻ, was appointed by Muṭahhar as his deputy.

The Ottoman government, Almighty God make its sultanate last for ever and give victory to its armies and servants, when it was told of the capture of Aden, nearly lost heart for fear that the cursed Franks would occupy it. For its port was extremely well defended and fortified, with incomparable equipment, war apparatus, cannon and guns; and if it fell into the hands of the wretched Franks, it would be difficult to regain it due to their knowledge of artillery and cannon fire and their care for ports and castles, in contrast to the Arabs who lacked such necessary knowledge. If the accursed Franks gained control of this fortified port, they would bring pressure to bear on the Muslims, prevent ships from India from reaching the ports of the Holy Places and perhaps aspire to taking Jiddah and its surrounding district, with harmful consequences for [233] the Holy Places and their outlying villages.

The minister entertained absolutely no doubts at all that he would have to expend every effort and do everything within his power to take Aden and save it from the Zaydī before the accursed Franks got there. The Porte had told him, 'We have to restore it to the control of Yemen as part of our duty; for it was the legacy of our late noble sultan. That was an important stimulus for us since he had maintained the port of Aden as a protection for the Holy Places against the wretched heathens and the heretical Zaydī as he had in general protected Muslims from religious heretics.' These were strong words of more value by far than priceless pearls to grace His Excellency's ear, hanging as an ornament from his esteemed lobe.[44]

As soon as his mounts had reached Mawzaʻ,[45] as he was travelling to Taʻizz, the minister made a detour to the port of Mocha, got together all the available small boats and loaded them with apparatus, equipment and troops whom he dispatched by sea to Aden under the charge of Commander the Admiral Khayr al-Dīn who was known as Qūrt Ögħlū (Son of a Wolf). He was a courageous and knowledgeable man, of sound judgment, especially in matters concerning the sea and naval warfare and in siege craft and artillery.

He had experience and understanding of such activity and had to his credit battles and victories over the Franks. He had had many encounters with them and was much wounded; and his bravery, knowledge and enterprise were renowned. He had been imprisoned by them several times and had been released; and, in turn, had taken their chiefs and leaders prisoner.

He sailed with this craft to Aden, departing from the port of Mocha on Saturday 28 Shawwāl 976/15 April 1569. After getting the admiral ready for Aden, the minister returned to his army in Mawzaʿ and was then busy fighting with the people of Mt al-Aghbar and capturing al-Qāhirah. Afterwards, he also equipped a land force against Aden to assist the admiral to which he assigned under Commander Māmāy some of the most courageous horsemen from a group well known for its skill in battle and combat. The commander was a brave and bloodthirsty fighter famous for the time when, as *kāshif*, he had conquered the bedu [234] by being invariably firm, brave and determined with such people.

By such means had Commander Māmāy subdued the country and eradicated the trouble-makers who considered it of little importance to kill for the sake of some drinking water, and took pleasure in murder and bloodshed. The commander had slain thousands of people and witnessed greater battles than that of al-Basūs![46] So he obeyed the command, untied his banner, got ready his horses, men and troops and set out by land for Aden to wrest it from the wretched enemy; and his departure from the minister took place on Saturday, 20 Dhū al-Qaʿdah 976/6 May 1569.

CHAPTER 9

[235] The minister's resolution to travel to Ṣanʿāʾ; and his consultation on the subject with the commanders

§ Once the minister had settled the affairs of Taʿizz, al-Qāhirah and the surrounding district, arranging matters there and appointing commanders and officers whom he could trust, he mounted his resolute charger, buckled on his doughty armour and set off to take Ṣanʿāʾ; for it was the country's capital and base for its army and troops, the place where Muṭahhar had taken up residence, fortifying it with his bedu and hillmen, with all the cunning and craft at his disposal. The Zaydī who had fought at Mt al-Aghbar joined him as well as every man jack among the mountain tribesmen who had taken the sultan's 'shilling',[47] in numbers impossible to calculate, with numerous weapons stolen during the days of unrest and with guns and cannon to raze mountains.

However, a lot of sheep do not frighten the butcher, and fine necklaces, however valuable, are worth more to people who appreciate them. So His Excellency assembled the Ottoman provincial commanders, the senior officers of the Ottoman army and those tribesmen he could trust who had knowledge of the numerous roads, with their position over water and provisions; their stretches of rough and easy going, their uplands and lowlands, their hidden secrets, their passes that were narrow or blocked, and their places to camp and rest. Once he had learnt all that and had checked the topography, the minister sought their advice as to the best route for conducting the huge army; a route that could provide forage for the [236] livestock and passage for human beings as well as for the oxen drawing the heavy guns; and he gained a full understanding of the different features of every route.

The most arduous task for the troops would be to carry the large guns on their shoulders over rocks and hills impassable by wheeled transport, to say nothing of tremendous mountains where all the tracks were rough, with stones both large and small, and high, towering ranges, the peaks of which just about touched the stars. There was nothing human or friendly there: the land was host only to gazelle and camels the colour of the desert: behind every rock lurked a pack of monkeys or a pride of lions. And Muṭahhar had already destroyed and razed to the ground villages built by the road, scattering their inhabitants all over the area. There was nothing there but the howling of jackals, the hooting of owls and the sound of crows; nor was there sign or trace of livestock.

After being informed of such conditions, the minister, understanding what terrors the Ottoman troops would have to endure, exclaimed, 'I consider we should approach 'Uthmān Pasha. After all he is Governor-General of Yemen. We shall consult him about undertaking such trials and tribulations. Perhaps he will be resolute and shrewd in countering the difficulty of such a challenging situation.' The remaining commanders endorsed his view as did the senior military officers, the *aghas* and other senior staff; and they reached this sound and fitting conclusion.

CHAPTER 10

[237] 'Uthmān Pasha's invitation to consultations and his obdurate refusal to come

§ As the sun drew the clarity of its light against the forces of the dark and, in true morning, spread from the horizon to conquer the army of the night, it filled furthest horizons with light and splendour; and the only darkness was that of the hair of buxom young girls and the kohl used to fard their eyes! Only then did the minister, sitting in the heart of his high *dīwān* among the commanders, the senior and the worthy, give orders to two of the official orderlies known for their intelligence and gravity, and their good manners and courtesy. They were both called ʿAlī and enjoyed high status within their unit. He ordered them to go to ʿUthmān Pasha and, with the utmost courtesy, inform him that they were to invite him to the sultan's official *dīwān* for consultations concerning what was feasible for them to do; for all the sultan's subjects who sought shelter in his far-reaching favour were obliged to fight against rebellion and wrongdoing within the land and districts of Yemen. Any mistake in direction would emerge from an exchange of views and the right course would be clear to the finest mind; for in a social community seclusion brings no advantage, and team spirit brings greater benefit to the majority than isolation.

The two orderlies proceeded to Taʿizz to deliver the letter, reaching ʿUthmān Pasha's residence before the sun had set. When they appeared at his door, he was rude and rough with them and offered no welcome. In a haughty and arrogant manner, he kept them at the gate for a long time without letting them in. He was a headstrong and intractable man, [238] supercilious and full of overweening pride. He always behaved in a very odd way, a creature of vanity, clad in disdain and hauteur. He had a noble and generous spirit and was a man of courage and daring but he would belittle the greatest gift. His horsemanship, the great display in his dress and his mount, and the precise arrangements in his *dīwān* and suite attracted looks and stares and created a great impression in hearts and minds.

Once they received permission, the two orderlies approached him and explained why they had been sent. They were polite in their explanation and courteous in their gestures. His reply, however, was as follows: 'He who appointed him minister has appointed me governor-general. Just as he is *sirdār* of the Egyptian troops who came with him, I am *sirdār* of the Ottoman forces that came with me. It is not for me to go to him; nor is it right for such as me to appear in front of him.' They each gave him all sorts of good advice but he persisted in his objection and was adamant in his refusal.

So they returned to His Excellency and relayed to him in great detail the reply he had given, whereupon the minister, after reflection, stated what was in his mind and gave his reaction to the excuses offered by ʿUthmān, with the words, 'It was up to us to judge who could sort out and reorganise the difficult situation in Taʿizz and its neighbourhood. If he is the man whom we judge suitable for the purpose, it is for us to decide what we ask and seek from him. As he has been appointed governor-general by the sultan and enjoys his favour, concern and protection, the more should he, with his suite, continue in his post and stay and look after Taʿizz.'

The minister had begun to prepare for the expedition, organising his officers and men and setting out to fight Muṭahhar when all of a sudden 'Uthmān Pasha moved his camp up-country, pitching his tents opposite those of the minister. He advanced with his suite to the main army, prompting the minister to realise that such obstinacy could lead to disorder and indeed perhaps to an unsavoury contest. Were conditions to deteriorate, the army might become divided; for two lions cannot get on in the bush and two swords cannot be kept in one scabbard. A small space was enough for a hundred poor men but the most enormous region could not satisfy two kings. The obstinate and painful dispute continued to cause rancour within their hearts. 'If there were therein gods beside Allāh, then verily both [the heavens and the earth] had been disordered.'[48]

CHAPTER II

[239] The minister's dismissal of 'Uthmān Pasha and the restoration of Ḥasan Pasha in his place as governor-general of Yemen

§ Once 'Uthmān Pasha had pitched his tents opposite those of the minister, his mamluks and his following joined him and his tents and encampment grew in number and size: some of the troops enlisted with him and a number of tribesmen enrolled. 'Uthmān Pasha began to threaten the Yemeni troops and Arab tribes who had not come over to him. He displayed anger towards the people of al-Qāhirah to whom the minister had granted protection provided they would not reach treaty terms with 'Uthmān Pasha, nor hand over to him the keys of the fortress. He began to claim that 'The minister will return to Egypt and none other than I shall be appointed as your governor-general. I shall deal with you severely afterwards, the outcome of what you have done and punishment for what you have committed.'

The tribesmen were frightened by this and some of the troops resident in Yemen came secretly to the minister with complaints about their situation, over which he commiserated with them but cheered them up, and sent them away happy and in good spirits.

Matters could only degenerate and, in consequence, a variety of futile and ugly things happened. On being informed, the enemy were overjoyed, displaying utter delight and joy at the argument between Muslims. Things nearly got out of hand and, after easing and calming down, the situation became complicated. Indeed, the minister was afraid that what happened during the attack on Malta in 973/1565/6 would befall him.

[240] To summarise: the late hallowed Sultan Sulaymān Khan, God bless his era with every mercy and favour and fill the meadows where he lies with sweet-smelling herbs, dispatched a magnificent fleet of more than a hundred

ships, laden with weapons of war and full of brave men, to conquer Malta and rid it of the Christians. He made Draghūd Pasha *sirdār* of the army and sent with them his minister, Muṣṭafā Pasha b. Isfindiār. However, an argument broke out between them while they were in enemy country which led to a difference of opinion. This gave victory over the Muslims to the Christians who found an opportunity to destroy an entire army. Draghūd Pasha lost his life and the rest were routed because of the failure to agree and make up the difference. They returned to Istanbul in defeat, losing in the war an incalculable amount of property, stores and lives.[1]

The defeat was notorious throughout Islam, a curse and torment for the late sultan to endure till he died, God have mercy on him, and his soul passed away suffering from such an affliction, a broken-hearted man. Indeed, every Muslim has become wounded and broken in heart because of this. 'The commandment of God must be fulfilled.'[2] Had the sultan, God have mercy on him, lived longer, he would not have left the people of Malta and their ruler walking in the garb of conceit. He would have invaded them with his troops and would have done all he could to wipe them out. Ottoman swords will surely take them. They will be taken, even if after a period of time, God willing, by the mighty Ottoman sword.

Let us resume our account. Once the minister realised things were getting out of hand and falling apart, he applied his shrewd judgment and sharp intelligence to correcting the problem before it gained control and to dealing with the emergency in the quickest and most effective fashion. He spent the night thinking about it, cogitating and turning over the matter in his mind; and eyes were dusted with sleep's antimony, save those of the stars which never close. So praise God who does not sleep.

[241] The white of morn rose, emerging through the grey, and, after long defiance, banished the darkness of night, as they called out the summons for prayer with greetings for the day's success; and morning burst forth its sway as the phantoms of the night took flight on black wings. Then did the minister open his *dīwān* and honour the *īwān*[3] with his presence, his commanders assembled beside him, the glorious army in ranks before him and his aides standing at his command. He took out of his laden treasure chest a bag of magnificent cloth containing an edict from the sultan, a noble Ottoman decree, which he handed to the clerk to the council. He gave orders for it to be read out to the large gathering, in loud tones, right to the end, with care and deliberation until everyone there had understood it. His noble instruction was obeyed, and the scribe read it out, word by word, to the mighty assembly.

The purport of the noble edict, the esteemed Ottoman order, was that: 'The Sublime Sultanate, Almighty God protect it on earth for ever, has entrusted the control of Yemen, its affairs, deserts and mountains, to his mighty minister and honoured counsellor, regulator of the world, shrewd director of the public's affairs, wise executor of mankind's interests, state minister of the Ottoman empire, Sinān Pasha, long live his ministry and support for his administration. And it has established him as personal deputy and *sirdār* of his esteemed glorious army, with all powers of dismissal, appointment, bestowal and promotion, quite independent of all and without let or interference. His government derives from the Ottoman state as do his orders. All who come into conflict with him or fail to obey him should be warned. He who warns has given notice'; and the sultan's monogram was at the top so as to emphasise its significance. This was one of the decrees written on the sultan's orders in Istanbul, rather than one of the documents containing his emblem given to the minister to write on as he wished when the occasion required.[4]

When the scribe had completed the reading of the noble decree in the *dīwān* and the parade had understood its significance, the minister asked of those present, 'Who is your *sirdār*?', to which they replied, 'You.' So he asked, 'Do you have to comply with the instructions it contains?' [242] 'Yes,' they replied. 'Can any governor, commander or anyone else in Yemen contradict me?' 'No,' they said. Then he pointed to one of the sultan's eminent *sanjaks*, Aḥmad Bey by name, who was commander of the Egyptian pilgrimage and one of the commanders with an Egyptian commission, whom he had directed to travel with the army. He was called Kūjuk Aḥmad because of his short stature. The minister now said to him: 'Had we wished to sack 'Uthmān Pasha, we would have done so but the sultan, God save him, has already dismissed him, and we have the edict for his dismissal, written at the Sublime Porte and summoning him there. The only reason for our delay is concern for him and the reinforcement and enlargement of the army. In that he has done nothing but damage to the army, and caused division, we must publish it and give orders for the imperial edict to be taken out of its sealed case.'

With the seal of the grand vizier, Meḥmed Pasha,[5] God save his rule and help his ministry, and on it the name of 'Uthmān Pasha, the minister handed it over to Aḥmad Bey, with the words, 'Go with the edict to 'Uthmān Pasha, give it to him and say that, if he is to obey the sultan's command, he should depart now, without any delay and without any military escort at all, and leave the entire army.' So Aḥmad Bey went off with the edict and handed it over to him; and the pasha at once obeyed the esteemed command, tying up his tent, in evident joy and delight, and heading for Zabīd whence he would travel to Mecca, and then to the Sublime Porte.

Aḥmad Bey returned to the minister and told him that he had carried out his orders and that the pasha had departed. His servants now dispersed completely and the minister summoned the former minister and governor-general, Ḥasan Pasha,[6] dressing him in a caftan of office and restoring him to his post in 'Uthmān Pasha's place. The public was averse to Ḥasan Pasha in view of his association, during his period in office, with an intermediary called al-Basakrī, his administration of Zabīd district and his extortion and impounding of public property. But, although the pasha had been oppressive and tyrannical as has been said, necessity drove him to act in such a way to meet the costs of the army. In any case, the minister made him governor-general only in name, with the semblance of authority which he did not allow him to exercise once he had understood his behaviour and character.

Almighty God heeded the prayer [243] of the oppressed to bring al-Basakrī to justice. The rod of his youth was broken; he was driven to justice to receive appropriate sentence, and so wrongdoers should not thrive. 'Those who do wrong will come to know by what a great reverse they will be overturned.'[7] Before he passed away and was swallowed by the jaws of death, Ḥasan Pasha came to regret his previous association and favouritism. He arrested and imprisoned al-Basakrī, punishing him severely and confiscating his property. He atoned for his wrongs in as far as he was able and made amends for part of what had been brought to him and the damage done to the populace by the association of evil men with rulers and the elite. Such damage rebounds on the sovereign and the rulers themselves: it ruins a once flourishing state, devouring everything in the land, destroying property and leading to hell-fire and a terrible end.

> When you are in a community, keep company with the best of them and do not befriend the worst, for you will become as bad as he. Don't ask about a man; rather ask about his companion because each man copies him with whom he consorts.

> Frequently literati quote these lines:

> It is for you to be with those with influence; for he who is with them will get ahead. Take care not to befriend the wicked, as you will lose your high place and be despised. The rise and fall of him who boasts offers a message, stark and warning.

It is said:

> Keep company if you can consort with free-born men; for his companion influences a young man for better or for worse.

It is also said:

> The character of a young man stems from that of his companions; and pay heed with whom you consort.

Sinān Pasha had been given some information about the disgraceful events during the disorder among the Yemeni mamluks in Ḥasan Pasha's time; so when he decided to restore him to the governor-generalship, he gave him advice in most emphatic terms, making clear to him the damage caused by his profiteering, with the words: 'You are a graduate of the sultan's palace education and belong to the cream of the Ottoman service; other commanders have had their education at a distance and have not had the honour to enjoy your advantage of proximity to that blessed presence. You have been within sight and hearing of His Majesty the Sultan and you have seen the splendid features [244] of his face in all their radiance. Others have not had the benefit of this privilege; nor has everyone attained such high rank. Any mistake of yours, however few in number, is too much; any fault of yours, however small, is for you a terrible shame. Your duty is to be perfect in all respects; you must display absolute fairness; freedom from injustice and oppression; reflection when faced with problems and sound judgment; distance from tyranny and aggression; and absence of cruelty towards any living thing, let alone human beings.'

The minister discoursed at length on such maxims and enumerated the vile and appalling ways in which Ḥasan Pasha had contravened such principles. An alert audience would have listened and the recital of such valuable advice would have pleased its ears. Perhaps it was just about enough and, God willing, may really have done the trick.

As for 'Uthmān Pasha, he had no sooner left the minister's camp than he began to slacken pace and linger on the way. Successive messengers from the minister reached him, urging him on and goading him, but only made him more dilatory and simply increased his hesitation and lethargy. In this way a long time passed before he reached Zabīd, which he was not able to enter, so he pitched his camp in the area outside. He began to froth and foam and fume with rage; and he fell into deep thought and distress. Messengers repeatedly came to him but letters coming from the minister, containing orders to travel and threats of the consequences, went unheeded by him.

After taking Ta'izz, the pasha had sent a courier to the Sublime Porte, followed by a second after his dismissal by the minister, and he now began to wait for the Porte's reply and procrastinate over the journey until the reply should come. The longer the journey, the greater the need for him to delay and wait. So he lingered until the reply arrived summoning him to the Porte and appointing Behrām Pasha,[8] son of Muṣṭafā Pasha, governor-general of Yemen. 'Uthmān Pasha was then obliged to carry out the sultan's instructions and to travel to the Sublime Porte, so he began to prepare for travel by land, loading his heavy luggage into trading craft which he dispatched by sea. He then set out on his journey using horses, mules and riding and baggage camels for his lighter effects. He travelled from Zabīd to Jīzān, and thence to Mecca.

[245] On his arrival at al-Sa'diyyah,[9] our lord Shaikh al-Islam, Guardian of the Holy Mosque, Sayyid Qadi Ḥusayn al-Mālikī went out to meet him with our lord, Sharīf Ḥusayn, son of our lord, Sayyid Ḥasan, Sharīf of Mecca, Almighty God help him and give him everlasting glory. Also with him were a number of sharifs from the Banū Ḥasan on horseback, including Sayyid 'Arār b. 'Ajil al-Numawī, as well as about 100 Turkish horsemen. They all went out to meet him at Malkān staging-post on Thursday, 3 Ramaḍān 977/9 February 1570, and they came upon the camp which 'Uthmān Pasha had pitched on his arrival. They continued on horseback until they met him and accompanied him to his camp where he was friendly to them and complained about the trials and tribulations he had suffered in Yemen which, thank God, he had now escaped. He gave them vast cloaks of *serāser* and *shayb*.[10] He spent a day there and then set off on his journey at night.

'Uthmān Pasha entered Mecca before noon on Friday, 4 Ramaḍān/10 February, in a large procession with much display containing some 200 horsemen and 400 camels, but it was strung out, faulty and weak;[11] and he came in from lower Mecca and left by the upper end for his camp. Then he chose to stay at the Qāyitbey[12] school which was vacated for him and which he had frequented and where he had given alms to the poor. He stayed in Mecca and celebrated the feast there, providing a splendid meal in al-Ḥusayniyyah at al-Ma'lāh. The dignitaries and important people called on him in droves.

On Saturday 8 Shawwāl/16 March, the pasha travelled to the holy city of Medina and visited the tomb of the Prophet, God bless him and grant him salvation, where he dispensed much alms, thinking that in the blessings from such alms lay the avoidance of misfortune.

Later he returned to Yanbu', and then left for Egypt and the Sublime Porte, dispensing generous gifts and escaping from difficulties. He continued to dance attendance, seeking a happy return.

CHAPTER 12

[246] The minister's circumstances after 'Uthmān Pasha had left him

§ After 'Uthmān Pasha's departure from the Ottoman camp on his journey, Sinān Pasha withdrew into his encampment and was left alone to his own business, free from argument; and the troops knew where to refer important matters.

The minister began to prepare for departure and assembled his official commanders for an exchange of views. They were unanimous about leaving Ta'izz and pitching the Ottoman camp in a place called al-Qā'idah,[13] at two stages from Ta'izz. He sent off ahead of him Ḥasan Pasha with the entire

Yemeni army while he appointed his deputies in Ta'izz and al-Qāhirah, and then advanced with the military forces that accompanied him, the troops surging like waves of the sea as they tramped the ground and made the mountain tops ring with their resolve; the inactive shedding their lethargy and the brave bristling with the terror in store for the enemy, with their lance tips aquiver as they marched from Ta'izz. Already he had marshalled his units and squadrons, ordered his commanders and notables, fastened his loads and mounts, and arranged his outriders to the fore.

In this formation the minister advanced as far as al-Qā'idah, on the second stage. His lofty pavilions had been erected and his bell tents spread as they arranged and decorated them; and they hauled and set up the guns and cannon. His arrival from Ta'izz took place on Saturday, the third day before the end of Dhū al-Qa'dah, 976/14 May 1569. He stayed there for a few days so as to select the road to be taken to Ṣan'ā'. Meanwhile, the Zaydī began to block the roads, convinced as to the value of their action, [247] forming pools in some by diverting streams, and making mires of others from water oozing from the loose earth of those parts; and some of the mountain paths they made impassable by rolling huge rocks and stones on to the tracks. They emptied the area of villages and settlements, leaving them razed, a quarry full of stones, devoid of light. Could spiders' webs stop a tremendous flood or the tails of foxes and rabbits stop a mighty army?

As the minister stayed in al-Qā'idah, examining the routes and checking tracks and distances, he realised that there were three obvious routes to be taken northwards.

The first route: Naqīl Aḥmar (Red Pass).[14] It is a defile between two lofty mountains, inaccessible because of its difficult terrain, devoid of all human life, with ascents and descents, and desert and plain where none but monkeys go and only wild animals and lions resort. It would be difficult to take the guns and cannon there, with the labour of carrying them on back and shoulder. The route was not lengthy but, in view of the hardship involved, would prove protracted, and, in that the pass was extremely tough going, it was regarded as unsuitable.

The second route: Wadi Suḥbān.[15] This curves like a snake, and anyone who takes it would risk being poisoned by the sting of vipers coiled in its dangerous crannies. It is much churned up, swampy and hard going for pack and load, where horses would wade up to belly and stirrup. It contains mountains that pierce the clouds and passes that pose mighty problems for the traveller. Once more, there is no pleasure there, only pain. This route is much like the first in proximity but worse in terms of hardship. It was decided not to use it and to avoid it.

The third route, called by them Maytam.[16] This is a long route containing both hard and easy going, but a better passage for the troops, despite its length, and easier for conveying the guns, despite the distance and the extent. Moreover, it was free of obstacles [248] erected by the Zaydī such as trees rolled down over it and overturned rocks from the high mountain ranges blocking its tracks. Waters from the streams had not been diverted over it to cause swamps; nor had it been turned into pools through which the tremendous army would not be able to wade. For they had not contemplated the Turks choosing this route and selecting such a low-lying passage.

The minister decided to travel via Maytam; thus befell the enemies of religion what came to pass. Among the good fortune and news that befell the minister was the announcement of the conquest of Aden. He therefore found al-Qāʿidah auspicious. Muslims displayed their joy and lost their uncertainty and despair. God's help must be sought, and trust placed in Him.

CHAPTER 13

[249] Arrival of the good news of the capture of Aden and the extinction of the fire behind the revolt

§ After he had equipped Commander Khayr al-Dīn, the admiral, and his brother, Commander Sinān, to seize Aden by sea, and Commander Māmāy, with a cavalry squadron and some heroic detachments, from the land, Sinān Pasha devoted his fine mind to maintaining contact with the troops and following every source for news of them.

Qāsim b. Shuwayʿ was the lame Muṭahhar's governor in Aden. He evinced his strange doctrine, characteristic of Zaydism, in which he displayed pride and arrogance, thereby diverging from the right path. The population of Aden, being Shāfiʿī, detested him, firm in the belief in the Holy Quran and the Sunnah, and strictly Sunnī. He began to construct a school in the name of Muṭahhar in which some of the Zaydī could study this execrable sect.

He had 1,000 Zaydī hillmen with him comprising 400 fighters and 600 musketeers but he did not trust in such a throng and turned to the Franks, inviting them to Aden. A small ship came from the latter containing some twenty Franks in the belief that they would give him assistance and succour, so he took them up into the fortress where he showed them the equipment, weapons and fortifications there, gave them the heavy cannon and agreed to assign them part of the sea so as to protect the town from the Turks. The land [250] would be the responsibility of the Zaydī and their people and part of the sea that of the Christians and their party. The Franks were agreeable to the plan and went off to bring Franks from Goa.[17] Ibn Shuwayʿ sent a message to apprise Muṭahhar of what he had done, which was appreciated, and he was praised and thanked for his action. Muṭahhar promoted him and acknowledged his excellent action in support of such a policy which will remain a disgrace to him and his followers until the Day of Judgment. Almighty God forsook Qāsim b. Shuway‘, rammed his cheating down his throat and overturned this base thinking of him and his troops. Almighty God got hold of him once and for all and made him taste ignominy in this world and everlasting punishment in the thereafter. Let a real lesson be taught.

Through divine fate and decree Admiral Khayr al-Dīn Bey was first to Aden and, as he stood off it, he saw far off in mid-ocean twenty sails belonging to twenty Frankish ships heading for the port.[18] Once the admiral was sure of the sighting, he set sail for them with his twelve ships. Then the Franks recognised that they belonged to the admiral, and, having such intelligence, began to sail away, with the admiral in pursuit of them for an entire day; and they got away.

For the admiral was frightened he would get far out to sea and lose the chance of taking Aden. So he turned round and returned to Aden and God saved the Muslims from fighting. The Portuguese Christians fled and the Zaydī were left with fire and brimstone. Such was the wondrous kindness of God and his perfect generosity for the Muslim people; for, although the accursed Portuguese had got into the great fortress of Aden beforehand, because of God's victory over heresy and contempt for religion, God ensured victory for the true religion. Glory to God, his Prophet and Muslims.

[251] The way Aden was captured from the Zaydī; and their defeat by those fighting in the name of religion

After arriving at the Aden coast, Commander Khayr al-Dīn made his base there, disembarking his cannon and searching for points of access to Aden fortress from the direction of the sea while he waited for the arrival of the army by land to complete his encirclement of Aden.

Suddenly, the commanders appeared as their spears and banners caught the eye; and, lo! Commander Māmāy arrived from overland, with the dashing troops and heroic cavalry of the noble Ottoman army, who surrounded Aden on all sides and began to approach its walls in the pitch dark of night in search of somewhere they could erect a scaling ladder, and a point appropriate for an ascent. For its walls were higher than the Pleiades and its method of fortification borrowed from a jewelled constellation as if the clouds were its turban and the moon's crescent a paring from its fingernail,[19] thrusting high into the sky, like the tip of the sun as it rises. They were higher than thunder and lightning, higher than [the stars] al-Suhā[20] and Capella; no shaft of changing time penetrates it; neither mankind, nor jinn, pollutes its virgin fortress.

Among those who circled the fortress and stood on its foothills was the captain Shukr, deputy to the late Ṣafar Bey, Admiral of Yemen,[21] who, in earlier days, while thinking of somewhere large enough to enter, if only a jerboa hole or a tunnel wide enough to reach the area, fell asleep over his thoughts, with slumber gripping his poor eyelids, and saw in his sleep the noble sayyid, known to Almighty God, Shaikh Bakr al-'Aydarūs,[22] one of the Yemeni saints, on him the mercy of the Most Holy King. He was based in Aden and famous for his manifest miracles and splendid and brilliant good deeds. It was as if the saint took him by the hand and conveyed him to one of the Aden forts called Shamsān,[23] incomparable in its high position save for al-Qamarān, and pointed out to him a path upwards, with the words [252] 'Go up from here. Do what you have set your heart on here.'

Shukr then woke up and was grateful for the sleep, rising from his rest in haste, and quickly he went to the spot pointed out by this generous spirit, accompanied by some brave soldiers. Ascending by a scaling ladder while people were asleep, they found in Shamsān three Arab tribesmen, their eyes closed in sleep and ears tight with slumber. Slumber had so completely overtaken them that they were as good as corpses. As they woke, all were taken by the sword and slain. Death was their lot. Their ranks were formed: the men were ready. Then the heroes ascended, the Ottoman *sanjak* was put in place and the victorious imperial flag was raised. The saviour Ottoman army grew bigger and the sun of victory shone from the direction of Shamsān; and shame and disappointment befell the enemies of religion.

Qāsim b. Shuway' fled to his fortifications, busying himself with his gang in his domain, defending his base with all his strength. And, lo, victory then followed from the sea. Commander Khayr al-Dīn, with all his troops from the seaward side, and Commander Māmāy from the land, aspired to attack Aden from every side, inspired by Almighty God. They stood firm in their resolve and intent in their determination; and it was with divine help and the assistance of God that the Ottoman army achieved victory and entered Aden on every military front, by force of arms from land and sea.

Once he realised the position, Ibn Shuway', agitated and confused, made himself secure in a ruined property, and began suing for peace. He asked for help but was given only defeat and deprivation. Ignominy was his lot, and despair, and his tribesmen had recourse to the grave of Shaikh 'Aydarūs in a bid to save their skins. Realising their vulnerability, Commander Khayr al-Dīn felt pity and compassion for them and gave them peace terms without thought of sword and spear; and they brought to him Qāsim b. Shuway' with his son and supporters and those who belonged to him and loved him.

Then one of them, an assassin in disguise, coming forward to kiss Commander Khayr al-Dīn's hand, struck him in the stomach with his dagger but the thrust did not prove fatal, only causing a broad wound. The thrust was clean, and his servants reached out and got hold of him, drawing out the weapon. They cut the culprit to pieces and dragged him away.

[253] Commander Māmāy came forward and cut off Qāsim b. Shuway''s head when charged with such treachery.[24] He wished to kill his son and all his followers but Commander Khayr al-Dīn restrained him from such action, issuing orders for them to be imprisoned. However, none of the Zaydī troops was to be killed but all were put into ships and used as oarsmen.[25] He then continued to tend to himself until, with Almighty God's permission, he recovered. No part of his body was free of wounds from his numerous battles with the Christians who imprisoned him on several occasions, but every time he was released.

The conquest of Aden on this occasion took place on blessed Saturday, the third day before the end of Dhū al-Qa'dah, 976/14 May 1569. They sent a messenger to the minister, while he was based at al-Qā'idah, giving him the news of the conquest of Aden and conveying Qāsim b. Shuway''s son, together with Qāsim's head and those of notables in his party, who had fallen to the swords of the victorious sultanate, together with the prisoners in their possession. The glad tidings found the minister in an advanced state of vigilance and anticipation, such news of the capture of Aden reaching him on the first day of the Holy month of Dhū al-Ḥijjah/17 May, that is, three days after the event, to be followed by the arrival of the prisoners and the heads. The army was absolutely delighted by the situation and celebrated by decking out the towns of Zabīd and Ta'izz and the entire Ottoman province. The morale of the Ottoman troops rose and the enemy was limp and broken.

Let fate be blessed and glad happiness remain with the minister, and glory and joy, thanks to Noble and much Forgiving God.

CHAPTER 14

[254] Sinān Pasha's appointment of Commander Ḥusayn as governor in Aden, with part of the army, his recall of Commanders Māmāy and Khayr al-Dīn to his side, with the rest of the army, and his dispatch of the glad tidings to the Sublime Porte

§ Once the minister had confirmation of the conquest and the Muslims were sure of the splendid victory God had granted them, he was obliged to report the situation to the Sublime Porte and the noble Ottoman government; for intense was the noble sultan's attention and concern and great his interest and preoccupation with the position. The victory fulfilled his objective in dispatching the victorious army and fully met his aim in spending the funds on such a purpose.

So the minister arranged for ʿAlī Jāwīsh, one of the imperial staff sergeants, with dispatches in his hand, to inform those in the imperial government he might meet as to the achievement of their goal so that Muslims should rejoice in God's victory and place their foreheads on the ground before Almighty God in thanks.

ʿAlī Jāwīsh arrived in Mecca in the middle of the holy month of Muḥarram, 977/July 1569, and was invested with an honorary cloak by our sayyid and lord, the Grand Sharīf, let Almighty God increase his glory, who gave instructions for the Holy Places to be decked out in celebration. The people of the Holy Places were greatly delighted by this, as was the entire population who maintained the decorations for seven days. Thanks be to God for such kindness and favour.

[255] Then the minister appointed as governor in Aden, to rule and keep it in good shape, that distinguished commander, noble lion and splendid warrior, his sister's son, Commander Ḥusayn. He arranged for him a noble Ottoman banner and a splendid imperial flag and enlisted with him about 200 troops. All the troops who took Aden were promoted and accorded various kindnesses and benefits, being invited to meet him and treated by him with care and sympathy.

He appointed a qadi by imperial edict in Aden and directed him to employ the Sharʿiah law on a sound and firm basis. They then travelled to the area and announced their plans for the place, making of Muṭahhar's school a pile of rubbish and a dump for refuse and filth. It still has not been rebuilt; its walls no longer stand, and none of its partitions or pillars survives.

It is strange that the divinely inspired shaikh, the learned spiritual guide, Sayyid al-ʿAydarūs, God help him and his illustrious ancestors, who gave us entry with his group to Paradise, passed by this school in Aden while Qāsim b. Shuwayʿ was digging its foundations. When he was asked, 'Shaikh, how do you find this school?' 'It shall be taken when it has reached the height of a knee,' he replied; nor did it reach knee high before it became a rubbish tip.

Such is the foundation of every folly. Almighty God does not allow foundation or root to the false. 'Falsehood hath vanished away.'[26]

CHAPTER 15

[256] The minister's journey, with his army, by the Maytam route to Ṣanʿāʾ

§ The Zaydī thought that the minister would choose either the Naqīl Aḥmar or the Wadi Suḥbān route because of their proximity to Ṣanʿāʾ and planned, once the victorious army was in the middle of the mountain path, to block the pass in front of them and overpower the troops from the mountain tops by hurling stones and rocks. They would not let them move their horses or use the cannon and muskets; and they would annihilate them in that way just as they had done with the late Murād Pasha in Wadi Khubān.[27] They began to make things ready with the help of thousands of tribesmen whom they stationed like crows on the mountain tops, but God rammed their deceit down their throats and thwarted their evil plans and thinking.

The minister chose the Wadi Maytam route which his vast army with its numberless men followed, since it was a wadi with room for horses and scope for the men to move and operate. Cannon and guns could be conveyed and cavalry and infantry could operate there. Although it was very long, it did not prompt much fear or pain. Despite its length, it did not take long to cover. Bold walking makes light of long distances. The choice of this route reflected sound judgment and good thinking on the minister's part, without benefit of adviser or counsellor. But Almighty God gave him inspiration and knowledge in this field which the wisest of men lack.

[257] The minister set out on the day of 'Arafāt[28]/25 May 1569, followed by the victorious army. The horn was blown and it was like the day when the trumpet sounds,[29] as they descended, once the sun had gained strength, to a place called al-'Alīq to wait for the arrival of the heavy cannon and their supply of gunpowder and cannon balls. Indeed, the pilgrims on the day of 'Arafāt were making their supplications to God while the minister was with his troops embarking on a holy war in the cause of God.

Then they continued their journey throughout the day and night, following the road on foot and horseback. They threw all their energy into the march, buckling to with zeal when they stopped and when they set off, until they emerged in a wide wadi, with pleasant air and a light wind, extensive shade and broad banks where they celebrated the Feast of the Sacrifice. Early in the morning, each one made celebration and sacrifice; and the troops fulfilled their duties there, with Almighty God keeping them from harm and danger.

They then continued their journey on the first day of the *tashrīq*[30] (11 Dhū al-Ḥijjah) and made excellent progress. But the heavy cannons caused them some delay as they watched out for their arrival. They waited until they caught sight of the cannons but, in the process, were delayed. They suffered successive delays and halts of this sort until they reached a place called Masjid al-Qā'ah[31] around which they settled while they made use of its facilities and space. That was in the middle of Dhū al-Ḥijjah at the end of the same year (end of May 1569). They found pleasure in visiting the holy shrines there and the tomb of one of the Companions of the Prophet, namely Jābir b. 'Abdullāh al-Anṣārī, God bless him.

He was a Companion of the Prophet[32] and is known for his glorious deeds and exploits. A man of manifest blessing and generosity, the great exchange stories about him with one another.

For example, in the *Meadows of Gold*,[33] Jābir b. 'Abdullāh went to Syria where he visited Mu'āwiyah who hid from him. Then he called for him, exclaiming, 'Mu'āwiyah, now have you heard the Prophet's advice, "Where someone has rejected anyone in want and need, God will reject him when he is in such need"?'

And Mu'āwiyah, God bless him, was angry with him, saying, 'And have you heard his saying, "You will meet after *'atharah* [favour] but be patient till you meet me at the *ḥawd*."[34] Or can't you be patient?'

Finally he said, '*'atharah* begins with *hamzah* and *tha'* forming the word from *āthara, yu'thiru, īthār* [choice, preference] which, when given, [258] indicates that he wishes to favour each of you with his portion of the booty and prize.' And Jābir replied, 'You have reminded me, Mu'āwiyah, of the selfishness of our times,'[35] and he left him, mounting his camel and returning to Medina. But Mu'āwiyah remembered him and sent him 600 gold dinars which Jābir returned, writing to him as follows:

> Indeed I prefer frugality to riches when I have the choice as I do water to a cold beverage. I undertake to obey when I am ordered but there are those who fail to do what they are commanded to do. I would wear the robes of shame were I to see wealth affecting my dignity.

I say that this was not Jābir b. 'Abdullāh al-Anṣārī, one of those who were frequently with the Prophet, but he shared his name, that of his father and his family. But the latter lived to reach ninety-seven years of age and died in 77/697 at the time of the pilgrimage; and I declare that the pilgrims do not pray over him.

But this Anṣārī who was a companion of the Prophet is someone else. Abū al-Fatḥ al-Yu'amarī mentioned him in his biography of the Prophet when the Prophet made a blessed reference to him concerning his young age at the battle of Uḥud,[36] with the words, 'It's not he with whom the *ḥadīth* is concerned. In an appendix to Ibn Fatḥūn, and with the support of the Imam Abū Yūsuf, concerning 'Uthmān b. 'Abdullāh b. Yazīd b. Ḥārithah, concerning his uncle, 'Umar b. Yazīd, concerning Ḥārithah, concerning his father, saying, at Uḥud the Prophet commented on the young age of 'Abdullāh b. 'Umar, Zayd b. Arqam, Abū Sa'īd and Jābir b. 'Abdullāh, not the one with whom the ḥadīth deals, and Sa'd b. Ḥibnah about whose son Ṭabarī[37] talked.'

CHAPTER 16

[259] An outbreak of fighting with some of the insolent Arab tribes; and their defeat at the hands of the heroic army

§ The victorious army went firmly on its way via the Maytam route, eschewing the roads via Naqīl Aḥmar and Wadi Suḥbān, while the Zaydī were frustrated in what they had attempted to do with these two routes, and their actions were in vain. They then began to follow the victorious army on its two flanks from the mountain tops, appearing to them like phantoms, causing terror and panic.

After descending near Masjid al-Qāʿah and settling there, the troops began to observe people to the front and rear. Some of the Arabs appeared like crows, firing clay bullets and snarling like jackals, thinking that in this way they would terrorise the sultan's army, fine horsemen [that they were], as they pretended to be monkeys and Satanic devils, just about frightening some of the children.

But the men regarded those movements and actions as rather idiotic and playful. The Ottoman troops took up their positions, refraining from beginning the battle but eager for them to come down into the wadi from the mountain tops so that the horsemen could manoeuvre and use sword and lance in cut and thrust. When some of them had descended to the foot of the mountains, with Satan letting them down by magic rope and other trickery, and the enemy was in the centre of the wadi, [260] the horses galloped towards them, in groups and singly. The troops attacked them whether on foot or mounted, at which the Zaydī held their ground for a while before scattering in all directions and getting torn to pieces. Their heads rolled around and their life and breath were snuffed out: those of them that got away escaped to the mountain tops and hid behind great rocks where they were inaccessible to the horses and out of reach of the guns and the long cannon.[38]

The troops then returned to the minister with the heads of those that had been killed, throwing them in front of him, let them rot, worthless and good for nothing things. The drums sounded in celebration and the horses tossed their heads in joy, in the general delight.

They passed their night till morning, the star of happiness shining for them from a glorious horizon of good fortune, as, from the enemy's pure blood, they circulated cups containing the evening and the morning's draught! They got themselves ready for the journey as true morning broke, all the commanders raising the noble Ottoman banner which flutters victorious in both east and west while the heroic troops mounted their swift chargers, galloping, with their riders, in their race towards battle.

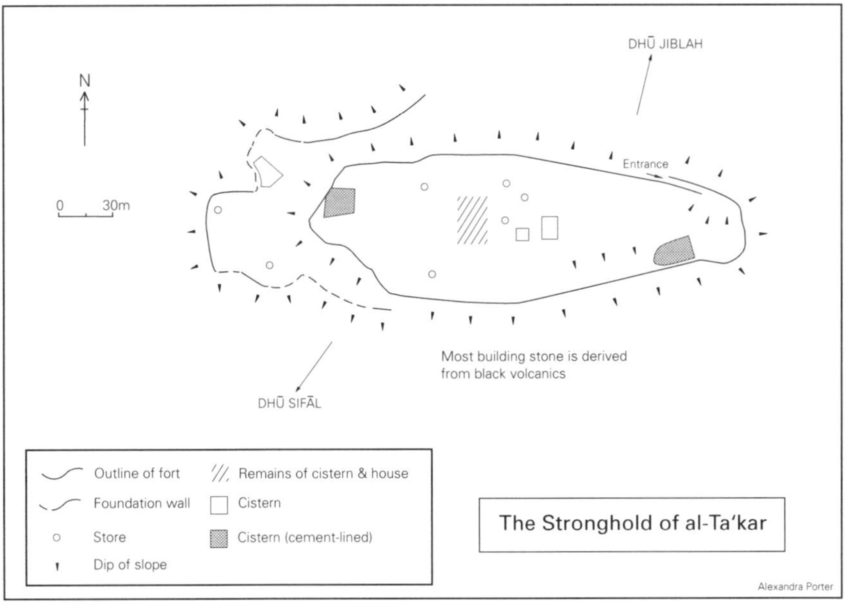

[261] The division of the road from Maytam, and the choice of the longer for the Great Army's route

After marching, in the illustrious minister's service, for two stages and stopping twice, the glorious army descended, on 18 Dhū al-Ḥijjah/3 June, into a broad wadi, fragrant with the scent of sweet bay and wormwood.[39] This wadi actually gives its name to Wadi Maytam, the name used for the entire route from the entrance, the name of part given to the whole. From there the road divides into two, one which is entirely under cultivation between two long mountain ranges, and the other which is long, containing twists and turns, with both ending at the castle of al-Ta'kar. The shorter road was all mud and mire into which the horses would plunge up to their stirrups and stomachs, the camels to near their haunches and men on foot to half their height.

The Zaydī had diverted water into this near road to increase the mire and they lay in wait on the mountain tops so as to hurl on to the Ottoman army stones and slingshot to make them weak and frightened and to impede their onward march.

The distinguished minister made his choice, sensibly deciding that the troops should take the long road in view of it being free of mud and, for the most part, without extensive mountain ranges and lofty fortresses; and it would be possible for the horses to move about with their brave riders. Once the minister had decided upon the long-distance route for his march with such a great army and the loads had been fastened for the journey; once the bugle had sounded and the rays of dawn had appeared; once the army and soldiers of the morning had defeated the forces of the night, and the stars had scattered their *darāhim* (silver coins) as morning's flags and banners opened; then in that field began the reckoning for the rebels who would meet their end in shame and error. Almighty God gave victory to the army of the people of faith over Satan's sect, as we shall recount, very clearly, if Merciful God so wills.

CHAPTER 17

[262] Meeting, battle and fighting, and contest with the dissident force

§ It was the mighty minister's practice during his travels to relax the reins of authority on the troops through noting places where there was no fear of the enemy, so that those who wished to go forward could do so and those who wished to delay could do so, while some of the loads could remain in the first staging place until the camels could return from the next stage and carry them to the camp. Indeed, he used to act in such a way out of concern for the army throughout the route, because of the loss of most of the camels during the journey, and because of the weight of the baggage.

Emerging from this staging-post during Friday morning, with ten nights of Dhū al-Ḥijjah remaining, 976/4–13 June 1569, they met the minister who saw that there were many packs of gunpowder, incendiary materials and weaponry[40] in the stopping place from which they had come, and that about 200 cavalrymen on foot had stayed behind to look after the loads. As he had about 500 horsemen with him, he brought his journey to a halt, with his suite, out of concern for those behind, since the entire victorious army had gone on with their march. But by then, the Arab tribesmen had descended from the mountains like a swarm of locusts, filling the wadi from which the army had withdrawn as they marched out. Their vast dark mass indicated a strength of some 10,000, comprising cavalry and infantry, musketeers and archers, whom Satan had led into deceit. They were bent on those of the victorious army remaining in the resting place.

Sharp anger and furious rage sparked and flamed in the heart of the mighty minister who wished to launch his small troop on those terrifying armed hordes but [263] the senior officers around him stopped him and made him stand firm under the Ottoman *sanjak*. They had with them three *ḍar-buzān*[41] left behind of the large cannon, so they were loaded with gunpowder,

1. Turkish gunner with a three pounder on either side of this rather droll camel, with a fuse in his left hand and his right poised to raise the breech for firing. c.1690. Marsigli, II, Plate XI, 29.

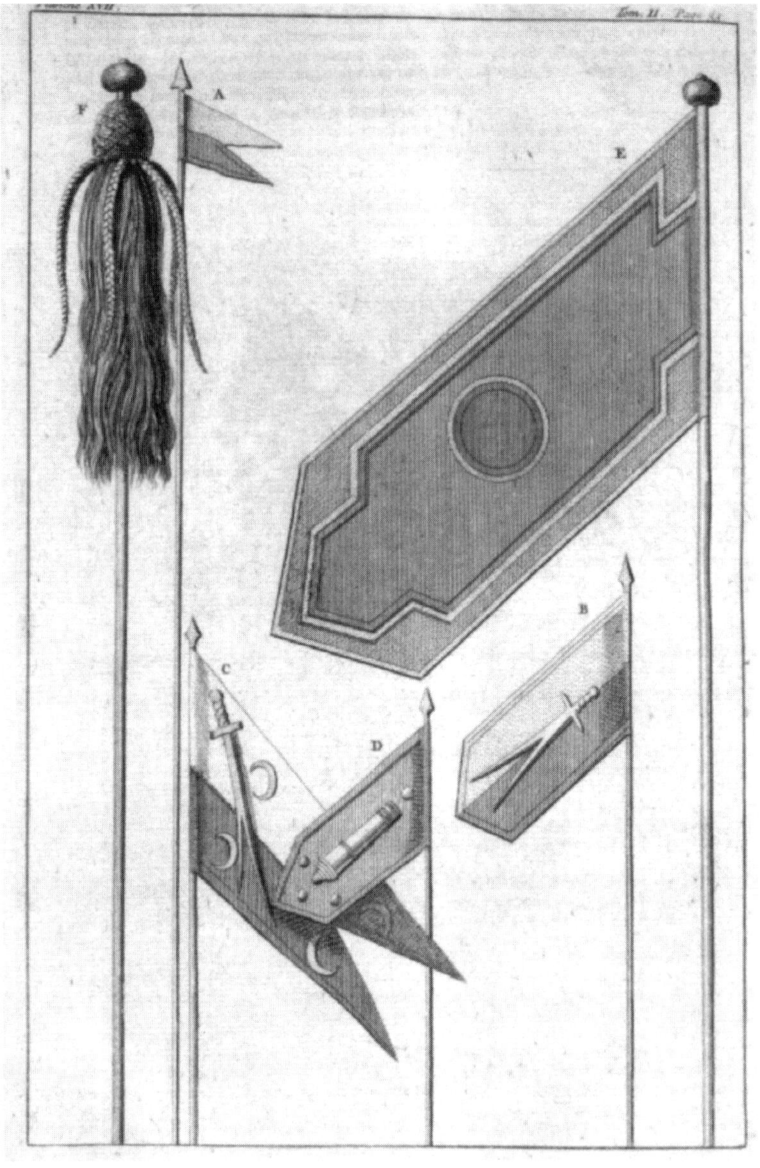

2. Turkish horsetail, banners and flags. The Turks made great play with such flags and penants. Even oxen, cannon or the most rustic cart would sport them.

From left to right: Horsetail, made by hand and dyed red indicating its Tartar origin. The number of horsetails to be displayed was strictly regulated. A grand vizier had five, a pasha of ministerial rank had three, a pasha in charge of a province two and a *sanjak bey* one.
Penant carried by Sepahi cavalry. Standard carried by cavalry. Flags carried by artillery and Janissaries respectively. Standard of Minister or Pasha, with gilded copper ball and embroidered everywhere with gold. Marsigli, II, Plate XVII, opp. 53.

3. Four methods of transport observed by Count Marsigli, which, mutatis mutandi, would have been used in Yemen. Marsigli, II, Plate XXIII, opp. 65.

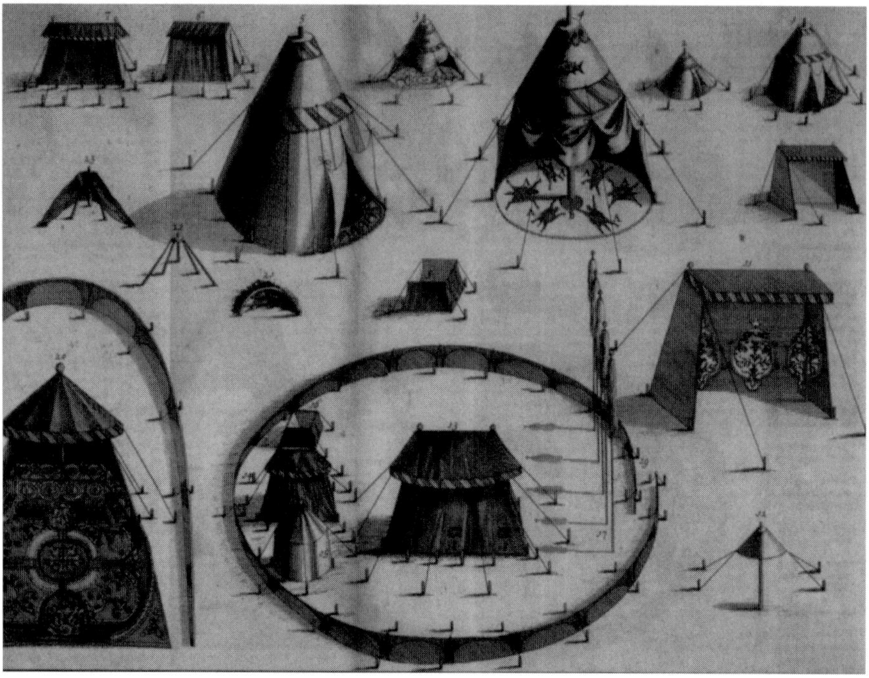

4. Different types of tent used by the Turks.

5. Tent of the Janissaries, displaying a Bursa rug.
3 and 4. Tents of the Janissaries, the latter enlarged to show sheepskins for sitting and *soffa*. Note the fish decoration on the latter.
2. Tent for the cavalry.
1. Tent for the Janissary *orta* or company.
20 etc. Grand Vizier's tent open to display carpet and low platform with cushions.
13 etc. Grand Vizier's encampment including tents for *dīwān*, sleeping quarters, latrines and display of horsetails.
10 and 11. Open tents, the latter enlarged, for Pasha to drink coffee.
Marsigli, II, Plate XIX, opp. 59.

5. Janissary on his way to war from a drawing by Nicolas de Nicolay.

Those who were to become Janissaries were collected by periodic levies from Christian families and brought up as Muslims. They were promoted through merit rather than privilege and formed the main Turkish fighting force. There is a strong resemblance to the Macedonian Phalanx or the Roman Praetorian Guard.
This figure wears a military cassock-like garment of blue cloth with long tails hanging to the back of his calves. His garment underneath, also of blue cloth, has close fitting sleeves. His *zarcola* or headgear, of white felt with huge feathers hanging to the rear like a fox's tail, is furnished with circles of gold at the edge and a band of gold, the length of the front carrying an insignia of silver guilt with gems. From the top of the hat hangs a sleeve to the shoulders in recognition of the Janissary connection with the Bektashi dervish order. The figure carries a long arquebus and scimitar, with a fuse wrapped round his right arm.
Chalcocondylas, II, Plate 9 and description opposite.

6. The Āghā Captain-General of the Janissaries from a drawing by Nicolas de Nicolay.

This senior official would have a large stipend from the sultan and be dressed in rich brocade or costly furs. He would also be given provisions for the regular entertainment of the Janissaries who owed him total loyalty. As the principle source of authority and support for the sultan he would be given a bride from the sultan's family as well as magnificently caparisoned horses.
The figure here appears on foot, dressed in a white turban, pleated at the top into pipe-like folds, carrying at the front an insignia of great value as well as a little feather. His costume befits a Muslim but would be of costly brocade, velvet or satin. His expression and carriage are those of great dignity and gravity befitting one in whom the sultan has placed great trust.
Chalcocondylas, II, Plate 4 and description opposite.

Nicolas de Nicolay was part of the suite of the French Ambassador who went to Istanbul in 1551.

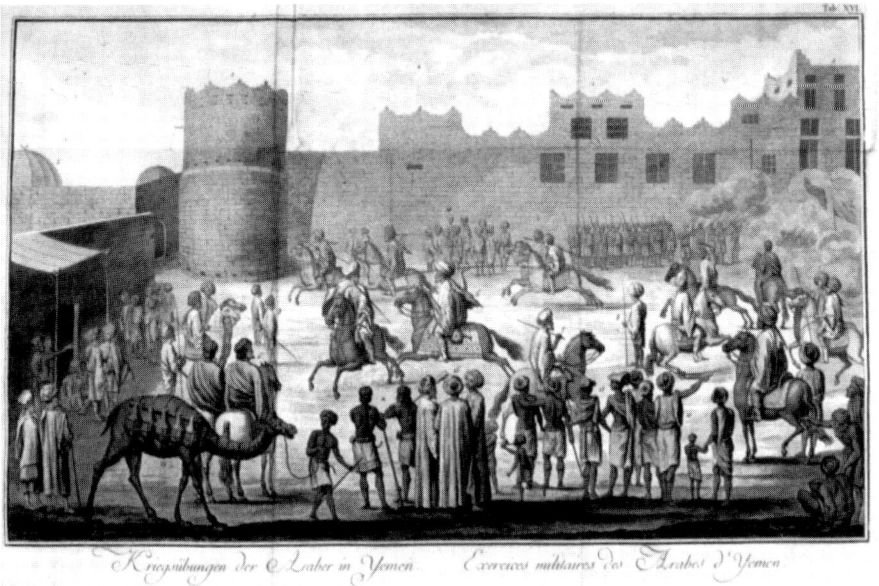
Kriegsübungen der Araber in Yemen
Exercices militaires des Arabes d'Yemen

7. Military exercises of the Arabs in Yemen from Carsten Niebuhr *Travels through Arabia* (Edinburgh, 1792).

The buildings and people depicted would have looked much as they did during Sinān's campaign. Of particular note are: the governor's palace facing the square; in the centre, the governor on horseback, sword and shield at his side, bare legs in his boots and wearing, in accordance with Yemeni custom, a large turban the end of which reached his shoulders; the guard in front of the palace some of whom are firing their guns; in the foreground to the right, some Indian merchants, and to the left, three of Niebuhr's party dressed as Turks.

8. Ta'izz from the north, as drawn by Niebuhr. The citadel of al-Qāhirah overlooks the town which in Niebuhr's time was still within its walls. The author describes its surrender to Sinān Pasha in [227]-[231].

Niebuhr was the only surviving member of a Danish exhibition to Yemen in 1762-1763. He published information about the country, previously unknown to Europeans, of which little in his 400 pages has been contradicted.

9. Copper engraving of a coffee tree, unsigned, from Dr Olfert Dapper *Naukeurige Beschryving Van Asie* (Amsterdam, 1680), 62.

A very early reference to coffee houses in Yemen is contained in [401] and [402]. By the early 1500's the drinking of coffee was no longer restricted to Sufi orders in Yemen; and by the time of Sinān's campaign it would appear that such coffee houses were well established.

10. Copper engraving of Mocha towards the end of the seventeenth century, from Dr Olfert Dapper *Naukeurige Beschryving Van Asie* (Amsterdam, 1680), 30. By this time the port had become more widely used and important than Aden.

Dr Olfert Dapper (1636-1689) was a Dutch geographer with a number of works, especially on Asia and Africa, to his credit. He expressed views that are typically Calvinistic and, unlike his contemporaries in the Netherlands, published his writings in Dutch rather than Latin.

11. Mt. Arafāt during Pilgrimage, from Sir Richard Burton's *Pilgrimage to Medina and Mecca,* (London, 1856) opp. 257. The scene is described in [453].

12. Stoning the Great Devil, from Sir Richard Burton's *Pilgrimage to Medina and Mecca,* (London, 1856) opp. 282. The scene is described in [454] where the *jamrat al-'Aqabah* refers to the 'Great Devil'. These details of Sinān's stonings more or less follow the rules described by Burton as applicable to the Ḥanafī school to which the Turks belonged.

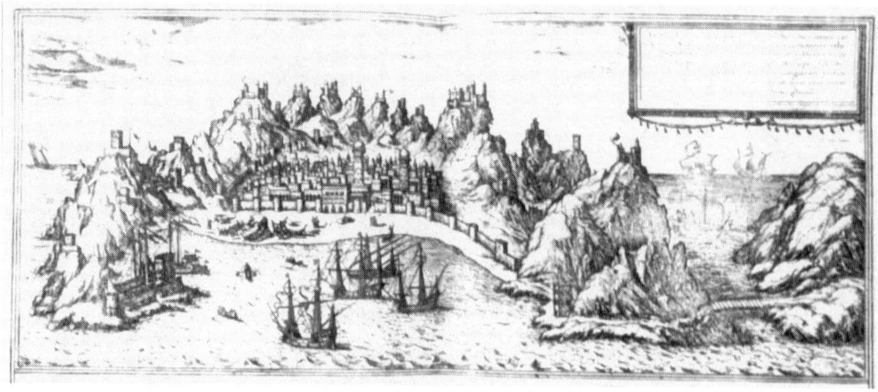

13. Aden in about 1572, from G. Braun and F. Hogenberg's *Civitates Orbis Terrarum,* 1572-1619, view 53. The island linked by a bridge is probably Mt. Ḥadīd.

14. View of Mawza', the ancient town inland from Mocha, by Henry Salt, from Annesley's *Voyages and Travels,* 1809. Salt was then British consul-general in Egypt. Mawza' would have looked much like this in Sinān's time and was on his route from Zabīd to Ta'izz. The Great Mosque is at the left of the engraving. See map 1.

15. View of al-Ḥutayb on Mt. Shibām in the Ḥarāz.
The third dā'ī al-muṭlaq or chief missionary of the Ṭayyibī Ismā'īlī, the Dā'ī Ḥātim b. Ibrāhīm (557-596/1162-1199), established his headquarters here and fortified the site. He was a prolific author and poet as well as warrior and organiser. He used to deliver lectures and hold assemblies in a cave below the fortress, visible at the top of the rocky outcrop, and receive *da'is* from throughout Yemen. His grave is within the white domed shrine at the centre of the picture and is visited with piety by Ṭayyibī Ismā'īlī. The top of the outcrop is reached by stone steps and holds a small mosque with a miḥrāb but without columns. There are also a couple of water tanks there. By Sinān's time the movement had been fragmented after victimisation by Imam Sharaf al-Dīn and his son, Muṭahhar.

16. View from above the *dāʿī*'s shrine at al-Ḥutayb.

17. A view of the Great Mosque in Zabīd in the Tihāmah where Sinān Pasha would have prayed. The entire length of the aisle incorporating the miḥrāb and entrance for the ruler, seen at left-centre, was constructed by the Tahirids at the end of the fifteenth century.

18. A close-up of the minaret of the Great Mosque at Zabīd which is attributed to Ayyubid times in the early thirteenth century. Some of the brickwork beneath the plaster is exposed.

19. The waterfall flowing into Wadi al-Ahjir basin by Wadi al-Khaltā. See inset to map 3. The Turks had faced tremendous difficulties in climbing such defiles and passes up the escarpment above which Kawkabān was situated.

20. View through part of the chasm or ditch, protecting Kawkabān from invasion. The inhabitants used to enter the chasm by a tunnel and cross by a temporary bridge which they could then withdraw. For the different ways with which the Turks attempted to deal with it and effect entry, see [415] and [416].

a flame inserted and fired with the explosive at that base crowd, causing casualties among those wicked people. The cavalry launched its charge against Satan's forces and many a cut and thrust took place in that field where the thick of the fighting whirled on and on.

The Arab tribesmen were cut to pieces and suffered much from blows and cuts from sword and lance. The fighting continued as the battle and combat raged with might and main from sunrise to sunset, from the break of day till the blaze of the sun had burnt their faces as if, at the arrival of those villains, hell-fire had thrown its flames and, at the coming of those scoundrels, cast its sparks. From the *zand*[42] of pebbles, the furnace of hell had thrown its fire.

The brave were about to lose their courage and the false win the day but for Sinān Pasha who was stout of heart and full of faith, sincere in his conviction, loyal in his belief and faith, clear in his advice, complete in his success, radiant in his grace for the spring of Islam and ardent in his damage to the heart of heresy. He represented his Lord in his support for religion as he begged for his support and strength, bright as a lightning flash, his chest as firm as a sword of steel. He stood firm till the face of victory rose forth and shone, and the wicked turned and fled as their armies were defeated and muskets began to fire at them with pellets of clay. This section of troops, small in comparison and composed of such people, had won, as the Zaydī took to their heels in flight to the hills and open country. 'Thus, with God's permission, does a small force win over a numerous one!'[43]

Before the thick of the fight, the minister had dispatched a brave troop, concealed with their muskets in the hills, to surprise and terrorise the Arabs and pitch them into a state of frenzy and turmoil whenever a party of them withdrew to catch the advance groups of the Ottoman army. That was sound judgment and really good thinking. For the Arabs, after their defeat, wishing to return, made their way from the mountains towards the Ottoman advance detachments whereupon the ambush aimed their muskets at them and, for a second time, they fled in panic [264] over their mountain passes, swords coming down on their necks till countless of them were killed and numberless dispatched to the fires of hell.

So God gave victory to Islam and thrust the nose of the depraved into the dust. God is to be thanked for numerous blessings.

Mention of the martyrs of the battle

Among numerous heroes and horsemen whose arms were stretched out to help both enemy and friend was Kadūk Farhād, a *kāshif* from Egypt, who suffered every grim horror while he fought and cut off heads; famous for his courage and help, known for his bravery and zeal, he put to death a number of Arab tribesmen in the battle and dispatched one of the Arab headmen, using his sword and mace against him and dismounting from his horse to cut off his head. Then a bullet hit him and snuffed out his life. He and the headman were both equal in death but were each to take different routes, one to Paradise, the other to the fire. So Farhād, the martyr, quenched his thirst with water of the blessed while the dull-witted headman burnt in the fires of hell. For Farhād died in honour, gaining his place as a martyr in Paradise; he had lived in comfort and died happy.

About ten of the soldiers also became martyrs and passed away, noble at the Day of Judgment, with friends by the *Kawthar*[44] and enjoying a fine reputation and glorious praise.

As for those depraved soldiers who were killed by the sword of justice, they were carried off to hell and a miserable end, without being counted and without being registered or recorded. Is anyone concerned with counting the dogs and wolves or can the gnats and flies be numbered? Or the number of stones, grains of sand or dust be counted?!

[265] The minister's favours to the troops who were present and his journey to take the stronghold of al-Ta'kar[45]

As he witnessed what such a small force had achieved in terms of bravery, courage and intimidation, the minister was encouraged by his troops and gave courage to them through many favours. He was relaxed in talking to them and at ease in discussion, treating them kindly and generously; and each of those then present had an increase in salary of one *'uthmānī*, as a general favour, apart from what he bestowed on their seniors and leaders, their horsemen and heroes, in the way of pedigree horses, sharp and thrusting swords and vast and magnificent robes. He remained in the same resting place for the rest of that day, relaxing with his entourage and drinking from the spring.

Then, at the end of the day, they mounted in the darkness of night and continued their way down, following the stream; and they made contact with the sultan's victorious troops, catching up with the imperial army. God delighted them with their victory. Hearts were quiet and thoughts dwelt properly on God. As Almighty God states in his true and virtuous book, 'And that our host, they would verily be the victors.'[46]

Thereupon the minister set out with the victorious troops from this place. He travelled for a stage until he pitched his lofty encampment with its high and extensive pavilions, with the commanders and dignitaries, in a place between Jiblah and the stronghold of al-Ta'kar, where he remained to organise the mamluks and troops. The forces of victory and success had welcomed his mounts; their brave foreheads bent down to kiss the dust at his feet; and the brave heroes fixed their eyes on his tent ropes.

CHAPTER 18

[266] The allegiance of the people of Jiblah, the conquest of the stronghold of al-Ta'kar and the surrender of those tribes; and the capture of the stronghold of Baḥrānah[47] and its obliteration[48]

§ After the mighty minister's camp had settled in the area between Jiblah and the stronghold of al-Ta'kar, the Arab tribesmen divided into two sections. Some of them opted to seek peace terms, submission and obedience, asking the minister for his protection and seeking the umbrella of his grace and favour. They brought trustworthy guarantees, assuring the terms for peace and offering reliable pledges which the minister agreed to accept, treating them with the utmost kindness and care.

The minister bestowed on them turbans and honours, with suitable rewards for all of them, and gave them guarantees for their children and assurances for their property and land. He called for trust among the Arab tribesmen and prevented any oppression or wrongdoing by the troops and soldiers as far as the people were concerned. He appointed one of the military police to be responsible to him for the markets and roads with instructions that no soldier should take anything from the populace without paying the proper price; nor should the troops obtain any goods from the market without paying a price acceptable to the traders. Anyone who disobeyed or was unfair, was aggressive or oppressive, would be given a sound beating and imprisoned for a long time; and there were those who were dismissed and banished and, in the heat of anger, burnt and crucified.

The people of Jiblah and some of the Arab tribesmen from the countryside declared their allegiance and the whole of the area was pacified.

As for the depraved rebels of the district, they congregated in the stronghold of al-Ta'kar, in alliance [267] with those who had come out in rebellion against the army, thinking that their fortresses would protect them; and they established their base on the summit of Mt al-Ta'kar whereupon the minister established a victorious base up against Mt al-Ta'kar, surrounding all its entrances and ways of access. All hopes of reaching it from the mountains above were cut off from below and none could reach its peak save men of the utmost determination.

But on the sheer outcrops of its flanks there were three collapsed towers which could be used as points of access to al-Ta'kar to which the minister dispatched by night a party of brave men, with heavy large cannon. From there they had instructions to fire on its population to divert them from the fighting below the stronghold, and to construct ladders from lengths of wood which he had instructed be brought there. The heroic men then clung to them as they climbed towards the enemy while the enemy were distracted from their guns by cannon fire directed against them from those dilapidated towers.

The Zaydī looked death in the eye, realising that they had been taken, and sought terms in exchange for their lives. The commanders advised the minister not to accept their appeal but to eradicate and get shot of them once and for all. However, Sinān Pasha displayed compassion for them and gave them terms. He put an end to the fight with them and sent someone from his entourage to take over the door to the stronghold, ordering them to come out one by one without arms or equipment; and he let them out to go wherever they wished. This was absolute mercy and kindness to them, and mention anyone else who has acted in such a way, especially after having enjoyed absolute control. But his object was admirable, to preserve people's lives; his intention towards Almighty God was admirable; and his actions were appreciated by God and by men.

This blessed victory took place on Saturday, 26 Dhū al-Ḥijjah 976/12 June 1569, and the siege lasted for five days. God is to be thanked for these splendid conquests; and to him are due thanks for victory for the forces of Islam and defeat for heresy, rebellion and evil.

After that, the minister appointed a *dizdār*[49] and a garrison in the stronghold of al-Ta'kar and strengthened it with cannon, weapons and funding; and he went off to take the district belonging to Idrīs the one-eyed, to cleanse those [268] roads of rebels and law-breakers and to complete the organisation of the populace under the umbrella of the sultanate in absolute peace and security.

The headquarters of Idrīs the one-eyed's country was the castle of Baḥrānah.

The aforementioned Idrīs had committed treachery against the Ottoman forces; for when the minister had pitched camp at al-Qā'idah on his first appearance from Ta'izz, he had sent nearly 150 musketeers to capture the stronghold of Baḥrānah; and Idrīs, with Luṭfallāh b. Muṭahhar, had sought refuge with them as they approached it, together with the troops with him. This the Ottoman troops had agreed for one night since they were unarmed and reliant upon some of the villages on their route but Idrīs had attacked them, killing about fifty of them while the remainder fled. Although this action had been attributed to Muṭahhar's son, it was with his agreement; and because of it the army bore a grudge against him as well as for his actions during the days when the Zaydī broke from their allegiance and undertook to run their own administration.

The minister sent troops to surround the stronghold of Baḥrānah and to kill those within, whereupon Idrīs the one-eyed and all his followers fled, leaving Baḥrānah and its neighbourhood absolutely empty. Ottoman troops entered it at the beginning of Holy Muḥarram, 977/16 June 1569; and the minister saw a good omen in the conquest taking place at the beginning of the year, with people being optimistic that the entire year would abound in different conquests and blessings.

Since the stronghold of Baḥrānah was of little advantage and of no value, in view of the possibility of damage by the enemy, the minister directed that it be destroyed, its structures razed and its foundations and walls torn down.

They left a bare plain over which a wind of ruin and destruction blew as if there had not been houses there and people had not passed by. It has become a refuge for owls, a home for spiders and a nesting-place for birds. In this way do the homes of the wicked fall into ruin where none but owls and crows survives.

CHAPTER 19

[269] The dispatch of the Dāʿī ʿAbdullāh to take the castle of Khadid; Muṭahhar's son's resistance and defeat; and the *dāʿī*'s victory over him and seizure of the town

§ The castle of Khadid was one of the impregnable castles which Muṭahhar had constructed in the days of his rebellion for his son, Luṭfallāh, may God disfavour him.

The Dāʿī ʿAbdullāh was adept at helping the Ottoman forces, devoting his heart and soul, as well as his supporters, to the task. He stood up in front of the minister and reported to him his desire to render a service to show his friendship for the noble sultanate, saying, 'I have with me among the *duʿāh* about four hundred fighters and I'd like you to send me to Mt al-Ḥubaysh and Khadid castle,[1] to seize them so as to help and assist you.'

Now the minister welcomed his words and accepted his service. He bestowed on him favours and recited to him verses containing advice, especially connected with war and ambush and concerning resolve, judgment and endurance, and the lack of fickleness and the need for firmness in an engagement, and other such precepts of war and such advice as men had given him. He tied one of the noble sultan's banners for him and assigned to him the tribesmen who had sought his protection when the citadel of Taʿizz was conquered and whom he had kindly taken on to the sultan's payroll as part of the Janad garrison.[2] From these he selected 100 men and enlisted them with him; so there were now 500 fighters who accompanied him seeking Almighty God's help against Mt al-Ḥubaysh.

[270] When Luṭfallāh b. Muṭahhar heard of this, he thundered and lightninged, and frothed and foamed, with the words, 'Is the Dāʿī ʿAbdullāh about to fight us? What has prompted him to do so? We'll make him taste the heat of sharp swords and we'll give him a good drubbing, on both back and

front. We'll take him prisoner and return him to captivity in a single night.'

When the *dā'ī* was told what the lad had said, he roared like a lion and his moustaches and hair stood on end, and he threatened the father and his offspring, quoting the verse:

> I shall unsheathe my sword from its scabbard after its long rest till tribe after tribe is slain. Each sword shall strike a head, and women at home shall cast their veils to stroke the backs of orphans' heads.

The *dā'ī* then immediately set out for Khadid, preparing his army for battle and displaying the strength of his forces. He had with him about 500 fighters, 400 of whom could be depended upon on such occasions and 100 of whom could not but whom he suspected of treachery and trouble-making. And Muṭahhar's son faced him with 2,000 of his father's special troops, each of whom he had selected and chosen for a day like this.

But the Dā'ī 'Abdullāh stood firm and his endeavour was worthy of thanks. He placed the 400 upon whom he could rely to his right and left, and to his front and rear, and the 100 about whom he entertained suspicions he made the vanguard of his forces. And indeed, the 100 aforementioned, at the first encounter with Muṭahhar's son's forces, joined them and treacherously became members of Muṭahhar's son's party; then Muṭahhar's son sent them to his father who reproved them for surrendering al-Qāhirah, seeking a truce with the minister and accepting a wage from him. They offered apologies to him which he did not accept; and they were rejected by him, by 'Abdullāh and by God and gained nothing but a black face, ignominy and ostracism. Each of them was counted a foolish traitor, with two faces and neither for God.

Then the Dā'ī 'Abdullāh and those of his army with him continued the battle, striking such extreme heresy with truth, trouncing them and beating them in the fight until the false lost the day and [271] turned his back. The Zaydī turned their backs and fled, and arrows and swords engaged their backs as they did so, and as they struck, one would imagine eyes and eyelids and recite over that misfortune:

> Our spears have pierced their backs with eyes over which swords have closed like eyelids.

Muṭahhar's son did not stop till he had reached his father to save and protect him from the *dā'ī*, and his troops went in all directions, scattered between dusk and dawn. After they had shown their backs in flight and rout, the Dā'ī 'Abdullāh captured the stronghold of Khadid and Mt al-Ḥubaysh which he fortified with the troops with him, and dispatched to the minister the news of his conquest and the abundant favours granted him by Almighty God. He advised him as to what he had done with the stronghold of Khadid, together with the weapons and equipment within it. Then Sinān Pasha decided to destroy its structure, raze its walls, uproot its foundations and level its building because its preservation would bring problems, in that brave men would be needed to save it from destruction, and the need was for men rather than the protection of a castle from those mountains. There was no alternative to levelling its walls, destroying its structure, removing any trace of it and extinguishing its fire.

So he sent a message to the *dāʿī* with orders to raze all trace of it, and so was heard the use of picks at its chambers: verses from the 'Chapter of the Convulsion'[3] were read over the walls of its buildings and all trace of it vanished. The echo reverberated throughout the district; the winds swept it away and dust obliterated it.

The *dāʿī* returned to the minister in triumph and victory, his efforts in the event appreciated and his loyalty sincere and blessed. A proud cloak of honour was spread over his back, and he was given thanks for his splendid help and applauded for his brilliant actions. He gained various promotions and favours and achieved his most extreme requests. He began to be mentioned in public and private; his higher standing was acknowledged among those tribes, and he attained a glory that did not fade among the people, whether by night or day.

Muṭahhar's son's defeat took place on 3 Muḥarram, 977/18 June 1569.

CHAPTER 20

[272] The minister's journey to conquer Ibb, Baʿdān and the stronghold of al-Shamāḥī,[4] and the battle that took place therein

§ When the minister had achieved his goal of conquering Khadid, the enemy had been defeated and peace and quiet had prevailed, he returned to take Ibb, a town of lofty houses that vies with long lances in the height of its buildings.[5] It lies on the skirts of Mt Baʿdān, a mountain the peak of which reaches al-Simāk and al-Naṣrān,[6] the summit of which only the sun and the moon surmount. At its foot is a wide valley with pure air and the fragrance for which sweet bay and wormwood are known, entered by a narrow pass like the neck of a pitcher. It is carpeted with anemone flowers and strewn with a bed of cornelians, 'a high garden with its fruits within easy reach.'[7] That valley was called Shabakah since it resembled a network, its trees entwined, its flowers entangled and its streams criss-crossed.

So the minister pitched his camp in that valley and filled that pleasure spot with his victorious army, directing against the foe his brave troops, his fighting forces; and then the false band, the weak, prejudiced sect, advanced to seize the narrow pass from the victorious army and to position against them on Mt Ba'dān stones and rocks, so that the sultan's forces should find no field for fighting and lose their equipment at every turn, as absurd and imagined disasters befell them.

Muṭahhar's son, who had fled from the *dā'ī*, rode with his cousin, Muḥammad b. Shams al-Dīn and 'Alī b. Shuway', equipped by Muṭahhar with what forces he could and furnished with [273] standards and banners. They were 20,000 or more in number as, mounted and riding, they approached their goal in procession. They sent messages to the tribesmen, who had acknowledged the minister's authority and been granted a truce to enter the ranks of the Sunnah and the community, urging them in coaxing terms and undoing all the good done to them, with the words, 'We don't ask you to fight with us; nor to expose yourselves against the Turks in any circumstances, but if you see us victorious and the Turks beaten, proclaim the truth and kill the vanquished; disclose the secret let none escape; and if we are beaten, then you remain loyal and deal with them as usual.'

Then they made their way to Ibb where they removed the populace and placed 1,000 men with muskets while the remainder climbed Mt Ba'dān, some of them blocking the road to the pass with many mounted tribesmen; and they began to kindle fire and discharge slingshot and granite.

Once the minister had observed the great throng and their recourse to that vast mountain, he went his splendid self to do battle with them, without concern for their immunity in their mountains, nor their attachment to their empty fancies, nor their faith in their idle thoughts; and he set the muskets against them.

That was on blessed *'Āshūrā'*,[8] the eve of the tenth of Holy Muḥarram 977/24 June 1569.

When the troops saw the minister making his way towards the battle, getting up and riding towards that ignorant mob, they went in a body with stones and arrows, and heavy cannon, and fired at their enemy at one discharge, attacking those heretics like brave lions.

The fighting lasted from the beginning to the end of the day, and the sword's blade grew tired with absence from its sheath. Then night separated the two sides and darkness drew a black curtain between each, with both on high alert. The young would have his hair turn grey as the air turned dark from gunpowder smoke; and the intensity of the night clothed garments in the black of pitch, unlit, [274] save for a flashing musket rap charging the sky as with a lightning flash, as they warned of death and blocked their ears against the din.

The noise of frightful thunder followed, causing the pillars and stones to shudder and hearts and throats to contract, till ears were deafened by it and the call of the muezzin drowned; and till daybreak's robe had concealed the night, twilight had smiled over the camomile flowers and the battle criers had called 'Come to arms', in place of 'Come to the good'.[9] And the fire of battle continued, burning and blazing: warriors in battle, cutting and thrusting; and sword blades clinging to necks and clashing. Between them still raged attacks, gallops and the cuts and thrusts of the fight. For the forces of Islam, with every sortie from the enemy, there was a harvest; for the heretics, in every engagement on the ground, there was a struggle. But the victorious army gained the upper hand, and its will was triumphant.[10]

Lots of brave men met their death and savoured the taste of battle. The sweets of paradise lured them on as they passed away in fragrance and basil, drowned in mercy and pardon.

Many of the heretics were killed, in numbers impossible to count, until a senior chieftain was killed. Notable for his great courage, he was called Abū al-Naṣr, and was hit by the lash of defeat. He fell prostrate on his hands and chest and went to hell-fire; and his fate was wretched. At that the Zaydī fled and withdrew to Mt Ba'dān, evacuating the town of Ibb which the sultan's forces entered and took over, and the warring sect reached the point of collapse. It was a conquest followed by conquests and a victory sweet with the fragrance of right.

The blessed conquest was on the day of *'Āshūrā'*, 10 Muḥarram 977/ 25 June 1569.

Then the minister returned to his base, his mind full of plans to get rid of the shameless tribe and, with sharp swords, to pierce its carcase. So he collected his noble thoughts and formed the lofty resolve to climb Mt Ba'dān with his army and to attack the sect of Satan. He had no thought for the muskets and stones they held, nor did he consider their numbers [275] hidden behind the rocks.

He selected 6,000 fighters and gave Ḥasan Pasha 1,000 brave men to destroy this false sect, calling among the troops for none of those braves to delay his ascent of the mountain to the Zaydī. He pointed out to them six tracks between the rocks to their base and commanded them to climb to those lairs. He himself chose one of the tracks which he followed without error, while the troops raced towards them, bent over the points of their swords. When the troops saw this bravery from the minister and witnessed his courage on the mountain as if he were flying, they raced with each other in the ascent, with fortune and luck as their aids. Nor did that unjust, arrogant sect believe that the troops would show such bravery, nor any of them take such a risk.

Then they fired the first volley from their muskets and discharged what they could from their thunderous *ḍarbuzān*. Then Almighty God saved those for whom a long life was written while he who could become a martyr in death passed over to him. The troops then followed, cleaving the heretics with sword and dagger as warriors embraced the brave, and the men made the forces of evil taste the direst of pain. They made their swords speak with clarity and candour, and their arrows quenched the thirst of their parched quiver. The enemy quaked in anticipation and fear: they wished to stand firm but were unable as they turned their backs in flight, leaping about like monkeys; and the victorious army won the day.

The Zaydī abandoned their tents and their pasture, their provisions and their weapons while the Turks spread out to seize the stock. They had suffered the most terrible defeat. Their time was up; their slaughter was complete; their armour was breached; and their spears were smashed.

The Turks captured the standard of Muḥammad b. Shams al-Dīn, with his clothing, his pipes and his drums while he himself escaped and abandoned his finery. Ibn Shuway' also just managed to escape on horseback and, abandoning all his hopes, did reach Muṭahhar's son. He threw away his armour, his helmet, his weapons and his cartridge, and then got down from his horse and took to his legs. Then he took off and discarded his clothes, hurling away his honour, as the verse says,

> He cast away his armour to lighten his load, and threw away even his dress and sandal.

[276] Someone had pursued him and been amused to collect what he found and put aside what he disliked. When there was nothing left for him to cast away, Ibn Shuway' took off his trousers, showing his rear to the man behind him and disclosing his ugly buttocks as he ran on, roaming about and screaming in that wide waste till one of his servants met him with a horse. Then he mounted its back and loosened the reins. So, although he escaped death from sword and arrow, he was ridden by lots of shame; and the man who had pursued him came back with his weapons, his trousers and his attire which he showed to the troops who talked about his habit when turning his back. This was the most remarkable thing told and spoken of him through ages of gossip.

Six hundred of the enemy heads were cut off and put to pen and paper, apart from those wounded in defeat and those of the slain who went unrecorded. Mt Ba'dān and the stronghold of al-Shamāḥī were taken in one day, with God's help.

That took place on 12 Muḥarram, 977/27 June 1569.

CHAPTER 21

[277] The minister's privileges for the troops in wage increases and individual monetary grants

§ After victory fell to the victorious sultan's army and the devilish troops of the false army were broken by the minister's organisation, courage and incisive judgment, he thanked God in His glory and might for His favour and implored Him to accept his thanks for His blessings and His generosity. For he acknowledged his own incapacity and modest judgment and performance while everything was due to His glory and understanding, as God gave victory to those among the faithful He wishes; for God possesses supreme grace.

He reflected upon the degree of cold and heat endured by the soldiers, the rigours of war and the travel by land and sea, their loss in life, spirit and pleasure in the taste of death at the Day of Judgment, and their scorn at offering wealth and property in the love of their sultanate. He understood that they deserved much in the way of reward, and were due plenty of favour and general kindness, so he raised each of the soldiers' pay by 2 *'uthmānī*, noting on his papers an increase in the sultan's emoluments and noble Ottoman pay, which he would enjoy throughout his life and with which he would construct his proud home. This he took from a supplement to the sultan's budget, which he himself had obtained over that given by the governorate, whereby there should be no deficit in the noble and generous budget; on the contrary, each successive occasion brought an increase in its size.

[278] And he gave these instructions, for, during the days of Muṣṭafā Pasha Qarah Shāhīn, funds had been transferred each year from the Yemen revenue to the Sultan of Islam, but, during its disturbance and instability, the Yemen province took 50,000 new gold dinars, from the cost of spices conveyed from Yemen to Egypt, by virement from the generous official accounts; and it had been organised on that basis for many successive years. This was increased in the days of Sinān Pasha to as much as 200,000 new dinars. That was a huge amount and a great deal of money and is still on the increase and growing, with Almighty God's agreement.[11]

The minister did not restrict himself to this general reward and the very generous grants but added to them thousands of dinars from the same funds to be divided among the many members of the army, whether senior or junior, commander or commanded; and he gave to each man from 100, 50 or 10 dinars according to his rank and status, to 2 dinars each per person. All of them were grateful to him, thanking him for his generosity and acknowledging his wonderful kindness. They prayed for his health and offered him pearls of fragrant thanks; they increased their love and affection for him and had full and loving trust in his sincerity. It was as is said in the wisest of sayings:

> The bird alights where it gathers grain and the dwellings of the generous are host to many visitors.[12]

What went against Muṭahhar's ambitions and made his soldiers shun him was his extreme meanness and excessive parsimony; for he would charge his neighbours for a hen's egg, take only a laying hen for the tax and collect date stones for himself in a bag or sack. Nothing was ever said of a gift made by him; nor was any deed of generosity, fitting or not, told of him.

> If a king is not generous, then he and his state will pass away.

Then how with one who was neither king nor son of a king; nor was he from the line of lowest royalty. No, he is a rebel; he has left the fold and renounced allegiance!

[279] I heard that in the days of his truce and during his peace and submission an important *jāwīsh* came to him with a magnificent honorary robe from the sultan, and favoured him with 50 dinars. When his drummers and pipers took up position by the *jāwīsh*, he gave them the 50 dinars but, after the *jāwīsh* had left him, he collected the drum and pipe players and made them give back the 50 dinars which he then placed in his safe!

That is the basest thing he could do and the vilest action he could take but he hoarded such treasure to the maximum extent and, so far as it was concerned, he was the sole keeper.

> If money is of no good to you save in its safe, then God's land and sea is your wealth.

It is also said:

> Your wealth is plunder against accident, or to be hoarded or inherited. It is best for you to use it in gifts and not get the worst of the three.

This stems from something concerning Abū al-Dardā' or 'Alī b. Abī Ṭālib, God be pleased with them.

> Your wealth is for you, or for your needs or for inheritance, don't become the weakest of the three.

Some have rearranged it with the words:

> It is happiest for you to enjoy your wealth when alive; for good and evil men will remain after you. If you leave it for the evil, he won't keep it and the good and his kind will increase the little they are left. If you are able, make use of it; for he who has the use of it himself is the one who is wise.

CHAPTER 22

[280] The appointment of Maḥmūd Bey al-Kurdī and Barwayz Bey to lay siege to the castle of Ḥabb; and their necessary and essential support in funds and troops

§ Mention has been made above of the castle of Ḥabb[13] and its impregnability, and how Maḥmūd Bey captured it from al-Naẓẓārī since it is the base for Ba'dān district and has control over its lands and towns.

'Alī b. Sharaf al-Dīn had been in the stronghold of Dhū Marmar when Muṭahhar had recommended he take charge of and make secure Ḥabb castle and become governor of Ba'dān and its districts. For Muṭahhar aspired to be left in the stronghold of Dhū Marmar and remove his brother, 'Alī, to Ba'dān which he had captured during the days of the revolt and where he had taken up his position.

When the minister had captured the province of Ba'dān, 'Alī had remained under siege in the castle of Ḥabb. The capture of Ḥabb castle would not be without difficulty; but most important was the capture of Dhamār and Ṣan'ā', for it was not possible to leave Ba'dān and go to take Dhamār and Ṣan'ā' because 'Alī would come down from Ḥabb castle, recapture Ba'dān district and really put at nought the hardship suffered by the sultan's army.

The minister decided to appoint two of his commanders known for their courage and bravery and give them orders to besiege Ḥabb castle while he would go and conquer the rest of the country, and then finally take Ḥabb castle. So he appointed for the purpose Maḥmūd Bey al-Kurdī who had been a *kāshif* [281] in Egypt. He was a brave and courageous man, known for his boldness and brutality, whom he had given a sultan's *sanjak* and who had accompanied him to conquer Yemen. The second was Barwayz Bey who was one of the *sanjak* commanders formerly in the province of Yemen. He was known for his courage as well as his bravery and ambition, famous among the tribesmen of those parts. He was noble-minded, had become commander of the Yemeni pilgrimage and possessed military knowledge and good luck.

With 'Alī b. Sharaf al-Dīn in Ḥabb castle there were 700 defenders, so Sinān Pasha ordered the two great commanders to take about 200 horsemen, lay siege to Ḥabb castle and take care of Ibb, Jiblah, al-Shamāḥī and all of Ba'dān district, an extensive area of great abundance and much produce. The majority of its tribesmen had come under control but the minister had not as yet come to rely upon them. They gave him the impression of loyalty while the power and capability remained with the sultan's forces; otherwise, they would suddenly withdraw, betray the community and be the cause of alarm and famine.

The two mentioned commanders set about this task and the minister gave them practical advice concerning the siege after he had himself gone round Ḥabb castle and examined its entrances and gullies and taken note of its heights and depths. He gave them the necessary instructions concerning the siege and handed out to them the funds and wherewithal required, together with the guns and cannon needed and approved.

In Ba'dān district, near Ḥabb castle, there were two strongholds of little value but of potential danger. They were the strongholds of Fanad and al-Mudawwarah. So he ordered their destruction, and they razed them to the ground, leaving a total ruin. The two commanders pitched their tents, encampment and quarters under Ḥabb castle and maintained the siege and watch they had been ordered. The minister bade them farewell and set out, with the rest of the sultan's victorious army, on their journey to conquer the remaining highlands of Yemen, attended with victory and help from God, who is to be gloried and praised, and protected by high glory and great honour.

CHAPTER 23

[282] The minister's journey to the town of Dhamār and its capture from the base invaders

§ After the minister had completed the capture of Ba'dān district and had ordered the siege of Ḥabb castle, he had to lie in wait for a while until he was free of such business.

Then he set out for Dhamār on 19 of Holy Muḥarram 977/4 July 1569, and encamped, with the army and commanders, and the rest of the dignitaries and senior officers, in a place called Wadi Sahūl,[14] seen as a good omen for getting on with things and the easy passage to the accomplishment of his goal, Almighty God willing; and they stayed there the whole day of 20 Muḥarram/5 July.

They left it on 21 Holy Muḥarram and descended into the foothills of the Samārah[15] pass which is a broad valley enclosed by two tremendous mountains, among the highest in Yemen, the sides of which interconnect and between which the path is extremely rugged. If Almighty God had not struck terror and alarm into the hearts of those base tribesmen, they would have caused a halt at the passes between the two mountains, prevented an ascent to them and a passage through them but, after observing the engagement at Mt Ba'dān, their hearts sank in fear and fright as they realised that they were powerless against the victorious army and lacking in the stamina and confidence for such a line of action. So they removed their sick and healthy from all the tracks and all of them gathered round Muṭahhar in Ṣan'ā'. Then the victorious army made their way through the Samārah pass without any hint of danger, travelling at their ease without crowding or haste.

[283] Sinān Pasha spent the entire day at the bottom of the valley until the army as a whole had advanced like an aggressive lion, come out of the narrow pass into the heights of Samārah, descended to its floor and cut across that rugged area. At the head of the defile they found an extremely strong and well-constructed fortress from which guns could fire in every direction and guard the road with cannon and *ḍarbuzān*. There the minister stationed a guard and outpost, fortified it with some guns and gave them an armoury, weapons of war, gunpowder, provisions and other requirements.

Then he went on to Wadi Yarīm[16] in which there was running water and much pasture. It was a very pleasant place where they stayed for six days, since the large cannon had got left behind in the Samārah pass; so they waited until they arrived and let their livestock rest. In it there was a stronghold called al-Dawrān which the minister saw was pointless to keep; so he destroyed it stone by stone until there was nothing left of it.

During this period the population of Dhamār arrived to welcome the minister and express their loyalty, bringing a lot of cattle which they slaughtered in honour of the victorious troops, some of whom divided the meat among themselves while the minister received them very politely, offering them every courtesy. Dhamār is a town rich in fruit, with excellent water and air, among the finest in the highlands, and with a strong fortress and vast orchards.[17]

Sinān Pasha then moved, with the victorious army, to open ground in front of Dhamār where he placed a guard in the fortress. He trusted the people of Dhamār and was good to them, and they informed him that Muṭahhar was in Ṣan'ā'. The minister decided to mount his horse and, with a group of the bravest troops mounted on horseback, to travel to Ṣan'ā' without delay, a squadron of horse riding on through night and day.

CHAPTER 24

[284] Sinān Pasha's journey to capture Ṣan'ā', and Muṭahhar and his followers' flight to Thulā

§ When the minister was informed that Muṭahhar had encamped outside Ṣan'ā', with his senior officers, grandchildren, relatives and children around him, it occurred to him to select 1,000 horsemen, mount with them on horseback, reduce the six-day journey from Dhamār to Ṣan'ā' to a day and a night and surprise Muṭahhar in his camp but, while he was having these thoughts and getting ready to take his gear, behold Muṭahhar was given this information by spies. Muṭahhar then fled the same night, with his entire camp and its people, his women, his slaves, the old and young, the new and ancient, and climbed up to Mt Thulā where he made himself secure, abandoning house and home and taking with him the greater and lesser dignitaries of Ṣan'ā'.

On the day after he had gone, news of his flight reached the minister who cancelled these arrangements and began his preparation for the journey, travelling from Dhamār with the sultan's troops of the victorious Ottoman army. Then after three stages they reached a place called Dhirā' al-Kalb, an extremely rugged and tough place inspiring misery and terror, a defile between two towering mountains which were a refuge to trouble-makers and Zaydī highway robbers. So the minister stationed there his advance and rear guards and placed on [285] the right and left guards for the road and its fort. He made suitable dispositions everywhere and controlled the mountain passes, with sure judgment and a great deal of thought.[18]

That day many of the camels got lost and many of the loads fell down. On it the troops suffered tremendous hardship and faced increasing and numerous trials but Almighty God delivered them and is to be thanked for His kindness which He bestowed at all times, and for His help which He had provided for them throughout such a long period. And, after three stages from Dhirā' al-Kalb, the minister, with the entire victorious army, arrived at Ṣan'ā', on blessed Monday 11 of happy Ṣafar, 977/26 July 1569.

Ṣan'ā' is a city of great plenty, with widespread buildings; and none other in Yemen is older in time or greater in extent. It is stated in *al-Rawḍ al-mu'ṭār fī khabar al-aqṭār* [The fragrant meadow in regional notes][19] that the founder and first builder of Ghumdān and digger of the well which today brings water to the Great Mosque of Ṣan'ā' was Shem, son of Noah, peace be upon him, because he went in search of a place without extreme heat or cold, without finding anywhere more temperate than this spot in the health of its air; and he saw the sun habitually striking it twice, at 8 degrees from Taurus and at 23 from Leo. He then adopted it for his town and established a population there. It is the capital of Yemen where, without exception, the kings of Yemen settled, and it is by a small stream flowing from the mountains to its north and passing by it on its way down to the city of Dhamār.[20]

Muḥammad b. Isḥāq,[21] in information concerning Sayf b. Dhī Yazan, one of the ancient kings of Yemen, mentioned that he had appealed to Kisrā to save him from the Ethiopians who had gained control over Yemen, and that Kisrā had furnished him with eighty men under the leadership of Wahriz who left with eight ships, of which two sank and six reached Aden. Sayf then collected those of his tribe he could and with Wahriz confronted Masrūq b. Abraha, king of the Ethiopians. Then Wahriz, with true aim, shot him with an arrow. All the Ethiopians were defeated but Wahriz was about to enter

Ṣan'ā' when he saw that the gate was not high enough for the banner to pass without being lowered, so he ordered the door to be smashed, and it was smashed. Then he entered hoisting his flag. It is said that they make cotton cloth not made elsewhere and shawls bright with the finest embroidery; and that in Ṣan'ā' [286] it rains only in June, July, August and part of September and only in the afternoon; so if a man meets his friend at noon and the sky is cloudless, he will say, 'Hurry up before the rain comes down,' because they have learnt that it must rain at that time.

When the liar al-Aswad al-'Ansī appeared in Ṣan'ā', the Prophet dispatched under his orders a man of the Azd or Khuzā'ah who went to Dāthawayh al-Abnāwī and hid there; and then Dāthawayh and Fayrūz al-Daylamī went off to murder al-Aswad.

His wife had detested him – indeed, he had forced her into marriage – and she made an arrangement with them. She had given him alcohol until he became drunk and fell asleep, so Fayrūz and another person went into him and found him on a vast feather mattress. They cut off his head and threw it with the rest of him to his attendants who deserted him and were derided out of shame and shock. The news reached the Prophet during the illness of which he died, and he said, mentioning al-Aswad, 'Fayrūz and Dāthawayh, who killed him, were good men.' That is the story that is told.

And Ṣan'ā' has many orchards and much fruit. It is far from the mountains in a level tract of land and is encircled by an ancient wall.

The minister won it in conquest and it returned to the territories under Ottoman rule and cities protected by the sultan. He had the *khuṭbah* delivered in the name of His Majesty the Great Sultan and sultan of all sultans, Selīm Khan b. Sulaymān Khan, Almighty God give him victory and everlasting rule and extend the expanse of his empire. The victorious army was stationed at the gate of Ṣan'ā' and, at brief intervals, a company of them would take its turn to attack Muṭahhar's people in villages which had not come under the sultan's rule.

CHAPTER 25

[287] The dispatch of a squadron against Qaṭrān and the destruction of his castle called Khawlān

§ Qaṭrān was one of Muṭahhar's senior deputies who possessed troops, power and strength. He used to march with 700 men with muskets in front of him, and around him not less than 1,000 other warriors, thereby giving him a total army of 2,000 (*sic*) men. He was a great trouble-maker and an almighty nuisance to the sultan's forces, following them, arresting all who got separated from them, blocking the passage of the supplies being brought to them and other such harassment.

Indeed, the aforementioned Qaṭrān owned a lot of Ṣan'ā' district where he had a strong fortress and an impregnable place called Khawlān which was extremely well fortified and defended, and was a veritable home for his devils and fiends.

He and Muṭahhar had agreed that, should the sultan's army go with the minister to Thulā district, Qaṭrān would follow them, rob the caravans on the road bringing supplies to the base from distant parts and road stations, and constrain the sultan's army so far as its equipment and food were concerned. This would disrupt the Turks and cause them hardship and trouble, and what with his occasional attacks on Ṣan'ā' and other remaining castles and strongholds, the minister would be frightened to stay in this area and locality. That was the aim of Qaṭrān and Muṭahhar; and they made their agreement with that intent.

Sinān Pasha had cottoned on to this vicious agreement, this unimaginative and oppressive plan; so, with his clear vision and sound judgment, he set off to block this nonsense and root out this obnoxious strategy. To that end he appointed Commander Māmāy, a brave *sanjak*, skilled in horsemanship [288] and a distinguished cavalry officer, together with a band of braves, a group of heroes, people of cut and thrust and of sword and spear. Commander Māmāy, with his heroes, followers and men, then made their way to Khawlān where Qaṭrān had entrenched himself in a castle with the finest fortifications and strongest defences. In front of it there was a deep ditch preventing all passage. It was loaded with musket and cannon, and with food and provisions. Commander Māmāy's aim was to attack them at once and to gain entry with men and heroes, but the Zaydī swept them off the castle with one volley from the muskets and cannon and prevented them from getting inside. Twenty-one of the soldiers fell, Almighty God granting them martyrdom and giving them a happy and blessed end. They passed into Paradise and were welcomed by houris and young men and covered in pardon and pleasure.

Then the victorious army set the cannon against them and struck them with fire and shot. The Zaydī realised that they could not sustain the position, nor stand firm in the face of sudden death, so they left the castle, in an apparent desire for battle for which the delighted Turks cleared an adequate space, but the Zaydī fled to the mountains, leaving the arms and grain in the castle. Groups of cavalry followed, catching some of them whom they killed where possible, with the rest fleeing to Mt Thulā and reuniting with Muṭahhar, in distress and full of shame.

Commander Māmāy returned to Khawlān castle which he found full of arms, food and grain which he divided among the troops. He destroyed the castle stone by stone until he had dug up its foundation, put out its lights and breath, and left it as an empty plain, hiding neither building, nor foundation; and men came to say, 'In this place there was a castle called Khawlān.'[22]

Commander Māmāy then returned in triumph and victory, happy and delighted with his load of the enemy's booty, to the minister who dressed him in a proud honorary robe and covered him with his generous gaze and splendid care.

The blessed conquest took place at the beginning of Rabīʿ al-Awwal 977/ 14 August 1569.

CHAPTER 26

[289] Ḥasan Pasha's foray into Wadi al-Sirr and his slaughter of the broken enemy tribesmen

§ Among the collection of castles near Ṣanʿāʾ is that of Dhū Marmar[23] belonging to Luṭfallāh b. Muṭahhar. It was surrounded by many villages in a large valley called Wadi al-Sirr in which there were a great many Zaydī sectarians, followers of Muṭahhar, all of whom caused trouble and robbed the caravans. So the minister appointed a company of the sultan's troops, to be commanded by Ḥasan Pasha, with orders to raid the villages and plunder the crops, men and women, boys and children they contained. He gave him instructions not to kill anyone but to take them prisoner and put them in the *kawrkajiyyah* and work the oars at sea, for there was a great need of oarsmen for the *kawrkajiyyah*.[24] It was his generous nature not to wish to shed blood; and only in very exceptional circumstances did he order the killing of those who deserved it; on the contrary, he would deal with them kindly. From first to last this was always his practice; and this is one of the best qualities and the finest customs.

Almighty God has never allowed kings, commanders, governors-general and others who shed blood to survive for long, and Prophetic tradition warns that the man who kills will be slain; for the intelligent have no need to be told of the fates of kings and sultans.

[290] Ḥasan Pasha submitted to Sinān Pasha by hearing and obeying, and exerted every effort he could to that end. Together with those selected by the minister, he made raids into Wadi al-Sirr, seizing the men and women, the young men and children he found there as well as the crops and grain. None he killed save those who resisted but he killed in battle and contest. Everywhere he seized booty and obtained property on an extensive scale of which he took what he could carry and left what gave him trouble. The latter he set on fire, without leaving it for those scoundrels.

He went round those villages and districts, putting the whole area to the sword and spending several days in the process. He roamed with his horses to right and left, to the front and behind, repeatedly attacking them and giving them a taste of gall. Time and again he broke them and left them like palm-tree stumps, in the depths of hell. 'Ah, what will convey unto thee what she is, a raging fire. Canst thou see any remnant of them?'[25]

The pasha returned to the minister in triumph and victory, bringing with him a lot of provisions and much booty, mature, young and child prisoners, whom he shared out among the troops, preparing those that were mature as slaves for the ships for captains to use in their galleys at sea. The good tidings spread and brought joy near and far: it rendered sterile land fertile and encouraged building through its message; everywhere it brought delight. Islam gained from its victory, and for heresy there was defeat and collapse. For people of the faith there was happiness and delight, and hands were filled with booty and gain.

A record number of prisoners was entered in the register. Cutting proof was furnished of the heresy's demise. In such matters there is nothing like seeing.

CHAPTER 27

[291] The minister's determination to enter Muṭahhar's land and conquer the stronghold of Shibām, one of the castles belonging to that arrogant fool

§ On 4 Rabīʿ al-Awwal the blessed, 977/17 August 1569, the minister struck camp and raised his tents and pavilions, organised his weaponry and supplies for the blessed journey, arranging his side cavalry and mounting his spirited Burāq.[26] He had drawn a curtain over the day with the blackness of his host and flooded the light with the whiteness of his swords, in an army whose columns collided with the mountain sides and whose van and rear contingents filled the plains and the hills as if its forces had kindled war's fire. The army passed along, as its squadrons of horse gave voice to its honours.

The minister's cavalry had turned their horse-reins to the fight a second time and events understood that they provided for him a rich harvest from the blades of his weaponry. So the minister continued his journey with his vast army until he came to a halt around the stronghold of al-Munaqqab[27] where he pitched his camp and settled; for this stronghold marks the border between the Ṣanʿāʾ region and that of the *duʿāh* who owe allegiance to the sultanate, root and branch.

Sinān Pasha maintained that position for three days for the cannon to complete their passage because of the difficulty of conveying them over the high and low land and of the uneasy passage over the uneven terrain. Once they had completed their journey and were nearly in position, the minister set out with the victorious army on 9 Rabīʿ al-Awwal/22 August, continuing the march and encamping in front of the town of Shibām where he pitched his camp and tents.

[292] Shibām is a large town, with extensive grounds, enclosed on three sides by mountains that rise to the sky rendering it inaccessible from those directions, with secure reservoir water and unclimbable save by foxes and rabbits. The fourth side facing the plain is defended by a wall of towering construction, built of strong adobe cast like iron, its length being 5,000 cubits and its width 15 hand-spans. At its ends are two bastions protecting it from hostile destruction and containing cannon and muskets. Those who wish to advance and shoot cannot draw near to it. One of the bastions is called al-ʿĀriḍah fort and the second al-Lubākhah, and they are loaded with weapons of war such as guns and the like.[28]

It is stated in *al-Rawḍ al-muʿṭār*[29] that Shibām is a mountain belonging to Hamdān in Yemen, and that from the town of Shibām to Hadramawt is four stages. It is a strong castle, extensive and populated, at the summit of an impregnable mountain which can only be climbed after effort. In its heights are many flourishing villages, farms, running water and much grain. It is said that when an earthquake occurred in Yemen, Shibām was entirely destroyed except for the house belonging to Ibrāhīm ibn al-Ṣabāḥ. He was very charitable, and it is said that he was saved from disaster through his generous charity.

The stronghold of Kawkabān is a point of access for whoever wishes to take Shibām, as al-Qāhirah is for Taʿizz. Kawkabān is a high fortress on the top of a lofty mountain, not climbed by any but mountain goats and not reached by any but the winds from the east[30] and the north. It is Muḥammad b. Shams al-Dīn's base, with control over Shibām, having it in range from behind and above.

Sinān Pasha was determined to take Shibām and dispatched there some of the tribesmen. They had a good look inside it, making a detailed assessment, and they found a stream of water flowing from within to the outside through which one could get inside. So they concealed there a group at night who got inside the canal by the stream and reached the stronghold's gate which was made of iron. There were guards around it whom they struck with the sword before opening the stronghold gate. The victorious army saw the stronghold gate opened and charged inside, entering and taking over the town. Sword battles broke out and the troops scattered [293] through the lanes. They killed those they found while some of them climbed to the top of the mountain where the tribesmen crowded round them, killing those who had become separated from their companions. Some of these were martyred; some of them threw themselves from the mountain heights and were broken to pieces; and others descended to safety to join the rest of the troops.

The battle between them intensified and the minister, seeing this, himself charged into Shibām with a section of brave troops. Shooting began against them from the forts of al-ʿĀriḍah and al-Lubākhah, so he detailed Ḥasan Pasha, with a section, to take al-ʿĀriḍah fort, and others to take al-Lubākhah fort; and they captured them, with those inside taking to flight.

Inside al-ʿĀriḍah fort there were about 100 Turkish prisoners together with the Dāʿī ʿAbdullāh's uncle.[31] ʿAbdullāh knew the place where they were imprisoned, so he quickly went to the prison and released his uncle and the prisoners with him who, as if returning to life in the world, went to the minister who treated them with kindness and took them on the pay-roll. The fighting continued until the two sides were separated by nightfall.

The sultan's troops took a great deal of booty which they found stored in Shibām and the minister returned to his base. He consulted his commanders over what to do with Shibām, collecting their views as to whether to destroy it rather than to leave it; for he could not control it before taking Kawkabān's fort which had it within range. Then he gave orders for them to destroy Shibām when dawn broke; and at sunrise the troops went to Shibām, burnt and destroyed what they could, ripping off the doors to the houses and the wood from the roofs which they brought as firewood for the base where it was badly required. In as far as they were able and could, they destroyed it.

From the best spoken of Shibām's history is the 'entry of Shibām', and also, 'We have opened your gates, O Shibām'. Its capture, and that of al ʿĀriḍah and al-Lubākhah, took place on 11 Rabīʿ al-Awwal 977/24 August 1569.

CHAPTER 28

[294] The minister's transfer of his base from Shibām to Mt Thulā and Kawkabān, and the Dāʿī ʿAbdullāh's request for permission to go to his territory and collect help for the sultan's army from his tribesmen and elsewhere

§ After concluding business in Shibām, the minister moved camp to the area between Thulā and Kawkabān[32] and summoned the commanders, headmen and senior figures to advise them as to his actions there. Thulā and Kawkabān were both extremely high and inaccessible, and equipped and fortified to the highest level; both were among the best of the Zaydī fortresses and supremely served by their impregnable position. He told them that the capture of such fortresses would require effort, strategy and trickery, a deal of care as well as lots of provender for the livestock and firewood for cooking. Both the latter were essential as were the fodder and the rest of the provisions.[33]

Shaikh ʿAbdullāh sought leave to go to al-Munaqqab and the rest of his district and ask his tribesmen and followers to convey to the army various supplies and the produce they required. He promised to get tribesmen for them whom he would bring under truce and from whom he would take hostages, as is the custom among the people there. When he had collected a band of willing tribesmen, he would go behind Kawkabān castle to encourage them to fight [295] there while the sultan's forces would fight them from the base with artillery and cannon; and perhaps they would win, take Kawkabān and be victorious.

The minister saw that what he said was right, sought God's blessing for the enterprise and agreed to let him follow that course of action. He imposed a limit of twenty days on his absence which the shaikh agreed; and with such generous approval, the shaikh departed for his people amid expressions of kindness.

The minister remained at the base with his troops and aides in their tented encampment. They were in need of food and firewood and of some essentials; so he asked if there were any villages and farms where such food and services could be found, and was told of a village called Ḥabābah[34] where there were plenty of livestock and resources. Its crops were standing in the field.

However, the Zaydī were exercising on horseback on the hills, their shapes visible from far off to the forces of Islam. So Sinān Pasha himself mounted in a small posse, very quickly took three artillery pieces, rode out to them and fired at them. As if by divine action he shot them dead on the spot. The minister then ordered the servants to make for Ḥabābah, cut down the corn they needed and rip off what doors and wood from the roofs they could. This they did successfully and returned to camp. They stored away what they had brought and for some time made use of it, in relaxation and good eating.

They were then again in need; so Commander Maḥmūd emerged with some horsemen and a number of servants and stewards, dispatching the latter to the same farms on the same mission while he, and the brave lions with him, were concealed in a place hidden from sight and fitting for such complete concealment. That took place shortly before daybreak before the flowers had opened their eyes, on 26 Rabīʿ al-Awwal 977/8 September 1569.

All that could be seen from the direction of the hills, when the servants had reached the farms, were figures masked in clothing, so the Zaydī launched an attack on the servants in the belief that they were solitary figures [296] over there, when suddenly Commander Maḥmūd, with his horsemen, became visible to them from his place of concealment and attacked them with sword and spear, in one solid mass. The Zaydī stood quite firm for a time, then bounded away in headlong flight after several of their heads had been cut off and prisoners taken.

The servants returned laden with prisoners and clothing and Commander Maḥmūd and his men had no fear of starvation. They then entered the camp and paraded the heads on spears which they planted at the edge of the plain. They then relaxed with the forage and crops they had brought, keeping their livestock from hunger and weakness.

The Dā‘ī ‘Abdullāh's absence grew protracted and his appointed time passed; nor did news come of the action he had promised. The troops grew restive in their base and each one of them hated the position he was in. However, the minister devoted time and thought to the matter, taking everyone's opinion and advice, courteous as he went to and fro, and relaxed with them in his enquiry. He implored God in His glory and praise, seeking His aid and guidance; for He is generous and open-handed and gives help where He wishes.

CHAPTER 29

[297] The generosity shown by the Dā‘ī al-Ṣalāḥ, confirming that he is a man of great honesty

§ The Hamdānī Dā‘ī al-Ṣalāḥ had been Muṭahhar's captain of the guard at al-Qāhirah when he submitted to authority, joined the community and donned the ceremonial of obedience and loyalty. He had seceded from Muṭahhar and his adherents and broken his allegiance to him and his sect; and made haste to offer his service and advice, to display friendship and good service, to atone for any faults in the past and to wash away any shame of dishonour. Before that, during the period of his allegiance to Muṭahhar, the latter had made him governor of Wadi Bawn in which there is a sizeable village called al-Ḥā'iṭ but, when he seceded from him and stood against him, Muṭahhar appointed somebody else over the wadi. Al-Ṣalāḥ used to be on intimate terms with the people of that valley who owed him for past favours and good deeds there, and he had experience and acquaintance with the business of that agreeable place. He nursed ambitions to take them over and make use of what they had to offer.

After the minister had exonerated him, he made him commander over the Shafālīt Arabs drawn from every tribe who draw the sultan's wage, who work for the troops on the march and at base and let their hair grow long. One of them is called a *shaflūt*.

He requested from the minister that he take a group of *shafālīt* and servants and with them launch a night raid on Wadi Bawn and the village of al-Ḥā'iṭ and bring what valuables and food they found there. The minister gave him permission for this; so he took a group of *shafālīt* and made his way across the barren mountain passes, enlisting those who were dear to him and recognised [298] his authority and allegiance. He invaded that place where he knew every village and farm. Every nook and cranny was known to him, and he had no fear of trouble from its people.

He encountered a small number of Zaydī there with a group of their vacillating tribesmen with whom he fought. He killed several, cutting off some of their heads and taking some of them prisoner, and driving away 1,000 head of sheep as loot and carrying off what booty he could as he went off, plundering the cattle and returning satisfied. All of it he brought to the minister who received him with many thanks and great kindness as he affirmed his faithful service, his trust and his sincerity.

In truth the members of the *du'āh* in that region are among the greatest enemies of wicked Zaydism, only supporting them on the surface to avoid coercion and rendering them no respect or consideration. Their enmity is continual and deep-rooted, ever rekindled and alight through close association and living. Thus God ordained between them of old and at present; and the damage they do each other continues.

CHAPTER 30

[299] Several skirmishes between some squadrons and a group of Zaydī

§ On 4 Rabī' al-Thānī 977/16 September 1569, a unit of the sultan's victorious armed forces emerged, comprising young and stalwart cavalry on long-bodied prancing chargers, riding defiant at the foot of Thulā, in search of battle and confiscating the animals, property and men they found at its base.

As none was visible to them and nobody caught their eye who might approach and chase them, they dismounted with confidence and let free their charges to graze under cover; they took out the bridles from their horses' mouths, some of them tethering their mounts in the usual way, when suddenly and without warning a group of Zaydī launched an ambush against them. He, who could, leapt on to his horse like a lion and attacked the enemy before the riders were ready; and they began the cut and thrust of battle.

The Zaydī horsemen spread out, double the size of the sultan's squadron, as they sprang upon those who had tethered their horses but, wishing to undo the horses' tethers, were unable to mount or bridle them. What a struggle broke out! What a network of swords and arrows developed! So the battle raged and the clash of weapons grew fierce; wounds multiplied and pain waxed. A number of Zaydī were slain, hastened to the fire by the angel of hell; and two of the sultan's troops met their death, delivered by Riḍwān [the angel of Paradise] to [300] Paradise.

Musket bullets continued to destroy armour and lances defile chaste shields before the two parties separated and the two groups withdrew. The horsemen returned to the *dīwān* with several enemy heads which they paraded in the square. Meanwhile, the people of Thulā and Kawkabān lit fires to tell the tribesmen that they had killed two of the sultan's troops. However, they did not celebrate the innumerable Zaydī heads that had been severed, but the tribesmen rejoiced with vain delight, excited and aroused. They spent the night in activity and burning, kindling a blaze of fire on the mountain tops.

Not long before daybreak, the unit employed another ruse to beat the enemy. They made a foray to the foot of Thulā without encountering anyone, so they dismounted from their horses and let them rest for the remainder of the night. Then, as morning forces drew their swords and sunrise displayed its brow; as the black of night withdrew to raze its clouds and the white of day rushed in to pitch its tents, then, the Zaydī horse came down from the mountain in search of battle and descended to the spot, spread out in a line. Only then did each rider from the squadron, agile on the back of his horse, thrust at them, with the power of his skill and the strength of his arms.

Heavy in aggression, light in the gallop: many in the encounter, few in number.

Then they went at the enemy for all they were worth and gave them a good drubbing. For a long time the fighting continued and the arrows flew. Men menstruated! Falcons and eagles hovered over the slain. Where the enemy emerged, fate came out to meet him, determined on contest with him. The horsemen galloped at him with their spurs, pouring their shot into the tumult-fire and maiming horses with their swords till the day's heat parted the two sides.

The sultan's troops returned after the utter rout of Satan's forces. The swords had been drenched in blood; death had watered the soil red; and they brought to the minister the heads of the slain. With that, violent fear convulsed the people of Kawkabān and Thulā.

CHAPTER 31

[301] Ḥasan Pasha's preparation to go behind Kawkabān and his summons to the *dāʿī* for assistance there[1]

§ The Dāʿī ʿAbdullāh's delay grew protracted and his appointment passed without him arriving at the base with his tribesmen, according to the plan previously agreed. The minister understood the weakness of the base tribesmen's resolve in coming with him to fight and their preference for ease over battle and contest. He realised that they needed a spur to stir their sleeping resolve and drive them to where they had plotted.

Now Ḥasan Pasha was called Ḥasan [i.e. splendid] by people in that he was governor-general of Yemen and superior to all the *sanjak* commanders in the service; and he was given such a name because he was endowed with the physical size, good luck and courtesy the name denotes.

The minister ordered Ḥasan to take the army of Yemen and the *muta-farriqah* of conquering Egypt, men of great standing and status, together with Maḥmūd Bey, lord of a noble Ottoman brigade, and travel to the *dāʿī*'s country. He should then escort the *dāʿī* and all his own tribesmen, together with other tribesmen and bedu under his authority, and go with him behind the stronghold of Kawkabān; and from there he should set siege to people in the stronghold while the minister would go, lay siege and fight them from his own side. In this way the Dāʿī ʿAbdullāh and the people under his authority and protection would be heartened by the Turkish forces. So 1,500 members of the Yemeni and Egyptian forces gathered under Ḥasan Pasha, comprising cavalry and infantry, and set out on 5 Rabīʿ al-Thānī 977/17 September.

[302] When Ḥasan Pasha had left the minister's base, he himself circled Kawkabān, examining its angles and corners and observing the secrets of its features. He was contemplating how he could enter the stronghold, and was thus engaged when the *āghā* of the Janissaries from Egypt and the *āghā* of the Janissaries from the Porte left him, together with about fifteen Janissaries, and climbed to the top of the mountain, near Kawkabān stronghold. They were far from Ḥasan Pasha and his military escort when a large number of horses and men came out at them from Kawkabān stronghold, cutting off the two aforementioned *aghas* and their sections and swarming round them.

The Janissaries realised that they were cut off from help, far from the troops and staring death in the eye, so they stood firm before the enemy, declaring, 'We shall fight. Then we shall kill and be killed but we won't die in vain.' Then they joined battle and had killed a large number of the enemy before the enemy swarmed over them, and they were slain in God's cause. Almighty God blessed them with martyrdom: they won Paradise and their souls gained mercy and compassion. They had risked their lives in what they did, Almighty God have mercy on them.

And it has been said: 'Risk is not recommended even when successful.'

This event angered Ḥasan Pasha when news of it reached him and he sent a message to the minister telling him what had happened.[2] The Zaydī were delighted by it and lit fires for it, demonstrating their joy and drive for victory, but God decides only what He wishes and God is merciful to those who believe in Him.

It had not occurred to Ḥasan Pasha that these young men would go and risk their lives, without seeking advice and permission from one of the *ʿaqils* [headmen], before throwing themselves into such a dangerous situation. But a man of sense would not undertake such a dreadful enterprise!

And Ḥasan Pasha went to the *dāʿī*'s country to encourage him in the way the minister had ordered. Information will follow as to what happened on the journey, if Almighty God so wills.

CHAPTER 32

[303] The minister's climb to the foot of Kawkabān to examine what route to take; Muṭahhar takes advantage of his absence; his attack on the minister's base and his defeat and failure

§ Having provided a detachment of troops for Ḥasan Pasha, the minister had the idea of climbing to the foot of Kawkabān to ponder its nooks and crannies, its paths and gullies, so that he could select the easiest for the ascent of the sultan's army and for its conquest and occupation. Accordingly, he went out with a squadron of horse, a force of brave men, and patrolled the foot of Kawkabān mountain.

Muḥammad b. Shams al-Dīn, aware of his action, hastened to protect the castle and ditch [chasm],[3] and, summoning the stronghold's occupants, warned them to be on their guard. He fired the large cannons and kindled fire to inform Muṭahhar in Thulā[4] that the minister had arrived at the foot of Kawkabān and was away from his base so that Muṭahhar might then raid it. For that had been their signal.

So Muṭahhar's generals, commanders and warriors bullied him into descending to the minister's base, realising that this was an incomparable opportunity and that they should exert every effort to fulfil their plans. They told him that he was a man of iron, with a heart like strong steel. Usually, Muṭahhar was not like that; on the contrary, as a rule, he was cowardly and indecisive. So he collected his sons, young and old, his attendants, generals and suite, and the weapons that he thought would protect him, and made up his mind to descend to the foot of Thulā.

He then mounted a donkey, as was his custom from the beginning, since his lameness [304] prevented him from mounting a horse. He was frightened that the donkey would slip, with him on it, as it tilted; so his generals held on to him as he sat on the donkey, terrified that he would slip and fall off.

Once he had left his house and taken hold of the donkey, it broke wind which he took as an omen for his downfall and a sign for his defeat and destruction. Then, seized by cowardice and alarm and struck by fear and fright, he went backwards and retreated; for he thought that, if he left his hovel, he would not get back to it; nor would he be able to regain his cave, once he had left it. But he lied to his troops and made light of the donkey's fart. The more his companions and friends encouraged him and gave him heart, the more he shied away backwards! Thus, backwards he went on his retreating donkey, recoiling without any advance. He was absolutely determined to go backwards!

However, from his cavalry, and especially his bodyguard and devilish partners in tyranny, his experts in outrage and tyranny, his co-infidels and co-aggressors, he selected 100 horsemen and 300 infantry. These their leader stupidly encouraged, with the words, 'Go and attack the camp and put on a bit of a show. If you find the place empty, occupy it; if you find it defended, then run for your lives. It is enough for you to talk of attacking the sultan's camp for rumours to spread that you've done so. Then you will have succeeded in achieving your purpose.'

Aspirations, even if only wishful, are sweet and, if they come true, then double is their pleasure.

So look at that misguided king who, with his army, pulled back because of a poor donkey's fart! Wonder over him and his weak-mindedness, his smug goal of idle talk during this long and widespread pretence, and his arrogant ambition for the crown; and draw a wondrous lesson from your age, for it is the greatest wonder of all.

Nights as you have learnt are heavy with child, and give birth to wonders![5]

Then the raiding party came out, descending in fury to the foot of Thulā, with its horses and men, thinking the minister's base to be a forest without a lion. The horse came in one force, followed by the men in formation. But, behold, the shaikh of the Gīza tribe, [305] prince of Egypt and scion of great commanders, emerged to meet them.

Descended from Arabic stock, the essence of courage, like a sword, with blade burnished till a jewel's liquid flows within.

The great commander al-Zaynī Ḥamād b. Khabīr had been left behind in the camp with his horsemen to act for the minister and was on guard watch and duty, ready for battle. He observed the Zaydī approach and advance by the side of the camp as they charged.

Commander Ḥamād rode among noble Turks, with Arabs on Arabs, among horsemen skilled in battle, with hearts hardened for the fight, armour of the finest steel, spears supple with honey, swords of the finest burnish. So the devil's band converged with heroes of the faith and the sword struck the hatred that lurked in their hearts. They embraced like brothers; the elite hugged the slave; and then contact was sundered. The band of infidels was sure of its end, and set on defeat and flight. They realised the endlessness of the suffering they faced and their inability to endure the strength of the pain they would meet.

So the Zaydī fled to the mountains that offered no protection, meeting as they left what broke and shattered them. They retreated, broken and destroyed. A number of them were slain or taken prisoner; some had their noses cut off; some riders were slain; and their coat-mailed corpses covered the void.

Commander Ḥamād returned to the camp together with a number of prisoners, bound and fettered and heads on spears after what had befallen them. Among the Zaydī slain were some of the chief generals of the lame and disabled Muṭahhar. Ḥamād had seized their horses, including some of the finest, bearing Muṭahhar's brand, as well as a number of others, and he returned to the victorious camp.

The sun began to set, with young girls slipping into their rooms and curtains relaxing their folds, as the minister made his way back to his splendid camp. Ḥamād advanced towards him to tell him the results of the battle and struggle, scattering [306] the heads of the slain in front of his horse and offering the prisoners bound and fettered in shame and ignominy.

Sinān Pasha praised Almighty God for this victory and thanked the Lord's kindness that the enemy had not been able to take his camp unawares. He recognised his inability to thank his great and exalted Creator and took heart from the kindness of Almighty God towards him on all occasions. That was on 20 Rabīʿ al-Ākhir, 977/2 October 1569.

CHAPTER 33

[307] The minister's customary climb to the foot of Kawkabān; Muṭahhar's dispatch to him of his general Farḥān, together with a group of Zaydī to his base; the outbreak of fighting; and the slaughter of Farḥān and most of the charlatan's soldiers

§ The great minister each day used to ride up to the foot of Kawkabān. He would take with him some commanders and horsemen of judgment and planning to examine the sides and features of that mountain, looking for some gully or opening through which it was possible to attack. That became his customary practice; that was the way he devoted his time; and spies covered his every move and conveyed to the cripple every new development.

When the night of 23 Rabīʿ al-Ākhir/5 October arrived, the minister went out as usual with Naṣr, lieutenant of His Excellency's horse. He left behind in the happy camp, to defend against Zaydī cunning, and their cunning is truly powerful, his nephew, the courageous horseman, the veritable lion, pride of the great commanders, Commander Muṣṭafā, God raise his status and let his spears and swords strike his enemies' chests. Together with him, he left the brave horseman, the great and valiant conqueror, Commander Qayt Āghā and a troop of coat-mailed Circassians as well as the Egyptian Arab shaikh of Gīza, the great and honoured commander, mentioned before in this report, Ḥamād b. Khabīr. He charged them with the care of the great camp and went off and forward to what faced him.

[308] Morning unfurled its banner and banished the forces of darkness with the sword of its light, flooding the earth with light and lustre; and the army of black night withdrew in defeat. Taking heart from the mighty minister's absence, the cripple dispatched a party of his misguided men to attack the encampment and appointed as their leader and commander, their envoy and guide, his slave, the general Farḥān. He attached to him more than 100 of his cavalry and about 500 sharpshooters[6] who descended to the foot of Thulā from its heights and attacked the camp with vim and vigour.

The defending commanders were hidden at the foot of the mountain where they were out of sight and absolutely hidden from the Zaydī until the latter advanced towards them, getting between them and the blessed camp; and then they surrounded them like a bracelet or necklace.

From their ambush point the horse broke them up, while from the base the lions burst forth from their lair. They completely surprised them and left them devoid of hope, caught unawares and at a loss. The Zaydī attempted to escape, but in vain. They were at their last gasp and in despair. Frustrated and ensnared, they fell into their hands. They were caught by their cunning and outwitted by their deceit.

With shining sabre, drawn sword and swift horse, the people of the Sunnah swarmed over the apostates who were absolutely broken. They were swept to the ground and across their minds flashed their fall into hell-fire on Judgment Day. The people of the Sunnah set upon their faces and shoulders, blunting their swords thereon. They broke their hamstrings and tore at their flesh; they made the blood spurt from their veins and ripped away at their bellies. They wreaked their blades on the low slaves, striking their necks with their swords.

They became desolate palm-tree stumps while their souls fell sinking to the bottomless pit. How many headless corpses and footless bodies! Throats were slit; a river of blood flowed; necks were hacked and noses cut off. Farḥān's back was pierced, as was his chest, by the points of lances. His innate joy was changed to grief and his head cut off. His life was finished and with it Muṭahhar's heart and vigour were broken as his hand and leg had been before. He burst into wild lament; and the scoundrel's army was shattered as always he had been himself.

They placed Farḥān's head with those of the slain on well-fashioned spears and paraded with them along the plain. He was tall, nay arrogant, in life, [309] and after death, he was more than a spear in length.

They crowned the spears with most of the slain which they then paraded; and that was the reward for sin.

When the great minister returned and was near to his noble camp, the aforementioned commanders met him, tossing and scattering the enemy heads under their horses' hooves, and giving praise and thanks to Almighty God. The minister thanked Almighty God from his knees, thus acknowledging what he owed his Almighty Lord for blessings and favours. And that is a benefit which God grants to whom He wills. And to Him are praise and thanks, at the end and the beginning.

CHAPTER 34

[310] Muṭahhar's arrogance; his dispatch of his two sons, al-Hādī and Luṭfallāh, with a group of horsemen to kill the minister; his sortie with them to the foot of Thulā; the killing of al-Hādī and the defeat of the remainder before arrival at the mountain's foot[7]

§ When news of the failure and defeat that had befallen Muṭahhar spread among the tribesmen, and they realised that he was the most abject coward, he decided to display a degree of courage and, if only for the one occasion, to show his presence among the Zaydī in the field with the cavalry. So he summoned his two sons, the misguided al-Hādī and the errant Luṭfallāh, who of all his worthless army were the fastest in flight. They arrived with ʿAlī bin Shuwayʿ and his crowd of vagabonds, who, on a former occasion in the time of Ḥasan Pasha, had been ignominiously cut to the bone and defeated near Zabīd,[8] and fled for their lives.

But, after such utter defeat and flight, they had counted on gaining the place in a brave charge, and began to boast about it among the tribesmen. So the cripple had selected them as his two wings, without realising that each of them had two wings for flight.

He put al-Hādī on his right and and Luṭfallāh on his left; and in front of them a band of fighters, a troop of warriors, marksmen, dogs of the forest, guerrillas and terrorists of every kind who never deal with honesty, devils who only fight with hell-fire in their fury for vengeance, thirsty for battle, surging for bloodshed and raring for the fray.

[311] Muṭahhar made a frightened and trembling exit from his nest,

indicating by this sortie that he had either revived or would be taken to his grave; and he made an exaggerated display of fire. With this in mind, he emerged from his cave, through the mass of smoke, as if it were Judgment Day. They fired at the sultan's forces with their guns and muskets, amid a sea of flags, standards and banners. They placed behind every stone someone to fire a musket and brought the long cannons into service. They made the earth and sands shake and the mountains and castles explode; they ignited the fires of war and caused the battle to begin. They deafened the ear with the explosions, like peals of thunder or clouds from the sky carrying darkness, thunder and lightning. The Apocalypse had come before its time; the Last Day had arrived before its hour. However, the truth emerged and the facts sprang to the eye.

The minister went to the scene himself and looked into every aspect of the battle. He thought that the base Zaydī would be bold enough to come down into the plain on this occasion although such an advance may not succeed; and he saw them standing on the mountain top and hiding behind the rocks while they fired the cannon, muskets and stones.

Then the Turks cast a volley of fire and staged a show of night stars at midday, hitting them with their long *ḍarbuzān* and cannon which made the mountains ring and the rocks explode. They showed them what an earthquake was like, how frail and slight were bodies and souls, and how the claws of death clutch the horsemen as prey. How many boys were bereft? How many children were orphaned? How many women were widowed? How many pregnant women aborted and emptied their wombs. How many bodies wore out and heads were cut off!

And Sinān, the mighty minister recited, while in the turmoil of the field, patrolling with his cavalry:

> I shall unsheathe my sword from its scabbard after its long rest till tribe after tribe is slain. Each sword shall strike a head and women at home shall cast their veils to stroke the backs of orphans' heads.[9]

[312] So here the flame of justice put out the fire of folly, and the people of the Sunnah triumphed and the heretics were fatally hit. Many of the Zaydī men and leaders were killed. Their folly failed and their men and horse were destroyed; and al-Hādī was hit by cannon fire and his soul snuffed out. His existence and his every action were erased from the page of life.

The cripple fled to his stronghold on his donkey, followed by his son, Luṭfallāh, on his horse, on which he sat as he raced with his retreating horsemen. The swords and fire of his weeping troops were stilled. Abjectly, they entered the defences on the crest of Mt Thulā; and behind Muṭahhar every artillery horseman called out bravely: 'Nay, but verily he will be flung to the Consuming One. Ah, what will convey unto thee what the Consuming One is! [It is] the fire of Allah, kindled, which leapeth up over the hearts [of men].'[10] The soldiers of the mighty Sunnī recited at him and his followers: 'Wheresoever ye may be, death will overtake you, even though ye were in lofty towers.'[11]

The banners of victory flapped, stirred by the wind, and in triumph did victory burst forth, ablaze with light. The callers to the good called out, 'Only God's forces are triumphant', and secrets were disclosed. 'The Romans have been defeated in the nearer land, and they, after their defeat, will be victorious.'[12] With thanks to God they conquered and pillaged, seizing enemy plunder. Night fell between them and the sky dressed in black; then waking lost its place and eyes were overcome by sleep. So the minister returned to his tent, victorious and triumphant, and broken Muṭahhar returned to his nest, shattered and routed.

When the enemy insisted on revolt, God insisted on victory for us.
How often in appeal they were held back from assaulting us but caution and assault were of no value,
God insisted that they die in shame, and they fled; and death and flight are equal.

God be thanked, the fires of untruth were extinguished, snuffed out and eclipsed; and the lights of justice appeared and shone, and were revealed. The people of the Sunnah arose with the help of sure religion, and their last prayer was to thank God, Lord of the two worlds.

CHAPTER 35

[313] The minister's conquest of the stronghold of Ḥabb al-'Arūs; Muṭahhar's wish to profit from his absence from his camp; and his defeat, betrayed and deserted

§ Among all the strongholds, castles and towers Muṭahhar counted as his during the days of his folly, were three strongholds, situated close to each other and closely connected with each other, the population of which used to rob the troops, in secret and quite openly.

One of them is the stronghold of al-'Arūs, beyond which lies Ḥabb al-'Arūs; and beyond them both the stronghold of al-Ẓafir, next to them, all in one line. The distance between each is just within a large cannon's range.[13]

As he passed by them, the minister made up his mind to seize them. They displayed to him weakness and the wish to be ruled, showing themselves as weak and ready for submission. They declared to him: 'If you take Kawkabān,

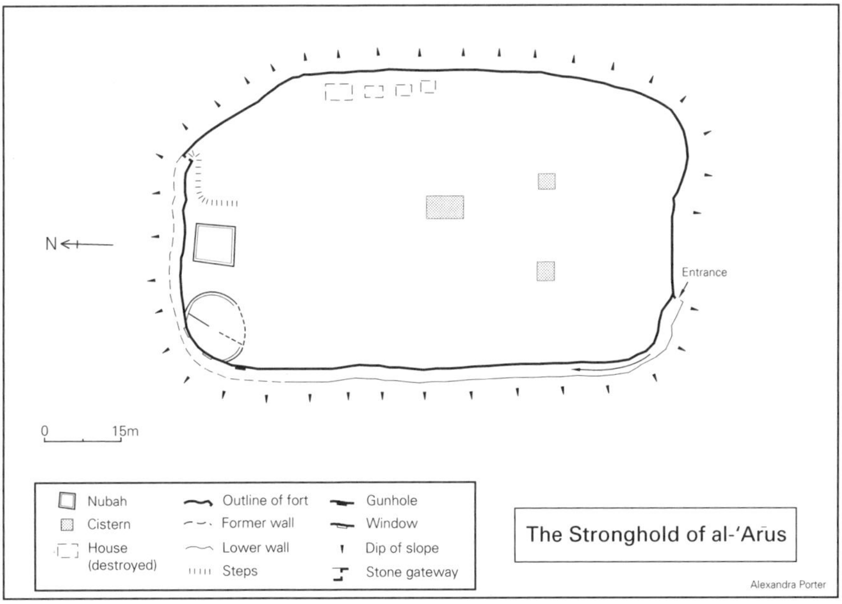

then we shall follow and submit and raise the flag of surrender to proclaim that we have submitted; for we are not opposed to you and your protection; nor would you find in us any harm or trouble as far as any of you are concerned. However, we cannot now hand over to you these strongholds lest we be accused of folly and treachery. But if you take Kawkabān, then we shall be willing to surrender them to you.'

The minister believed what they said, because he had no wish for bloodshed and was opposed to the loss of life, [314] as indeed is the practice of the merciful. And he reacted: 'If we take Kawkabān and Thulā, then these forts would hold no value. Then they would really have to submit and come under the sultanic banner by force.' So he left them on condition they caused harm to none, commit no highway robbery, nor supply the lame Muṭahhar. However, once he had begun to do battle with the people of Kawkabān and Thulā, war had broken out and the call to arms had been issued, he was told that the people of these strongholds were wreaking havoc on the land, committing every outrage to cut off supplies to the sultan's forces and joining the cripple's army in large numbers.[14]

So Sinān Pasha showed them that they had broken the contract with him and brought harm to his army and soldiers. In return for their aggression, therefore, he would shed their blood, arrange their death and extinction and put a stop to the continual mischief from those tribes. So he dispatched there some *ḍarbuzān* in haste and wrought havoc among them; for they had begun to help the foolish Muṭahhar and assist the charlatan group. He realised that the capture of the central stronghold was the nearest way to shatter the lot of them and the most forceful way to break their centre and knock them for six. So he advanced towards it and positioned the victorious army against it.

> They made for the stronghold and went round it. They encircled it with a handcuff rather than a bracelet.
> The enemy were routed when they saw an ocean vast enough to swallow the sailors.
> Their excuse for flight was clear. Can night stand against day?

The brave men clung to the walls of the stronghold and climbed to its top without thought for the fire and stones hurled by those villains which each met on the face rather than the back, and on the chest, not the rear. They made their way up like birds, with each other's help, without heed for accident or care for the death for which they were prepared. For they must hoist the sultanic banner at the top of Ḥabb al-'Arūs and wreak revenge and havoc on the stronghold population whose homes and property they destroyed, and of whom all trace was removed from the slate of life. They became as a harvest blown by the winds, phantoms without spirits, devoid of all sign of good or success in life. White armour and brown spear did for them in [315] punishment for what they had done and as reward for their folly. However, the majority had lost their wits; for they were oppressed and confused.

It was then that groups of soldiers plundered the grain they could find as well as the camels and mules; and they found a lot of firewood of which they were in need and to which they helped themselves with enthusiasm. Then the Zaydī women carried it to the guard post above, each of them carrying the wood tied to her neck by a rope made of palm fibre.[15] That was the harshest of their bitter lot, the most severe and tough. The Turks found in the stronghold a cistern full of water which they pierced at its base in an open place so that the water flowed out in a stream. The enemy plot had failed; the loyal were delighted and the enemy distressed.

After that the minister ordered the dismemberment and destruction of the stronghold, stone by stone, till it became a tale to be retold. In this he intended to exact compensation for the damage to the sultan's forces and to deny support or vestige to the enemy there. It was not long before its quarters became a waste, its outline obscure, and a ruin from top to bottom. There was an advantage in its destruction and sound reason for its flattening and dismantlement; for such action would bring an end to the mischief of the other two strongholds in that neither, because of the distance between, could have contact with the other.

The minister returned to his noble camp as was his wont, with triumph and victory running by his august heels.

Then, behold, during his absence, a strange thing happened, considered by the *ʿaqils* to be the most wondrous. It concerned the people of Kawkabān who, from their proximity to the camp, perceiving that the minister had left by night and observing that the noble camp was without the cavalry horses, ranged the cannon from the heights of Kawkabān and lit fires to warn the people of Thulā of the minister's absence from his camp with his fighting horse; for this was the signal between the people of Kawkabān and Thulā for the exit of the minister from his camp and his absence from his tents and pavilions.

Muṭahhar was jubilant over his absence. He collected his remaining tribal fighters and his troublesome guerrillas, in the belief that he would make the most of this opportunity, calling: 'This is the time for war; so, horse, brace yourself.'[16] His plan was to attack the sultan's camp in the morning [316]; so he collected his evil devils in the hope of achieving this goal. Others came to his aid, confident of their power, but when the Turks in the base, who were on their guard for such an assault, caught sight of them, they drew their swords, mounted their horse and advanced their cavalry and chargers.

The Arab tribesmen came to meet them on their Arab horse, attacking the wagons[17] and tents, but those in the base rode against them, lions meeting death on their chests. The soldiers mustered; ranks were formed; swords were unsheathed; the harvest from bronze armour drew near; the fight wore out the horses, exhausted by the chase and galled in the fray; swords were blunted with use; the enemy surrendered to the sabre's wound and arrows prised souls from their bodies.

Then the Arab tribesmen turned their backs, confirming their defeat and flight, and returned to the shelter of the mountains while the people of the Sunnah struck them from behind with swords and arrows, seeing, in their backs after the battle, faces with eyes and eyebrows, and foreheads with lines and features.

Again they tore the horses from them and struck the heads from numerous chiefs; while the remainder fled with Muṭahhar in disarray to the stronghold nest of Thulā, after so many trials and tribulations.

When Sinān Pasha returned from the conquest of Ḥabb al-ʿArūs, the base detachment met him with the horses they had seized and the spears bearing the heads, and gathered beneath his horse's feet, each lion bringing its prey. The faithful were delighted by the victory that they had seen come to pass. Their eyes were full of the pleasure of conquest and multiple triumph.

That took place on 25 Rabīʿ al-Thānī, 977/7 October 1569.

CHAPTER 36

[317] The sultanic army's ascent to Bayt ʿIzz from Kawkabān; their defeat in the first place, then their ascent a second time on a day appointed for Ḥasan Pasha and his detachment to ascend from the other side; their failure to achieve their goal; and the arrival of the news that the stronghold of Durām in the sub-district of Wadi Khubān had meanwhile been captured[18]

§ When Friday, 26 Rabīʿ al-Thānī/8 October arrived, the minister decided to go with a military detachment to the area of Kawkabān and climb with them to the stronghold of Bayt ʿIzz which he would take by storm. This mountain of Kawkabān is of tremendous height and of difficult ascent, its rugged track making ascent impracticable. Its extensive massif contains many strongholds, lying at some distance from one another, well fortified, and among the strongest castles in the area; and this stronghold was the closest to Thulā of those belonging to Kawkabān and the most useful for the Zaydī people.

So the minister assigned a party whom he selected and picked for his service, with instructions to mount with him by night, to try their utmost to take Bayt ʿIzz; and he took with him a number of *ḍarbuzān* and some strong tools and weapons. He set out on the night of Friday 27 Rabīʿ al-Thānī/ 9 October and arrived the same night at the foot of Kawkabān where only the stars, Taurus and Cancer, repair.

He advanced the infantry, then the trusty cavalry, then the *ḍarbuzān* gun carriages and weapons. They then climbed up the mountain to the best of their ability on [318] that terrain, hanging on ropes as best they could, until the horses found no way up; so the men dismounted and clung on to the rocks, climbing up between the boulders till, with the onset of darkness, they could find no way further; nor could they light flares for fear of waking the people in the stronghold from their sleep.

So they waited patiently for day to break and the dawn call to be given, 'Come to the Good'. The morning disclosed their faces and the millstone of war began to rotate like cups of wine with the morning meal as those in the fort became aware of them, fully realising how they had been taken by surprise.

The Zaydī then emerged from their stronghold and showed they were ready to resist. They occupied the top of the mountain, spreading out behind the rocks like cockroaches and beetles. They began to roll the rocks and the large stones over the advancing soldiers beneath them, when one stone would make a number of others roll with it, smashing the horses and men it met, and grinding down the brave soldiers in its path. The soldiers could find no way at all up the mountain; nor could they find any means of getting to the top; and about ten of the brave detachment went under the stones, together with about seven of the horses and mules.

So the minister gave the order to fire the *ḍarbuzān* at those rolling down the rocks from the top of the mountain, to keep them engaged and hurl flares at them, 'throwing up sparks like castles',[19] so that they should taste the torture of fire. So they fired a volley at them, burning them to a cinder in God's fire and adding to the mayhem. They killed thirteen of the Zaydī whom they had quickly shot, passing them from fire to fire as they went.

Among those engulfed in the flames, going to hell and damnation was Qāsim, captain of the guard at Bayt 'Izz, Sayyid Bahhāl, minister to the rejected Muṭahhar, the general Jābir b. 'Āmir, minister to Muḥammad b. Shams al-Dīn, and others of the Zaydī sect carried from the House of 'Izz to the House of the Vile, deep in hell. Their remains disintegrated and fell down to the lowest level below.

Then the victorious army withdrew, the banner of peace flying over their heads, and returned with the great minister to the blessed encampment, thanking Almighty God for their safety which is the most important prize of all.

[319] The minister had been kept waiting for news of Ḥasan Pasha after he had equipped him with a detachment of 1,000 men, without any knowledge of what had happened to him in his absence. The news came to him that he had gone behind Kawkabān and camped at its foot, and that he had agreed with the *dā'ī* that they should ascend Mt Kawkabān from behind.

Then the minister thought it right to send a message to Ḥasan Pasha, together with his troops and those of the *dā'ī*, since they had arrived behind Kawkabān, for them to ascend from their side to 'Izz stronghold on an appointed day, so that the minister could climb, together with part of his detachment, from his side to those in Bayt 'Izz. Those in the stronghold would be at a loss and taken by surprise, and the stronghold would be captured from either side or both.

The commanders were unanimous in supporting this view. So His Excellency sent Ḥasan Pasha a letter in which he stated:

> We shall undertake the task of climbing to 'Izz stronghold from our side on the night of Monday 14 Jumādā al-Ūlā/25 October so as to attack those inside in the morning; so that night you climb with your forces from your side and attack those inside in the morning, so that it should be possible for us to conquer the said fortress at the agreed time.

When that night arrived the minister mounted, escorted by some picked infantrymen; for there was no task for the horsemen on the mountain. And he took with him some *ḍarbuzān*, travelling at night as far as the foot of Kawkabān. The soldiers tackled and clung to the rocky surface, climbing up till they came near the top of the mountain. They found that some of the tracks, which they had used before on the first occasion, had been blocked by structures on which guards and defenders had been posted who spotted them and began to roll down stones from above.

They had dropped them from the edge of the mountain from which they had to roll only a short distance before one stone rolling from above would take with it several others in its path. So those in its way as it fell would be shattered, whoever they were. Moreover, at night they could only guess who was rolling the rocks at them since they were unable to see who was hurling them down [320] from right and left.

During the night terrifying noises multiplied, louder than thunder and lightning flash, produced by the rolling of these rocks and the explosion of stone against stone, until daylight appeared and dawn broke, and faces became recognisable. The banner of light spread, bringing forth the day, as night's black army was overcome, turning its back in defeat. Dawn drew its sword, polished and resplendent, filling east and west with a panoply of light, and, at sight of sovereign sun's sword unsheathed, the army of stars scattered in defeat.

At sight and contact with each other, a violent battle broke out between them on that memorable day. Sinān Pasha and his troops stood firm but found no way of ascent. Throughout the entire day, in God's just cause, the Turks put all their strength into the fight and had begun to fire from below with the *ḍarbuzān* at the Zaydī while from the mountain top the latter hurled stones and rocks which rolled down upon them. All hit on their way they smashed; anything hit as they came down they broke and shattered. And from below the cannon poured forth volleys of fire on the mountain tribesmen above, discharging over them from their mouths showers of fire and smoke.

The minister stood firm, disdaining defeat. He remained with his detachment in that position, taking pleasure where death fell and drinking cups of death as they were of water while their tongues recited, 'Why should we not fight in Allāh's way'.[20]

The appointment with Ḥasan Pasha passed as they waited and stood firm until the end of the day. They did not slacken their efforts to attain their goal; nor did they gain any success in their fight. About ten of the righteous souls met their end under the rocks, conveyed by Almighty God to Paradise in the hereafter, to live in gardens watered by rivers flowing beneath. Of the brazen infidels, the wicked devils, a large number was slain, driven from fire to fire and made to enter hell and a terrible end.

[321] Then, as day passed by with its soldiers and night took over with its army and banners, and the lowlands and plains assumed black turbans; and eyes lost their sight as the antimony of sleep laid them to rest; then did Sinān Pasha return with his detachment to the blessed camp. He let them have a

good rest that black night after the day's ordeal suffered in battle, more severe than the sharpest pain, in seeking from God triumph and victory in His universal kindness.

As the minister was again afflicted by such distress, he entrusted his situation to God who sees and hears all and waited for the joy from the fulfilment of His purpose and the clarity of conscience, in the expectation of news and blessing from Almighty and All-powerful God.

And in no time did a message come with news of the conquest of much territory and a great castle, thus dispelling the great sorrow the minister suffered as he handed the business to Almighty God; for He brings blessings for the governor and for the faithful.

> Or don't you see that patience is paired with thanks and that they are treasures in ease and hardship.
> So thanks when great blessings befall you and patience when the ups and downs of fortune afflict you.
> I have not seen the like of thanks to preserve blessing and a help in trouble like patience.
> Thanks should be given for the rain but for which the meadows would not cast their scent.
> Gold is not prized but for its purification in the blaze of the furnace.

The subject of the message lay in Wadi Khubān, the place where the late Murād Pasha was defeated and his soldiers massacred. The castle, called Durām,[21] is fortified and defended, of powerful construction, solid and indestructible; and it is in the hands of one of Muṭahhar's supporters called Muḥammad b. Sa'īd, a pig-headed tyrant and wretched outcast from the village of Madal, one of the districts in Wadi Khubān, whom Muṭahhar had made governor of Durām and chief over the tribes of that area. The Ottoman governor in that area had not confronted him, and he and his tribe had remained in rebellion in those parts.

He had a local friend from the population of Madal called Shaikh Muntaṣir al-Muraysī [322] who had been loyal to previous governors-general and who had been one of the most loyal and obedient shaikhs. Then, when the revolt broke out, a tense period of trial and tribulation when Yemen had been without an Ottoman governor and the Sunnī were weak, Muṭahhar had seized this Shaikh Muntaṣir through deceit, perfidy and trickery, imprisoned him in the stronghold at Shibām, put a collar round his neck, fettered his legs and written on his fetter, 'life sentence'.

> The collar is the necklace for men and the fetter the anklet for every hero.

When God allowed the minister to conquer Shibām stronghold, God took charge of its houses and settlements; for He is all-powerful. Muntaṣir was among prisoners whom the minister freed from prison and put an end to their punishment and suffering; so he went up to Sinān Pasha, advised him as to his rectitude, real sincerity and absolute loyalty and allegiance to the Ottoman state, and asked his permission to collect those tribes that acknowledged his authority and go and lay siege to the stronghold of Durām. For he knew its paths and river beds and was familiar with its hills and plains.

The minister agreed and gave him permission to do as he wished, with instructions to travel to his territory and tackle that wadi, with its high and low lands. So he went to his territory and fulfilled his commitment, mustering the tribesmen who owed him allegiance and causing uproar in the whole of Wadi Khubān. He laid siege to the stronghold of Durām for twenty-seven days exactly, attacking and entering the stronghold with his resolute sword. He killed Muḥammad b. Sa'īd al-Madallī with his sharp sword; and with him, he killed his son and twelve of his shaikhly relatives, sending their heads to the minister on the tops of poles. The Arab tribesmen of Wadi Khubān expressed their submission and entered into the sultan's control; they installed in that area an Ottoman provincial commander. That great and important victory took place on 27 Rabī' al-Thānī 977/9 October 1569.

CHAPTER 37

[323] The affairs of the Dā'ī Shaikh 'Abdullāh, and his movements during his absence from the campaign

§ It has already been reported in Chapter 28 how the minister pitched his great camp by Mts Thulā and Kawkabān to conquer them by sword and spear, by cannon and *ḍarbuzān*, and asked the Dā'ī Shaikh 'Abdullāh, commander of the Hamdānī *du'āh*, to travel to his territory of al-Munaqqab. He should invite the tribesmen to submit to the sultan's authority, gather troops from those tribes who owed such allegiance, and travel with them to the rear of Mt Kawkabān. There he should begin the battle while the sultan's forces would fight on this side, so as to facilitate the mountain's conquest.

The Dā'ī Shaikh 'Abdullāh asked for six days to carry out the task, not more. The minister was surprised by the speed with which he promised to return and gave him twenty days. So he went early in Rabī' al-Awwal/mid-August and, when his absence became prolonged and no news of him came back, the minister dispatched some of his troops with Ḥasan Pasha to go round to the back of Kawkabān, give his attention to the *dā'ī* and what had happened to him during this time, and obtain reinforcements from him and the tribesmen he had gathered.

Ḥasan Pasha had set out with his splendid troops on 5 Rabīʿ al-Thānī/17 September, as previously related

[324] Shaikh ʿAbdullāh had made many promises over mustering a lot of troops, the loyalty of the tribesmen and the capture of the towns but the time for his arrival passed and there was absolutely no sign of him. He had been too hasty as far as the *duʿāh* were concerned. Now the reason for his delay was that he had found all the tribesmen observing the state of the campaign and waiting for who would win so that they could follow the winner. While they vacillated between the two, their promises of sincerity were not to be believed and they were to be regarded as liars; and, after a time, their fealty became fragmented. In all events, it was feared that they would not stand firm and would incline towards those whom they favoured.

A brief report concerning the Dāʿī Shaikh ʿAbdullāh would show that, after leaving the sultan's victorious camp on 6 Rabīʿ al-Awwal [sic]/19 August,[22] he had camped at the village of al-Lu'lu'ah which was in his own territory. He then moved to a bastion also called al-Ḥaḍūr, euphemism for a place devoid of settlement – like calling the black brown!

Then on 8 Rabīʿ al-Awwal/21 August he reached a district called al-Ḥaymah where there were a number of strongholds, the largest of which was called Yanāʿ.[23] Then the people of Yanāʿ came and entered the sultan's authority, following Almighty God and rejecting rebellion. The tribesmen of the al-Ḥaymah districts entered the sultan's allegiance without fight or conquest.

Then the *dāʿī* moved from al-Ḥaymah and reached Hamdān al-Ḥarāz and the people belonging to him, where he got hold of 300 men with muskets.

Then on 11 Rabīʿ al-Awwal/24 August, he reached a fortified mountain called Ānis, where its population, when invited in the minister's name to be subject to the sultan's authority, accepted his orders and submitted, rejecting Satan's rule and offering their repentance. They joined the ranks of the faithful, glory be to God and let Him be thanked and praised.

Then he moved to the territory of the Banū Ismāʿīl, a people from a mountain higher than Shāmah and Ṭufayl,[24] with two strong castles which were among the possessions of the late Sultan Sulaymān, Almighty God cover him in mercy and compassion and water his epoch with all generosity and forgiveness. [325] Two men of old, of Arab tribal stock, called Shāyam and Sabāʿah, built them, after whom the two castles were named. During the period of rebellion and enmity, their population entered the authority of the Zaydī people of treachery and sedition.

When Shaikh ʿAbdullāh called them to the sultan's authority, they answered his call. They apologised on the grounds that they had no reason to revolt, and the minister accepted their apology. He accepted the intercession of his *dā'ī* on their behalf and thanked him for his endeavour. The tribe responded to such acceptance with intent ears and attentive hearts. The objective was gained and they thanked God for its attainment.

Then the *dā'ī* went on to the tribes of Sāri' district, travelling with haste and staying in that vast area, with its broad and extensive wadi inhabited by Arab tribes who before then had never entered the sultan's authority, nor worn the cloak of submission and obedience. However, their rulers were Zaydī and their former allegiance was to those trouble-makers. They were eight tribes: the Banū al-Azraq, Banū al-Shadīd, Banū Muḥammad, Banū Walīd, Banū al-'Awādī, al-Daḥādiḥah, al-Ja'āfirah and al-Majādīn.[25]

Shaikh 'Abdullāh sent a message to them summoning them to authority and using every persuasion at his disposal. He indicated to them that the minister would protect their country and he offered reassurance over their property, lives and children. The minister would exempt them from tax for two years without argument or falsehood. He would look kindly upon their good deeds and pardon their errors, and meet them happily and generously when they arrived. He would award them a customary honorary cloak and reward them in wonderful and generous ways.

They appreciated that their safety was of the first priority and their entry into the shelter of the sultan's authority would afford them greater security. By such means they would be delivered from death and capture and be free from murder, conquest and subjection. So they submitted and sought his trust and protection which they were granted, relaxing in the shelter of peace under the sultan's authority.

Near them was a strong fortress with mighty buttresses, of ancient construction and broad proportions, called Qarn al-Masjid, which protected its people from harm. They also joined [326] the tribes in submission, unanimously yielding to authority. They were accepted, felt secure in their entry and achieved their goal.

After the *dā'ī* had fulfilled his objective with those tribes, entered them within the authority of the Sultan of Islam and bestowed upon them peace and security, he visited a village near Mt Tays[26] called Sūq al-Qifāf, winning over the rebellious Arab tribesmen through personal contact and acquaintance and recommending them to join the agreement to lift the rebellion. He made his aim to win over the Arab tribesmen on Mt Tays to the minister and to give them a stern warning against wickedness and rebellion. Some of them yielded to him, coming to visit him as he handled things with judgment and common sense, and God's command who is high and great.

CHAPTER 38

[327] The submission of the population of the beleaguered Mt Tays; and what happened to Ḥasan Pasha and the victorious army troops with him

§ As for Mt Tays, it is among the highest mountains nearly touching the sky, nay al-Simāk [Arcturus], and, in its tremendous height, rivals al-Jawzā' [the Gemini]. It whispers to al-'Ayyūq [Capella] and its *burj* [tower] dwarfs the *burj* [constellation] of al-Ḥamal [Aries]: indeed the *tays* [billy goat] and al-Tays [the mountain] are higher than al-Ḥamal [meaning both kid and the constellation Aries!].[27]

Hearkening to the stars, so that when they moved, we thought they were listening to it,
as if its *abrāj* (towers) on every side were their *abrāj* (constellations), and their *simak* (the two stars Arcturus and Spica) its shoulders.

Within it are Arab tribesmen of extreme coarseness and enormous size, men like towering mountains who prefer the hard ground to the softness of a bed and who spread out a bed of thorns for the best of rests. The minister was still winning them over with kindness and treating them with the most generous sympathy and courtesy, acting with great charity towards them and capturing their hearts with tremendous generosity when their shaikh and chief, their overlord and commander, Shaikh 'Abd al-Qādir al-Nuzaylī, approached him. He was a man whose rank and power they respected and whose authority was beyond question.

Sinān Pasha received al-Nuzaylī kindly, showering favours on him, dressing him in a sultanic honorary robe and mounting him on a horse with a splendid saddle. He heaped unforeseen [328] and totally unexpected favours upon him. Man is enslaved by charity and from love of charity come bonds of obligation!

Do good unto men and keep them in bond.
How often has a good turn been answered in kind.

That handsome action and deed of extreme kindness led to the honoured Shaikh 'Abd al-Qādir yielding to the minister along with the tribesmen of this mountain of Tays. Mt Tays, with its environs, its villages and its districts, became one of the annexed possessions of the noble sultanate and protected Ottoman regions. Its population prayed in the sultan's name and replaced the tatters of treachery and rebellion with the legality of submission, in the comfort of security and the raiment of faith.

In such a way Muṭahhar's back and his unjust body of tribesmen were broken, and, in like manner, the people of Kawkabān were crushed, weakened and desperate, rocked and convulsed. For this mountain is within shooting distance of Kawkabān, can cause the destruction of buildings therein, and cause its structures to shake. That can be counted among the brilliant conquests and shining pieces of good fortune, an impressive victory stemming from the minister's good judgment and decisive and effective planning.

As for Ḥasan Pasha, he, together with Maḥmūd Bey, chief sultanic commander, and some 1,000 soldiers, had gone to relieve the *dāʿī*, during the time news of him was awaited, as has been stated, on 5 Rabīʿ al-Ākhir/17 September, and had reached Wadi al-Ḥaymah on 10 Rabīʿ al-Ākhir/22 September. He had captured four of the strongholds in the area, of tremendous strength and impregnability, height and elevation, inaccessible save to the Pleiades and visible only to the Gemini, as if they were pillars of the sky, to hold it over the earth.

[329] One of them was al-Maṣnaʿah belonging to the Banū Shaqā'iq.

The second was the stronghold of Ẓafār assigned to the Banū al-Aḥbūb.

The third was the stronghold of the Banū Sūdān, belonging to the Shaikh of the Banū Suwayd (because of their brown skin).

The fourth was the stronghold of ʿAttar, belonging to the Banū al-Aʿḍab.[28]

These strongholds used to be within the sultan's domain before their people rebelled at the time of the revolt and gave their allegiance to the cripple Muṭahhar in his defiance and folly. But now those paths and wadis have returned to the sultanic authority they enjoyed before, for which God be thanked. The people have been pardoned for their crime, forgiven for their deceit and treachery and granted a clean sheet, thanking Almighty God for His kindness in His great bounty and seeking His pardon and forgiveness, and His favour, generosity and benevolence.

> Whoever seeks pardon for his crime from his superior, should pardon the man below him.

Ḥasan Pasha continued, on 5 Rabīʿ al-Thānī/17 September, in the direction travelled by the Dāʿī Shaikh ʿAbdullāh, and they met in the village of Dayr Rijum on 24 Rabīʿ al-Thānī/6 October. The two of them travelled with their troops to a territory called Sahl Bāqir containing numerous Arab tribes and soundly constructed fortresses, fortified against strangers; of these the pasha gained the allegiance of the people of three, donning them in the clothes of security and protection. The first was al-Jālid the large, the second al-Jālid the small, called the two Jalids; and the third was the stronghold of al-Kāhil.[29] All were Zaydī castles belonging to the foolish Muṭahhar but their population gave in and submitted, choosing peace over war. So they acknowledged his power and thrived, handing over the stronghold keys to Ḥasan

Pasha. They surrendered, offering symbols of acceptance and submission as they did so. Then they were kindly received in audience and in every way taken into the fold; and [330] the keys were returned to them.

So they gained the advantage of profitable trade and, in return for surrender and submission, were left in their strongholds. From such security they gained all they could ever desire: there was peace in their villages and countryside; they were content as a result; and tranquillity obtained.

This had befallen Ḥasan Pasha and the Dāʿī Shaikh ʿAbdullāh at the end of Rabīʿ al-Ākhir/11 October.

Then they moved to a stronghold belonging to Muṭahhar called Hubaynī which surrendered and submitted to the troops of its own volition, saving its population from contest and battle. Its population gained prosperity for themselves and their property and the army put an end to their combat and slaughter, agreeing to receive them in peace. The aforementioned stronghold was added to the victorious Ottoman possessions and they were granted peace and security. They were enfolded in calm and tranquillity in the real shelter of His Majesty the Sultan. They were free from the worry of fear and aggression. God grants blessings; from Him come help and reliability.

That took place at the beginning of Jumādā al-Ūlā, 977/mid-October 1569.

CHAPTER 39

[331] The fighting between Muḥammad b. Shams al-Dīn, ʿAlī b. Shuwayʿ and Muḥammad b. Raḍī al-Dīn, and Ḥasan Pasha, together with the victorious army and those behind beleaguered Mt Kawkabān[1]

§ After Ḥasan Pasha and the Dāʿī Shaikh ʿAbdullāh had completed the conquest of the strongholds and tribes that have been detailed, the last being Hubaynī, they spent some days making sure of the tribesmen who had made peace. Then the Dāʿī ʿAbdullāh went off to check on the rest of the tribesmen and travel to the back of Mt Kawkabān so that he and Ḥasan Pasha could climb from behind the mountain, attack the Zaydī and completely surprise them.

Ḥasan Pasha took up this position while the Dāʿī ʿAbdullāh went to the foot of Mt Kawkabān and descended into a wadi called Ḍayʿān where he saw serried ranks and a mob of tribesmen whom Muḥammad b. Shams al-Dīn,[2] the contemptible ʿAlī b. Shuwayʿ, and Muḥammad b. Raḍī al-Dīn had mustered. And goodness they were like locusts swarming in the place, ready for the fight and contest and ignited for battle. When the *dāʿī* caught sight of them, he sent off a message to Ḥasan Pasha with the utmost speed, urging him to come and informing him of the terrifying thing he had witnessed.

Ḥasan Pasha became most agitated, and, abandoning the loads and baggage and taking men and horse, rushed to the attack and sped, with his suite, in a detachment over that waste. Men and horse, they answered the call of the Dāʿī ʿAbdullāh [332] and advanced towards him in sections and squadrons. With Monday's dawn (after twenty nights of Jumādā al-Ūlā had passed)[3] they came upon them, on foot and mounted, with cutting sword and savage lions. The numbers of the enemy did not worry them as a butcher is unconcerned over a lot of sheep, or a skilled hunter over a herd of wild calves. Then they clashed and struck; they smashed and ground; they ripped and rendered; they scattered without any fear; they used sword and javelin; they sharpened their sword blades; and they launched arrows like the wind. They slashed skulls and heads and extracted souls and spirits; they waded in a sea of blood; and they did not give up till they fell in God's cause.

> Other people sleep on pillows while they pass the night on lean chargers, and
> their domes break the day in blood as if they were ships on the seas.
> Nor would wolves eat one of their wounded, so full of broken spear shafts
> would it be.

Men held their ground against men. The slow made haste to run, and the powerful mixed with the insolent, a blend of light with darkness. The Turks then made their noses bite the dust and put their thousands to flight. They reduced thousands to hundreds as sharpshooters, the mail-clad corps, shot their devils with their firebrands, flying at their inmost hearts with their arrows while the Zaydī reaped from the spear's harvest such fatal fruit and drank cups of death bitter with gall.

Of the Zaydī leaders Muḥammad b. Raḍī al-Dīn was killed, his head cut off and his life extinguished; and many of the leading Zaydī figures lost their lives while others were severely wounded. About thirty heads were impaled on spears and some twenty of their horses seized, together with numerous coats of mail and shields, and several muleteers and riders. And of the victorious army two *kushshāf* and ten brave infantry soldiers advanced to Paradise in the clash of youth and spear as their insolent foe advanced to the torment of [333] hell-fire and the misery of the hereafter.

The sword swept shanks and shoulders; the spear pierced chest and eye; and the arrow struck throat and eye. No tent could afford screen from the mêlée as the raging sand blotted out every view. One of the seven tiers of the earth was missing and a tier was added to those of the sky. The fighting and slaughter continued, and the bloodshed and carnage, and the destruction and havoc, until the veil of darkness separated the two sides and the sky's flame fell to the earth. 'And by the night when it is stillest.'[4]

All battle abated and war's eyelids inclined to sleep; and each side withdrew to its base, bound up in the exact state of its affairs, each counting its dead and adding up its fallen, the bereaved mourning them and weeping over them. To God have they returned, in whose hand are good and evil.

The victorious Ottoman army ascended to a high mound, overlooking far and near, and placed a protective guard in a tower. All watched their lines of sight against a surprise attack from the enemy till they were overtaken by sleep, exhaustion or inertia.

Then Ḥasan Pasha was minded to dispatch details of this engagement to the minister; so he took counsel with his senior staff on the matter who advised him to take the action he wished. However, they asked him, at the same time, to seek help and reinforcements through the dispatch of more men and equipment so that they could climb Mt Kawkabān and attack its population from behind with musket shot and fire.

So the pasha wrote a report describing the situation, as to what had befallen them in those mountains and plains. This he gave to one more stealthy than the night at its darkest, to take in all haste, a phantom of deepest pitch. The man ran on, guided by the stars which he chased as he sped through the night, and even the day. Cutting through wadis and bush until he reached the minister, he discharged his commission, informing him as to events and relating what had happened in every detail.

Sinān Pasha paid attention to what he said and questioned him as to exactly what had happened. He was informed as to events as he gave his ear to the account and took to heart what the man had to say as he listened. He then went off to apply [334] his sound judgment and good sense to the arrangements he put into force. He commissioned a squadron of brave cavalry, men of experience in battle, to go in two movements, one after the other, so as to arrive in two waves, with repeated advantage, as the troops arrived in succession, a surprise to terrify the enemy with every minute, a cause of panic, fear and horror for their hearts. The first troop went on 8 Jumādā al-Ūlā/19 October, and the second on 9 Jumādā al-Ūlā/20 October, spreading out in the width and breadth of the wadis and capturing hearts and souls with their numbers.

Ḥasan Pasha and his detachment continued to protect their camp and defend their busy station until reinforcements arrived from the minister. They were encouraged and, with the arrival of their requirements, revived and refreshed. In fact, before the arrival of reinforcements, they were frightened, faint-hearted and miserable; for they exaggerated the numbers of the enemy and became like a white spot on the hide of a black cow. They were frightened that the enemy would attack them and come at them from every side. They were in a confused state as they guarded the station, the pitched tents and the grounded baggage. For the enemy were too numerous to get rid of by sword or fire; nor could any, save the Dear Conqueror, overcome them.

So Ḥasan Pasha pitched his *dīwān*, mustered the brave and courageous military and sought their advice as to what to do in that place and what practical course to adopt. Some suggested that they burn the baggage, slaughter the camels and go into battle together. For, if they succeeded in defeating the enemy, they would recoup their losses and replace what they had burnt and blown up. Then if they were killed, they would win the state of martyrdom and, in another abode, gain the ranks of blessedness. Their baggage would not be left for the enemy; nor would those base fools derive any value from it; nor those dimwits any pleasure.

The rest did not agree with this view, saying: 'This is pure cowardice and folly! What are these Arabs save crows, a thousand of which can be driven away by one stone in the field? If they didn't cling to the mountains and boulders and hide behind the rocks and stones, we would really mow them down. We would not be able to put a number to them. [335] My view is that we fight them beside our loads and baggage, and that we should not be separated from our livestock and camels. God will grant victory to whom He wishes; and He is kind to whom He prefers.' They approved this view, unanimously agreeing it was best; and all opinions that followed they rejected as vain.

During this period the reinforcements arrived from the minister and they realised that Almighty God was kind to them. Indeed, He is all-powerful.

They relaxed in agreement, swore by God to go ahead. They undertook to launch one fierce attack against the enemy and not to flee from such martyrdom. If there were fierce fighting and they were frightened out of their wits, they would stand firm and bear the heat from sword and dagger. Any of them who turned tail, they would deal with and slay before killing the infidel enemy. They committed their souls and wealth in God's cause, victory to the Ḥanafī[5] creed and help to the Sunnah. They understood that God had asked from Muslims their souls and wealth in return for Paradise, and they swore to such on oath. They committed themselves to it in their hearts and with their tongues, and they confirmed their words by swearing allegiance.

They left the large guns in the camp with Commander Maḥmūd, lord of an Ottoman brigade, and, on that oath and agreement, advanced to battle. They launched on the enemy a fierce attack, head on, certain that to remain in this world was extinction whereas fighting in God's cause was to endure. They learnt that death in bed was indeed a death of foolish cowardice and they continued to keep the promises they had made in public and private, fighting the 'battle for God's cause in ranks, as if they were a solid structure'.[6] Had the Turks a field for battle and earth on which horses could manoeuvre, they would have crushed the enemy under their horses' hooves as they attacked, at once and for all. But they were on rough ground, useless for horses, inaccessible to them because of the rocks and stones. Despite that, the enemy was unable to stand their attack; nor had they any defence against their assault but, overcome by it, fled in utter disarray. The enemy divided and scattered, fleeing pell-mell to the sea where they drowned!

Ottoman troops chased behind them, killing masses of them, until their swords broke. They tied up some of them tightly by the shoulders and drove them to market as does a butcher, making them tread like cattle for slaughter [336] before night led the defeated to the village of Turyādah where they were far from the victorious army and had realised what war with it meant. People of virtue had won virtue and more, and with truth had achieved their higher aim in levels of bliss.

Ḥasan Pasha returned with his accompanying troops to his camp where they remained free from the hapless enemy's treachery and hypocrisy, and delivered their affairs to Great and Almighty God who is the absolute lord and victor.

Aḥmad Bey, called Jitr Qīl,[7] was an Egyptian *kāshif* who proved his bravery that day in action, penetrating the heart of the enemy in safety. He took the risk of going among them without disguise and openly. He showed that his intentions were good in that dark and empty air which was black with the grime of dust. Then Almighty God granted him safety and ensured his survival, and he returned with several heads, and people were thankful for his stand.

Six soldiers in the victorious army met their martyrdom that day, leaving the abode of vanity for that of delight, finding enjoyment in the Paradise of Eden under which flow rivers in joy and delight, and exchanging for the same castles Paradise without blemish.

As for the defeated enemy, its slaughtered were innumerable and its prisoners bound securely with chains and belts; and it is for God to determine events.[8]

After morning had revealed the scene and morning criers had made the call to drink; after the sun had revealed from its veil the Ottoman insignia and the morning standard had spread its white banner far and wide; after night's soldiers were defeated and broken, and morning's army spread in victory over the dark; then did Ḥasan Pasha and his united troops mount to pursue the rest of the hapless enemy army, searching for them across rough country right up to the village of Turyādah. They were happy to reach it and ready for battle when ordered to enter, but the heretics had realised they were there.

The Zaydī had intended to stand firm for the contest and fight and approached with their sharp scimitars, swords of iron, slings and firebrands. But they did not stand firm; nor did they hold out but [337] scattered and fled, abandoning their equipment in the village and fleeing. For fear they would be hurt, they had chosen to flee rather than to stand their ground. Nor did the Ottoman army dare to plunder the village, fearful of a plot, lest the soldiers disperse and the enemy return in force against them. So they abandoned the village to the Arab tribesmen who in no time had plundered it, reduced it to nothing and seized what the enemy had left in the place.

By a strange chance the Ottoman army had run out of gunpowder but they then found, among all that the enemy had left as they fled, five loads of gunpowder which they took and divided among the gunners. Save for the gunpowder, they did not interfere with any of the stuff the enemy had left in the village when they fled. This was help from God for which He be thanked!

The victorious troops continued to chase the vanquished till they took refuge on Mt Ḍulaʿ where they closed in on them from the direction of the wadi and discharged at them their cannon and lion fighters. Throughout the day they fought them till the sun could no longer be seen and night had fallen, and it was dark, with darkness spreading its wing; and all was black as pitch.

Then the enemy fled to Mt Siwwān where the Dāʿī ʿAbdullāh chased them with his horsemen, attacking and destroying them, breaking and smashing them. So the enemy were defeated and fled, scattering without fight or battle. The Dāʿī ʿAbdullāh took possession of Mt Siwwān where the Ottoman army gathered and was joined by Maḥmūd Bey with the loads and baggage, the camp equipment, tents and carriers, carried on the camels and mules among the soldiers and warriors. Then they pitched their tents on the top of Mt Siwwān and, with the utmost care, set up camp.

They were delighted with the victory bestowed upon them by Almighty God and thanked God for the blessing and great benefits He had brought them. They began to express their surprise to those of them who had advised the burning of the equipment and to blame them for that view which had proved to be at fault. There is no victory save from God who is powerful and generous.

CHAPTER 40

[338] The victorious army's ascent to Mt Kawkabān, Muḥammad b. Shams al-Dīn's flight within the stronghold burnt by fire; ʿAli b. Shuwayʿ's flight to Thulā in distress and disappointment, and the capture of some of the strongholds and villages[9]

§ The victorious army was encouraged by the defeat of the routed enemy who had disappeared from sight as darkness sank with the brightness of day, understanding that they were of no avail against this experienced force. The majority had scattered over the mountain tops and rocks, while the army of Islam was determined to pursue them to the mountains and hills and eradicate them once and for all. The troops were determined to climb Mt Kawkabān, even if it really was with the stars, and to climb it, even if it was in the sky, or indeed above it; and they leapt like gazelles as they united in the cause of the faith.

On 15 Jumādā al-Ūlā/26 October, with the Dā'ī and Āghā 'Abdullāh al-Hamdānī, they took the route called al-Qillah while Commander Maḥmūd and his suite took the Turbah route and Ḥasan Pasha and the rest of the troops took the middle route between those two. They travelled halfway through the night, taking those paths with men and horses, absolutely bent [339] on the infidels and bursting into loud laments against them. Then they found, after travelling part of the way, that the Zaydī had blocked with large stones the Turbah and middle route, by rolling huge rocks into them. And they had not left any space for passing.

As for the Dā'ī and Āghā 'Abdullāh al-Hamdānī,[10] they had taken the Qillah route which they had found to be wide all the way. So they had followed it, climbing to its top without excuse or delay and reaching a place called 'the head of al-Mikhraf' while the troops set to climbing and making their way up the escarpment.

Commander Maḥmūd, Ḥasan Pasha and their companions returned from the blocked tracks to this open one. This was the only route the Zaydī had neglected to block with their crushers and pounders; and that was God's fate. Planning can be no substitute for fate; and when fate decrees, the eye is blind and wisdom negligent.

After the troops were all at the head of al-Mikhraf and each of the soldiers had completed the climb, once they had gathered there with their arms and equipment, with kind help from Almighty God, the Zaydī became aware of them as day broke, and realised that the victorious army, bristling with arms, was with them on the mountain. No sooner had dawn drawn its sword in the morning than dark fate and charging horses overtook them as the guns and cannon hurled fire, 'striking sparks of fire'.[11] The battle raged till the sun was high in the sky when the Zaydī took to flight without standing firm or making a stand. Muḥammad b. Shams al-Dīn took refuge inside the stronghold of Kawkabān while 'Alī b. Shuway' fled to Thulā and reached Muṭahhar in shame and exhaustion.

During the engagement countless were killed, with defeat for the Zaydī who received neither relief nor help. When news of this great victory and enemy defeat reached the minister, he thanked Almighty God for His kindness, victory and support, going to great length in his thanks to the noble

Benefactor so as to gain more blessing in the future, and resting his forehead on the earth in [340] praise of God. There is no victory save from God; and the minister experienced God's continual blessing and favour, realising that he only enjoyed such victory because of his Lord's blessing.

At once Sinān Pasha made haste to climb Mt Kawkabān from his own side, setting off with tremendous speed and letting nothing distract him. Those he had selected to go with him moved to follow and join him with all speed and without delay. They marched at night as dawn first broke with the release of its lucky white-winged bird till they began the siege of one of Kawkabān's impregnable fortresses called Bayt 'Izz, a vile, horrible place of evil and oppression; nor did its people realise that they were surrounded like a ring on a finger, and had no place for retreat or sanctuary for escape.

The infidels kept up the fight and battle, the confrontation and killing, the engagement and resistance, the suffering and perseverance, until there was no fight in them and they became a target for arrows and spears once the wall was breached and an attack launched. Those who could took to flight while the rest were dispatched to hell-fire. A devastating battle was fought until the end of the day when fighters were tired and weary and weapons clapped out and finished. The sultan's *sanjak* was raised over the wall and the place was radiant with light after its deviance in apostasy from the splendour of Islam and the Sunnah. For God determines events: to Him are due thanks at the beginning and at the end, and for Him is Judgment Day.

That took place on 16 Jumādā al-Ūlā/27 October, on the same day as Ḥasan Pasha and his party ascended from his own side to another strong fortress, surrounded by a well-built wall, called Ḥajar al-Rakānīn,[12] one of the stronger castles belonging to the people of Kawkabān. Ḥasan Pasha surrounded and did tremendous battle with its inhabitants, firing the heavy cannon against them, launching attacks against them and shattering them with muskets and *ḍarbuzān*. The soldiers scaled the wall, raised the victorious sultanic standard and put the stronghold's population to the sword. They tore them out root and branch and those who fled lived only to be killed another day.

God has fulfilled his promise to Muslims for successive victory. It was a severe day for infidels when these strong fortresses were taken and their authority and lands left their control. With that the back of the terrible cripple was broken, [341] as well as that of Muḥammad b. Shams al-Dīn; and 'Alī b. Shuway' went down to the lowest of the low. They burst into loud laments and were seized by depression and despair. They realised that the infidel army was defeated and broken, and that of the Sunnah people, with the help of Almighty God, was victorious and triumphant. The noble Ottoman sultanic sword is long and famous and its *sinān* [spear head][13] makes light work of Yemeni swords, when they clash in fight and show blunt against its resolve, over which one should be wary.

CHAPTER 41

[342] Appointment of Ḥasan Pasha to lay siege to Kawkabān; the raising of the large cannon to the heights of the same mountain by ropes and hawsers; the capture and destruction of the stronghold of Shamāt; and the rescue of the commanders imprisoned in Kawkabān at that time

§ God in His splendour had favoured H.E. the Minister, of mighty status and rank, with the capture of these strongholds on the heights of Kawkabān, thanks be to Almighty God for His blessing in the victory of the Sunnī people and the rejection of heresy and rebellion. Sinān Pasha then set out to capture the fortress of Kawkabān which is of sure and impregnable construction and of absolute strength, solidity, power and might. It is surrounded by a deep and ancient ditch [chasm], impossible to bridge and cross, due to its great width; and the fortress's population have a tunnel through which they can descend into the depths of this ditch.[14] They have only one means of entry from above, impassable and uncrossable for others, for which they place in position pieces of wood when they need to. They then lift them up so that there is no path or access to it. So if an attempt were made to block the ditch with stones, the fortress people would go down into it by means of the tunnel and lift them out to prevent it being filled up with such stones. And they possess some large cannon [343] with which they fire at anyone approaching the ditch. So none can get anywhere near to the ditch save at night when he is in a state of absolute terror.

So the minister selected a number of young warriors for the siege of the fortress and made Ḥasan Pasha their *sirdār* in the area, while he returned to his noble camp to arrange for the heavy cannon to be taken up to them by night when it was pitch-black. It was the most difficult task to raise those great cannon between those rocks. However, man's determination will raise mountains, and it is nothing for strong determination allied to skill. The higher the degree of determination, the higher and greater the qualities of men, and God praise the author of the verse,

> He possesses such qualities, the greater of which are without limit, the smallest greater than time.

The minister was very considerate with his troops, winning their hearts with his great energy, good actions and kindness and dispersing bags of gold and carnelians.[15] He ordered them to raise the large cannon to the heights of

Kawkabān, so the men carried them on the nape of their necks; and making little of such weight, they conveyed them on their backs through the gullies. They got them up by means of various devices and pulleys. They helped each other in the task; for cooperation makes light of difficult work.

When the heavy burden is borne by many shoulders, its weight is light to bear.

During Sinān Pasha's stay in his victorious camp, there were various duties with the troops, and the local people to calm so that none should suffer at the hands of another; and such would include road maintenance, security from theft, the arrival of caravans with foodstuff and provisions, the encouragement of the troops scattered among the villages, the strengthening of Ḥasan Pasha and his party on the heights of Kawkabān through the dispatch of regular supplies, reinforcement in numbers and weapons, and frequent extra equipment, as well as countless other help.

Along the route taken by the artillery lay a stronghold called Shamāt[16] at a great altitude, equipped with troops for battle, the population of which was so frightened and afraid – for they realised what they had missed and done without through their fear of the army – that [344] they had broken down and handed over the stronghold to the minister, and offered their submission. The minister clad them in robes of protection, treated them with kindness and courtesy and conveyed them to the best of positions, granting them rations and handsome funds; so they left with their entire population, descending from their mountain top to its foot and leaving their homes empty, bewailing the end of the builders and seeking for their occupants elsewhere to live.

The minister gave directions for Shamāt to be destroyed and its walls razed, for the remains of its walls to be flattened, its foundations to be uprooted and its structure to be levelled; and he set picks at work in its chambers. It then ceased to be counted as a stronghold and became as if it had never existed. Now the minister gave such directions for fear its people would renew their rebellion should the devil seduce them from allegiance to the sultan and it become a refuge for their future protection. He saw the matter through to the end, and its end became as it was in the beginning.

When the mighty army gained this great victory, following its former conquests, and the wretched enemy's defeat came in the wake of successive disasters, as Almighty God's continuing blessing and bounty for the Sunnī people came in steady succession, they thanked Almighty God for His abundant good-will and successive blessings. They understood that victory came through Almighty God who delivered it to those among His servants He wished, as previously foreordained, and that the Sovereign Lord was one and without partner, who brings life and death with His benign hand. For He is all-powerful.

After Muḥammad b. Shams al-Dīn, with the people of Kawkabān and those who had joined with them in rebellion and were fighting, realised that the sultan's forces had brought up the guns and cannons to the top of the mountain, they were panic-stricken and lost all their double-dealing and trickery. They were certain that they were taken and knew that they would taste the pain of dishonour as punishment for what they were doing, and they were extremely agitated. They knocked at the door of peace with all the strength at their disposal.

They had with them six of the important *sanjak* commanders whom they had imprisoned in wells after capturing them during the rebellion and revolt and granting them protection. They had behaved treacherously towards them and tied them up, putting them into iron fetters and prison. That was during their occupation of Ṣan'ā' and other parts of the country.

The fires of rebellion and lawlessness blazed; and then after their absence [345] at the bottom of the well for a number of years, their sojourn in prison with the prisoners, and their endurance of terrible torture, they now released them from prison,[17] taking off the fetters from their legs and the iron collars from their necks and heads. They decided that they would put them to use with the minister in calling off the battle, stopping the fight and contest and retaining the rest of the men and possessions. So they clothed them and put them into good spirits by smooth talking. They got them ready in secret at night with some of the men and released them near the minister's camp, leaving them as they fled to the mountains.

These commanders then approached the camp and raised their voices in Turkish so that the guards should not think they were Zaydī and use their muskets and arrows etc. against them. The guards felt safe with them and asked them, 'Who are you?' And they introduced themselves. They then got near to them and that night took them to the minister who welcomed them and was delighted with their release from Zaydī hands. He made them sit down in his presence and chatted to them; and they chatted to him. They were six of the *sanjak* commanders:[18]

First. Head of the Treasury and Supervisor of financial matters in Yemen. Maḥmūd Bey, nephew [sister's son] of the former governor-general of Yemen, the late Qarah Muṣṭafā Pasha, God have mercy upon him.

Second. Of old commanders in Yemen, Shāh 'Alī Bey, called Shaikh 'Alī Bey.

Third. Of old commanders in Yemen, Qizilbash[19] Meḥmed Bey, brother of Aḥmad Bey who was martyred during the days of Murād Pasha. It is said that they were called Qizilbash because they were Persian commanders and that they were warriors famous for their swordsmanship.

Fourth. Of the old *sanjak* commanders in Yemen, one called Urayq Ḥasan

Bey, a brave dare-devil whose fame was widespread throughout Yemen.

Fifth. Of the old commanders in Yemen, one called Qarah Kawz Bey, who, among the commanders, had great wealth which Muṭahhar seized, leaving him without anything.

Sixth. The chief minister to Murād Pasha, by name Ḥusayn Bey, whom [346] the late Murād Pasha recommended be a *sanjak* and was quickly appointed a sultanic *sanjak* by the Sublime Porte. When the late Murād Pasha was killed, he was among those taken prisoner, and Almighty God decreed his release with the others. That was in the book already recorded, and within Almighty God's knowledge already ordained.

Sinān Pasha approached them and showed his kindness and esteem as he talked to them, and bestowed horses and weapons upon them as well as silver coin and fine [lit. brown] spears. He put them completely at their ease, entertaining them and providing them with the finest lodgings; and he made them forget completely their period of ordeal. That was Almighty God's favour towards them, together with his continuing kindness and fine regard for them. In such a way adversity precedes comfort and joy takes the place of sadness. Neither stress, nor sadness endures; this is the custom of the age and an aspect of time.

> Don't ask for relief in difficult times, for they would not endure were you to ask.[20]

The release of these commanders from imprisonment by Muḥammad b. Shams al-Dīn took place on 17 Jumādā al-Ūlā/28 October in the same year as is recorded in writing.

The rest of the commanders remained in prison with Muṭahhar in Thulā, Almighty God enable their release from misfortune, when Almighty God in His glory and height is pleased to let them go.

CHAPTER 42

[347] The battle between the people of trapped Thulā and the sultan's forces; the submission of some of the strongholds voluntarily, and some by force and compulsion; and the minister's destruction of those strongholds he thought necessary when forcing such compulsion

§ On 20 Jumādā al-Ūlā/31 October the minister ordered his encampment to be moved near the edge of the strong fortress of Kawkabān. So his victorious camp, by the help of Almighty and Glorious God, was established near the ditch, which the troops were to fill with stones and pass over for the siege of Kawkabān fortress.

On 21 Jumādā al-Ūlā/1 November, the population of Barāsh stronghold, to the west of Kawkabān from the district of al-Ṭawīlah, came to the minister in search of peace and a reprimand. Of all those strongholds on Mt Tays, it was most the strongly fortified and impregnable; its population had not sought peace along with the rest of the mountain people and had behaved badly towards the sultan's troops at the time they had passed that way. So they apologised for what they had done in the past and asked for protection. The minister accepted their apology and granted them protection; and they entered the fold. They put an end to dispute and disgraceful behaviour, asking some of the commanders to intervene, and the minister agreed to listen to such pleas.

However, the stronghold was [348] in the way of those wishing to climb to Kawkabān, so the minister gave orders for it to be razed and destroyed, and dismembered bit by bit, for fear it might bring trouble in the future and its people might rebel anew. So he directed its immediate destruction, especially in view of the history of rebellion and bad behaviour on both their parts.

The intelligent reflects in his heart on the ups and downs before they arrive.
So, when calamity comes, he is not overtaken, as he had foreseen it.
He had already seen that one thing leads to another, and so took the end for the beginning.

On 22 Jumādā al-Ūlā/2 November, a tremendous battle broke out between the people of Thulā and the victorious army who were in their noble tents within the blessed base.

The reason for such was that, as the number of captured strongholds grew, whether by force or through their populations seeking protection, the more devastated the cripple Muṭahhar became; nor was he able to control such feelings; so, he decided to play tricks and games on the sultan's troops. He appeared to launch sorties against them, in this way pretending that he was capable of fighting, and he mustered men as if he was about to attack the warriors. But this was empty posturing of the most fanciful kind, the caprice of a confused mind.

Thus he collected the Zaydī with him on Mt Thulā, gathering a further mass of them from around the mountain. He ordered them under the cover of darkness to hide under Mt Thulā and appear in the morning to the Turkish troops in a display of strength and lack of concern over the numerous strongholds that the minister had taken in such a short time. So they carried out his instructions and concealed themselves behind the rocks on the mountain opposite the plain. They comprised about 200 horsemen and 1,000 on foot, bristling with weapons and brandishing swords and spears.

Then as dawn discarded night's dress and morning from the east inhaled the clearest air; as morning drew its cutting sword against the army of darkness, so night retreated to the west in complete defeat. Then did the Zaydī attack one side of the sultan's tents thinking they were unheeded and that the Turks were still farded with the antimony of sleep. They did not understand that they were more wary than [349] crows, more alert than eagles, and fleeter than an arrow on target. In the verse of al-Mutannabī:[21]

He sleeps with one eye closed, while with the other he watches against disaster.
Thus, while awake, he takes his rest.

So the sultan's troops made haste to get ready and prepared to fight the guilty enemy, pouring on them arrows, heavier than a downpour of rain. The horsemen moved on to the field and set to with sword and spear, lance and pole. The engagement was fierce, with the army fighting like lions, army charging army; and the minister was personally in the precious camp.

Wading into the blaze in the heat of the tumult, as the war nakedly rages,
with a charger of perfect beauty racing like a flash flood from the hill side,
and an Indian sword, its blade glistening like water over an ant under water, sweeping,
and destined for the heart of a rider whom chain-mail would not protect,
with the will of one determined in war and not one faint-hearted and cowardly,
as if, ranging in its midst and dust, he had covered noon with a screen,
a wild lion, on the back of a doughty steed, attacking with arrows, in the clothes of a knight.

Then the minister, mounting his horse and seizing his sword and spear, entered the field and, in the heat of battle, slew a number of the Zaydī. But they at once withdrew to their mountains, still full of their cunning and trickery, and took their stand on the mountains like monkeys where the sultan's forces fired at them bullets of flame.[22]

The minister returned from the field, and before him were ten of the enemy's heads on poles as he praised and thanked God and sought further help and succour. He and the faithful rejoiced in God's victory; and let Almighty God help him and through him destroy the heresy of his enemies.

[350] On 23 Jumādā al-Ūlā/3 November, people arrived from the district of Ḥarāz, from the stronghold of Shibām – that is Shibām al-Yu'fir called Shibām Ḥarāz,[23] one of the *dā'ī*'s tributaries, at the minister's encampment, the object of triumph, glory and honour, seeking his protection from attack and entry into H.M. the Sultan's dominion; and the minister responded to their plea, agreeing to protect them and their property and receiving them with honour and splendour, and thus welcoming the administration of their affairs, their security and the realisation of their hopes.

On the first day of Jumādā al-Ākhirah/ 11 November, came a delegation from a tribe called the Banū Qawī to the minister, in his Āṣāf-like[24] wisdom, who sought protection for their stronghold and begged his favour by giving them security. This stronghold of theirs was called Ḥidād Banī Qawī in the district of al-Ḥaymah, and Almighty God is glorious and powerful. So the minister accorded them a good reception and took them under his noble wing. He gave them everything they hoped for and placed on their shoulders robes of honour, adorning their persons with ceremonial and honorary dress.

None of them was censured for what he had done, whether he had acknowledged or denied his wrong. The minister addressed them with words of forgiveness and pardon – let God pardon what has past – seeking to attract the rest of the rebels among the Arab tribesmen and to win over their hearts, wary in view of preceding bad behaviour, and setting aside evil for what was better. He removed from their hearts and spirits trial and tribulation; for that is the practice of the intelligent among people of discernment and sagacity in their doings, great or small.

As is said:

> A hint is enough for an intelligent man; another is summoned by a strong call; and the third by a reprimand without the stick. Then the stick is the fourth course. Then the sword is brandished to threaten. Attack is the last one, the device of the eager.

As is also said:

> For the hostile there are degrees of acumen. Trickery, then peace, then struggle. [351] Men can defeat a thousand by stratagem whom he cannot defeat by arms.

When news of that protection, with honour and esteem, reached the people of Rawmān stronghold in the district of Ḥarāz, they took the initiative in coming to the minister and appeared one and all at his door. All of them, great and small, cast down their weapons and sought protection for themselves, their children, their property and their livestock; and the minister met them with the utmost courtesy and made them understand how full of great kindness he was.

He had filled their hearts with joy and respect and sent them back to their stronghold, happy and delighted, feeling secure for themselves and their property, relaxed and trusting; and wishing him well in all they said, thankful for the kindness and courtesy he had shown them.

That was on 5 Jumādā al-Ākhirah/15 November of that year, let God give it a good end.

Then on 9 Jumādā al-Ākhirah/19 November, a delegation called on the minister from the people of Nahād stronghold in the district of Ḥarāz, for themselves, their followers and their children, declaring submission and obedience, and rejecting revolt and rebellion. He welcomed them and showed them respect, agreeing to their request and desire on condition that their stronghold be destroyed, as he doubted they would remain penitent, something he thought and guessed might happen. To that they agreed; and they obtained protection and began to dismantle their stronghold and the buildings therein. Then they moved far away. Almighty God brought to an end that iniquity of theirs and safeguarded Muslims against their double-dealing and treachery.

Then during the rest of the month a number of strongholds were taken by extending peace terms at the request of their population; and the minister agreed to grant protection on condition that strongholds with potential for danger be destroyed but that those that posed no problem could be left. There were four of them:[25]

First. The stronghold of Da'lah. [352]
Second. The stronghold of the Banū al-'Amrān.
Third. The fortress of Mu'ad'id.
Fourth. The stronghold of al-'Aqabah.

The people of these four strongholds came and became subject to authority, asking for their protection for themselves and their children, for their slaves and their property; and the minister gave them such a blessing. They brought valuable presents and were given proud robes of honour to wear; and they went off in good spirits, with calm minds and happy hearts. He allowed them to keep their strongholds in their own hands; nor did he order their demolition and destruction. For his noble mind was reassured as far as they were concerned.

After that, the population of twelve strongholds from different districts came to him, seeking protection in the expectation of a courteous and generous welcome. They brought to him gifts and presents, everything of good quality whether old or new, seeking to attract his noble mind and gain his high favour. The minister agreed to grant protection on condition they destroy their strongholds with their own hands and adopt other places in their stead where they would live, like all the noble sultan's subjects, Almighty God render him victorious, seeking shelter in his great shadow, and secure from killing, imprisonment and fetters. So they accepted these conditions, and he had contracts written for them. They then returned to their strongholds and destroyed them according to the agreement. These were the twelve strongholds:[26]

First. The fortress of Thunaynah belonging to 'Udayn, around Jiblah.
Second. The fortress of Ẓifrān, in the district of Waṣāb.
Third. The fortress of Qabḍān.

Fourth.	The fortress of Raymān, both in the district of Yarīm.
Fifth.	The fortress of Qaylah, belonging to the *nawāḥī* or sub-districts of Suḥbān.
Sixth.	The fortress of al-Qufl, belonging to the *nāhiyah* or sub-district of Maḍraḥ, the place where the late Murād Pasha was martyred, God have mercy upon him.
Seventh.	The fortress of Shakhab (near al-Nādirah), a strong castle in the sub-districts of Banū 'Ummār.
Eighth.	The fortress of al-Miqrānah in the district of Radā'.
Ninth.	The stronghold of Damt, also east of Radā'.
Tenth.	The fortress of Sānah in the sub-districts of Waṣāb.
Eleventh.	The fortress of Rājid, also one of the thirteen strongholds in the district of Waṣāb.
Twelfth.	Arayshah.

Their populations destroyed ten of the well-fortified castles, razing them completely, in accordance with the minister's instructions and his honoured wishes, and entered the protection of the august sultan, under his authority and care and the shelter of his broad empire. In such a way, their intelligence and religion guided them to him, and they rejected their devils from then. God is He who guides and directs. He whom God guides will not be led astray; and he whom God directs will not be scorned.

CHAPTER 43

[354] The battle between H.E. the mighty minister's *Qarāghul*[27] and the Zaydī forces, the ambush made on the latter by the cavalry, and the killing and driving to hell of Abū Dāwūd b. al-Hādī

§ On 2 Rajab 977/11 December 1569, the cripple Muṭahhar was informed by his spies and bullies, messengers of his evil and revolt, who were working to his disadvantage while they thought they were doing him favours, that Sinān Pasha was absent from his honoured camp in the area of shattered Kawkabān,[28] waging war to seize and destroy its castle stronghold. So the poor cripple, realising that the brave cavalry were absent from the noble camp, mustered a band of his wretched men whom he led astray with his cunning and prattle, claiming that his devil had seen in the stars that he would gain victory over the Turks that day. Would that he gained not his wish, nor achieved his desire.

Now the bravest and most distinguished of the officers he had to rely upon, a man with a well-wrought coat of mail and valiant heart, was General

Abū Dāwūd,[29] who was joined by a contingent of men on horse and foot, together with archers and lancers, all encouraged by lies and falsehood and promises made by Satan which could only be deceptive.

The minister had understood their cunning and could imagine what was running in their minds. He prepared a squadron of cavalry and brave warriors and directed them to go in the middle of the night to the foot of Thulā and hide there behind the rocks till nigh daybreak. If people came down from the mountain, they should wait till they reached the bottom and got into the plain [355]. They should then charge from their rear and drive them on to death, leading them to die. They were to reap their harvest and prepare for their slaughter, advancing against them with their swords and eradicating them once and for all.

So they obeyed the minister's order, hid for half the night behind every large boulder and, when the heralds of morning called out, 'Come to the good', as dawn drew its white sword and morning donned its robe of eastern white, defeating the army of darkness and spreading its flags and banners, then the misguided Zaydī came down.

The Zaydī spread across the plain with their Indian swords and doughty spears, attacking the mighty camp, heedless of the serpent's poison concealed from them. No sooner had they gained the centre of the plain, than the cavalry fell upon them and the ambush squadron struck their shoulders with their swords, arrows and firearms while those in the camp advanced to their front, encircling them as a bracelet does a wrist. Their slaughter was sweeping; and they killed the general Abū Dāwūd, hurling him to the ground, in the open, and, carrying his head high on a spear-pole, they returned to the camp in victory and triumph while the Zaydī went back weak and defeated. None of them escaped save those for whom it was written they would die on another day; nor did any avoid the sword save to reach death, broken and defeated.

As the minister came back to his camp at the end of the day, a figure of peace and dignity, on his return from the foot of Kawkabān, the cavalry, who on his high command had been hidden, advanced to meet him. They were carrying on their spear points the heads of the dead which they then rolled beneath the horses' legs, for their owners to suffer public contempt in this world and woe in the next.

And the Zaydī continued, defeated and exhausted, suffering a succession of calamities in which they were defeated and taken prisoner. But each time the lame Muṭahhar was responsible for such incitement, careless behaviour and successive defeats, then he would spread among the tribesmen that he was fighting, making all sides and areas believe that he was keeping up the contest and struggle, and convincing his tribes and supporters that the battle was evenly waged. He would recount to them that he had read in the stars that his rule would come. But let Almighty God prove him a liar now and in the future in his clever delusion and fancies; for God is strong and skilful.

CHAPTER 44

[356] The arrival of news of the demise of Ḥusayn b. Shams al-Dīn; the death of his brother al-Hādī by mighty artillery; the killing of al-Bahhāl, a leader of the tyrant people; and the arrival of Sayyid Nāṣir b. al-Ḥusayn al-Jawfī under truce and his entry under the sultan's authority with a group of people of the faith

§ Shams al-Dīn b. Sharaf al-Dīn had three sons, all of whom were scoundrels, as if they were firebrands who loved revolt and trouble and spread universal harm and damage.

As for Ḥusayn, he along with ʿAlī b. Shuwayʿ were founders of the revolt and rebellion and pivots of injustice and oppression. They were the pair who had attacked Aḥmad Bey Qizilbash and mustered against him a band of cowards and riff-raff when Murād Pasha dispatched him with supplies for Ṣanʿāʾ. They had ambushed his passage at Dhirāʿ al-Kalb, cutting him down and killing him, seizing the supplies and causing widespread damage. News of that came in chapter 27. Refer to it if you wish to read it again.[30]

His brother, al-Hādī, was extremely misguided, and the trouble he brought to great and small well known. Their brother, Muḥammad, possessed intelligence and discernment, strength and vigour; and he will resume [357] his allegiance and go against that gang, as will be explained, God willing.[31]

Ḥusayn b. Shams al-Dīn was afflicted with a protracted illness, suffering from dropsy which consumed him and wore him out; and his demise came on 11 Shaʿbān 977/19 January 1570. Then God brought an end to his evil for Muslims and got rid of his harm and damage; he made him a lesson for people of sense, drove him to the tortures of hell-fire and brought him to hell and damnation.[32]

As for his misguided brother al-Hādī, the head of the misguided people and heretical leader in damage and disorder, he was struck by a large cannon which blew off his head, snuffing out his spirit and quenching his fire. He went from fire to fire, from ruin to perdition, and was assigned to hell and damnation.

Despite his youth, he was a strong pillar of the revolt and a founding guide in the outbreak of this tragedy. So Almighty God got rid of him for good and burnt him in hell; let him remove his evil from all believers and blot out the picture of his inanities and the image of the damage he has done. The eyes of believers were delighted by his demise as they rejoiced when in this way victory and happy triumph came to them.

Muḥammad b. Shams al-Dīn had an in-law who rivalled him in delusion and helped him with men and funds, providing him with sons, servants and men. His name was Sayyid al-Bahhāl. With numerous warriors and known for the ferocity of his fighting and combat, he was a real prop for Muḥammad b. Shams al-Dīn, and for the exhausted cripple a crutch and aid to rely upon. He was one of the pillars of Thulā and Kawkabān, one of the evils of the treacherous period and a sly chap who would slink in his furtive and deceitful way like a real fox.

One night he left Kawkabān heading for Thulā stronghold without attracting any attention in the dark. He passed some sentries as they patrolled round the troops from the onset of dark till just before daybreak, seizing anyone they found and looking out and lying in wait for the enemy; so, when they caught a glimpse [358] of al-Bahhāl, they attacked him with spears and arrows and struck him with their swords and lances, making him taste death and slaughtering him as sheep are slaughtered. They drove him to hell and damnation and carried his head to the minister, hurling it beneath the horses' hooves and the feet of the mules and donkeys. Almighty God put an end to the evil of that devil and Muslims rejoiced in the victory of God who offers the best help and protection.

With that Muḥammad b. Shams al-Dīn's sting was plucked and Muṭahhar's back was broken and, with his death, the heresy defeated. Every cripple is twisted; and God helps by His favour upright religion, and drives away from His straight truth every stoned devil!

Coinciding with these events was the arrival, at Sinān Pasha's, of Sayyid Nāṣir b. al-Ḥusayn, one of the Sharifs of Jawf, submitting to the sultan's authority, in search of the shelter of the Ottoman sultanate, grasping the skirts of its pardon and forgiveness and inhaling fragrant gusts of Ottoman compassion!

This sayyid was famous for his courage and bravery and known for his sense of honour, horsemanship and archery, seeming to clash with thousands and to yearn for his own death, thereby being termed mad by those who witnessed his frenzy in battle. However, a wise man would not be so negligent with himself, nor would he expose his head to the sword, to take suicidal risks. Only the rash or crazy undertakes such things when he loses his sense. But this man was known for such and threw himself into many dangers. In this respect, cowards among the tribesmen say:

> If I had two heads, I would keep one in store and meet sharp swords with the other.
>
> If I charged into battle, bold and fearless, I wouldn't give in to cowardice, during times of adversity.

But I've only got one. If I lose it, I shall not find another.

Moreover, he was the cousin of 'Alī b. Shuway' but between the two of them enmity [359] existed so that each of them wished to kill the other, and wished to destroy him sooner or later, as happens with family enmity.

The minister, once he caught wind of this and understood the clear struggle between them, intrigued for someone to suggest to Sayyid Nāṣir that he seek asylum with him and ask his help in every dangerous enterprise he might wish. If he could hasten to his fold before the minister took possession of the land, then he would obtain from him all he wanted. But if he waited for the victorious army to occupy the country and its famous castles, there would be no advantage in such neutrality; nor would there be any point in submission once the country had been captured, as protection for the hopeless is unacceptable, and surrender for infidels after punishment has been imposed is denied and unacceptable. For that reason, what appears to be submission and surrender in the future cannot be approved.

Sharīf Nāṣir realised that this attitude was correct and gave it his complete approval, undertaking to come to the minister and tread the sultanic carpet in his surrender to Almighty and Great God.

He sent a message to the minister seeking his favour in granting protection and in pardoning him for his crime of rebellion which the minister then agreed to grant. He granted protection and undertook to meet his expectations. When the minister approached him, at times the sayyid turned red with embarrassment and at times yellow with fear and dread; so the minister stilled his alarm, calmed his spirit and eased his conscience, receiving him in an open and relaxed manner. He presented a smiling and lively face and spread over his shoulders a robe of honour, saying to him, 'Let God pardon what is past'. He filled him with delight as he dressed him in an honorary robe of *zarbāf* [gold velvet][33] and silk brocade; and he granted robes to all his suite in accordance with their rank. He was courteous to all, distributing among them dinars and dirhems [gold and silver coin] and hoisting for them flags of kindness and compassion.

Then he sent them to the guest-house and had spread out for them, with extreme kindness and generosity, a great banquet. So they ate and drank and were absolutely delighted. Then he brought to him and the dignitaries in his party pedigree horses with excellent golden saddlery and stirrups [360] and silver reins of the purest metal. They plucked from the tree of love its succulent fruit and became amazed at that fair bounty and those kind hands. They went back to their homes, happy and secure, returning to their people, confident and full of cheer. They were, as is said:

So they returned, full of praise for what you are worthy of; even when they were silent, the sacks of gold will heap praise on you.

With that the cripple's back was broken as his leg was broken; Muṭahhar, his military staff and people were depressed and frightened. They were struck by a fatal arrow right in their very hearts. All that is attributable to God's help and His approaching victory, to His help for the Sunnī people against every rebel and doubter. Thanks to God who is close at hand and watchful, attentive and easy of access.

CHAPTER 45

[361] Muṭahhar's lies, stratagems and deceit; the spread of his lies and humbug among his band of devils; the invitation to the people of the Jawf and Ṣa'dah to join him, misleading them with his cunning and deceit; their arrival; and the minister's appearance at the battle, with their flight from his grasp to the mountain tops[1]

§ It was this cripple's habit and practice, which developed with his crooked character, to lie, falsify and deceive, and to dive into a sea of deception where he would lay traps to leave no doubt that he was a cheat; and to make quite clear that he was the greatest trickster and fraud of all.

He is a fount of lies. If you were to throw the least of him at mankind, they would all become liars.

Throughout these battles, although he was entirely broken and depressed, defeated and overcome, Muṭahhar personally was not seen to be weak and broken; nor did he appear without power and in trouble; but, to avoid blame, he hid from sight and concealed the fact that hundreds of his troops had been killed. However, when his gang killed a single Turk, he would publicise the fact among the bedu and the entire population.

It was the custom in that country, when fighting broke out, for the victors to light [362] fires on the mountain tops, indicating and displaying joy in their victory throughout the countryside.

Every time Muṭahhar was beaten and defeated, and in any battle broken and destroyed, he would light a great fire on his mountain from dusk to dawn, to display to the tribesmen his utter joy and delight, in the pretence that he was the victor when in fact he had been broken and defeated.

Among his tricks and stratagems, and the deceit that he evinced from his heart, was the occasion when he sent a message to the people of the Jawf and Ṣa'dah[2] and the outlying tribesmen to the effect that:

The Turkish troops are weak and exhausted and have been afflicted and struck by disasters. A great number of them have been killed and we have taken a great deal of booty from them. Only a small band and weak group of them survive who cannot fight and endure contest and battle. So come to us, so that we can share with you their booty and plunder and bless you with the weapons and equipment they have left; then enjoy this booty and fill your bags with the finest pearls, worth dinars and dirhems, in place of scraps of fodder and mean bits of food.

He filled their ears with such prattle and spun for them such nonsensical tales; so their veins throbbed with avarice and they believed the idle talk that reached their ears. They responded to the call of the lying cripple, thinking that indeed he was the victor he claimed in these battles. They did not realise that, had he been victorious as he claimed, then there would have been no point in his call for them to get into such hopeless situations. Does one leave his prey to someone else? Does a dog call another to his quarry once he has it within his grasp?

But they are stupid and ignorant tribesmen, without intelligence, indeed careless, who have been deceived by nonsensical talk and believe empty falsehoods. Taking leave of their senses and proceeding on their rash way, they reached Thulā to endure trial and tribulation, driving ahead those whom they found on their way and in that way swelling the number of their forces.

Does the butcher take fear at the number of sheep? Does the shepherd take the increase in his stock but as a blessing? God have mercy on Nābighah al-Dhubyānī,[3] when he says:

[363] We used to regard every bit of white as fat [i.e. we had no experience] when we faced Judhām and Ḥimyar,
until we met the tribe of Bakr b. Wā'il with its 80,000 men, some in armour, others not.
Then when we crossed our weapons with each other, their hilts would not be broken.
We gave them a draught as they did us, but we were more patient in facing death.
At a time of crisis we could not distinguish the colour of our horses from clay, till bay was counted as blond.
It is not known for us to return them safe, nor to have them harmed should be counted wrong. We have won, without uncovering a lady's veil; nor did we plunder anything save studded iron [i.e weaponry].
Had we wished that sort of thing, their ladies would have become as merchandise.
There is no good in folly without sense; so when things demand, they can be corrected.

There is no good in sense without the urge to protect purity from being sullied.

They could not reach their perilous goal before they had covered hills and dales, slippery stretches of rocks and forests, and had been afflicted by all sorts of harm, with each day bringing loss of people and property. God kept fortune away from them and caused trouble on their way.

No sooner had they reached Thulā, in the belief that they had exchanged oblivion for life, vigilance for sleep, hardship for comfort and trouble for calm, than Muṭahhar came out to meet them and welcomed them with delight, greeting them with smiles, an open heart and high spirits. He was kind and hospitable with them, inviting them to join him and looking after them. He flattered them greatly and was courteous to them; and most of them were moved and sympathetic. He directed them to pitch their tents in a quarry at the foot of the mountain opposite the minister's encampment, in a place which scattered stones made inaccessible; nor could the great cannon reach it. They had piled up rocks in front of them, barricading themselves behind some great stones so that the fine horses could not leap upon them; nor could the mighty guns reach them. Indeed, it was difficult to get round those bends and the going was between those twists and turns. And they had prepared behind each rock men to fire small guns, hidden behind the rocks like a cache of fire in the stones, allowing an excellent line of fire.

[364] The first a passer-by would know of the fire was when it hit him. Only the vagabond, only the rash vagrant would tread there. Even after such preparation, every one of them, taken unawares and under attack, would have run off to the mountains like a monkey, abandoning camp and cooking pots, and lost with the force of panic and alarm; and they did flee, with a hiss like the devil's at the sound of the call of prayer, with a cry like the bray of a donkey at sight of a hyena in the plain. But despite their flight, once they reached Thulā, they lit fires to display their victory, with their lies and chicanery among the tribesmen. Then, when other mountain tribes watched them, they also treacherously lit fires, screeching like monkeys on the rocks and hopping like birds to show their delight and joy. All that was lies and double dealing; and God knows what is in men's hearts.

Once the minister had been told of the arrival of this large army and this massive gathering, he resolved to meet and fight them; so he left his noble pavilion and mounted his men on their beloved horses, brandishing their lengthy spears. He assembled the weapons, sharpening the sword blades and rubbing honey along the spears. He mustered his troops; raised his flags and banners; arranged his squadrons and stirred his lions; and he put his troops into ranks on the field and stationed them where the cavalry could operate.

Sinān Pasha stood in the centre and set out the two wings, arranging the army in a most dazzling display, most attractive to the eye. Then he displayed the standards and banners, and, with the beat of drums and kettledrums,[4] it was like the Day of Judgment when the trumpets sound and the ground is shaken by a quake. The sky almost moved from side to side as the cavalry sported their horses before him, bent on striking the enemy in the jugular. They longed for engagement and for entry to the fight, and, warming up for the fray, drew their swords and sabres.

They carried the hearts of lions within their breasts and tied their turbans on their moon-like [i.e. handsome] faces.
They took on the day of tumult, determining by the sword faster than fate.
A people who when they wore armour looked like a day-cloud full of rain.
When they terrified you, you encountered every evil and when they brought you protection, you gained refuge.

[365] Sinān Pasha sent a message to those boors to call them to line, so that they should mount their horses, and he invited them to the field so that they could put their claims to the test; and then the claimant can be honoured or despised.

The minister's call for the horsemen to appear was repeated, as was the invitation to the battle and fight, but no Zaydī uttered the slightest sound; nor appeared for the contest at his polite invitation. But, terrified, they kept silent, shaking with utter dread, and, instead of fighting, they took to their heels and fled to the mountain tops. They sought refuge in the stronghold of Thulā, thinking that it would protect them from disaster. In such a case Abū al-Ṭayyib al-Mutannabī has said,

Whenever you chase in a people's wake, their skulls and bones lie untended.
You hurled at them a sea of iron, that left its waves on land behind them.
In the morning their coverings were silk, but in the evening dust.
Those of them who had in their hands spears, now have in them red blood.
Thus, should one who seeks the enemy do, and your example should point the way.

The minister and his forces continued in the field till near sunset, waiting for the enemy to come to them for battle and the fight. After a long wait, as the ranks got tired of such a lengthy delay and evening was about to strike, with any hope of the enemy coming falling to a 'may' or 'perhaps', the news came of their flight from the encounter and their escape from any thought of meeting.

God insists that those who take to flight die despised; for death and flight are equals.

If they had held on, they would have died with dignity and glory, but in battle endurance forsook them.
For such lives, to perish would have been better; and captivity of more value than flight.
Their strength stands firm on the blue of the spear heads, nor have their brown spears drunk their blood, as, frightened in their dreams as they sleep, terror strikes as they wake with the dawn.
[366] They concealed their deceit within their breasts in bad faith, and the evil of their concealment and deceit enfolded them,
their homes were far away from them and they remembered. The homes of those reviled are better denied.
The horses of fate have galloped on in frenzy, a memory for them and those among them who remain.

When the minister was certain of their flight, with the victorious army he returned in victory to his mighty and populous encampment, passing the night in ease, calm and pleasure, while his wretched enemy passed it in fear, with nightmares in his sleep.

So when he is awake, your swords alarm him, and when he sleeps, his dreams will have unsheathed your swords.

CHAPTER 46

[367] The size of the mighty army remaining with the minister, and of the vanquished one gathered with Muṭahhar; the two attacks launched by the cripple during the beginning of Ramaḍān/7 February; and his defeat and descent into disappointment and despair

§ With the start of Ramaḍān 977/7 February, it occurred to the mind of the twisted cripple, and those who shared his sick and arthritic view, to launch an attack on the minister. He thought he had been strengthened by those of his enormous army who had come from the Jawf and Ṣaʻdah,[5] and that victory came from strength of numbers, without realising that it came from maintaining steadfast hearts, and not from mere numbers, if fear plays round and occupies the heart. For how often does a small force overcome a large one with God's permission, especially when one betrays his sultan, with his sectarian followers from infidel and oppressive tribes, his motley of renegades and rebels and his band of vicious apostates? Victory comes only from God.

The minister counted the detachment remaining with him, taking the roll of those warriors who were present. He excluded those who had reached martyrdom in battle, those who were absent, those for whom the mother of books had stated their time had come, and those who had remained to guard the [368] occupied land; nor did he count those assigned for raids and dawn attacks against the rebellious tribes, or those surrounding the stronghold of Kawkabān for its siege and attack.

The troops round the minister in his guarded camp and his great encampment, living in his accustomed glory and good cheer, amounted to 1,200 fighters, both on horse and foot, and warriors whom Almighty God inspired to drive away the unjust. Every day half of them would take their turn to climb up to Kawkabān to assist the troops stationed there in its siege. Their purpose in climbing up was to cooperate in filling the ditch by throwing in stones and large rocks, so that it would be filled in and allow a track and path across.

On the next day the other half would climb up and work in the same way.

And the minister assigned to each half an *āghā* commander with whom the troops would ascend and return at the end of the day: most days the minister would accompany them in their ascent, with his suite and mamluks[6] for the task.

As for the wicked Zaydī troops and the people around Muṭahhar on Mt Thulā, there were 1,000 horsemen and 8,000 men on foot, of whom 4,000 were musket and artillery men and 3,000 fighting with spears and full armour. However, Almighty God had made them weak-hearted, docile and submissive and afflicted them with every sort of illness and disease.

> Noble steeds and spears are of no account or value, unless noble mounts are riding them.

The most they used of weapons was shouting, on encounter they cast them away, in surrender, escaping to the mountains and leaving dust on the wind. That was their way and habit; that was the way they fought and went to war. That was their only recourse, but they were obstinate and arrogant, and persisted in their delusion. They knew the truth but did not recognise it. 'Lo! those who garner sin will be awarded that which they have earned.'[7]

[369] So Muṭahhar gathered his vain trifling finery, his mock army and contrivance. He got his troops into rank and order, hurling them into their sinful way and setting his targets, without care. He encouraged them, exuding his magic and attracting their ear. He assigned them a leader whom he swore to bring victory and made them promises, but the devil will only delude them. So they began to come down and ride to the plain again, loosening their reins. That was at the onset of Ramaḍān/7 February.

As Sinān Pasha witnessed their suicidal courage and bravery, he gave orders for the troops to stand firm and feign disregard, and to bide their time over any movement, so as to encourage the wretched enemy to complete their descent into the plain. The mighty army could wait no longer and flew with a bound on to the backs of their horses, kindling the fires of war. The minister rode behind them with his mighty band playing the drum and pipe, intoxicating the troops with the sight, as if they had drunk wine; and the battle broke out and raged on. The eyes of fate watched; from all sides arrows rained on the men; fighting was fierce; army clashed with army; and the angels' forces joined with those of the devil.

> A suckling camel, when he nudged his way to the fight, could not stand to face a determined force.

The fighting and battle continued from dawn till after noon. Countless Zaydī were slaughtered while few of religion's loyal were martyred. Many horses lost their riders and many were killed on the plain. Swords were broken in the fight and spears shattered. That people's blood began to flow like running water in those valleys and the dead were seen as uprooted palm stumps.

When afternoon came the Sunnī people gained victory and the heretics were defeated in death and capture, with destruction and subjection in their train.

> Pursuit joined them to battle where one of their weapons was flight.
> They passed, limbs racing with heads, as they fell, pell-mell.
> [370] When day withdrew its light, darkness was twofold, the night and the sand-haze,
> then the darkness lifted and the sparkle of tempered swords and the day did shine.
> If they had escaped the spears, the desert would have caught them with pangs [lit. spears] of thirst.
> They would see death before and behind, and, perplexed, they would have no option but death.
> Who asked for the fight? It is this Sinān, the horses of God and the finest swords.

Spears kept driving through their chests from behind and swords kept striking their shoulders and heads till night fell between them. Darkness dropped the favour of her skirts over the scene, and eyes were farded with the pitch of night from the darkening gloom; and, between sight and the scene, a jet-black veil imposed its fabric of night as it fell.

The victorious army returned to its noble encampment, with the winds of victory fluttering on the points of its long spear heads, as the minister returned to his mighty pavilion, with victory and triumph streaming from his noble stirrup. Discarded enemy heads rolled towards him, and faces of victory, joy and good fortune turned his way. And he dispatched the heads for display in front of Kawkabān stronghold so that its people could see the shame and disgrace that had befallen their supporters, as a result of the pain Muṭahhar had brought them in this world, and worse and more enduring in the next.

The minister set about in his glory and majesty, discipline and command, sending units throughout the region, preparing the troops to control the country and borders, and giving protection to those tribes and bedu who came to him. He had given top priority to the capture of Kawkabān and, after its capture, to that of Thulā, from the chief cripple and imposter in the world. This was the objective over which he talks to himself, over which he passes the time, his constant companion.[8]

With the arrival of Friday, 5 Ramaḍān/11 February, the two sides viewed each other and met, [371] as the tribesmen with him in Thulā came down, led on by shame and driven by the devil, till they drew up in line on the field. As is said:

They would have advanced, had there been none to capture; they would have fled had there been none to follow.

The minister, together with his troops, went out to them; and rider and horse raced towards the fight and charged, the flashing splendour and the massive force, with tremendous will and swords drawn for blood. He drew up the men in their positions, posted his warriors in ambush to left and right as God's troops joined in the fight against His enemies; and they waited for God's victory to descend from His lofty abode. The two sides merged in battle and contest.

What stayed most were their bodies as they tumbled to the ground and their spirits departed.
Slaughter raced on faster than they, so that neither death nor old age could strike them.

How many heads were scattered and lives cut short, how much blood shed and life taken before the pebbles had turned to carnelian, the sands of the plain turned red and the dust had struck its course.

The land narrowed so that one in flight saw man when none was there.

The horses were active from morn till night and the Sunnī folk won the field over the infidel foe, with many slain and their heads cut off. Although many were killed in the fighting as it went on and on, it was not obvious, so numerous were they. No decrease in their number was seen, however many of them were killed.

When the spear points completed their toll, they overdid their task,
and they [the spears] left them in the dust as if their heads were at war with their bodies,

[372] corpses stretched on an earth of blood while white stars were in a dark sky, and limbs belonging to known fathers have left their offspring as orphans.

And the rest of the tribesmen fled and scattered along the mountain paths and elsewhere, with some of them climbing up to Thulā and Kawkabān and telling what they had seen. None can speak like an eye-witness!

The minister maintained his stoutness of heart, mounted in the heart of the field like a towering mountain, overwhelming without being overwhelmed, a vast ocean, crashing the enemy with waves of its mighty tide.

Then, as the sun's sultan inclined to set, its colour wan as that of a sad lover, and 'streaks of raven-black'[9] appeared from the west, the minister made his return to his noble camp. Enemy heads had been cut off, hoisted high on lofty spear heads and paraded before him, with horses captured, equipment removed and skulls cut off. Then he prayed to Almighty God in thanks, abasing himself before Him in public and private, denying any power or ability of his own; for he recognised that this was God's wish and doing. He reviewed those lost, made holy in God's service and martyred, of whom there were nearly twenty who had risen to the highest heaven.

As for those of the infidel troops and followers of Satan whom the angel of pain had thrown into hell, there must have been more than hundreds, whose heads had been cut off, souls extinguished, and lives snuffed out. Those whose fate was unknown were beyond counting, beyond estimate and enquiry; and those killed and slain were not few in number. Nor did their number lessen through killing and slaughter; for they were like insects, types of scorpion and viper and the lowest form of creature, among the ill-fated and squalid, the vile and goaded.

Dogs have decided to rule; then to whom is left the care of young sheep and goats?

CHAPTER 47

[373] Muṭahhar's request to change the battle ground; his boldness in appearing to fight; and his trouncing and defeat, and his flight with his army like monkeys to the mountain tops

§ During the middle of the month of Ramaḍān/February/March, Sinān Pasha was told that the tribesmen were robbing travellers on the roads as an earnest of rebellion, and taking advantage of his own preoccupation with fighting the people of Thulā and Kawkabān. They saw there was a timely opportunity, in the tradition of the tribesmen of those parts and the custom

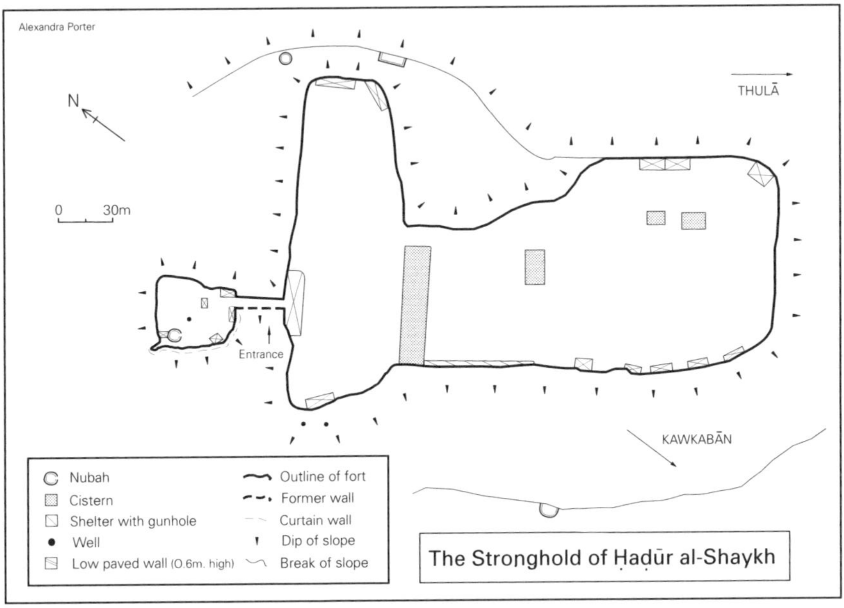

The Stronghold of Ḥaḍūr al-Shaykh

of the ignorant tribes of the area. For, when far from the restraint of the sword, they set about trouble and harm without thought for the punishment; nor heed for what the distant future might bring. On the contrary, they were captives of the present, blind and deaf to what things might lead to.

So the minister prepared a detachment to control the roads, cut off the heads of those breaking the law in the area and disciplined those bent on treachery and misrepresentation. For this task he dispatched the most skilled horsemen he had and the bravest of brave men around him, men of sound judgment and sagacity.

And Muṭahhar was given this information which caused him to gloat and be deceived. He thought that, through lack of assistance, the mighty army was few in number and weak. He saw that this was an opportunity to fight them and expected the pawns to be picked off when separated from the rook. He asked the minister to change the field of battle and appointed of his own accord an alternative place for the men to take the field; for he regarded the first venue as inauspicious and thought that he would beat the minister [374] by changing and renouncing the place. But he did not realise that grounds and places have no effect on the course of the battle, and that all of that depends upon fate and divine decree; for staying and fleeing turn on what God has put in men's hearts and God brings victory to whom He wishes.

Muṭahhar selected, as a place for the battle and field for the chase, a quarry with much stone and hard ground where movement for charging horses would be impracticable, and Arab tribesmen hid behind every rock, each on guard with a musket and the colour of dust and pitch; nor could his figure be recognised by a man on horseback so that he could observe him at will. That was a gloomy spot on the slopes of a mountain with a fort called al-Ḥaḍūr[10] in which bedu devils had gathered and settled. Muṭahhar had brought them there and they had hastened to settle; and he had summoned and mustered the tribes without exception. He had organised them as a body in those mountain paths where they had collected in that extremely restricted area so that the valleys and plains resembled a moving snake.

The minister responded to his request and went along with what he, in his warped mind, wished. He personally set out with his men and his remaining warriors and troops, with his pipes playing, his kettledrums beating, his banners hoisted and his flags flying; and he set the sword blades and arrow heads against the enemies' chests.

The answer to the letter I sent was obtuse; and its signal to those watching obscure.
The desert was uneasy about what it declared and there was no end to the emptiness there.
There are three letters of importance that it spelt, a charger, a slender lance and a sword.
Spears are broken, and there are many of them; men in the army are also being killed and they are a mighty force.

On the morning of 18 Ramaḍān/24 February, the two armies clashed, and the two masses met. The tribesmen launched their attack, calling their men to their fate; and the Sunnī cavalry responded, hurling at them their iron spear heads. They surrounded them from the front and behind; then with the blades of their swords they opened for them the doors to their death and showed them their faces reflected in the blazes of their horses. The stout clothing of leather was stripped from them as they wrenched [375] at armour with sword blade, cleft iron with iron and inflamed the sword in blood. They destroyed them in the open, dishonoured them with nakedness, stripped the fallen of their arms and clothing and seized their booty, cutting the equipment off them. No sooner had the army achieved its purpose than many of the mamluks brought to the minister the leading captives, followed by the army leaders. 'And thou wilt see mankind as drunken, yet they will not be drunken.'[11]

The killing and fighting went on till those in error lost the day and turned their backs in flight to the mountains. The numbers of the slain equalled the pebbles and sand, crushed under the horses' hooves and mules' feet. The wretched cripple's nephew was slain, one of the greatest and bravest of his cavalry and the strongest to fall while fighting before him, Muḥammad b. ʻIzz al-Dīn, whose father was one of Sharaf al-Dīn's finest sons. The father had combined strength of character with sound intellect, and had been captured and equipped for the Sublime Porte, during the days of Muṣṭafā al-Nashshār, to quieten the rebellion in the province, but when they reached Yanbuʻ, he had been taken ill and died, his glory draining away to its end. So, after his death, they cut off his head and dispatched it to the Sublime Porte and threshold.

The son had grown up at his father's feet, and was very like him in bravery and courage, as well as fine language and ability. Then terrible disasters befell him and cast him to the claws of ill fate and the mouth of death when God willed the time appointed for him and arranged for him to meet his death at the hand of those people, as had been fated.[12]

On this side one of the martyrs was the *sanjak* commander of the minister's household who had been given warning of it; for he had had a dream in which it was foretold. He had willingly grasped the award of martyrdom, knowing that it was God's will that he was one of the blessed, and passed in victory to Riḍwān, attaining joy and bounty and reaching the highest heaven. And a contemporary recited to the minister this verse in consolation:

May you survive, and we give you consolation; may you live that we console none for your death.

Then the minister returned to his camp, with victory and success at his side and in his van; and triumph had stretched over his head the gift of its screen while plunder and horses were left to be taken. [376] His eye was attracted by none of these things; nor had he any desire for them. There were stallions the size of bastions, shining chain mail, with gilded helmets, steel swords of celebrated antiquity and clothes to dazzle the eye. The prisoners were paraded before him in fetters and iron collars, and the heads of the slain on the ends of spears and long poles.

After reaching his camp, the minister bowed down in prayer to God as he thanked Him for His blessings in the realisation that he had fallen short in his thanks for the kindness and generosity God had bestowed on him. He knew that these were blessings from God and overwhelming deeds of His kindness which He continually brought him, and he acknowledged His own absolute failure and shortcomings and made just compensation by blessing His name and generally exalting His deeds, in the words of the poet who declared:

Leave things to God in submission as submission is best for the servant.

CHAPTER 48

[377] Some of cheating Muṭahhar's stratagems, lies and deceits with which the mountains were nearly sundered; and his false visions to which men and women were subjected

§ In Chapter 45 an account has already been given of the deceit of this cheating cripple who, in his cheating, could beat even the false prophet, of how he was enveloped in the web of his deceit and how he was full of lies and trickery. Such was his custom as he grew up, his nature which governed his every moment, and his practice which he never gave up, and indeed is still current with him.

Muṭahhar's strength failed with the numerous losses he sustained and more of his troops were slain than those who opposed him; the funds and treasure he had collected were dispersed, and he came under siege in the stronghold of Thulā, in deprivation, humiliation and distress. He would watch for the claws of death to snatch him and anticipate when the ruin of contempt would break him as he waited for calamity's blows to pound him.

He was at a loss and depressed over his predicament: immersed in his thoughts, he veered backwards and forwards; and he turned to his inventive lies and his various clever stratagems and deceits, thus to save himself from destruction and offer the strongest incitement to the ignorant in their foolish bigotry.

So Muṭahhar[13] wrote separate letters to the bedu clans, the tribal shaikhs, the hostile tribes and inciters to rebellion and revolt, to the tent and town dwellers, and the bedu and the villagers. With flowery and showy messages, he sought their help, asking them to join [378] the troublemakers, and making their weak and feeble minds believe him to be a man of dignity and authority, with whom Almighty God was much concerned. They were to see him as one of those the Prophet watched over in his sleep and, in his dreams, spoke to him and encouraged him in his mission for his people; giving him directions as to what to do for the people of Islam.

Surely the holy Prophet had nothing to do with these lies and fantasies and how grave are this charge and insolence to Almighty God and the Prophet. Then he fabricated the lie that he had seen the Prophet in his dream who promised victory over the Turks and ordered him to enrol the tribes against them, with the words: 'Their state has now passed and their power among men has been broken.' He filled them with such rubbish, lies and fantasies. For the state will survive to the Day of Judgment; and it is necessary for the nation to force them to battle and destruction.

After that, rule will return to you and the sultanate will be in your hands. The

> mamluk commanders will obey you and depend upon you. If you take this great step and reach this lofty state, then make my people your concern, lift them from evil and injustice and serve the people of Yemen. For I am concerned for them; I value them and care for them. Once you have the responsibility for looking after them, then you shall remove from them the land tax for three years[14] and exempt them from any arrears. You will pardon them for anything they have done in the past for people other than yourself. Extend a pardon to them and dress them in robes of honour.

And the lying cripple went on - but surely the Prophet's high position had nothing to do with such lies. 'O Prophet of God, how can you make your people believe me over this message? How can they trust me in the words I pass to them about you?'

And the liar maintained that the Prophet had said:

> The signal for it is an eclipse of the moon on the night of the fourteenth of Shawwāl/[22 March].[15] This is a signal about which there can be no doubt or confusion; when that occurs, the people will know the truth of this dream and they will respond to the call to arms imposed on them. Whoever does so after witnessing the sign will be a Muslim. Otherwise, I shall have no truck with him on earth or at the Day of Judgment.

The cripple took advantage of the moon's eclipse forecast in the almanac chart for that night. Then he produced it in that mean manner, making it a signal for this great occasion. He had no fear that he would be thereby revealed [379] as a liar since the bedu are ignorant and their intelligence is extremely weak. They would think that it came from a knowledge of the supernatural for which Almighty God's help must have been sought and that the Prophet must have passed on the information; for news concerning the prediction could only have come from Almighty God either through divine inspiration or a true dream. They did not know that the simplest of astronomers can obtain it from the almanac or that a chart containing it is available for purchase in the market by those needing to know of it. But it is possible that tribesmen from that part of the mountains and bedu of that type had not heard about the invention of the almanac and were unaware of its method of calculation.

So they were fascinated by the letter as the devil approached them with such lies, diverting them from the true path. And the lying Muṭahhar, not content with such deceit and fabrication, dispatched to each tribe an appropriate amount of money for use on the land tax on the appointed day and time, so that they could escape the noose of submission to the sultan, show that they had come out in rebellion, kill as many Turks as possible, and cause damage and mayhem in the land. In addition to the letter and money that he sent, he sent hair from his daughters and women, and people of his village and relatives, together with their outcry against the Turks for robbing them and subjecting them to unlawful treatment.

> So where is the fury? Where has passion gone? While these men degrade women of high status,[16] taking them off to evil haunts where they can take their pleasure, while they force them into adultery and deflower chaste virgins, you swell out your clothing and fill your saddles and your stomachs. You eat, drink, dance and play music. You do not defend your women against such shame; nor do you take any risks to avert such shame. Have you not heard what happened to Ṭasm and Jadīs and those noble[17] tribes?

And the lying Muṭahhar continued with such calumny and enlarged on such disgusting slander.

As for the story of Ṭasm and Jadīs,[18] they were two of the original Arab tribes who existed before Ismāʿīl was born. They were Arabised Arabs. Ṭasm was the son of Lawth b. Iram b. Sām b. Nūḥ, peace be upon him.

[380] And Jadīs was the son of ʿĀbir b. Iram b. Sām b. Nūḥ, prayers and peace be upon him. They had many sons and descendants. Their home was in Yamāmah where there was much fruit and produce, grapes, palm trees and rivers, tended gardens, lines of castles, ease and plenty, with agriculture and stock farming.

There was a king in Ṭasm who ruled with terror and oppression. His name was ʿImlūq, and he humiliated and maltreated Jadīs, subjecting it to trials and tribulation. He continued to do so until a woman from Jadīs came to him called Huzaylah, daughter of Māzin, who had quarrelled with her husband called Māshiq. He had divorced her and wished to take his son away from her. But the woman rejected the idea; so they took their dispute to ʿImlūq; and the woman said to him: 'O King! This that I have borne is nine years old. I have given birth to him and raised him well till he was completely weaned, his character formed and his beauty apparent. His father wished to take him from me by force, rob me of him and leave me alone.'

Then her husband said: 'I have paid the entire dowry, and I have gained nothing from it save an ignorant boy. We have come to the king for a solution. Let him do what he can.'

Then ʿImlūq took the boy from them and, putting him in the care of his servant, sent them away from him, at which Huzaylah said: 'We came to the one from Ṭasm to judge between us but he produced an unfair ruling for Huzaylah. By my life, You have judged today, neither with piety, nor wisdom in judgment.'

Then ʿImlūq was told what Huzaylah had said, and was annoyed. He gave orders that no woman in Jadīs should be married and conducted to her husband before being carried to him for deflowering; and they had no option but to obey him. They suffered this humiliation for a long time and were still subject to it when ‘Ufayrah, daughter of ‘Ufār al-Jadīsī, sister to al-Aswad b. ‘Ufār, was married to a man from Jadīs. When the night came for giving her to her husband, her companions conducted her to ‘Imlūq for him to possess her, as was his custom, while they sang with the tambourine:

Begin with ‘Imlūq, then get up and go,
and start the morning with something attractive.
A virgin has no other course.

[381] When ‘Ufayrah went into ‘Imlūq, he deflowered her and let her go. Then she came out to her people, splashed with her blood. Her robe was split in the front and at the back, and she said: ‘There is none in Jadīs more humiliated. Or is this what happens to a bride?’

She went to her house without going to her husband’s house and recited as follows:

Is it right for young girls to be defiled while you men are as numerous as sand.
Should your bride appear walking in blood in the morning as she is conducted with the tambourine to her lord,
and you are not angered by this, then you become women for incense and the bath.
Here take marriage robes and dress. For what befits you are robes and kohl.
It is shameful and wretched for one who makes no defence and struts about among us like a bull.
If we were men and you were women, we should not have remained in shame.
So die in dignity, be steadfast in meeting your foe in the fight, raging in conflagration like firewood,
in which shall be destroyed he whose day has come and he who has nobility and breeding will be safe.

When the Jadīs heard about this, they were inflamed with rage and beside themselves with fiery anger and concern. Their anger would have just about razed the heights and set entire mountain ranges and chains alight. They met to organise arms and war and determined on battle and fight.

Then al-Aswad b. ‘Ufār, who was their accepted leader, said to the people: ‘O people, obey me in what I command wherein lies present honour and an end to shame. For in truth the Ṭasm deserve no respect at all from you; for the king reigning over them is the person that has humiliated us by his authority over us. Were that not so, they would be in no way superior to us; and if we were to refuse to have anything to do them, we could take vengeance on them.’

Then they replied: 'We agree with what you have said but our Arab brothers have greater numbers and equipment than us. Were they to win the day, we would have neither goats nor sheep left to us.'

To which he replied: 'I have an idea and I swear by God that you'll follow me, Jadīs, or I shall fall on my sword and kill myself.' So they replied: 'What is this idea?'; and he said: 'I will prepare a meal for 'Imlūq and his people of Ṭasm, and invite them to it. When they come, trailing the skirts of their cloaks and mantles, we'll come out against them with our swords. [382] Then I'll kill 'Imlūq while you'll each kill one of them.'

So they agreed on it and al-Aswad produced a lot of food and slaughtered a hundred camels. He ordered his people to bury their swords in the sand where he was preparing the food, telling them to begin by killing the leaders. Then al-Aswad invited 'Imlūq and his people to dine, and they accepted his invitation and came towards him, trailing their garments. After they had taken their seats, the Jadīs began to draw their swords from the sand and then slew 'Imlūq and his companions to the very last of them. They passed into their houses which they plundered and killed the rest of them inside. But one of them called Riyāḥ b. Murrah al-Ṭasmī escaped and reached Ḥisān b. Tuba' whom he asked for help against the Jadīs. So he dispatched with him an army to al-Yamāmah.

Al-Aswad b. 'Ufār, who was king of Jadīs at the time, came out to meet them. Their army was not powerful and most of Jadīs was emptied with the slaughter. Then al-Aswad b. 'Ufār and his survivors fled to Ṭāyy', and when they took shelter in their homes, they granted them asylum in face of Tuba' and his army. They remained with them and their descendants are known today in Ṭayy'.

Sayyid Taqī al-Dīn al-Fāsī al-Mālikī, qadi of Holy Mecca,[19] related this story in his book in which he collected the rulers of Mecca during the period of Ignorance and Islam. His death took place in 832/1428/9.

Let us return to the cripple's lies and deceptions on the bedu rabble tribes in the desert. The letters from this charlatan reached them containing such double-dealing and deceit, details of which have already been given. The request for assistance was clear and the essence of their Arabism touched which they were urged to sustain by every means. Their ardour stirred within them and the fires of kinship were kindled.

They took the matter to heart and unanimously decided to break allegiance and revolt, and for the second time to break with the sultan's authority; and they began to spread havoc in the land and commit themselves to wild and wanton destruction. They committed robbery on the roads, encouraged banditry and made use of the money that reached them with the letters to break agreements and violate treaties. This was anticipated by Muṭahhar's promise to absolve them from dues and land tax, and to exempt the rich and the needy poor; and it arose with the order from the Lord of all mankind, in his mercy [383] for the people of Yemen, for Muṭahhar's agreement to help them out of support for religion; and other groundless nonsense and vain, hare-brained, empty-minded fancies that are worst in people with the intelligence of a spider's web and softer than a toy sword compared with a real military one!

Then the bedu became agitated and volatile and returned to their former folly with a vengeance, demanding their due from the promises of the swollen, lying Muṭahhar. They were on the point of explosion. The roads were cut; fear spread through the land; mayhem was everywhere; and, after the period of calm, there was renewed revolt.

They came up against war with God and his Prophet, without rest or quiet; for God helps the faithful with His victory, generosity and favour. He makes the cunning of the infidels rebound against them; 'and the evil plot encloseth but the men who make it'.[20]

CHAPTER 49

[384] Goading and restlessness displayed by the rebellious Arabs; the violation of agreements and slaughter of people; and the actions of immoral al-Qaṭrān and ill-starred Ibn Nushayr

§ The rebellious Arabs took leave of their senses and were deceived by the letter sent to them by the cripple Muṭahhar and, believing the rubbish and lies fabricated by him, started to cause trouble and turmoil. They cut the roads and terrified the countryside and population, some of them taking to revolt willingly and with pleasure, others being driven to it against their will and under pressure. There was a general rising and they set up a remarkably united front. Most of them were among those who had been offered protection and had been pardoned for their killings by the minister. He had been extremely kind to them but his only reward for such kindness was more trouble and turmoil and the recourse to treachery and revolt. This is the practice of vicious people and the custom of those who do not differentiate between good and ill behaviour! Abū al-Ṭayyib al-Mutanabbī spoke the truth when he said:

When you honour a noble man, you own him, but if you honour an ignoble man, he rebels;
and to put bounty in the place of the sword is as harmful to nobility as to put the sword in the place of bounty.[21]

Relevant to the killing in battle, the opportunism and the revenge, is what al-Mutannabī also said in his poem to this effect:

> Whoever knew the world as I did will not hesitate to plunge his sword without mercy.
> He will find no mercy if taken, and, in causing them to die, he commits no sin.

[385] But the minister did not treat them harshly or severely, but with real patience, kindness and leniency, so that his kindness would be a heavy blow to them afterwards, retribution for their insolence and pride and an agonising end for their treachery and betrayal. 'And whoso doeth good an atom's weight will see it then, and whoso doeth ill an atom's weight will see it then.'[22] As has been said:

> If somebody wrongs you and you have the opportunity, then kill him with kindness and not with rejection.
> If his wrong is repeated, then his reward will come from God before Judgment Day.

While Sinān Pasha was busy with the siege of Kawkabān, the tribesmen took the opportunity to make manifest their revolt, causing trouble and turmoil all over the place. They came out against Ta'izz, al-Ta'kar and Dhirā' al-Kalb, making a general call to arms. Commander Khayr al-Dīn Qurt Oghlū [Son of a Wolf] and Kūjuk Aḥmad Bey were based by the Ḥabb stronghold when they were surrounded by tribesmen from Ba'dān and people from Jiblah. They set up positions against Dhamār and Ṣan'ā', rewarding with abuse those who had treated them well.

They had asked the minister, on his way by Dhamār with his tremendous army, for protection and sought his pardon for their rebellious activity before that; and he had accepted them, engulfing them in his most generous kindness and enfolding their shoulders in the mantle of good-will. He was extremely generous and respectful with them, but now with insults and malice they repaid his favours and acts of friendship. They rewarded his pure charity with ingratitude and evil.

'Alī b. Nushayr from Dhamār, let God drive him to hell, was among the shaikhs and chieftains living in Dhamār who had abandoned the killing and capturing and to whom the minister had granted protection. They had submitted to the sultan's authority after revolt and betrayal, had been generously and well treated, and pardoned for their crimes during that period.

While the minister was passing through the area, 'Alī b. Nushayr had approached him with every appearance of peace and dignity and expressed his extreme regret for the rebellious activity of those villains. [386] Because of his misleading talk and his own good opinion of him before the disturbances, the minister had directed that he take over the administration of Dhirāʿ al-Kalb and Dhamār, defend the roads from loathsome robbers and be police chief for the region. So he obeyed and guaranteed to the minister that he would fight off heresy and disorder, bring to an end suspicious behaviour and traces of evil then current, set out on the right path and put into practice the precepts of the ancient and holy Shariʿah.

So the noble minister approved this undertaking of his, and this man gained a mighty position and important standing. The minister dresssed him in a robe of honour, gave him a great salary and covered him with clouds of great favour. He became one of his greatest intimates and most important agents and officials until letters from the cheating Muṭahhar reached him, containing his counsel of cunning, deceit and chicanery. Betrayal was deep in ʿAlī's character, and hypocrisy and treachery were two faults within his nature. So immediately that charlatan obeyed the order, accepting and submitting to it, and starting his mischief and deception. He agreed to the absurd business, but God's strength cannot be resisted.

Among the maniac cripple's generals was one of importance called Qaṭrān the mad. He was a brutal warrior, a man without manners who filled that region with heresy, novelties, treachery, cunning and deceit. He agreed with ʿAlī b. Nushayr to gather the tribesmen together and set off to capture Ṣanʿā'. They would cut off all supplies to the Turks so as to weaken them and make them surrender the city to them in return for and in defence of their lives. So they collected the forces and mustered the troops and established a base against Ṣanʿā'. They prevented all supplies from reaching Ṣanʿā', completely cut off the roads, and terrified townsfolk and bedu throughout the population, spreading mayhem in the countryside. They declared rebellion and, after the period of calm, incited to revolt, putting all their efforts into spreading trouble as broadly and deeply as they could.

ʿAlī b. Nushayr occupied the district of Sanḥān, taking its population by force and calling upon them to revolt; and they heeded what he said, opting to submit and obey his orders while Qaṭran occupied the district of al-Ḥaḍūr,[23] gaining authority over its people through lies and misery.

These are two broad districts which had been governed by the sultan's *kāshif*. When the minister required [387] a substantial army or a large force, he would go to one of these two most important districts, relying upon the compliance of the population of both and the delegation of their business to those of their tribesmen under authority. But their two peoples took advantage of this unexpected development to evince their hidden treachery and rebellion, and displayed the evil and oppression in their hearts.

As for Qaṭrān, the *kāshif* Māmāy had destroyed his stronghold, broken his support, got rid of his following and killed many of his men. He had escaped slaughter and fled from the grasp of the Turks but this rancour remained in his heart, hatred in his breast and passion in his chest; and he was waiting for the opportunity, a wait that produced the height of torment.[24]

As for ʿAlī b. Nushayr, he had shown ingratitude, behaved immorally and rewarded good deeds with ill faith, extinguishing the light of obedience with the dark of revolt. God punishes each for his actions, and makes him suffer for his injury and ignorance. A rotten line inclines to evil; and when one from it appears sound, no reliance can be placed on him!

The building will be in danger after a time if the base is not sound.

These two cut off the roads to the minister and stopped all supplies to him, allowing none to pass to the Turks while Qaṭrān sent messages for preparation and revolt to the townspeople of Ṣanʿāʾ. But Satan's promises are only misleading. He provided them with letters to win them over, asking them to rise against the Turks stationed in Ṣanʿāʾ and drive them out completely. In them he recounted Muṭahhar's lies and fancies, and his fabricated dreams and intrigues, up to the last lies detailed and recounted by that lying charlatan.

Absolute uproar broke out among the population as they absorbed the information. They consulted with each other over it and fell into utter perplexity. Some of them advised others to break allegiance and make clear their break while others stopped short of that, not relying on such disquieting talk. However, after lengthy discussion and dispute as to which was correct, and a great deal of difference of opinion, they decided unanimously that at the time they would be neither for nor against the Turks in the fighting and battle line; and they sent a message to Qaṭrān informing him as to the opinions expressed and as to what the entire population of Ṣanʿāʾ had agreed.

Now inside Ṣanʿāʾ there was no apparent disorder but riots were expected [388] to break out and things were spinning out of control. People remained at loggerheads: vehement hatred, hidden in the mind, lay concealed; and, on the surface, agreements and pacts remained but they were fragile and lacked force.

The dog Qaṭrān had gained possession of Dhirāʿ al-Kalb and, right, left and centre, had cut the roads to the Turks, preventing even a bird from flying. News of the minister ceased; those Turks separated from him were killed; others who stood with the rebels were received, prepared and sent to Muṭahhar; and yet others of them who were in the citadel guarded the fort and themselves and the fighters defended themselves as best they could.

Qaṭrān went to great lengths to frighten and terrify the Turks guarding Ṣanʿāʾ and to cut off their supplies. He and the rebel tribesmen with him ascended Mt Lawz and caused a great deal of din and uproar, lighting fires, causing violence and aggression and inciting people to outrage and terror. Villages and towns waited in dread and everything became disturbed, after having been set in order in as far as such had been possible.

But truth is supreme and unsurpassable, and falsehood is sure to vanish. It is obvious that truth surmounts and overcomes falsehood, protecting, defending and guarding its people.

> However an aggressor gets his way over a people, he will surely meet his defeat.

CHAPTER 50

[389] Near-outbreak of revolt in Ṣan'ā'; and Almighty God's suppression of its evil, with the extinction of its fires, affording escape and avoidance of harm, and an end to its wrongs

§ At the edge of Ṣan'ā' there was a mighty castle[25] where, because of its strength and impregnability, the governor-general used to live. Inside, for his protection, there was an arsenal and gunpowder magazine, and beside it a large prison where criminals were confined. When the minister went to take Ṣan'ā', he stationed there a *dizdār* [constable] in command of about seventy soldiers whose duty was to guard this castle where the arms and gunpowder were stored, together with the prisoners. He appointed *dizdār* over them an *āghā* called Khiḍr Bey.

But residence in the castle became too irksome for Khiḍr Bey because of it being the residence of the governor-general, so he resided outside it; and the castle became administered like a fortress with an *āghā* as constable of the garrison and a *kedkhudā* [steward] according to the custom of fortresses. They (the latter) lived inside the castle to guard it but the *āghā* and the rest of the soldiers lived outside the town. Then the *āghā* acted the grandee and became tyrannical and unjust with the townsfolk, who made accusations against him to the minister and recounted his tyrannical and oppressive behaviour with the population. The minister therefore dismissed him and appointed Yaḥyā, a member of the Porte's corps of *jāwīshiyyah*, to govern them.[26]

Among the prisoners who were responsible for a lot of crime and discord was a rebellious individual called Turk Māmāy, one of the first Turks living in Yemen, at whose door was laid much trouble and strife; and the minister had put him in the castle's prison [390] with the rest of the prisoners, and, in the prison, he began to spy on the prisoners as to their thoughts and intentions. He had continued to urge them to rebellion and revolt when Qaṭrān came out in rebellion, and he would advance its feasibility to the prisoners, making them realise how close it was to breaking out. They were to take Muṭahhar's side through Qaṭrān and break faith with the sultan, smashing their fetters, killing the guard, opening the castle door and swearing allegiance to Qaṭrān.

Qaṭrān would come to them from outside Ṣan'ā'; they would help him to enter the castle; and he would take possession of the city. Satan had enticed them to this adventure and brought this scheme to their minds, recommending they take such a risk and throwing them into such a fatal imbroglio.

So Turk Māmāy dispatched a letter with a black slave who was allowed access to him, which he directed him to take to Qaṭrān on Mt al-Lawz and bring back his reply. Inside the letter was a declaration to be taken to Muṭahhar that they would support him from Ṣan'ā' and open the castle's gate to Qaṭrān. Then if they were to carry out such action, they should be among Muṭahhar's intimates.

Qaṭrān was delighted by this and entertained the black slave, sending the message to Muṭahhar. Delighted by it, Muṭahhar promised that he would offer them every kindness and give them everything they wished. He would give Turk Māmāy any town he wished and give him authority throughout the land. He guaranteed this with a fanciful oath and swore some fearful lying pledges. He put his ugly signature to it and sent it to Qaṭrān.

So Qaṭrān then sent the letter to Turk Māmāy who was delighted when the letters from Qaṭrān and Muṭahhar reached him with that slave of his. He read it to the prisoners, of whom there were about 200, who agreed with the rebellion and sent a message to Qaṭrān that, 'We'll prepare the files and hammers, and we'll cut the chains and fetters before midday on 26 Ramaḍān/3 March. We'll attack and kill the the castle doormen, and we'll open the door for you; be there outside Ṣan'ā', so that we can let you into the castle. Then you'll get in and win the day.' For they considered noon to be a time for inaction and a nap, and that the matter would be clinched. [391] God's will will be done, and God will protect Muslims from rule by heretics. He will ram such vicious deceit down the throats of the agitators; for God watches over His people.

Then Turk Māmāy sent off the letter containing the plan with his black slave to Qaṭrān, and they were informed as to the arrangements.

When 26 Ramaḍān/3 March came, the prisoners severed their fetters and Turk Māmāy went, with a group of prisoners, at noon while people were asleep, and approached the doormen, three of whom were fast asleep and the fourth awake. The fourth fled when he noticed them sever their fetters. They came to the door while the doorman ran to waken the *āghā* and the rest of the soldiers and tell them what the prisoners had done. So they got ready all their weapons and advanced to the door where they found Turk Māmāy with about ten people who had seized the swords belonging to the three sleeping doormen and cut off their heads. They opened the castle door and went outside Ṣan‘ā’.

But they could not find anyone to come into the castle; nor did they find there any call or answer. Then their spirits fell as their effort failed. Their treachery was manifest and they were killed on the spot. Then the Turks seized control of the door and prepared the guns to kill any who resisted them. They returned to the remaining prisoners whom they found had returned to the prison, each placing his leg in fetters as it had been. The prisoners began to apologise and swear on oath that they had not followed the rebels; nor had they agreed to revolt. And they resisted.

Then the commander tightened their fetters and restrained them, conscious of their treachery and deceit. He and the guard post with him were prepared for battle and knew well how to defend the area, the wall towers and the mountain limits where they realised the prevalent negligence, shortcomings and neglect.

Then Qaṭrān, with his accompanying bedu, reached the foot of Mt al-Lawz, turning up for those with whom they had made arrangements, but it was in vain; and Qaṭrān was distressed. His plan had been foiled. He was sorry about Turk Māmāy who had been buried beneath the rocks. Victory had eluded him; and he wept over him and over the prisoners killed with him who had chosen treachery at that time. He sent to the charlatan cripple the news of the punishment that had taken place, and of the failure of the stratagem devised by him. The latter was much put out and from that suffered great distress and pain.

CHAPTER 51

[392] The minister's receipt of the news; a brief mention of his constraints over troops and money; his involvement in planning and preparation; the dispatch of Qarah Kawz (Black Eyes) Bey to fight Qaṭrān and the wicked ‘Alī b. Nushayr; and their death by triumphant sultanic sword and delivery to hell and infamy

§ Sinān Pasha was governor-general of Egypt when the noble sultanic decree reached him to go to Yemen and extinguish the fires of rebellion, with the bestowal of the rank of minister and the letters of reference thereon. He undertook to obey the noble sultanic order without reluctance, delay or hesitation and presented himself with as many of the Egyptian army, mamluks and salaried soldiers as possible, for whom he made financial provision from the sultan's funds available in the Egyptian treasury.

He had dispatched to the troops their salaries until the end of Dhū al-Ḥijjah of the current year, that is '76/15 June 1569. He had left over from the salaries for '77 expenditure for the soldiers for seven months, until the end of Sha'bān '77/6 February 1570. He would require the salaries from Ramaḍān/February/March of that year but he had before him the noble sultanic decree to the governor-general of Egypt that he should dispatch the troops and money required. His successor as governor-general in Egypt was Iskandar Pasha the Circassian who was preoccupied with the collection of the sultanic revenue and was collecting it for the Sublime Porte. He had sent nothing to the minister for the equipment for Yemen, nor the salaries for the victorious sultanic troops with him.

[393] As for the troops with the minister, there were approximately 4,000;[1] with 'Uthmān Pasha, who had travelled before him, there had been more than 3,000; and with Haṣan Pasha, predecessor to 'Uthmān Pasha, there had been 1,000. This did not take into account the rest of the sultanic troops in Yemen prior to the outbreak of the revolt, and afterwards; nor the issue of the noble sultanic decree for Iskandar Pasha to dispatch later to the minister the troops coming from Syria and Turkey, whom the minister had relied upon.

The minister had depended upon them and had set out for Yemen. When he arrived, however, he had found only 1,000 of 'Uthmān Pasha's fighters of whom about 300 returned with him; and of Ḥasan Pasha's troops and all those in Yemen, he found only about 1,000. The rest of them had gone under the sword in battle during the rebellion, and many of them had died of illness and disease. The minister had divided those who were left to look after the country and fortresses in which he placed guard posts and guards, although not on a scale to protect them. About 1,000 remained with him at his base on Kawkabān. For these numerous troops were scattered throughout the country and some of them were killed in the struggle while others were induced to flee to the heretics. As for the *shafālīt* and the loyal tribesmen, they could not be relied upon; they augmented the size of the forces, nothing more.

When news of the evil Qaṭrān's activities and those of the absolutely worthless 'Alī b. Nushayr reached the minister, he was extremely troubled and entrusted the matter to God; for God is all-powerful. He began to ponder as to who was capable of averting this sedition and calming these trials and tribulations. He displayed neither weakness nor shortcoming. His heart stood firm and he was patient and dignified.

[394] The dispatch of Qarah Kawz [Black Eyes] Bey to fight Qaṭrān and Ibn Nushayr; and the deaths of the two Zaydī

While Sinān Pasha was pondering as to whom it was appropriate to appoint to calm the sedition, his choice fell upon Qarah Kawz Bey, one of the *sanjak* commanders who had fallen into the hands of Muṭahhar and then been imprisoned by him in Kawkabān in the care of Muḥammad b. Shams al-Dīn. He had then been released by Muḥammad b. Shams al-Dīn's mother[2] along with the commanders who had been in prison with him. This Qarah Kawz Bey had tasted the pleasures and sorrows of the period, experiencing the time's trials and strengths and meeting suffering and joy. He had tasted hardship and blessing and had worn garments of honour and disgrace and boasted symbols of plenty and of want.

Qarah Kawz Bey was brave, brutal and courageous, a man of experience and energy, but his possessions, old and new, had gone and everything had been lost. He had become poverty-stricken, naked, and weak in strength. However, he was experienced in the country's affairs, knew everything about the troublemakers, and possessed knowledge of the tracks through wadis and lowlands. So the minister invited him and looked after him generously, spreading for him the carpet of hospitality and honour!

The minister raised him up, after he had been cast down low by time; and he gave him all he needed in the way of arms and weapons. He mounted him on lean horses and mustered for him a troop of warriors, a small group of guerrillas, whom he equipped for battle with 'Alī b. Nushayr and Qaṭrān. They then went off and crossed the land, over easy and hard-going terrain, at a swift and strong pace. With their horse hooves, they struck and kindled sparks like fireflies, as far as Ṣan'ā'.

They sought help from a group of subject tribesmen and recruited a number of men with muskets, in that way augmenting their number in a bid for help and victory. The governor of Ṣan'ā' sent word throughout the town for all subject tribesmen on the sultan's pay-roll to come with musket and weapon, take the sultan's wage and leave for Qaṭrān with Commander Qarah Kawz Bey.

There came from the town itself [395] and its outskirts, and from Sanḥān and its districts, those remaining in the noble sultan's service, in crowds to the *dīwān* in Ṣan'ā'. Commander Qarah Kawz Bey registered them, gathered them all together, and gave them wages. He then left with them and the Turks[3] who had joined them, while Qaṭrān and 'Alī b. Nushayr, at receipt of the news, gathered their devilish rebels who had come out in revolt against the victorious army and fortified themselves on Mt al-Lawz.

Qarah Kawz emerged with his detachment to fight, went to the foot of Mt al-Lawz and made his base there. From his observation of the troops with him he realised there were few Turks and that the majority were tribesmen who had indicated their loyalty and taken the sultan's wage. However, he had no confidence in them and thought that the tribesmen would act treacherously as they had done beforehand on many occasions. He found no strength of resistance among these Turks against the large number of rebel supporters of Qaṭrān and Ibn Nushayr; nor did he find any advantage in engaging in battle, but, on the contrary, certain collapse and defeat.

So he acted as God said 'and be not cast by your own hands to ruin'.[4] He then returned with his detachment to Ṣan'ā', and pitched his camp outside the wall, sending Aḥmad al-Ṣawbāshī to the minister to explain the situation. He was a mamluk belonging to the minister whom he had put in charge of his other mamluks, charged, with Qarah Kawz Bey, with this service. He was one of the horsemen famous for his strength and bravery. So Qarah Kawz Bey said to him: 'Go to the minister and tell him the whole situation in the utmost detail as you have seen and witnessed. For the position is critical enough for me to send you, as there is no clerk to write a detailed explanation for the minister. You shall be my letter to him.'

And Aḥmad al-Ṣawbāshī accepted the task and went at once to the minister without fear of robbery on the way. He spent a night in the saddle deep in the dark, quoting to himself the saying:

> I must give no rest to the camel and its saddle, and I wear the desert and the dark and the coat of mail.[5]

When he reached the minister he told him the story and unburdened himself as to the distress and agony he had witnessed. However, the minister did not approve what Qarah Kawz Bey had done [396]; nor was he pleased over the bey and his companions' failure to engage against Mt al-Lawz. So Aḥmad al-Ṣawbāshī apologised to him on behalf of Qarah Kawz Bey, that 'our heads would have gone in fighting the sultan's enemies, simply and willingly, but we are anxious for the honour of the noble sultan; so we have saved ourselves for the day of victory, God willing'. Then in that way the minister appreciated their apology and forgave them for not hurling themselves to death. He helped them with other horsemen, and with clothing and dress for the tribesmen who had submitted, so as to win over their hearts; and Aḥmad al-Ṣawbāshī handed them over.

Qarah Kawz Bey and his companions debated as to what they should do. Qarah Kawz Bey said: 'Let us first send messages to the tribes who have submitted, winning them over by sending them the clothing. Let us have confidence in them and likewise send clothing to all those of standing, and gain their confidence so that they will put an end to their ill behaviour towards us. At least they will be neither for us, nor against us. Then we can go to our foes and fight them, putting our trust in these tribesmen.'

But this view did not satisfy the majority of the Turks with him; nor did the minister's mamluks who had come with Qarah Kawz Bey approve it. They said, 'Sending clothing to the tribesmen will not win them over. It would be cowardly and craven of us, and display fear of them; nor would we put an end to their evil in that way. On the contrary, had we shown weakness and lack of strength, they would have displayed the deceit they harboured. But they have supported the enemy against us. So there is no value in humouring them now. The first thing for us is to begin the battle and not to display any weakness or lack of spirit on our part. Let us take the initiative against them before they do so with us. For if we win, the tribesmen will join us from all sides in submission, yielding to us, voluntarily, to serve us; for they will be forced to appear to obey us. But, if we lose and they win and gain victory over us, we would have been armed with sword and spear. We would have fought until we were killed in God's path, without showing any shame or weakness; and we would die nobly on our horses' backs. We would gain a fine reputation among people and win mercy from Almighty God. In summary, we shall not return to the minister without victory; failing that, news of our martyrdom in God's path will reach him.' They stuck to this approach until they left [397] Ṣan'ā' and descended into a broad plain, courageous in their preference for this policy over any alternative.

And behold, a great cloud of dust appeared at the foot of Mt al-Lawz, dust which obscured the sun's light, behind which nothing could be seen; and behold, behind this dust was Qaṭrān, 'Alī Nushayr and their insolent soldiers. They had been ordered to get to Mt Thulā and present themselves before Muṭahhar; and he was excessively kind to them, entertaining them and promising each that he would marry him to one of his daughters. Qaṭrān would become chief of all his generals, dismissing those he wished and promoting and demoting those he wished, while 'Alī b. Nushayr would become his deputy in rank. They would both operate with his authority, stores and posts.

They returned from this audience, with confidence in his promises, and reached Mt al-Lawz, convinced that they would both return with their troops to Ṣan'ā' and assume the privileges, having been seduced by Satan in this vain fancy.

They then came down to muster their tribesmen from the top of the mountain to its foot, as far as the plain. Then the dust rose, and they did not know who was in front of them. And behold it was Qarah Kawz Bey, 'Aḥmad al-Ṣawbāshī and the cavalry with them in that field.

So the two forces met each other without planning or deliberation. Heated tempers spiralled; fires from strong wills blazed; and the cups of death circulated between the two sides. The white of day was darkened with the pounding of hooves; and the blackness from the night-like haze was lit by the sparkle of sword blades. The soaking from the torrent of muskets and arrows seemed to come from the clouds. The sun's eye paled before flashes from the spear shanks before being eclipsed; and chests boiled with the blood within them, like pots on the fire. The mamluks attacked the rebel tribesmen, carrying, lifting and shedding much of their blood.[6]

Battle had broken out and fighting raged. Wounds multiplied. Star-like arrow-heads broke as human frames were cleft. Wells of blood met their end as virginal armour was deflowered by men's swords. How many mean bedu were slain, with the moans of hell in their ears? How many wretched rebels fell, brought to hell-fire for their crimes?

> [398] 'Their backs were turned in shame, and he who wore the helmet became she who wore the veil.
> They were defeated in the plain as they beheld an ocean of tumult in which seas would drown,
> and their excuse, for their flight was clear. Was night to resist day?

Among the rebels slain were Qaṭrān, and 'Alī b. Nushayr, like him, head of the forces of injustice and aggression, and a large number of those who had led the troublemaking and terror. And the Turks carried their heads on spears and paraded them through the villages, bringing them to the minister and hurling them at his feet, in humiliation. Thank God for victory by the faithful over Satan's forces, the defeat of the heretical army and the downfall of the rebels. God's help must be sought and in Him confidence can be placed. There is no power and no strength save in God, the Sublime, the Great.

CHAPTER 52

[399] The siege of 'Alī b. Sharaf al-Dīn in Ḥabb fortress in the principality of Ba'dān; and the martyrdom of several commanders with Khiḍr Bey the admiral and their arrival in the higher abodes in Paradise

§ After the minister had conquered Mt al-Aghbar and the stronghold of al-Qāhirah, seizing Ta'izz districts and mountains and the principality of Ba'dān, his adversary did not stand to face him but, on the contrary, continued to flee from the encounter while the victorious army maintained its pursuit of the enemy; and 'Alī b. Sharaf al-Dīn, Muṭahhar's brother, was under siege in Ḥabb fortress.

Sinān Pasha saw that eliminating and driving out the enemy was preferable to remaining behind and taking Ḥabb fortress. So he appointed Maḥmūd Bey the Kurd to lay it under siege. He was brave and brutal but generous and open-handed. The minister dispatched with him about 300 troops who sur-

MILES TVRCICVS
clasſiarius.
CC.
Kriegsleuth auff dem Meer.
KRiegsleuth zuſtreiten auff dem Meer/
Mit Handtpogen vnd ander Wehr.
Künnen Durſt vnd Hunger tragen/
Vnd groſſe geſehrligkeit wagen.

1. Hand coloured woodcut of a Turkish soldier of the navy by Jost Amman from *Habitus praecipuorum popularum, tam vivorum quam foeminarum singulari arte depicti,* 1577. Note his weapons and the blue cloth of his uniform underneath his overcoat.

Amman was born in Zurich and moved to Nuremberg in 1560. He is acknowledged as the best print maker after Dürer and took a great interest in the activities of the German nation.

2. Aquatint of a mamluk exercising by Luigi Mayer from his *Views in Egypt*, 1801-1804.

Mayer was a talented artist in the suite of Sir Robert Ainslie, the British Ambassador to Istanbul, in the early part of the nineteenth century. Sinān Pasha's private mamluks would have loved such panache and display.

3. View of al-Qāhirah, the inaccessible citadel overlooking Ta'izz. Its surrender to Sinān Pasha by the Dā'ī Ṣalāḥ is described in [227] to [231]. The citadel was reached by a zig-zag track and comprised a princely residence, a prison, some cisterns, and some agricultural land. Niebuhr reckoned that in his time it could contain a garrison of some 500-600 soldiers.

4. A view of the citadel in Ṣan'ā', known as the Qaṣr al-Ṣilāḥ. It is possible that the large hewn stones fitted together with fine joints are of pre-Islamic Sabaean vintage. Arrangements for the building are described in [285] and [286]. Sinān arrived there on 11 Ṣafar 977/26 July 1569.

5-8. The stronghold of al-Ta'kar, an ancient fortress overlooking Dhū Jiblah from the south. See map 2 and [265]-[267]. Sinān captured the fort after a five day siege involving cannon and ladders which is dramatically described by the author. It was used as treasury and summer palace by Queen Arwa of the Sulayhid dynasty in the sixth/twelfth century. The Queen is buried in a handsome tomb in the mosque she had constructed in Dhū Jiblah.

5. View of the fortress on the mountain top skyline from Dhū Jiblah.

6. Final approach to the fortress, central on skyline, from north. The guide climbs the final terraces.

7. Looking westward along the site. The guide examines the entrance to a store framed by masonry blocks. Note the remains of the rendered water tank. Adequate grain stores and water tanks were vital to withstand long sieges.

8. Guide standing amid masonry ruins. Note the terracing reaching to the skirts of the fortress.

9-12. The stronghold of Ḥabb, a heavily defended fortress in Ba'dān, regarded as one of the four strongest in Yemen. See map 2. The fortress eventually surrendered to the new governor-general, Behrām Pasha, after its commander, Muṭahhar's brother 'Alī b. Sharaf al-Dīn, had been tricked into eating a poisoned quince, allegedly when intoxicated.

9. The main gate to the fortress.

10. View across the storage chambers, carved out of the rock. There were fourteen openings, each wide enough for a slender Yemeni to enter, with a capacity of several thousand tons of grain, which would explain how the population would have been able to withstand over a year's siege. Farah, 39.

11. View of the fortress from below.

12. View across the fortress, with the *qubbah* or dome containing 'Alī b. Sharaf al-Dīn's tomb.

13. View of the 'Āmiriyyah in Radā', east of Dhamār, an important town under the Tahirid dynasty (859-923/1454/1517) which had amassed a considerable fortune from the Indian trade. The construction of this teaching mosque was completed by the sultan 'Āmir b. 'Abd al-Wahhāb, in 910/1504. Sinān ordered its *sanjak* commander to reinforce the Turks fighting the rebels at the Samārah pass. See [407]-[408].

14. View of Thulā, Muṭahhar's base, with the fortress known as Ḥuṣn al-Ghurāb, the fortress of crows, on the top of the outcrop. See map 3. Its stone glows like amber and it contains some ancient mosques. The ramparts of the town are said to date from Muṭahhar's time. The Austrian scholar, Eduard Glaser, assisted by local climbers and a strong rope, climbed up to the fortress in 1873.

15. The Great Mosque at Thulā.

16. The teaching mosque at Thulā named after the Imam Sharaf al-Dīn. Muṭahhar is buried in the *qubbah* or domed chamber with exquisite workmanship.

17. View across the site of the stronghold of Ḥaḍūr al-Shaykh towards Thulā. See map 3 and [374]. High on the massif, the fortress controlled the road to the north and commanded excellent views southward towards Kawkabān and eastwards to Thulā. Muṭahhar's father, Imam Sharaf al-Dīn, was born there in 877/1473.

18. View of the southern part of Shibām, an historic city at the foot of the escarpment below Kawkabān. See map 3 and [291]-[292]. The entrance through its wall can be seen in the foreground. The view looks northwards towards Thulā the outcrops of which are clearly visible.

19. View of Shibām from the east, with Kawkabān visible on the edge of the escarpment above. The track to Kawkabān, now in places overgrown, wends its way up the escarpment. An arch supporting the track can be seen near the summit. It crosses the chasm which played an important role in the long siege of Kawkabān.

20. The basin of Wadi al-Ahjir, showing the escarpment to the south east of the Ḍula‘ massif, down which the nearly vertical wadi passes descend which, manned by Zaydī hurling stones and firing weapons, proved for the most part impassable to the Turks. The inset to map 3 shows the beginning of the track westwards along the top of the escarpment.

21-26. Kawkabān, the historic fortress town above Shibām, the extensive siege of which proved the key to Sinān's campaign. See map 3. The town dates from pre-Islamic times and boasts ancient mosques as well as vast water tanks and grain silos. The views here help to convey something of the dramatic beauty and historic and strategic importance of the town.

21. View of Kawkabān from the north. In the foreground are the Qishlah or Barracks built by the Turks in 1895, during their second occupation. The chasm, largely filled in, can be imagined directly in front of the fortress, now crossed by the *maḥmūlah* or bridge.

22. The entrance to the fortress of Kawkabān, with its beautifully dressed local stone of glowing amber.

23. The Jāmi' al-Kabīr or Great Mosque in Kawkabān, founded by Imam Sharaf al-Dīn in the sixteenth century. Note the semi circular wall of the *qiblah* and the steps leading to the large water tank.

24. The Masjid al-Sharīfah or mosque named after the Sharīfah Muḥsinah, the second mosque in Kawkabān with a minaret.

25. One of the impressive water tanks constructed by the Ayyubid leader, Ṭughtakīn, after his successful siege of Kawkabān in 1190.

26. Stars of David and magnificent pre-Islamic inscription above door to al-Shūnah or the Granary, constructed by the Turks, some 13 to 18 yards in size, with entrances from the roof, used for storing different types of grain.

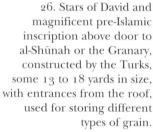

27. View of Bukur, the fortress connecting Mt. Ḍula‘ with the rest of the vast Maṣāni‘ range. See map 3. It was at the limit of Muḥammad b. Shams al-Dīn‘s authority with Muṭahhar. The town was entered by the tiny *maḥmūlah* or bridge, seen on the skyline leading to the fortress buildings to the left.

28. View of Shamāt. See map 3. After its surrender, the fortress was destroyed on Sinān's orders because of its position by the artillery route. Later Kulābī Bey, with a detatchment of thirty, was ordered to rebuild it, because of its strategic importance. Enticed into a picnic outside its entrance, he was murdered by a group from Kawkabān, acting on the orders of Muḥammad b. Shams al-Dīn. See [343]-[344] and [412]-[414].

29. View of the stronghold of al-'Arūs or the Bride, an important stronghold of great strategic importance to Kawkabān, with its own bluebeard legend. See map 3. A proverb states, *al-makhāzin Kawkabān wa mifātīḥha al-'Arūs.* Kawkabān holds the stores and its keys are al-'Arūs. See [313]-[316] for Sināns capture of al-'Arūs and its two sister strongholds. The mountain contains sulphur deposits within its caves and some allegedly pre-Islamic columns.

30. A powerful Portuguese cannon at the fort of Reis Magos in Goa pointing towards the Mandovi river. The fort was built between 1551 and 1554 to guard the northern side of the estuary leading to Goa which Afonso de Albuquerque had captured for the Portuguese in 1510. Successive viceroys took their vows of office here.

rounded Ḥabb fortress, ensuring that none could either enter or leave it. For there was only one road to it, and it was at a great and towering height, bumping against the star Aries, transfixing Arcturus and impeding the Milky Way.

Hearkening to the stars, so that when they moved, we thought they were listening to it,
as if its *abrāj* [towers] on every side were their *abrāj* [constellations], and their *simāk* [the two stars Arcturus and Spica] its shoulders.[7]

[400] The governor of Ta'izz was Commander Aḥmad known as Kūjuk Aḥmad Bey because of his short stature. He was one of the commanders protecting Egypt and was rash and at times boorish. His administration of Ta'izz could not be admired and was termed 'the rule of Qarāqūsh'. Now this Qarāqūsh was governor of Egypt during the days of the Fatimids.[8] He had some strange rules, often quoted as examples, such as when someone removed another's eye, and they took the matter before him. The offender was his treasurer. The ruling was that he had to have his own eye removed (an eye for an eye); but he said, 'I am your treasurer. If you remove my eye, I will be not be able to examine the coins.' To which Qarāqūsh replied, 'True, but we must do justice to the offended.' He thought for a while and said, 'Bring the marksman and we'll have his eye removed in place of this one. For aiming arrows, more than one eye isn't necessary. Indeed, if he were to shut one of his eyes and aim the arrow with only one, he would be in the same state!'

Aḥmad Bey was similar to Qarāqūsh in his rule. He had been Commander of the Pilgrimage[9] in 976/1568/9 when he had been angry with the late supervisor of the caravan, Qadi Zayn al-Dīn al-Jazayrī al-Ḥanbalī who was a polite, learned and intelligent historian whom the ulema had authorised to become a mufti and teach for his *madhhab* [school of Islam]. Moreover, he was a grave and elderly shaikh; but Aḥmad Bey held no respect for his grey hairs and gave him a violent beating, and then placed him in irons and made him walk an entire stage, with increasing ill effect on his body and well-being. For that he will get his just deserts from Almighty God in payment for such an outrage. Aḥmad Bey did not die but for the invocation of God by the shaikh.

Tell him who has grown strong at my expense and did not fear the angel there to observe his acts.
I have hidden arrows for him at night, and they will hit him.

After the people in Ta'izz had made accusations to the minister against Aḥmad Bey's government, he dismissed him from Ta'izz and sent him to Ba'dān to lay siege to Ḥabb fortress with Maḥmūd Bey the Kurd, and he appointed as governor over Ta'izz in his place Qurt Oghlū [Son of a Wolf] Sinān Bey, brother to Khiḍr Bey the admiral. Then [401] Sinān Bey arrived in Ta'izz and Aḥmad Bey went to Ba'dān and was stationed by Ḥabb fortress until he met his death there afterwards. The earth of each drew him to it, and the fate of each preceded him to the place where he feared to find his grave.

And where a man is fated to be buried, he cannot die and be buried elsewhere.

Information concerning the death of both of them will come soon.

As for Maḥmūd Bey the Kurd, his military policy in the base around Ḥabb fortress was of no avail, and the minister was apprised of the fact; so he sent Khiḍr Bey the admiral to be *sirdār* over these two commanders, over the other commanders and all the troops under orders to besiege Ḥabb fortress. Khiḍr Bey reached the two of them, bringing the heavy guns from Ta'izz and al-Ta'kar, against the minister's instructions, and began to fire them at the population in Ḥabb fortress who were unconcerned because of the height of this fortress, an account of which has already been given.[10]

Khiḍr Bey and his companions maintained their siege of the fortress until Muṭahhar's letters reached the tribesmen of Jiblah and al-Shawāfī[11] and the population of Ba'dān who were the most evil of the people of those parts. Muṭahhar urged and pressed them to revolt. Previously, they had been in rebellion and had been the cause of Ibb and Jiblah's capture, where Ottoman troops had been slain during the time of the late Murād Pasha, till his own martyrdom, Almighty God have mercy upon him, which has already been related.[12]

The devil had incited them to unrest and led them to rebellion. They had embarked upon troublemaking and mayhem, cutting off the supplies to the people in the camp. They had put them under siege when they themselves were laying siege, and had put them under extreme pressure. The Turks were scattered in Ibb and Jiblah in coffee houses and places of entertainment, pleasure and idleness.[13] The tribesmen caught them unawares, in coming out in dispute and rebellion, surprising them with broken agreement, treachery and outrage. They killed Turks everywhere they found them isolated; and only the commanders and a few of the sultan's troops remained round the tents of Khiḍr Bey the admiral.

The minister had forbidden Khiḍr Bey to disperse his troops, or to give them permission to enter the coffee houses in Ibb and Jiblah. They were not to go there for recreation, nor to resort to those tribesmen. [402] They were not to show trust and affection for them but were to stay in his camp and not to be separated from him in enemy country. But Khiḍr Bey contravened his noble instructions and everyone who asked for permission to visit Ibb or Jiblah was given it.

It was also his instruction not to fight the people living in Ḥabb fortress, nor to convey and discharge the heavy guns against them, so that they would escape such affliction. But he was to put them under siege so that they should be constrained by the siege and hand over the fortress to him with a demand for peace. However, in that respect he contravened the minister's instruction. He asked for the heavy guns from al-Ta'kar and Ta'izz and began to use them to strike Ḥabb fortress, to absolutely no avail, save loss of gunpowder and the toing and froing created by the guns.

His order was also not to make a habit of using the tribesmen from those parts; and neither to register them for wages, nor to allow them to approach, since there was no confidence in using them. But in all of this he went against the minister, and there were numerous contacts with them. They then played him false over the need for them. They did nothing but cause him harm and were against him afterwards. Every time he was guilty of contravening the minister's instructions, the admiral had said: 'If we capture Ḥabb fortress, he will forgive us for going against his orders.'

As the situation dragged on and the pounding by the guns was of no avail, as a great deal of gunpowder was used to no end and his error became clear, Khiḍr Bey sent a message to Sinān Pasha, apologising for the offences for which he was responsible and seeking his pardon for the mistakes he had made, and the minister responded by accepting his apology and in his esteemed letter to him gave him various forms of encouragement and instruction.

Now Khiḍr Bey was one of the reliable people in the service of the noble sultan, and for that reason had been selected to conquer Aden, as has been related.[14]

He was brave and courageous, with military knowledge concerning such things as the capture of strong fortresses, along with good administration. However, good administration was of no help to him without the help of judgment, and when judgment is missing, then administration is of no use; for when fate steps down, the sighted become blind.

[403] Be calm at heart; for your time is arranged for you as to the things you like and the things you hate,
and, when you are fated for things, and you flee from them, you are in fact heading towards them.

Among the mishaps was the Ottoman governor of Dhamār's need for gunpowder; so he sent to Khiḍr Bey asking him to send him some loads of gunpowder for his use in battle with the enemy should he require it. So Khiḍr Bey sent to him loads of gunpowder with Commander Barwayz, one of the sultanic *sanjaks* in Yemen, and with him equipped horsemen to protect them.[15] However, when they had reached Dhamār with the gunpowder and wished to return, the rebels blocked their passage and prevented them from doing so.

Now Barwayz Bey was a warrior known for his courage and bravery, and he had with him about fifty courageous horsemen, but the rebels swarmed around him and stopped him from returning to Ba'dān, so he remained in Dhamār. Among the troops whom Commander Khiḍr had got together was a person called Bālī Āghā, an evil chap much given to intrigue and one of the old Turkish commanders in Yemen. He was related by marriage to the Zaydī, had children by them and was intimate [16] with them. No trust had been placed in him when he came to the minister. For he was treacherous, frightened and on the look-out. However, he had approached Commander Khiḍr Bey and presented himself to him during the absence of the minister, who was preoccupied with the fight against Kawkabān.

Khiḍr Bey received him warmly and gave him every attention, taking him on to the sultan's wage-roll and into his confidence. He made him his confidant, companion and adviser, and appointed him agent for the Arab tribesmen.

Then he brought to Khiḍr Bey a group of Zaydī rebels and double-crossers who appeared to offer their submission; and he took them on the wage-roll and into his confidence. But this Bālī Āghā and his Zaydī companions were spies for 'Alī b. Sharaf al-Dīn against Khiḍr Bey about whose circumstances they were writing to him; and they were turning some of the troops against him till about 900 of the fighting Turks and tribesmen, feigning submission and sympathising with the rebels, adopted his position.

So Bālī Āghā sent a message to 'Alī b. Sharaf al-Dīn informing him that the 900 fighters supported him whereas Khiḍr Bey had only 150 fighting troops with him; and they asked 'Alī to come down from [404] Ḥabb fortress to fight since they would stand with him and get shot of the Turks to the very last man.[17]

Then 'Alī b. Sharaf al-Dīn sent messages to Jiblah, Ibb, Ba'dān, Banū Ḥubaysh and the people of al-Shawāfī to assemble on 17 Ramaḍān/23 February for battle with Khiḍr Bey. They should encircle him while 'Alī came down to them from Ḥabb fortress. So they accepted his order and were prepared for action. The majority of the tribesmen came out in rebellion, broke their agreement and blocked the roads. All the Turks who were isolated were slain and as many of them as possible were murdered.

On 27 Ramaḍān 977/5 March 1570, the rebel tribesmen arrived and surrounded Commander Khiḍr's camp while 'Alī b. Sharaf al-Dīn came down, and the battle began. There were 8,000 tribesmen, and with Khiḍr Bey there were 150 men but they stood firm for battle, with Commander Maḥmūd the Kurd on his right and Commander Aḥmad on his left; and the remaining Turks fell into line in front of and behind him.

They were certain they would die and approached martyrdom so as to gain places in Paradise. The battle drew out and the arrows flew. The blood of heroes flowed as a torrential stream. Every Turkish horseman had to face 100 and more misguided enemy horsemen. The enemy attacked on foot and on horseback, with spears and arrows, the dead as well as the fighting, in sections and as a mass; the battle raged; and every conceivable sacrifice was made.

Those martyred on the Sunnī side, Riḍwān[18] received into Paradise, while those heretics who died, Mālik was quick to convey to hell-fire. In the end the three commanders were slain in God's cause. They had created havoc among the enemy and cut down numbers by sword before each of them died a martyr and was admitted by Almighty God to gardens in Paradise under which rivers flow. May God be pleased with them and they with Him; and may He kindly let them look upon His noble face in the hereafter.

Of the noble troops about half were martyred after slaughtering many more than twice as many of the enemy. The remainder withdrew, striking the enemy with their swords [405] as they found a route for flight. Such is war: charge and retreat; retreat and charge; defeat and conquest; death and capture!

Whoever thinks he can experience wars and not be hurt is wrong-headed.

The Zaydī stole the equipment, arms and shields left in the camp and got hold of three large guns, as well as what goods, furniture and heavy loads they could find. Such is the way of the world and the way of errant and wicked time.

A day against us and a day for us; a day for us to to be hurt, a day for us to enjoy.

CHAPTER 53

[406] The minister's engagement with the massive disorder that had broken out in the country; the dispatch of commanders Shaikh 'Alī and Ṣafar Rayyis to look after Ta'izz and Aden; the dispatch of Qarah Kawz Bey, Barwayz Bey and Aḥmad al-Ṣawbāshī to fight the troublemakers in Naqīl Samārah; and the slaughter of the wretched heretics

§ Once news of the martyrdom of Khiḍr Bey and the Kurds Aḥmad and Maḥmūd reached the minister, he was very distressed. However, he did not display his distress to the troops to save them from fear and despair but convened his *dīwān*, with every appearance of confidence and lack of concern, with the words: 'H.M. the Great Sultan, Almighty God grant him victory and long rule over his kingdom, possesses in each part of his empire more than 1,000 mamluks better than Khiḍr Bey and Aḥmad Bey and Maḥmūd Bey the Kurds. And, by grace of Almighty God and the blessed noble sultanate, I am able to appoint from the military each day the equals of these commanders who have passed to the mercy of Almighty God. The sword of the sultan, God grant him victory, is long. I must cut off the head of ʿAlī b. Sharaf al-Dīn and capture the stronghold where he has fortified and protected himself. Once I am free of matters in Kawkabān and Thulā, then I shall eradicate the discord and rebellion.[19] When will the sun fail those who dye cloth?' 'Those who do wrong will come to know by what a [great] reverse they will be overturned.'[20]

> [407] Laylā will come to know what kind of debt she has taken on and what kind of adversary will sue her.

Then Ṣafar Bey the captain turned up, a brave and courageous sea captain, accompanied by 100 brave sailors. The minister made him *sirdār* over them, dressed him in an honorary robe and ordered him to go by way of Liʿsān[21] to Mocha. There he should take the grabs [coasting vessels] on the sea shore as far as Aden which he should defend against the enemy; for the defence of the port of Aden was of the greatest importance.

Then the minister summoned Commander Shaikh ʿAlī who was brave and brutal, with long experience in Yemen and one of its *sanjak* commanders. He had governed a number of its towns and knew the conditions and idiosyncrasies of the country, its roads, its river beds and its water holes. The minister gave him a detachment of 100 fighters and made him *sirdār* over them. He dressed him in a robe of honour and ordered him to go by way of Liʿsān to Zabīd, taking with him the troops who had come from Egypt; for fifty soldiers had arrived there from Egypt. He was to go with them to Taʿizz and defend it; and he was to defend al-Qāhirah, al-Taʿkar fortress and those districts.

Then he summoned Commander Barwayz who was a brave and courageous man of spirit, renowned in Yemen for his valour, courage and swordsmanship. He was also one of the old commanders in Yemen where he had held a number of posts: he had been commander of the Yemeni pilgrimage[22] and other such things. He attached to him Qarah Kawz Bey, previously mentioned in connection with the engagement with Qaṭrān and ʿAlī b. Nushayr; and he also attached to him Aḥmad al-Ṣawbāshī, one of the minister's mamluks, also previously mentioned in connection with the engagement with Qaṭrān. With them he attached cavalry and infantry, and awarded them honorary robes.

He sent an order to the *sanjak* with authority over Radāʿ,[23] Commander Aḥmad Bey, and another to the military commander with authority over Dhamār, ʿAbdī Bey, along with the military detachments of those commanders, to proceed in a troop and do battle with those wretched, filthy rebel tribesmen gathered in Naqīl Samārah. They should prepare the road for the passage of caravans and traders, make the districts secure, and calm their inhabitants,

[408] eradicating the basis of the rebellion, root and branch, and cutting off the heads of every open heretic they could. All of them then went off where he had directed and travelled with feelings of security, peace and triumph, and with the help of Almighty God.

As for Commander Ṣafar the captain,[24] he and his companions reached the port of Mocha where they found three grabs ready on the sea shore; so they dragged them to the sea and loaded them with the equipment, arms and guns and set off with them for Aden which they reached in safety. He and those sent with him stayed to look after and defend it by land and sea. They met neither harm nor wrong there. The minds of Aden's people and those of its districts were assuaged and assured as to the deceit and double-dealing of the enemy: they prayed for triumph and victory for H.M. the sublime sultan and the blessed minister, and for everlasting happiness, glory and victory.

As for Commander Shaikh 'Alī, he and his companions had travelled by way of Li'sān as far as Zabīd. There they saw the troops who had arrived from Egypt and whom the commander of commanders, Iskandar the Circassian, governor-general in Egypt, had equipped, without, however, paying their wages or taxes. He had said to them: 'When you have reached Yemen, the minister Sinān Pasha will pay your wages.' And he forced them to travel; and each of them was burdened with expenditure and spent everything that he owned, selling his weapon and his accoutrements. They reached Yemen without a penny to their name and stayed in Zabīd, eating like rats and living on debt.[25]

> I was like a lion, my food was what I hunted, but now I became like a rat and live by borrowing.

When Commander Shaikh 'Alī saw them in this state he was embarrassed by their situation and realised that they were not fit to travel. They had neither weapons nor anything in their hands. They were six months in arrears of wages; and there was no money to spend on them, either with him or in the Zabīd treasury, or with Sinān Pasha. So he sent a message to the minister advising him as to the position and waited for his esteemed reply with his instructions.

The report with details of the situation reached the minister but there was nothing in [409] his treasury which he could produce for spending on these troops, as has already been explained. So he pondered the matter and realised that he had some clothing and goods stored in Zabīd. He decided to let them have them although, in view of their requirements, there was not enough to spend on them. So he wrote to Commander Shaikh 'Alī with instructions to sell all the implements, clothing and furniture he had stored in Zabīd, get the proceeds, borrow what he could and spend all of it on the troops. He should arm them, giving to each of them a musket and gunpowder, to be provided for them from the armoury stored in Mocha. He should not delay and travel with them where directed.

When the minister's esteemed letter reached Commander Shaikh 'Alī, he started to sell the equipment. He sold it for a paltry price due to the dullness of the market, the paucity of demand and his need for the money. However, he did not hesitate in the business and raised a loan which, with the proceeds, he spent on wages for the troops for nine months. They were encouraged by that; and he then armed them, giving them muskets, and took them to Ta'izz, using them to guard Ta'izz and al-Qahīrah and its districts, and al-Ta'kar. He eradicated the rebel tribesmen from the area which was brought under control in accordance with the minister's arrangements, sound judgment and effective thinking.

Muslims were reassured; the populace gained confidence; and people relaxed in the security of the noble sultanate, praying for the continuation of the sublime sultanate, God make its shelter a comfort and a bounty.

As for Barwayz Bey, Qarah Kawz Bey and Aḥmad al-Ṣawbāshī, they and their companions reached Dhamār where they met 'Abdī Bey, *sanjak* of Dhamār, who was a brave warrior, together with the victorious sultan's troops and about 1,000 tribal fighters still under authority.

There were three places where the Zaydī rebels could be expected to gather, the first of which was Ba'dān, with 'Alī b. Sharaf al-Dīn; the second was Naqīl Samārah; and the third Yarīm.

[410] So they went to Yarīm where the Zaydī were collected, to be joined by people from Naqīl Samārah. There were about 10,000, divided between cavalry, infantry, musketeers and archers. They pounded the earth with their hooves and forced asunder the chain-mail circles of iron! They knew nothing of religion or the world; nor had they any intelligence or viewpoint. They had renounced God and his Prophet and taken over control; and they had submitted to the dreadful devil and violated the blood of Muslims and their property; and that is worse than to drink wine.

So the victorious army launched their attack against the enemy, with their banners spread out above them and wielding their famous sabres. Every horseman had his fervour and his spear as he blazed with his pride and his honour, his pace and his will, every racer his charging wings in his flying squadrons; everyone was true to his aim and fired his arrow right for the kill; everyone cut the enemy's head as he struck, returning blow for blow; every hero destroyed the worthless with true aim. No commander was slow to kindle his heroes, nor did his men offer him any delay. He had ignited the coals with all and attracted white, red, black and blond, with sabres cutting and horses whinnying.[26]

They came in a mass darker than pitch, deep enough to block the light, during a night of clamour, bright with star-like spears, before the battle morn revealed its sparkling sheets of metal. Lions approached lions; the strong urged to combat; the lancer drew his spears and hurled; the scabbard unsheathed its blade; the sea of armour surged with the hatred raging within the troops; the earth groaned with the striking of hooves and woke the sky to ease the force of its pain.

The strength of the clash turned from enemy chests to their backs as the killing and slaughter, the bloodshed and murder, moved from their van to their rear, till they turned their backs in flight and defeat. They abandoned themselves to flight from the greatest victory, showing their heels without thought for their end in the abyss left by the encounter.

The slaughter was tremendous and the carnage terrifying. Only the fall of night, with its curtain of darkness, saved the rest from the sword; only darkness, lowering over them its curtains of pitch, rescued them from the fire.

God gave victory to the Sunnī people and forsook the heretics and rebels, inflicting on them death, slaughter and capture on a grand scale. Thanks and praise to Almighty God for the outcome; and Muslims in the districts of Radā‘ and Dhamār were reassured. [411] Traces of the wretched heretical rebellion were severed as groups of them escaped from Yarīm and Naqīl Samārah. None was left save ‘Alī b. Sharaf al-Dīn and those from Zaydī tribes who had gathered with him in the fortified position of Ḥabb stronghold, in the principality of Ba‘dān. Details of the evil, defeat, slaughter, capture and disgrace that happened to them will follow; for that is the reward for sinners. Thanks to God, Lord of the worlds.

CHAPTER 54

[412] The reconstruction and fortification of the dismantled fortress of Shamāt; its safeguarding through the posting there of Commander Kulābī Bey; his removal from his threshold through Zaydī treachery and deceit

§ Among the collection of forts captured behind Kawkabān and Mt Tays was the fortress of Shamāt. It has been stated that its population had asked for protection which they were granted on condition they abandoned and destroyed the fort; for it was on the road to the base and its people were said to have been rebels and to have plundered the caravans bringing supplies to the sultan's army. When they brought news of its destruction, they had not finished the task; nor had they completely demolished it, but left some of its dwellings and walls. So the minister was afraid that the Zaydī would rebuild it at the nearest opportunity and restore its fortifications. It was possible that thieves within would prevent the caravans from returning to the base with supplies, with every requirement of the troops for supplies to be brought to them.

So he decided to rebuild and fortify it, and place there soldiers to ensure that the Zaydī did not lay their hands on it; and he appointed for the purpose Commander Kulābī Bey, a tall dolt of a man but courageous and brave who was extremely naïve. The minister had selected him for his courage without observing that he was rather a fool. He gave him a detachment of thirty soldiers, with muskets and weapons, gave him some cannon, and ordered him to rebuild that part of [413] Shamāt fortress that had been destroyed, and guard it.

Commander Kulābī had taken sufficient provisions and travelled to the place in question which he rebuilt and fortified, and where he remained as governor. That constrained and disheartened the Zaydī but the former population of Shamāt approached him, displayed their former submission and gave him a terrific welcome. They began to ingratiate themselves with him and asked to entertain him but all that was deceit, hypocrisy and lies.

They brought a great number of sheep and cooking utensils, and laid out a great cloth to which they invited him and his company; and he said to them: 'Come and be our guests in the fortress.' And they replied: 'Come out to us in the open where there is plenty of room for spreading out the food, and between us there can be bread and salt.' They slaughtered a lot of sheep, heated a lot of cooking pots and brought all sorts of food; and they continued to entice him until their copious flattery deceived him.

Because of his naïveté he was thus deceived and emerged with his companions after they had hesitated to come with him. He forced them into it, with the words: 'These people wish to meet and be behind us. Let us use them in our service. There will be no revolt or deceit from them.'

They were taken in, in the way he had been taken in, and emerged with him from the fortress into a broad area where they had spread carpets and decorations, calling out, 'Let us make today a day for relaxation and pleasure, for entertainment, happiness and joy. For how long can you be worried and anxious, constantly fighting, suffering and at war without taking a break from this upheaval with a day of ease and joy, pleasure, laughter and fun?' To which the Turks replied: 'Yes. We shall do that; and let us have a day when we'll have a bit of entertainment and a spot of fun and pleasure.'

A soul is refreshed by the atmosphere, don't give it cause for worry.
Perhaps time has caused you some harm, let not you and time suffer.

They did not realise that these words were as ointment hiding sores, that there was poison in the fat and fire in the coals. For Muḥammad b. Sharaf al-Dīn had sent from Kawkabān a group armed with guns who lay concealed from the Turks behind some hills; and that, when they were seated at the feast, [414] they would come out with guns and fire at Kulābī Bey.

Kulābī Bey had been chewing a choice morsel of meat which he was about to swallow when he was shot in the heart and at once fell prostrate on his face. He had met his appointed time and moved to the mercy of Noble God, transferred to stages of happiness. When his companions saw that he had passed away, they lost all control and began to split up and scatter. Some of them clung to their commander and took martyrdom in God's cause while others took to their heels in flight and roamed over the mountain side.

The tribesmen seized hold of what the Turks had brought to Shamāt fortress and went to extreme lengths of treachery and betrayal. The Turks used to be described as treacherous by the Arab tribesmen and were known for their double-dealing and trickery because of their occasional ill treatment in the past and their failure to keep their word. But the Zaydī tribesmen were now among the most treacherous of men on earth and were the most disloyal where all Arab tribesmen were concerned. They were regarded with contempt and shame and known for their sheer treachery for all time.

When the minister was told exactly what had happened, he displayed neither concern nor attention. Nobody referred to it; and it was completely ignored. None asked about it or gave it thought. But he maintained his pressure on Kawkabān and his constraint on its population through the siege, firing the great guns at them and seeking help from God, Unique and Triumphant, against those wretched heretics in waiting for the hour of victory and triumph.

CHAPTER 55

[415] Muḥammad b. Shams al-Dīn's displeasure at the length of the siege; his knocking at peace's door; and his submission after extreme ignominy and humiliation

§ An account has already been given of Kawkabān fortress, its height in the sky along with Saturn, and the deep encircling ditch or chasm[27] cut into the granite rock through the bottom of which there was an entry into the fortress; and how every time it was filled with stones and rocks, they would enter it from the bottom and take them out by the opening. There was despair over filling the ditch and they thought they would make a bridge from wood. Its pieces would be joined together by rivets, which they would place over the ditch at night. The troops would cross over it as far as the town wall which they would then climb by ladders without thought for being killed or fired at by the people in the stronghold. They would launch a single assault and capture the stronghold.

But the country was short of wood and timber and they had to go to the trouble of carrying long poles from Ṣan'ā' to the base at Kawkabān above; and they brought to them planks and timber, nails and iron hoops. They constructed a bridge of the same length as the width of the ditch, and went on with their task until it was complete. They carried it to the ditch at night and decided to put it over the ditch for them to cross over. However, the people in Kawkabān discovered the fact and brought the cannon and *ḍarbuzān* near to the ditch at which they began to fire, volley after volley. Meanwhile, the sultan's troops fired at them with cannon from outside the ditch and crawled with the bridge to place it over it.

Many from both sides were killed by the cannon. [416] After they had brought forward the bridge and placed it on the edge of the ditch, one of its ends broke and it fell inside! The task over which they had laboured was not complete; and they had lost a lot of money and numerous lives. So they returned to the base. But the minister was determined to construct another bridge, whatever the cost to him, and not to abandon the capture of Kawkabān. Once he arranged to dig a tunnel in the mountain to connect with the bottom of the ditch and thence to the fortress. This he would fill with gunpowder and set alight. However, boring a hole in the hard granite rock over that extensive distance required funds and equipment, so he directed the builder to construct a broad wall at the edge of the ditch behind which the troops could gather and construct another wooden bridge, without being hit by enemy gunfire.

When Muḥammad b. Shams al-Dīn heard about the minister's determination to take Kawkabān, and that he did not expect to draw back from it, however long it took, he realised that every besieger wins and every besieged loses.[28] So he began to knock at peace's door, to pay any price for submission and obedience, and to ask for protection. Towards that end, he put out feelers to find out what was in the minds of his associates and the people of his stronghold; for they had met and discussed the matter in secret. They reported: 'A large number of our commanders, leaders and men have been killed; and it is clear to us that this minister will definitely not leave us alone unless he and his companions cease to exist. You have learnt that we have not the strength to meet him, that his siege has lasted a long time, and that our weakness has grown. For those of them we have slain, replacements have come from Egypt. Only Almighty God can get rid of them.' And they agreed that some of their leaders should relate this to Muḥammad b. Shams al-Dīn, with the recommendation that he should ask for peace and urge submission.[29]

For this purpose they selected his minister, Muḥammad b. al-Ḥasan al-'Ayyānī, who approached Muḥammad b. Shams al-Dīn, with the message for him. 'A view has been expressed which I would like to convey to you.' And he laid it before him. To which Muḥammad b. Shams al-Dīn replied, 'Tell me what you have. Perhaps it will coincide with mine.'

So he went on: 'It is well known to you, that during the time we were subject to the Ottomans, we were extremely safe, enjoyed peace of mind and lived in bounty, the reason for which was our faith in ourselves, our children, our property and our people. Then discord broke out. We were ambitious to rule and we behaved arrogantly with the Turks around us; then Satan recommended that we rebel against the sultanate [417] and leave it. When we did so, the country became disturbed, people's blood was shed and some things went as we would wish, others did not. Events followed for which we were responsible before Almighty God and situations occurred in our time, the shame for which will last for ever.

'Then, when their sultan became annoyed with us, he sent his minister to us with these troops whom we have not the power to resist. Those *ashrāf* and commanders have been slain who are buried in the earth. They were the elite of the world and the flower of society. None of them is left save you. Your brother al-Hādī and your cousins have gone together with numberless of our own people and commanders; and the Turks will not leave us until they possess the country. So our opinion is that we save ourselves, our children and our property, enter within Ottoman jurisdiction and seek peace from them. Then we can relax in peace for ourselves, our servants and our people.'

Muḥammad b. Shams al-Dīn paid great attention to his speech, the content of which pleased him and accorded with his thought. When it was finished, he answered: 'By God, for some time I have been agitated by this opinion but kept it to myself for fear that I would be accused of cowardice and weakness. However, since I have been found to hold it, I must send you to the minister so that you can conclude the matter with him and agree a truce with him.' And they agreed upon it and parted on it.

Ḥasan Pasha's camp surrounded Kawkabān and had its stronghold under siege. He had there about 1,000 troops of every kind. All of them had stormed ahead with the siege throughout the war while the killing and fighting continued.

The minister's base was below Mt Kawkabān, and with him were the commanders and the rest of the troops. Every so often he would climb up the mountain and give them what orders he had to give and arrange what he had to arrange over the tunnel, the digging, the filling of the ditch with rocks and earth, the making of the bridge and such-like. Then he would return to the base. There was no flagging over the siege and the fighting but the troops with him had become lax; however, they were in awe of the minister and did not show their listlessness.

News of Muḥammad b. Shams al-Dīn's request for peace reached Ḥasan Pasha and some of the *sanjak* commanders but none of them was able to pluck up courage to report it to the minister. They wished to put it to him but they did not dare to do so.

Now Qadi Shams al-Dīn al-Sa'ūdī, the scribe, Almighty God preserve him, was imam to the minister and had access to him. [418] The minister treated him as a confidant, would talk to him at night and drink with him; and during their time together, he would put a number of ideas to him, seek his advice as to what he thought right, and would pay attention to what he said. He would be received by him, as he was informed as to his secrets and kept his affairs discreetly from strangers and those who were not privy to them; so one night the qadi said to the minister, having seen him complain as to the cruelty of time and his inability to attain what he desired, 'Let Almighty God lengthen the days of your state, minister, and ease every hardship and difficulty. I'd like to raise with you an important matter I'm afraid to put to you. I'm frightened that you'll rebuff me, or that I'll trouble you. Fear stops me from coming forward but sincerity prompts me to shoulder the task. I'm caught between two stools.'

Then the minister replied: 'Say what's in your mind. Don't be afraid; for I rely upon your sincerity and your friendship.' So he continued: 'Let God give victory to those who follow you, double your power and strength. It must be clear to your clear judgment and your sharp mind that the fortress of Kawkabān cannot be taken by force; nor can it be captured through attrition and conquest. We have no gunpowder left for the guns, and the roads have been cut and supplies are finished.

There are few troops as they are scattered throughout the country, some of them to keep an eye on the area that has been captured, others having been sent to subdue the rebels and those who plunder the roads. Others have been martyred in God's cause; yet others still have fallen sick and died or remain unwell; and others still have fled and moved far away from us. All we have left now are about 1,000 men, apart from the Arab tribesmen who are under our authority, the *du'āh* and such-like.

'The priority is now for me to write a letter to Muḥammad b. Shams al-Dīn with my advice. I shall remind him of our power and might and advise him to seek peace, submit to the authority of the sublime sultanate and obtain his release from this siege and protection for himself, his children and his people. This advice I have put before you since none of the commanders has the courage and pluck to tell this to Your Excellency.' The minister thought for a long time and, with his penetrating power of thought, realised that the argument was sound. So he gave him permission to put it into effect on his own initiative without informing anyone about it; so the qadi set to and, on his own initiative, wrote a letter to Muḥammad b. Shams al-Dīn as follows:

[419] In the name of God the Merciful and Compassionate.

Thanks be to God, Lord of the two worlds, prayers and peace be upon our most noble lord, Muḥammad, his family and his companions, this letter is from one devoted to God who takes shelter under his wing and gives advice for his sake and the family of his prophet, desiring to look upon his face, as God has said, Glory to him who said 'surely pure religion is for Allāh alone';[30] and as the Prophet said, religion is sincere advice.

Sayyid Muḥammad b. Shams al-Dīn, the peace, mercy and blessing of God be upon you. Let God remain in your mind and religion and arouse you from the sleep of negligence.

Understand, my brother, that you are observed by the Ottoman family whom kings and sultans obey and who rule most of the inhabited world. They have no shortage of people or funds. They are not in need of these lands. But their glory and honour has protected the honour of the Holy Shari'ah and supported the sublime Ḥanafī faith; and God by whom alone they have sworn not to withdraw from the fortress, and with him alone, even if they have to stay there for years. Their power and might, their strength and capability, and their conquest of kings, have no fear of you.

Now I give you this advice; and God is the best of witnesses. God has fated they take the fortress by force. That is very obvious. Then what a trial will befall its population! What degradation will fall upon those who are inside, the *ashrāf*, the high born, the women, children and men! What slaughter and capture there will be, what plunder and theft and disgrace among the tribes! Only the good-for-nothing would find satisfaction in that. Only the stupid and irreligious would not despise it. I implore God to reunite the two sides and reconcile you, for the good of the country and the people, and the preservation of blood, property and lives.

Sayyid Muḥammad, you are a man of intelligence; so pay attention to this letter, and write to H.E. the Minister, Almighty God grant him victory, seeking his protection now, forgiveness for what has happened in the past and submission to H.M. the Sultan, let Almighty God make his sultanate last for ever; and let your answer be given at once. So if you do this; for the minister is patient, I think that he will not reject your request but will stipulate that the sermon and currency be in the name of the sultan; and my view is that you answer at once and he will issue authority for you to have the standard your father[31] had in the past. When this happens, you should send someone you trust for the minister to meet and receive an honorary robe from him. Then you should meet him yourself and don the robes [420] of agreement.

And by God, again by God, I am giving you this advice, with love for the family of God's Prophet. Only God knows what is between us; and if you do what I have written to you and ask the minister's permission to stay in Kawkabān, he will not stop you, and will grant you all you wish. God speaks the truth and He shows the way.

When the scribe had finished the letter he put his seal to it and prepared it for Muḥammad b. Shams al-Dīn, and it reached him. He was delighted with it and replied to the scribe's letter as follows:

In the name of God the Merciful and Compassionate.

God bless our Lord Muḥammad, his distinguished family and his rightly guided companions. The peace and mercy of God and his blessing be upon the shaikh, the most illustrious, illustrious, perfect, ideal, noble, lover of the most noble members of the Prophet's house, rising star in the Two Cities, who acts upon His saying, 'Say, O Mohamed, I ask of you no fee therefore, save loving kindness among kinsfolk',[32] devoted to the good members of the Prophet's house, Jamāl al-Dīn Abū al-Sa'ūd the scribe, God give him happiness in the Two Cities etc.

We are informed as to the esteemed message and are clear as to the sound advice contained therein which satisfies his religion, his honesty, the sincerity of his convictions, the purity of his intention and his love for the people of his noble house.

Illustrious shaikh, you understand the true traditions for people of the Prophet's House such as that of the ship 'I am leaving with you what you should grasp so that after me you do not err' [*ḥadīth*] and 'every relationship and pedigree is broken save my relationship and connection'. Thank God Who has made the shaikh one of those who understand their truth and protects the meaning of kinship among them. All that he advises me in his message concerning blessed peace is agreed and is immediately acceptable.

Perhaps Almighty God will make peace between Muslims. We are of those who love peace and long for it; nor do we have any hesitation. You will have known the affection, sincerity and love which existed between our late father and Özdemir Pasha. When our father died,[33] Almighty God have mercy upon him, we made our uncle Fakhr al-Dīn Muṭahhar our father in place of him. He was our blessing and our mainstay. Peace will not be complete until he too has entered into peace with us as well. He is keen about it [421] and agreeable to it. So quickly arrange for peace also between him and the minister, so that peace can be complete, if Almighty God so wills. And thus Muslim blood can be saved.

We have arranged, for the completion of the business, our minister, Sayyid Muḥammad al-'Ayyānī, to go to the minister, God give him everlasting favour in this respect, and discuss with him some of the matters orally; for writing is not equal to the purpose. Let Almighty God choose for us and for Muslims what is for the general good and in the general interest, if Almighty God wishes and in peace.

Issued on 12 Holy Dhū al-Qa'dah, 977/18 April 1570.

Then Muḥammad b. Shams al-Dīn made ready his minister, Sayyid Muḥammad b. al-Ḥasan al-'Ayyānī, and Yāqūt al-Ḥibshī the drummer,[34] together with the letter he had written to him, as follows:

In the name of God the Merciful and Compassionate,

Thanks to God, Lord of the two worlds, and God bless his Prophet Muḥammad, his family and his excellent, pure companions.

His High and Noble Excellency, His Sublime and Mighty Presence, the Most Mighty, Noble, Magnificent, Glorious Blessed and Unique, who has acceded to the most glorious heights and received from the ministry its radiance, Sultanic Minister for Islam and Muslims, Executor for affairs and decrees in the two worlds, His Excellency Sinān Pasha, let God enhance his position and raise his power and status, we offer to his high presence and position, the most radiant peace and the most flattering greetings, respects and salutation.

We bring to his esteemed knowledge that the honoured and noble Sayyid Muḥammad b. al-Ḥasan al-'Ayyānī has been authorised to place before His High Excellency the message recorded, to be discussed orally with him, and to bring the reply to it; and we await the reaction to the meeting with His Excellency. It will be within his esteemed knowledge that high-minded people and the holders of important posts devote themselves to bringing peace to the country and the people, and long for the Muslim community to regain the peace and guidance it had in [422] life and the hereafter.

You will know only too well what is recorded in the *Saḥīḥ Muslim*.[35] 'For the world to cease is lighter for God than the killing of a Muslim.' And in the traditions, 'to spare the blood of a thousand is regarded as lighter than to shed sacred blood'. Within your noble knowledge are many such examples but Almighty God settles the affairs of all of us. Peace be upon Your Highness, and the mercy and blessing of God.

Issued by Muḥammad b. Shams al-Dīn on 12 Holy Dhū al-Qa'dah 977/18 April 1570.

So the two messengers arrived at the minister's base and those who were looking after them hurried with them to the noble pavilion. They were 'Alī Jiblī likalk and Ḥasan, the interpreter from Ḥasan Pasha's party laying siege to Kawkabān fortress. Their arrival at the minister's took place on 13 Dhū al-Qa'dah/19 April; and they handed the letters for him in secret to Qadi Muḥammad the scribe; and the qadi sought permission for them to enter from the minister who had secretly been on the look-out for the arrival of someone from Muḥammad b. Shams al-Dīn's base to seek peace. He was on tenterhooks over the business; however, he gave no impression of so being but, on the contrary, behaved haughtily and showed lack of concern although within himself he was quite different; and he deferred his reception of the visitors for a time.[36]

Then, after they had given up hope, the minister allowed them to enter. He was courteous with them, made them relax and treated them kindly. He dressed them in robes of *serāser*, entertaining them and ordering them to withdraw after he had taken Muḥammad b. Shams al-Dīn's letter. However, he did not read it in their presence, but sent them to the guest-house, and then invited them at night, talking and relaxing with them. And they explained to him that Muḥammad b. Shams al-Dīn had sent them so that, out of His Excellency's mercy, they should seek for him pardon and peace; and they should ask for protection for him, his property and his sons.

Muḥammad b. Shams al-Dīn would submit to the authority of the noble sultanate, a friend to its friends and an enemy to its enemies; and he implored that he would also give protection to his uncle Muṭahhar. He begged the minister to grant a pardon for him as one who had submitted to authority, a friend to the noble sultanate's friends and opposed to its enemies.

The minister hid from them his joy but agreed what they asked from him. He stipulated that Muḥammad b. Shams al-Dīn should give a hostage, either his son or brother, who would reside in Ṣan'ā', as the taking of hostages was customary with the people of the country.

This was agreed, and with that both sides expressed their extreme joy [423] and delight. And the minister dispatched with them someone to go to Muḥammad b. Shams al-Dīn and make him swear on a copy of the Quran that he would not act disloyally and that he was true outwardly and inwardly to the noble sultanate; and he should take the hostage from him. For the purpose, he appointed Qadi Muḥammad the scribe who went to Muḥammad with the two of them. And they set out on 12 Dhū al-Qa'dah/18 April.[37]

When Qadi Muḥammad the scribe reached Muḥammad b. Shams al-Dīn with the minister's letter, he was very much delighted at his arrival. He made a great fuss of him and was kind to him; and a contract for the truce was made between them. Muḥammad b. Shams al-Dīn wrote a resounding letter and swore to him on the Holy Quran; and he handed over to him as hostage his brother, Sayyid 'Abd al-Qaddūs who moved to Ṣan'ā' with his people, sons and family, and remained there as hostage. Muḥammad b. Shams al-Dīn sent to the minister a great deal of food, edibles and grain. The camp was filled with it and the victorious army was loaded with it, after the great dearth in the base and after the arrival of twenty camel loads of forage.[38] Thanks to God for this blessed peace.

Sinān Pasha bestowed on Muḥammad b. Shams al-Dīn a sultanic standard and registered sultanic credentials for him, on behalf of the noble sultanate, on one of the numbered documents sent to him from the Sublime Porte with the *ṭughrā'* of H.M. the Sultan on blank paper, for the minister to write what essential business he might wish during his blessed journey to the land of Yemen. A copy of what he wrote follows:

In the name of God the Merciful and Compassionate.

Thanks to God, Conqueror of hearts, Moderator of worries, Forgiver of sins Who has declared for him who who has sinned and erred, if he has repented, sought help for his sin and been afraid 'Allāh forgiveth whatever may have happened in the past'.[39] Prayers and peace upon our Lord Muḥammad, settler of the community's affairs and protector against every grief and affliction, sent to all the worlds as pardon, entrusted with the fulfilment and support of treaties, to whom was revealed, 'Fulfil the covenant of Allāh when you have covenanted, and break not your oaths after the asseveration of them';[40] and upon his family and companions, acting with God's guidance and devoting themselves to the security of His people and the repair of His country, we thank Him for including us with those to whom He declared in the holy declaration, 'We have set thee as a viceroy in the earth.'[41]

We have succeeded in establishing religion, in observing the Sunnah and religious duty, 'from the *jihād* in God's path to the Day of Judgment'; and we have been blessed [424] with the service of the two Holy Cities of Mecca and Yathrib.[42] To us have submitted most parts of the populated earth from the east to the west. We rule the capitals of the Turks, the two Iraqs, the Arabs and the Persians and have included within our empire the kings of Egypt, Syria, Iraq, Kurj, Turkey and Daylum,[43] and our troops have gained clear victory and firm and mighty conquest whereby they have followed and ruled, where they have cleared and shed blood and slaughtered; and, when they have fought the enemy, they have won, conquered and destroyed.

We thank Him for the compassion, kindness and goodness He has bestowed on us, as He has granted us victory over those who made their rebellion and tyranny plain, urged us to pave the way for justice which is the basis for prosperity, and has imposed on us the far-reaching aim of defending against tyranny, injustice and aggression. etc.

When it came to our noble ears, and was reported at the threshold of our Sublime Porte, as to how, in the land of Yemen, some of the mountain people had rebelled and departed from the ways of guidance for lawlessness and troublemaking, and how they had rejected our authority and come out in revolt, and had terrorised the country and people, especially so far as he and his father were concerned, who had throughout his life till his death been under the authority of our father, the blessed martyr sultan, the sovereign victorious king, Sulaymān Khan, God bathe his time with mercy and compassion,

and when the kingdom came into our noble grasp and we inherited the earthly possessions through the kindness and generosity of God, the sons of theirs did not follow the path of their fathers in submission but withdrew their hands from the community, received our noble directions with neglect, and fought with our mighty army in those regions, abandoning subjection to God, His prophet and those who rule, and evincing an absolute aversion to the Ḥanafī faith,

then we were obliged by our far-reaching aim to check the troublemakers and curb the rebellious faction, and to assure the security of humanity and calm the populace who had been entrusted to our care by Almighty God, defending them from oppression and easing their lives in the shade of our noble state, and letting them enter the extensive protection of our justice.

So issued our noble and undisputed order, our lofty and far-reaching edict, to our esteemed minister, our magnificent guide, the mighty seat of the constitution, manager for the affairs of nations, fighter in God's cause, upholder of the word of God, executive for men's affairs with his strong intelligence, solver of the people's affairs with his sound judgment, intimate with the affairs of court of the illustrious king, Sinān, [425] long live his justice and let his heart rejoice.

So we appointed him *sirdār* of our victorious army, provided him with our troops to render victory and joy and instructed him to put right the damage to matters in the land of Yemen by extinguishing the fire of suffering and revolt that had broken out there.

But when the mounted forces of our ministerial counsellor reached those regions, Muḥammad b. Shams al-Dīn set out to resist him but was worsted in the advance of our victorious army until they laid him under siege in Kawkabān fortress and everywhere had him hard pressed. Then he took alarm at the strength of our weapons and asked for protection. His weakness became clear, and he asked to return to God the Generous, and repented. He deferred to the authority of our triumphant state and acknowledged his error. He sought refuge with this minister of ours and sought his good offices at our noble gate, asking that he should obtain the honour and dignity his father had held.

So when our minister understood the reality of his situation and received his reassurance that he would refrain from his misdeeds and outrageous behaviour, he made him subject to pacts and agreements and imposed on him conditions and limits including the surrender of one of his brothers as hostage with us in the fortress citadel at Ṣan'ā'. The hostage was to be the eldest of his brothers, 'Abd al-Qaddūs, to reside there in honour and dignity, in turns with his brother, 'Abdullāh, on whatever basis their brother, Muḥammad, should choose and decide. Another condition was that we should retain the stronghold of al-'Arūs and the countryside connected with it, in return for the standard he would be granted and which would make him an object of honour among men.

Our enemies must be his and our allies his. He must be at peace with those at peace with us, and at war with those at war with us. Should any of our troops flee to his side, he should return them to us. Neither he, nor his brothers or supporters, should enter into friendship with Muṭahhar, either secretly or openly, as long as he remained in rebellion and beyond the pale.

We have authorised and approved this treaty and truce proposed to us in draft by our minister and awarded to Muḥammad b. Shams al-Dīn the area his father had, that is Mt Tays, the territory of Shamāt, al-Ṭawilāh[44] and Bayt 'Izz and, with genuine good-will and general kindness, granted him an annual stipend of 600,000 ottomans [*'uthmānī*]; and we have made him maintain the same obligations of fealty and submission to our noble state held by his father.

We have directed that this notice be put into effect and that it be accepted and obeyed, in its exact terms or meaning; and we have applied our noble cipher above, as guarantee of its authenticity.

[426] Issued 10 Dhū al-Ḥījjah 977/16 May 1570.

Then 'Abd al-Qaddūs, Muḥammad b. Shams al-Dīn's brother, arrived to meet the minister who awarded him an honorary robe and undertook what was due of him. He then prepared him for Ṣan'ā' to reside there. The situation was under control; the problems ceased and an end was put to the war and fighting. God is to be thanked for calming the unrest, for arranging matters in the land of Yemen and for removing the trials and tribulations; for He is generous and merciful to mankind, kind and open-handed.

CHAPTER 56

[427] Muṭahhar's earnest appeal to the minister for peace and submission, to show fealty and regret, and to renounce resistance; the minister's agreement to his request after repeated demand

§ After peace had been established between Muḥammad b. Shams al-Dīn and the minister, and established on a handsome basis with the best of provisions, aspirations were satisfied, and peace and quiet were general; agreeable conditions obtained, hearts were calm and souls at rest; and north and south were in clover. Then did Muṭahhar's spirits burn and blaze, and his anxiety raged with pangs of fear and failure; for he realised that he was caught beyond doubt and that any of his tricks or wiles were of no avail. So bitterly he knocked at the door of peace and displayed his impotence, sorrow and contrition.

But the minister made no answer to Muṭahhar's request, as he placed no trust in what he said because of his repeated treachery, deceit and deception. In his doubt over helping his distress and his distrust of what he had said, as with the liar who appeared at the entrance to his house, shouting at the top of his voice, 'Muslims, fire! fire in my house! Almighty God have mercy on you', so that all should run to him with a full water skin, an iron pick or something, to put out the fire and destroy the part of the house in flames. But they did not find anything, so they returned, sorry that they had left their beds and run about in the roads in the stones and mud. [428]

He and they went through the same procedure; and they realised that he was a liar as his lies were famous among them. Then one night Almighty God fated that his house should catch alight; and he went up to the roof and began to shout at the top of his voice, 'Fire, fire!' and it was for real! But nobody came to his aid. People just laughed at his shouting and scoffed at him. He continued shouting until the fire caught him and he burnt. So that is why those with sense stopped people from getting used to telling lies, so that it should not become a habit; and then none believed him although it was true.

So, when Muṭahhar repeated his request for peace, and the minister gave no response to his request, he clung to the skirts of his nephew, Muḥammad b. Shams al-Dīn, sending a messenger to him to convince him in the matter; and Muḥammad sent another with that of Muṭahhar to the minister, entreating him, on behalf of his uncle Muṭahhar, to agree to his request, accept his regrets and let him enter the sultan's authority. He pledged as surety for Muṭahhar himself, his wealth, his children and his country, so that Muṭahhar should be included within the noble sultanic protection and that the sermon and the currency be in the name of the great sultan, Almighty God give him victory.

Muḥammad b. Shams al-Dīn had dispatched his relative and brother-in-law, Sayyid Muḥammad b. al-Ḥasan al-'Ayyānī, with his letter to the minister, and this Sayyid Muḥammad b. al-Ḥasan was a man from a fine and kind family, of handsome behaviour, happy mien, pedigree and descent.

A copy of the letter which the envoy brought from Muḥammad b. Shams al-Dīn:

> In the name of God the Compassionate and Merciful, thanks to God, Lord of the worlds, the prayers of God on our lord the Prophet Muḥammad and all his companions, and fragrant and absolute peace which continues to cast its excellent breeze over the noble presence,
>
> the highest, most excellent, mighty, glorious and unique and treasured excellency, commander of great commanders, greatest of ministers in magnificence and glory, of the highest of all degrees who merits honours and radiance

from the ministry, secretary to the sultan of Islam and Muslims throughout the empire, who undertakes the good of the community in all cities, helped by God Whose help is sought, the mighty minister, Sinān, God increase his standing and glory and inspire his good judgment and justice, to whose distinguished seat [429] and high and noble position is addressed

the issue of this statement, containing his serious opinion and honoured and clear belief, that our elder Fakhr al-Dīn Muṭahhar has entreated you, by my intercession out of my love for you, to accept his apology for his past errors; for Almighty God gives pardon for sins. He is happy with what is to be accomplished by Sayyid Muḥammad b. al-Ḥasan al-'Ayyānī concerning the restoration of the noble Ottoman law and his submission to its sublime authority. I who love you have received a letter from this venerable sayyid, let God extend his life for us, so that he can remain of value to this noble Sayyid Muḥammad.

For there is no doubt that your noble excellency has the welfare of Muslims in his heart as is the custom of people of high rank and high-minded aims concerning the welfare of the world and religion, and which our elder Muṭahhar clings to, Almighty God preserve him, in accordance with the former practice between him and the early pashas. For he has been faithful to such, until the violation occurred on the part of Riḍwān Pasha.[1] Then occurred what took place among popular hooligans and troublemakers while Muṭahhar maintained his customary behaviour in self-defence. Nothing else happened. Were normal conditions to have resumed, security would have have been restored to its normal state, and the struggle and the insolence would have been lifted.

Both of us, as Almighty God knows, will exert every effort, for the good of Muslims, to extinguish the blaze of rebellion, by putting out its flame, if Almighty God so wills; for Almighty God is responsible by virtue of the Quran and the lofty position of the Prophet, for gathering hearts to His satisfaction, and for extinguishing the fire of rebellion through the relief of His kindness and approval, and complete peace, and the general prayers of the noble pasha, and the mercy and blessing of God.

This is issued on 20 Dhū al-Hijjah, the last month of 977/26 May 1570.

When the minister was informed of this letter, and that of Muṭahhar, he took counsel with the army chiefs and community commanders, who were tired of fighting, had had their fill of battle, and realised that peace was in the best interests of all, especially after repeated requests and degradation. Then all advised acceptance and were happy to have the requested peace. So H.E. the Minister was made absolutely certain of their support and gave his complete approval to their wishes. He agreed with them in the matter and dispatched to Muṭahhar [430] the great commander and perfect horseman,

Maḥmūd Bey, lord of a sultanic brigade, and the noble and most honoured commander, Muṣṭafā Bey al-Rumūzī,[2] treasurer of the state of Yemen, so as to make Muṭahhar take an oath on the Holy Quran and reach blessed peace with him. And he wrote a letter for them to take to Muṭahhar, a copy of which follows:

> In the name of God the Compassionate and Merciful, thanks be to God and peace on those who follow the true path. The most learned to cast light on the pages of existence and the most magnificent flower to scent the world with its calyx and blossom thanked God Who has succeeded in bringing to His guidance those men of integrity He loves and removing them from wrong by selecting them for His favour, from the path of error; and peace and prayers upon the Prophet the suns of whose message have shone and illuminated the corners of existence; and the moons of his guidance have risen and filled with justice every being, and upon his family and companions the guidance of mankind, lights for darkness and the stars of the right path to lead away from error and sin.
>
> And so to continue. So after you knocked at the door of peace with your sparkling letter, and repeated such a request in bright language, turning away from the revolt of which you have been accused towards friendship and harmony, and entrusted yourself to your nephew, Sayyid Muḥammad b. Shams al-Dīn, displaying obedience to the sultan of sultans; then we gave our agreement to that, and acceded to your request and hope.
>
> We have furnished for you two great and mighty commanders, Maḥmūd Bey and Muṣṭafā Bey, commanders of a sultanic province and lords of a noble Ottoman *sanjak*, to swear with you on the Holy Quran and make a kind and blessed contract, to the effect that the sermon[3] and currency throughout Yemen will be in the name of His Majesty the great *Khunkyār* [sovereign khan] Almighty God give him victory, make his noble rule everlasting and extend his ample and broad shade; and to the effect that all the area conquered by his former commanders shall return to his noble possession as it was formerly; and that thirty men with pay shall reside in the stronghold of Ṣa'dah while the town will remain yours on the understanding that you hand over every instalment of its tax to the noble sultan's agents; and any delay in an instalment will be followed by the dismissal of the person responsible there, and he will have no authority afterwards. Al-Ṭawīlah, with its surrounding area, will be ours as will [431] the area of al-Ẓāhir, 'Amrān and its districts.[4]
>
> All that was formerly under the noble sultan's control will return to us. You shall release those commanders who have been imprisoned; and, as for the castle of Ḥabb and those who have taken control of it, the matter will remain between ourselves and those rebels inside it. God will decide between us, and He is the best of rulers. However, we insist that you give no assistance to those

within; neither do you correspond with or support them. The sultan's sword is long; and God speaks the truth and points the way.

Issued on 15 Dhū al-Hijjah 977/21 May 1570.[5]

So, Muṭahhar was delighted at the arrival of the two commanders, and went outside the stronghold (of Thulā) to meet and welcome them. He was extremely generous with them and entertained them, bringing them gifts; and he was generous and kind with their servants, making a kind of apology for his former behaviour during the rebellion and fighting. He swore on oath that all of that was without his orders, and without his knowledge and complicity. They accepted his apology and were satisfied with his admission and denial.

Accept apologies from him who brings them, whether he is truthful in what he says to you or lying.
He who pleases you on the surface has honoured you, and he who opposes you in secret has obeyed you.

Then Muṭahhar gathered his relatives and his household, his servants and his suite; and, fetching the two commanders and their attendants, he had a large feast spread out. Then he brought a copy of the Holy Quran and the two commanders made him swear as to the contents of the minister's letter. So he took such an oath for them among those gathered and donned an honorary sultanic robe.

Assent was reached; agreement was obtained. Discord was lifted; hypocrisy ceased. And the two commanders returned to the minister and informed him as to what had happened down to the last detail. Both sides were filled with delight and joy. Thanks to Almighty God all trouble and distress had ceased, and thank God, Lord of the worlds.

CHAPTER 57

[432] The minister's return to Ṣan'ā', news of the arrival of Behrām Bey and the battles that occurred during that period

§ It is known that, after the completion of the peace agreement with Muḥammad b. Shams al-Dīn, and his uncle Muṭahhar, the minister returned to Ṣan'ā'[6] with the army where he pitched his mighty camp and began to send troops to the outlying districts to restore peace. Now the new governor-general whom the sultan, God bring him victory, had appointed to the province of Yemen in place of Ḥasan Pasha, had arrived at Zabīd at the beginning of Dhū al-Ḥijjah/7 May. He was a commander of mighty commanders, a man who put orders and decisions into effect, gifted in the use of sword and word, the mighty pasha Behrām, who was ever victorious with the noble royal armies. He was an excellent young man of virtue and talent, of good judgment and organisation, and of good character and much intelligence.[7] His father, the late Muṣṭafā Pasha, known as Qarah Shāhīn, was one of the governors-general of Yemen, and his brother, Riḍwān Pasha, Almighty God lengthen his days, was governor-general of Yemen also; and reference to both of them has already been made.

When Behrām Bey was appointed governor-general of Yemen, he decided to travel there from Egypt where Iskandar Pasha the Circassian was governor-general, formerly lord of Diyār Bakr and Wān,[8] who had been unconcerned over sending Behrām Pasha and had not prepared for him the forces as was necessary. He had given him a detachment of only 600 soldiers, recruited in Egypt from those without weapons or strength. He had provided them with just enough cash [433] for their journey to Zabīd. They lingered long on the way, consumed all they had with them and sold their clothes. By the time they reached Zabīd they were naked, hungry and poor, destitute of everything.

Behrām Pasha was embarrassed by the situation but did not find in Zabīd any sultanic funds to spend on the troops; so he went with them to Ta'izz where the governor was Shaikh 'Alī,[9] one of the *sanjaks* released in Kawkabān, as has already been indicated. The minister had been kind to him, strengthening his position and appointing him *sanjak* of Ta'izz.

When Behrām Bey reached him, Shaikh 'Alī met and received him, and collected all the Yemeni army at his disposal, some 800 cavalry. He also mustered about 700 of the infantry fighters along with their muskets and swords. When the Arab rebels heard about them, they rallied together, the tribes mustering and gathering in Naqīl Aḥmar while Behrām and his troops mustered in al-Qā'idah.

As the Arab tribesmen understood that the Turks were weak, which was the opposite of the truth, they came down from the mountains for the fight and were seen to race to battle. Then the Turks came out against them, on their horses, piebald, chestnut and black, racing among them like ships in a battle at sea. Behrām Bey began to encourage them and goad them on, encouraging them and enthusing them against the rebels till the fighting became fierce; and the truth was revealed. Precious souls were lost as army was enmeshed with army.

Then Behrām Bey took up the sharp sword with his attendant troops, without pausing to wait for the rest of the army. Spirits were about to expire;[10] and daggers were thrust into bodies. Battle was joined; fighting was interlocked. People advanced; battle reigned. Swords were gorged with blood; and enemy bodies were impregnated with spear poles as heads bore fruit and became pregnant.

The hungry bird hovered rapacious above the enemy heads and the eagles of death swooped down.
Blue arrows had more than their fill and eastern steel disowned its scabbard.
Many were the young whose lives were ended by the sword. Many were the old whose white beards were darkened by blood.
Their corpses had filled the field which its birds and jackals had divided.
Jihād, by God's command, in the victory of His religion and in the power of generous God, in anticipation of His reward!

[434] Swords became blunt as spears engaged throughout the fight, from beginning to end of the day; then, when the sun returned his sword rays to their sheath and replaced his burnished blade in the scabbard of his setting, did the wretched enemy army withdraw, broken and blunt, under the skirts of darkness, protected by the lowering of darkness's curtain from the eyes of the horsemen, whose eyelids were smeared with the black of kohl.

The enemy were only saved by withdrawal while the victorious army maintained its place and lit its fires to display the blessing of victory and triumph. They counted the enemy dead which exceeded 160 in number. The rest of the fighters had scattered among the mountains and were of no avail; and the heads of the dead were hoisted on the spear tips as hands were clapped to frighten the enemy on their way; and the song of victory was sung:

They said that he pierces two knights with one stroke on the day of fury, and you do not see him weary,
and in answer, I declared he could pierce a line of knights, a mile in length.

In complete victory and triumph, and with the defeat and rout of the enemy, the defeated went up to Naqīl Aḥmar[11] with the mighty army in pursuit. But they were unable to climb the mountain; nor to ascend such peaks, because of the difficulty of the road and the roughness of the approach, and because of the large rocks rolling over them as the enemy hurled stones at them from the mountain above.

So H.E. Behrām Pasha pitched his tents and formed his encampment by the *naqīl* [pass]. He dispatched a report to the minister, telling him of his great victory and mighty conquest and thanked Almighty God for such a great blessing and marvellous fortune. He apologised to the minister for his failure to reach him and reported his circumstances and what had happened to him. And he asked the minister for troops to help him achieve victory over the remaining enemy, so as to eradicate them from the face of the earth, without trace.

The minister was delighted at the messenger's arrival with the letter, and his anxiety over his business and affairs lifted. He thanked Almighty God for

His beneficence and help, and for His favour and benevolence. Then he prepared a magnificent honorary robe for Behrām Pasha, as he was pleased with him and held him in good [435] favour. He assigned him some brave commanders, men of knowledge and experience in fighting mountain people of trickery and deceit. The commanders were Barwayz al-Farīs (the knight), the courageous champion, Aḥmad Bey, *sanjak* of the region of Radā', and 'Abdī Bey, famous in those parts for his courage; and he appointed, as commander-in-chief over them, the great commander Maḥmūd Bey.

Then they assembled with their troops and people and arrived at the minister's *dīwān*. The minister greeted them with kindness and gifts and gave them honorary robes and presents, encouraging them and increasing their pay; and their spirits revived. They left him in glory and honour, accompanied by good luck, blessing and peace.

When they reached Naqīl Aḥmar they found it overrun with rebels and full of agitators and scoundrels. They did not find within themselves the strength to drive them from the road because of the rough and difficult ground, and the defile, so they sent off to the minister a request for reinforcements with whom to drive off such an enormous mass of enemy forces. Even if the enemy had had their hands tied and the mighty army had been ordered to execute them, they would not have been able to carry it out. And how? For the Zaydī had different kinds of weapons, muskets and gunpowder. Only God in His glory and majesty would have defeated them, and no mortal could overcome these people, and scatter them and tear them to pieces.[12]

CHAPTER 58

[436] The minister's dispatch of troops with Ḥasan Pasha in support of the commanders who had gone to H.E. Behrām Pasha's aid, the defeat of the enemy troops, the meeting of the troops with Behrām Pasha and the taking of hostages from the Arab tribesmen

§ The report by Maḥmūd Bey and the other commanders whom the minister had sent to help Behrām Pasha reached him, telling of their failure to reach Behrām Pasha owing to the large number of tribesmen whom only Almighty God could count in Naqīl Samārah,[13] together with their request for further troop reinforcements to climb this pass. Now the minister was angered by the news, and dispatched a reprimand over their failure to carry out his instructions.

He wrote to them, disparaging the number of Arab tribesmen who, because of their treachery, had fallen victim to cowardice and lassitude; for the traitor is fearful. He encouraged and heartened them; and, as reinforcement, he dispatched to them a party of his mamluks, augmented by an attachment of troops, and placed as commander-in-chief over them Ḥasan Pasha. He equipped and prepared them, with care, instructions and help; and they travelled, guided over the right course, impatient and braced to meet the enemy.

On reaching the commanders, they launched a single attack against the enemy. They came at them like thirsty camels and did justice to their encounter with the swords with which they wore them down, with the spears with which they put them to flight, with the swords, burnished like the sun, with which they beguiled them and through the destruction to which they led them. Each of them stopped them in their tracks with his arrows and blinded them with the sand-haze from his horse on whose withers he crouched. They drove the enemy masses from their position and gave them a taste of hell-fire from their muskets as they chased them to the very depth of humiliation. [437] The evil they had brought upon themselves from their rebellion had engulfed them; so they fled to the four winds, scattering in every direction, disappearing without trace.

The mighty army continued its way down from Naqīl Aḥmar,[14] the focus for victory, triumph and peace, until they came in sight of Behrām Pasha's base and met his troops with delight and joy. They met the commanders and the governor-general in happy intimacy and thanked Almighty God for the defeat of the rebels, the rout of the revolting tribal troublemakers. There were repeated entertainments and mighty banquets, to display joy at the victory over the enemy and the reunion of friends and loved ones. And that continued for days.

Then they travelled to the district of Ba'dān and invited the Arab tribesmen of those parts to become subject to the sultan, stipulating that the shaikhs of each tribe provide hostages, as is the custom in those lands, and that the hostages be imprisoned in Ṣan'ā'. They remained on such business until they had taken hostages from about 100 tribes, all of whom they took over and introduced to the fold. They took over hostages from the shaikhs on whom they could rely, and only a few of those who had been in revolt refused to provide them; and they were far away from the noble sultanic lands.

The roving tribesmen and the victorious army began to seize them till they had put them out of range, and they had gone off to their mountains and distant strongholds. The rebellion had died down completely in those parts and, of the rebels, only 'Alī b. Sharaf al-Dīn remained, indeed well and soundly fortified within Ḥabb castle.

Then the victorious sultanic army proceeded to lay siege to that sturdy fortress; and victory is in the hands of Almighty God Who bestows it on those He pleases, and the issue is for those who fear God.

One of the wonders of Almighty God's dispensation are the seven regions into which the inhabited portion of the globe is divided, raised from the surface of the oceans which surround the earth, each region being related to one of the seven moving stars; and the region of Yemen is related to the planet Saturn. Now Saturn is a planet the effect of which we feel through Almighty God and which can be appreciated in revolution, evil, killing and the like. So it is less often that these areas are free from revolt, due to that stellar effect, coming through Almighty God's decree and ordained by the Mighty and Knowing One.

CHAPTER 59

[438] H.E. Behrām Pasha's journey with his military detachment, on the minister's orders, to capture the castle of Ḥabb; the minister's arrival at Dhamār to be near him; the defeat of ʿAlī b. Shuwayʿ and ʿAlī b. Ḥusayn and their Zaydī companions; the death of ʿAlī b. Sharaf al-Dīn; and the taking of Ḥabb castle with the help of Almighty God, and His victory and clear triumph

§ When they had overcome the Arab tribesmen of those parts and taken their hostages, save for those who had made themselves scarce and scattered, and were far from village or settlement and house of mud or stone, the minister gave orders to Behrām Pasha and the Islamic forces with him to go and lay siege to ʿAlī b. Sharaf al-Dīn the Imam, who was fortified in the castle of Ḥabb. They should inflict the utmost damage on him and revenge those late commanders who had treacherously lost their lives there, Almighty God have mercy upon them and let fall on their remains the eternal rain of mercy and pardon, and place their spirits inside a green bird[15] to reside under the throne of God, and roam where they wish in Paradise in nobility and glory.

So H.E. Behrām Pasha left to carry out this task, accompanied by his military detachment. He made his base under the castle of Ḥabb, encircling it and pitching by it his mighty tents and pavilions. With it he engaged the heretics into the strictest form of *jihād* and sent a request to the minister that [439] his noble encampment to be near to, and not distant from, his own so that he could seek his advice and help; thus he would be encouraged and not be isolated.

So the minister departed from Ṣanʿāʾ and camped at Dhamār. From proximity to the settlement of Dhamār he would be within sight and earshot of Behrām Bey's camp.

An account of the stronghold of Ḥabb has already been given, with its difficult access and height, the way it touched the constellation of Gemini with its ranges and spurs, and the failure of the upper stars to reach the height of its circlet of bastions and strongholds. It had never been taken by force; nor had any king been able to capture it. Indeed, Maḥmūd Pasha[16] and others had taken it through treachery, trickery, deceit and cunning but, if God decided something, He prepared the way for it. When He ordained something, He made it and opened its door.

Among the causes was the fact that a Turkish qadi and a *shaflūt* tripeseller were captured by the Zaydī and kept as servants in Ḥabb castle as is the practice with Turks who are imprisoned; and their cell was near the gunpowder store. So the qadi and his companions thought up a stratagem through which they would contrive to blow up the gunpowder. And they saw a fissure in the upper part of the cell; so they took a cat, to the tail of which they tied a long fuse, the end of which they set alight. They then lifted the cat to the fissure within the cell and pushed it into the store. It ran through, with the lit fuse, on to the loads of gunpowder, and the fire took hold. It took away a side of the stronghold and raised it to the clouds in the sky! The entire mountain was convulsed in a colossal quake and many of the buildings were destroyed. All of the gunpowder went and with it the back of the people in the castle was broken. They knew that they were taken and realised who had done that to them.[17]

So they took the qadi and his friend and trussed them up by the shoulders and legs, deciding thus to punish them. Then they bound them up as tightly as they could in that position, and rolled them from the heights of the mountain to its foot. They were shattered and their remains disintegrated. But they resigned themselves to God and bore it; nor did they perish without donning the glory of compassion; and they were transported from the bottom of the mountain to the highest heaven through stages in Paradise, victorious in the rank of martyrdom and compassion and attaining the highest approval and mercy from God the Merciful and Compassionate.

This glad news reached the mighty, high and honoured minister to coincide with his noble dismounting in Dhamār. [440] It was received with the utmost delight and was a sure signal of victory and triumph, indicating God's mercy on those pious martyrs; for they knew that they were in Paradise and the wonder of the hereafter.

Then the minister sent off to the Governor-General of Yemen, Behrām Bey, and the military detachment with him, urging them to surround and encircle the castle of Ḥabb so that gunpowder should not reach the people in the castle from outside. They obeyed his order and reinforced their encirclement of the castle but those inside became aware of the fact and were put on their guard.

ʿAlī b. Shuwayʿ and ʿAlī b. al-Ḥusayn were hidden in the environs of Radāʿ

among rebel tribesmen and errant Zaydī; and they had loads of gunpowder with them which they intended to get to ʿAlī b. Sharaf al-Dīn in the castle of Ḥabb to replace the gunpowder in his possession that had been exploded. The minister was aware of the situation, and sent to Behrām Bey a couple of his personal mamluks, known for their bravery and horsemanship, ʿAlī Ṣawbāshī and Aḥmad Ṣawbāshī.

They were horsemen famous for bravery, fortitude and strength, of seasoned swordsmanship and horsemanship, lethal to their opponents. With them the minister included 300 horsemen. He had picked the best of the troops and selected the pick of the elite. He raised their spirits, selecting both horses and mares for them, and awarding them the best of pay. He armed them with instructions and directions, with words of encouragement and support, bade farewell and saw them off.

They began to strike the ground and make the stones ring with their horses' hooves. They raced on with their journey as voices mingled with whinnies and the wide beds of the wadis ran with the *rakūb* [mounted section]'s embrace. They aimed for the sky, then borrowed from its stars the slender spear points. They tore out the earth with the force of their steel horseshoes. They kept to their way, driving the dust like a banner above them; they continued their course with the help of lightning flashes, and struck on like the swing of a sword in its flashing and light. On they went, as they sped to higher things, in the company of victory and conquest, till they had wrought disaster, in the pitch-dark night, on ʿAlī b. Shuwayʿ and ʿAlī b. al-Husayn; and they drove towards them and their rebel companions, invoking their death.

The mighty army made a great advance and hurled at the enemy stone and iron. They flayed them with their batons, with punishing blows, and their sides ached and hearts fell. [441] Those who could, escaped; and those who were not hit, fled. The remainder became prey for swords, then beasts. Their arms and old equipment were plundered as they flew pell-mell in all directions and were scattered to the four winds without leaving behind any sign or trace.

The victorious sultanic army then returned, the sovereign's banners of glory flying above them, with heads raised on their spears and the plundered horses and arms. The faithful were happy with God's victory and calamity was the lot of the heretics and misguided. The roots of the outrageous and terrible rebellion had been cut. Then the minister thanked Almighty God and, before his Creator, gave vent to words of impotence and shortcoming, recognising the blessing and many favours of Almighty God; and he abased himself before High and Mighty God, yielding to His strength and power and recognising that God is in all respects omnipotent.

And to complete the victory for Glorious and Excellent God, to shout the signs of God's power, for the mighty and felicitous minister in his reconquest of the lands of Yemen in their entirety, remained the destruction of 'Alī b. Sharaf al-Dīn. He was in his fortified castle in a place where birds cannot reach and even imagination refrains from a visit. He had adopted al-Iklīl [a star in Scorpius] as rival, al-'Ayyūq [Capella] as companion, al-Jawzā' [Orion] as belt and al-Jabhah [the brow of Leonis] as forehead,[18] but when God commands and prepares the means, and ordains something, its difficulty is overcome and the truth disclosed.

> You will not be far from achieving what was hard when fate obliges; and if God does not protect you from what frightens you, then neither stronghold will be a defence; nor armour a curtain.

The outcome of the story, in which trifles filled hearts till they were sick, was that there were two *shafālīt* among 'Alī b. Sharaf al-Dīn's intimates who were very close to him and enjoyed access so that he trusted them with his food and drink; and he had drunk a great deal and was still intoxicated. They had been at his service throughout the war, their names being Nuqayr and Buayr; and one of them went down to H.E. Behrām Pasha, obtained access to him and confided, 'I have a secret', and Behrām allowed him to sit.

Then he said to him: 'I will feed 'Alī b. Sharaf al-Dīn with poison for you. [442] What shall I have from you?' Then Behrām Pasha replied: 'You will have from us dignity and respect. We shall give you any important position you wish for.' So the man said: 'We are two servants in the service of this man. We have agreed to poison him and we have prepared for him a poisoned quince. When he sees it, he will take it from us and eat it; and after that he won't survive.'

Then Behrām Pasha replied: 'We'll give you 1,000 gold coins, and your friend 1,000 gold coins.' So the *shaflūt* said: 'Take heed of an appropriate time and attack the stronghold; and you won't find anyone to stop you. Be there at that time and do not forget it.' And he left him, went up to the castle and entered upon 'Alī b. Sharaf al-Dīn who was absolutely drunk. Then he said to him: 'What have you brought us from below?' So the *shaflūt* produced for him the quince, and he immediately wanted it. So he ate it all and immediately collapsed on his face, prostrate and dead. He was carried off to hell-fire and damnation. Then the crier arrived at the house; and they burst into loud laments, in distress and pain.

Then behold the mighty army had climbed the mountain where there were 100 of them at the highest gate to the castle. They asked for protection for themselves and were given it. So they came out of the castle in one movement, and Behrām Pasha granted them protection. Then they disappeared in flight and saved their skins. The troops entered the castle and surrounded what was within. They took the stores and property they found as well as the weapons and food. They found there all the guns that the Zaydī had seized from the late Khayr al-Dīn the admiral; and the capture was complete, and God put an end to fighting so far as the faithful were concerned.

The news of the capture reached the great minister and was for him the best of spoils, and he thanked Almighty God for His continual benevolence, and for His successive generosity and blessings.

The date for the conquest of the castle of Ḥabb this time was 5 Rajab the unequalled, 978/3 December 1570.

He wrote to those of ʿAlī b. Sharaf al-Dīn's party who had asked for protection, in confirmation of assurances granted by H.E. Behrām Pasha; and calmed their fears to some extent, granting them security and peace.[19]

[443] The blessed conquest of all possessions in Yemen which had been under the control of the noble Ottoman sultanate, God give him everlasting victory, was complete; and indeed there was an increase, with a number of strongholds and towns, villages and *qasbas* [forts], taken for the first time. The minister's judgment throughout the campaign had been sound and pertinent, and his appraisal during the battles with the rebel tribesmen felicitous.

When Muṭahhar heard the details of the situation and of the treachery and nemesis that had befallen his brother, violent fear took hold of him and his stomach muscles contracted. Determined to make absolutely certain of the arrangements and agreements, he sent a request to the minister to be allowed to undertake the administration of Ṣaʿdah and be entrusted to hand over the tax imposed on it to the sultan's treasury. The minister was to appoint a military guard detachment from the sultan's army in Ṣaʿdah stronghold for its defence, on behalf of the noble sultanate, against any aggressor, wrongdoer or any failing to enter within or observe the sultan's authority.

So the army would look after Ṣaʿdah, together with its surrounding districts; and it would be for Muṭahhar, on the customary basis, to deliver its tax annually, as usual. With that, absolute justice would prevail, the rebellion would die down and dispute would cease. With that, communications and contacts would be complete.

Sinān Pasha responded to Muṭahhar's request and apprised him as to the depth of his hopes for it. He spelt it out in an agreement in which he confirmed former treaties and contracts, and he appointed a guard detachment of thirty people who would occupy the bastion in Ṣaʿdah stronghold and protect those regions and places from rebels and aggressors. And he imposed on Muṭahhar the tax for those lands due to the noble sultanic *dīwān*, on the condition that the sermon and the coinage for all those districts would be in the name of the noble sovereign.

His objectives had been met and, with the conquest in the sovereign's name, he had achieved his utmost goal, diligently, resolutely and with no effort spared. He had completed his blessed task with good reputation and to good purpose. Since he had no further ambitions within the country, he decided to return from Yemen to the Sublime Porte and kiss the noble Ottoman threshold. So he put arrangements in train, with God's blessing and care for every aspect and stage of the journey.

CHAPTER 60

[444] Sinān Pasha's transfer of the Yemen state to the great governor-general, the revered Behrām Pasha; his return from Yemen; and his passage through God's holy city, undertaking the Muslim pilgrimage and visiting the grave of the Prophet, upon him most excellent prayers and peace in favour of the people of the two Holy Cities and those who live there

§ The minister had decided to depart from Yemen when its conquest in the sovereign's name was complete and those rebel leaders who had incited rebellion were quiet. So he summoned the governor-general appointed by the noble sultan, he being the commander of noble commanders, lord of the abode of happiness and nobility, defender of nations through the sharpest of swords and speech, mighty lion, brave and energetic warrior, Behrām Pasha. He was son of the mourned and late, the holy and felicitous, blessed in this world and the next, who has reached the abundant mercy of his God, Muṣṭafā Pasha, known as Qarah Shāhīn, Almighty God give him peace among the highest and bless all his children and grandchildren.

At his arrival, the minister received him with much pleasure and gave him useful advice, loading him with counsel, arrangements and much secret information. He advised him as to matters of order and administration and the care and control of the troops, so far as was necessary and affected his responsibilities; and he gave him information as to matters he needed to be informed about and alerted to. [445] Behrām Pasha received it with every courtesy and submitted with every grace. Then H.E. the Minister handed over to him the entire country, its plains and mountains, its buildings and ruins, its ravines and hills, its ports and coasts, and its highlands and its lowlands.

And Behrām Pasha received them with a relaxed mind and happy heart and he appointed there his agents and *kushshāf*, his administrators and his experts. He asked help from Almighty and Blessed God in carrying out such duties and in providing justice and security throughout the coastal plains and mountains, in as far as he was able. He would remove and eradicate oppression and injustice, placing his trust in God, the fount of unseen blessing.

The minister set about preparations for the journey and got ready what he needed for the purpose, offering choice to the soldiers and troops, who were like raging lions, as to going with him and returning to Cairo, or remaining in Yemen on generous wages. There were those who wished to go with him; and there were those who had lived in Yemen and enriched themselves, largely from tax collecting. So he made his decisions, gave them his directions and put them in good heart. Then he embarked in ships and craft which he had prepared and put right, with equipment and supplies, and where he put his loads, belongings and luggage, leaving some of his horses to follow by land later with the Yemeni mounted sections.

He set sail and put out to sea after the feast of al-Fiṭr on 4 Shawwāl 978/1 March 1571. He was accompanied by winds which blew in his favour and fortune smiled upon him and led him on. He embarked with the words: 'In the name of Allāh be its course and its mooring.'[20] It sailed on, away from port and anchorage, and went far out in the deep-sea waves, crossing unheard-of distances before landing at the port of Jiddah the populous where it anchored in absolute safety.

His happy disembarkation on safe land took place on 18 Shawwāl/15 March; and the total of his sea voyage was twelve days, from the port of Mocha to that of Jiddah, excepting the days of his embarkation and disembarkation. This was also seldom true of other governors. And with him arrived sixteen ships carrying the rest of the returning troops, *sanjak* commanders, *aghas* and other subordinates.

In Jiddah he was met by one of the chiefs of Mecca [446] of the greatest standing and splendid quality and consideration, of the purest pedigree and noble line, of high status and handsome deed, the Guardian of the Holy Cities, head of the learned ulema, our lord the Qadi Ḥusayn b. Abū Bakr al-Ḥusaynī, God renew his good fortune, prosperity and noble and blessed service. He had been told of the minister's arrival, the day before, by a message shortly before he reached there from al-Qunfidhah.

So he rode at once during the night to reach Jiddah in the morning and arrived there before the minister had disembarked. And he went on board and met him in the most friendly fashion. The delight at their arrival and meeting was mutual. The minister unloaded for Qadi Ḥusayn a fine, radiant robe and a beautiful Khusrawānī dress[21] and disembarked with him.

Then our lord accommodated him in the Dār al-Sa'ādah [House of Happiness], our lord, the Grand Sharīf's house in Jiddah, and accommodated the commanders and *sanjaks* in houses nearby; and our lord, Sharīf Ḥasan, ordered a tremendous great banquet, and indeed it was a vast feast, containing every kind of food and drink, sweet pastry, confectionery and citrus, prepared by the minister Sharaf al-Dīn Abū al-Qāsim b. Qarqamāsh by order of his master, as well as about 1,500 plates, or at least 2,000.

Then the minister personally took his place at the banquet and summoned the *sanjak* commanders who had arrived in his suite; and they were: Muṣṭafā Bey b. Ayyār Pasha, Ibrāhīm Bey, his sister's son, Commander Māmāy Bey, Commander Ḥamād b. Khabīr, Arab Shaikh of Gīza in Egypt, Sallāq Aḥmad, 'Alī Bey and other *aghas*. They sat down at the banquet with all the victorious soldiers who had come. They ate as they brought in to their order; and there was no end to the banquet till they got up from it and were succeeded by seating after seating till the food was taken away and what was left was given to the sailors, the oarsmen and the poor. And the minister robed Sharafī Abū al-Qāsim in a caftan.

Then arrived our lord and master, lord of the Dār al-Sa'ādah [House of Happiness], scion to glory, honour and sovereignty, father of coat-mailed warriors, the pride of ferocious lions, his noble and high excellency and shining and radiant star, our lord Sayyid Ḥusayn, son of His Highness our lord Sayyid Ḥasan, Almighty God give them everlasting victory and help them with happiness and good fortune. With him were the mighty hero Sayyid 'Arār b. 'Ajil b. 'Arār [447] and all the Turks, Banū Ḥasan leaders and personages who came to congratulate the minister on his arrival and victory over the vanquished foe.

They came to him and brought greetings from our lord Sayyid Ḥasan since he had directed them to remain under the minister's orders and undertake whatever he needed from the port, whether great or small. So the minister received them with respect and consideration, and with gestures of generosity and honour, giving splendid robes of honour to our lord Ḥusayn b. Ḥasan, and Sayyid 'Arār, as well as dazzling honours.

He bestowed on them kindnesses and talked to them courteously while they and their companions remained in Jiddah looking into the minister's requirements and attending him on most occasions till he had satisfied his requirements and made preparations for his voyage to Egypt by sea. He dispatched his loads and luggage in boats and sent off some of his mamluks and men. The remainder of his troops had come from Yemen; and he distributed among them some of the custom dues and gave them permission to return to their country. Some of them did not wait for the pilgrimage but voyaged by sea; others waited to carry out the ceremonies and gain the recompense and reward.

After a few days Ḥasan Pasha, the former governor-general in Zabīd, arrived together with Kaylān Bey, former treasurer of Yemen, whom stubborn Muṭahhar had released from prison, and Maḥmūd Bey, treasurer before him, also released from prison and fetters. They had each begun to tell what he had suffered in prison and the violence and ill treatment he had met. There were many angry expressions as people were affected by what they said and the suffering that they had endured. How God had relieved them from pain! and how Almighty God's kindness had brought joy and ease after hardship and trial! For Almighty God has fulfilled his promise to man and humanity. (But lo! with hardship goeth ease, Lo! with hardship, goeth ease.)[22]

There came from Mecca to welcome the minister the great, most noble and glorious efendī, mighty qadi of God's Holy City, our lord Muḥyī al-Dīn Efendī b. Ḥājī Ḥasan Zādah, Almighty God preserve and increase his noble house, and the great commander and man of law and knowledge, Commander Qāsim, *sanjak* of populous Jiddah, charged with the running of the waters of the well of 'Arafāt to Jiddah, who received from the minister a splendid and radiant welcome, full of smiles and laughter, as well as [448] a happy sunny countenance. The minister presented them with magnificent robes of honour, with bright floral patterns, and had them nobly seated in high honour.

The minister displayed the height of courtesy with great and small, rich and poor. He assigned to many of the *faqihs* and the poor regular money from the income from the port of Jiddah, and made various improvements for some of the *faqihs* and sultanic troops who had such regular benefit, giving them kindness and honoraria to an extent unknown before from ministers and noble commanders.

He then made his preparations to travel to the Holy Sanctuary, God increase its honour and status, with dignity, justice and respect. He was wearing the *iḥrām* for the twin[23] pilgrimages since that is better for the Ḥanafī Imam, God be pleased with him.[24] Then our lord and master, bearer of banners of nobility and high rank, His Highness Sharīf Ḥasan b. Abū Numayy, Almighty God grant them both everlasting glory and victory and raise their noble dignity and standing, sent to him 400 camels to carry his loads and 100 other stock, comprising horses, mules and riding camels. His Highness had vacated for his accommodation the school of the late sultan al-Ashraf Qāyitbey, Almighty God water his epoch with true mercy and compassion; and he had directed that many houses be vacated for the *sanjak* commanders and the rest of the victorious army. So many houses were vacated and made ready for their accommodation.

The minister set out from Jiddah after the afternoon prayer on Friday, 4 Holy Dhū al-Qa'dah 978/30 March 1571 and reached Ḥaddā in the morning where he stopped at Ra's al-'Ayn [the head of the spring] where al-Sharafī Bū al-Qāsim b. Qarqamāsh had prepared a meal of dried fruit and dishes which some of Sayyid Ḥasan's servants laid out in front of the minister. Then he robed him in a caftan and was charming with him, dividing with his companions such pastries and the like. After the afternoon prayer, he rode off from Ḥaddā, together with our lord Qadi Ḥusayn, with whom he travelled and conversed. When he reached a place called al-Shāqah our lord Sayyid

Ḥasan's mounted advance party arrived to meet him, God give him everlasting glory and victory, and Sayyid 'Arār b. 'Ajil arrived, kissed the minister's hands and told him that our lord Sayyid Ḥasan had arrived to meet him.

Then the minister welcomed them. He was delighted with the arrival of His Highness and displayed his delight at his approach. They approached with the horses in a cavalcade but they formed one large line as they halted, [449] about 300 horsemen and many soldiers.

From among them our lord Sayyid Ḥasan advanced, with Sayyid 'Arār and Muḥammad b. Yūnis and about fifty horsemen belonging to his private suite, while the minister waited for him to approach amid clapping at the sight of their horses as they greeted each other. The minister walked on the right and began to exchange pleasantries. Each took pleasure in the company of the other. The minister gave him two magnificent honorary robes, the one of *shayb*, the second of *serāser*; and he girded him with a splendid gold sword, inlaid with gems.

They continued to chat till the approach of sunset; then Sayyid Ḥasan and his suite went off to a palm grove while the minister went off to al-Hudaybiyyah,[25] where he conducted his *maghrib* prayers, after which he mounted and went on with his suite till they passed a place called al-Muftaraq where he dismounted and, with his suite, slept till morning broke. Then he said his prayers and mounted, together with our lord, Sayyid Ḥusayn al-Mālikī, travelling as far as al-Riyya' where our lord, Sayyid Ḥasan, caught up with him with his horse and men. So they met up and continued their journey till they entered Mecca by al-Shabīkah where our lord, Sayyid Ḥasan, Almighty God give him everlasting glory, left him in lower Mecca and went to his residence.

The minister and his suite continued until they dismounted at King al-Ashraf Qāyitbey's school, God water his epoch, whereupon the *faqihs* and dignitaries called on him, in waves; and he would stand for them, acting courteously with them and greeting them kindly. Then he conducted the *ṭawāf*, and I was with him. He conducted it with devotion and dignity, and he walked quickly in accordance with Prophetic tradition. Then he walked to al-Ṣafā and the *sa'y*; nor did he in any way neglect good manners, custom or normal practice. The he conducted the *ṭawāf* of arrival a second time but postponed the *sa'y* of the pilgrimage till its appointed place.

The Khwājā Kamāl al-Dīn Abū al-Faḍl b. Abū 'Alī laid out an excellent large meal, the last word in size and excellence, by command of our lord Ḥasan, Almighty God give him everlasting glory. He ate, and divided it among the commanders and troops; and dressed the Khwājā in an honorary robe of *serāser*.

On Monday, 7 Dhū al-Qa'dah/2 April our lord and master, Sayyid Ḥasan, Almighty God extend the shade of his blessing to the minister, arrived at the Qāyitbey school, to extend his greetings and sat with him for a long time. He asked for permission to go to the revered Grand Sharīf, [450] our lord Abū Numayy,[26] who was in the east, God give him everlasting glory and blessing as well as everlasting rule for his state and authority. The minister granted permission, and he went off to his father, Almighty God lengthen their years and celebrate the pillars of their glory and victory. The minister gained the absolute confidence of the people of the country by that gesture and removed from them doubts and misgivings, but only after the hearts of many had been about to falter from ignorance, misunderstanding and anxiety. But God in His light and might maintains His sanctuary secure from every revolt and disturbance.

Then on 10 Dhū al-Qaʿdah/5 April the minister went to inspect the work at the well of ʿArafāt, together with the *sanjak* commanders, each a horseman and former hero. The supervisor of the work at the well was a model commander and pick of the elite, Commander Qāsim al-Bawṣnawī, deputy for Jiddah the populous. He had gone down to where the work was complete, that is near the pool of al-Sallam, and had prepared for the minister a large meal with various Turkish dishes which had put him to a great deal of expense.

The minister had criticised this Commander Qāsim for God knows what allegation made against him; so when the minister arrived at the work site and Commander Qāsim was spreading out the meal for him, the minister wished to stop him but the commanders interceded with him: Commander Sallāq Aḥmad and Commander Māmāy came forward and kissed his hand over it. So the minister received it from them, and he, the commanders and the troops partook of the meal and drank the sugared drinks.

Commander Qāsim produced five horses and mules, with their bridles, saddles, stirrups and horse-cloth, and armour and helmets which he brought to the minister; and he produced an honorary robe and implored the minister to put it on him and let the people think that he had given it to him; so he did so and the people thought that the minister had put it on him.

Feelings were aroused and the fires of hatred burned, and the minister arranged for someone to inspect the details of his work throughout his stay in Mecca. However, the minister had noticed nothing against Commander Qāsim due to the pleasant manner in which Commander Qāsim treated the person set to inspect him, the brief span of time and the extent of the work.

Then when they had finished the meal, the minister returned to Mecca, with the horsemen racing in front of him, displaying the finer points and finesse of their horsemanship. The high degree of their skill is illustrated in this verse:

> [451] As if they were planted on the back of the horses from the strength of their resolve rather than any harness.

The minister began to attend to the institutes and to visit the traditional places and the shrines, giving alms to the poor and charity to the weak, in his general charity and kindness, and included most of the deserved in his bounty and compassion. He was of tremendous service to them and they filled the four quarters of the area with their prayers for him. During that period he visited Ḥirā'[27] the place where the Prophet's chest was cleft and the spot where the revelation of the spirit began, and Jibrīl, the prayers and peace of God be upon him, brought down to him the Holy Quran.

Then he continued with his commanders and his senior army officers, and paid an early visit to this noble and ancient place. On his return from the visit, our lord the Shaikh al-Islam arrived, Guardian of God's Holy City, about whom all talk of his glory and majesty, the moon of the world and religion, Sayyid Qadi Ḥusayn al-Ḥusaynī al-Mālikī, teacher at the sultanic school of Sulaymān and holder of other Sunnī posts. And the qadi met him in his garden in Abṭaḥ. He had prepared a splendid banquet, suited to somebody like the great and mighty minister and big enough for his large suite, indeed more than enough to satisfy them and their like, Almighty God willing.

So the qadi had the banquet served out before him while the minister, his commanders and senior military officers took their seats before it. The dishes were like chrysolite and turquoise, filled with the choicest food such as *lawzīnaj* and *faludhāj* [almond and honey cakes], grilled lamb and chicken, *muhallabiyyah* [spiced meat and rice] and *ma'mūniyyah*, *sikbāj* [stew cooked in vinegar], *rashīdiyyah*, *sharābiyyah* [fruit syrups] and *kilāj*,[28] many of which were impossible to name or describe properly in their beauty and variety.

The minister sat this lord of ours on his right and began to chat to him pleasantly. He was delighted with the excellence and quantity of the food, and with the grace of the setting. He charmed him with his conversation and interesting talk, telling him among other things: 'Our lord qadi, you have spent in one hour five years of your income from your official posts on the cost of this banquet.' Then he ate at his ease and with good cheer; those present ate; and the troops sat down and ate; and they took away what they wanted. Then he gave to the poor and there was still a lot left over. Then the minister went down to his lodging in the school.

[452] After a few days, the minister went to Mt Thawr[29] and visited the Prophet's cave. He climbed the mountain with vigour and energy despite the roughness of the track and the difficulty of the ascent. He entered by the opening over which the spider wove its web and in which the dove hatched its eggs. Through this opening the Prophet had entered the cave, the much visited place in which the Prophet hid himself with Abū Bakr, may God be pleased with him. The idolaters had followed them to the opening, and then saw the dove's nest and the spider's web, but Almighty God had kept them

away from His Prophet and his companion within the cave, in that insignificant way displaying His tremendous power, as the poet of the Burdah says,[30] Almighty God have mercy upon him:

> the blessing and nobility the cave contained to which all the unbelievers were blind.
> Verily the Truth, Prophet Muḥammad and the Believer, Abū Bakr, were in the cave but went unseen,
> and they who chased them declared there was none inside.
> They thought the dove and the spider for the best of mankind did not weave and did not protect.
> The protection of God saved them the need for doubting the strongest armour [i.e. the Prophet Muḥammad] and the highest castle.

In general it is thought that the lawful child enters by this opening, but, as for the child of adultery, he is caught in it. But there is no ground for that; for he who enters needs experience, and if a rock juts out in front of his face and stands in his way, it would prevent his body from going through; and he would be struck by it because of his stupidity and lack of sense. But if he went over to the left side he would find some room and easily get inside, without any trouble.

During our time and before, many people have got caught up in it. The masons in Mecca had been summoned and broke some of it off so as to enlarge the opening. Because of them he was able to make his way but, because of the situation, only a very few dared to enter the cave.

The minister returned from his visit to Mt Thawr, and he was full of energy, despite the length, roughness and difficulty of the route, while the rest of the commanders and troops were exhausted with climbing up and going down. The reward of the journey was gained, thank God.

And so then the minister continued to visit the famous sites and well-known shrines, giving alms to the poor and courtesies to the great. He went out at night [453] and walked by the Holy Mosque, treating kindly the poor and weak he found there, giving alms in secret and doing favours, till the days of the pilgrimage arrived. That was on Thursday the 30th at the end of Dhū al-Qaʿdah. The noble *waqfah* [stand at ʿArafāt] took place on the Friday, with absolute felicity for the minister, his good intention and sincerity. Almighty God enabled him to make the greater pilgrimage, and that day corresponded with the Prophet's pilgrimage during his last and farewell pilgrimage, and it was the best pilgrimage as has been told in previous accounts on the subject.

The commander of the Egyptian pilgrimage was the pride of the commanders and pick of the elite, Murād Bey, secretary to the late Maḥmūd Pasha, who arrived in Mecca with the Egyptian caravan on Saturday, 3 Dhū al-Ḥijjah/28 April, to be met by their excellencies the *ashrāf* [descendants of the Prophet] at al-Jawkhī's spring, as usual. He pitched his tents at al-Ma'lāh and did not stay at the Qāyitbey school as he usually did, since the minister was staying there.

After him arrived the commander of the Yemeni pilgrimage, together with the rest of the minister's heavy luggage, and some of his horses and equipment. Then the commander of the Syrian pilgrimage caravan, Riḍwān Pasha b. Muṣṭafā Pasha, arrived, later than usual owing to having met some rain and flooding on the route which had hampered him on his customary journey. He entered Mecca the day people ascended to 'Arafāt, that was a Thursday, 8 Dhū al-Ḥijjah/3 May, and put up at Minā where, in accordance with the Sunnah, he said the prayers of midday, the afternoon, dusk, the evening and the morning; nor did he abandon these Sunnah and their community. The reason for that is that these Sunnah have inspired multitudes after being handed down a long time ago.

He then went to 'Arafāt where he stayed and laid out a large meal for the poor and the great. He prayed in the Namirah mosque,[31] between noon and the afternoon, then returned and stood at the foot of Jabal al-Raḥmah [the Mount of Mercy], in prayer and supplication to Almighty God. He wept and made weep those standing at that noble place, abasing himself before Almighty God and rubbing his face in the dust before his glorious and exalted Creator.

He and all those standing by that mighty spot prayed for the continuation of the great sultan, the most magnificent and noble sovereign, sultan of Arab and non-Arab sultans, king of the lands and seas, [454] sultan of Turkey and the two Iraqs,[32] Sultan Selīm b. Sulaymān, Almighty God make his sultanate last for ever and let his rule never die.

When the imam moved on, the people did so with him, and the imam at the place that day was our lord, the late deceased Muḥyī al-Dīn Muḥammad b. Khiḍr Shāh b. Muḥammad b. Ḥājī Ḥasan Efendī, the qadi of Mecca the sublime, who died there in 979/1571/2, Almighty God let him dwell among the highest and make him among the noble of this faithful town.

Then he reached Muzdalifah[33] where he spent the night after praying between dusk and evening and did as God said (But, when you press on in the multitude from 'Arafāt, remember Allāh by the sacred monument).[34] He spent the night in prayer and asked God's pardon for his errors and misdeeds, seeking from the Eternal forgiveness for sins and the acceptance of wrongs. For the Prophet has promised his community that God will pass over the errors of those of his servants who stand in supplication to Almighty God in this place, and that Almighty God will accept good deeds and acts of charity in atonement for error. Then they will forgive those who have sinned against them with the permission of the All-Knowing King.

The minister and his suite then moved with the rest of the pilgrims to Minā and stopped near the mosque of al-Khayf[35] where he threw seven pebbles at al-'Aqabah,[36] ceasing the call of '*Lubayk*' [here we are] at the first of them, and calling out *Allāhu Akbar* with every stone. They slaughtered about two hundred animals, both sheep and camels, which the poor seized without opposition. It had been a year of drought and famine, so with that, the poor were satisfied, praying for God's acceptance. Then he shaved his head[37] and took off his *iḥrām* in the first *taḥallul* or sign of completion. He had performed the pilgrimage, as has been said, and the twin pilgrimage is better with our ulema, God be pleased with them, than enjoyment and performing only the pilgrimage itself.

The minister then moved to Mecca, making the final *ṭawāf* of departure, which signifies the completion of the pilgrimage, when the second *taḥallul* takes place (when sexual congress can resume). He carried out the *sa'y* and returned to Minā where he stayed for two days and carried out three stonings during the afternoon. He threw them at the first which is opposite to the mosque of al-Khayf, then the second, then at al-'Aqabah, on each occasion seven stones.

[455] Then hurrying on, Sinān Pasha rushed with the first party to Mecca, stopping at Muḥṣab,[38] as is customary.

Then he entered into the *ṭawāf*, and carried out the *ṭawāf* of return. He then returned to his camp, without omitting gifts of charity and alms, various deeds of kindness, the provision of food and clothes for the poor, and payments for many of the poor in secret. His days were spent in service and his time consumed in acts of devotion.

Among the acts of charity which he carried out in Mecca, he constructed an area around the circuit for the noble *ṭawāf* which he furnished with dressed stone like that of the noble *ṭawāf* which was an area contrasting with the rest of the mosque because of the path running from one side to the other; and the path, 3 cubits wide, was covered with a layer of small pebbles, like the rest of the mosque. So he paved it with dressed stone like the *ṭawāf*. The worshippers there felt the improvement because of its superior surface and greater resemblance to the rest of the mosque. So it became like the rest of the mosque save that between it and the circuit was another strip where copper columns had been placed from which hung candles around the circuit.

And also, among his aesthetic improvements, was the well which he refurbished at al-Tan'īm[39] for pilgrims and those travelling with caravans passing from every direction; and they began to drink and draw water from this well, filling their water skins and bowls with its sweet water; and the numbers of pilgrims and travellers who prayed doubled, because of the minister, let God register reward for that in his (Sinān's) noble records.

Also among his endowments was an arrangement he made for the Quran to be read in his name by thirty Quranic readers throughout the year, one of whom would recite a part[40] of the Holy Book daily, completing the whole Quran each day, as a display of repentance in his noble pages. He paid each individual 9 gold dinars every year; and he made a similar arrangement in Noble Medina, most excellent prayers and peace be on her citizens.

[456] He was responsible for other good deeds by digging wells on the Medina road, at places where people crossed or required water, for charity towards the poor and stipends, posts, honoraria and such-like. He appointed many of the religious and teaching dignitaries to posts in the noble sultan's *dīwān*, Almighty God protect them, since none of the sultans or ministers before him had arranged for such benefits and activity to be initiated; and let God Almighty give him good reward for his charity and extend over him the protection of his favour, generosity and benevolence.

And on Friday 17 Dhū al-Ḥijjah/12 May the minister came down from his encampment in al-Abṭaḥ,[41] pitched his tents at Sabīl al-Jawkhī, made the Friday prayers and set out, after his farewell to the Noble Sanctuary. He maintained the stance of the frightened and weak and wept, drawing tears from those watching his departure as he displayed his torment and suffering. He implored Almighty God for approval and the recognition of His creature before him in his shortcomings and weakness. He was generous in the alms he gave, going backwards till he had left the gate of al-Ḥazwarah.[42]

He then mounted and went to his camp, giving alms to the right and left. As night fell, he went to al-Tan'īm and put on the *iḥrām* for a separate *'umrah*. He went and made the *ṭawāf* at the Sanctuary, made the *sa'y* and shaved. Then he entered the Holy Mosque and, at night, repeated the *ṭawāf* of farewell, hidden from people. He withdrew from the Sanctuary of his Lord and made his supplication to God, enumerating for him the good deeds he had done for him and acknowledging his shortcomings before him.

He then returned to his encampment and set off, accompanied in the peace of Almighty God for the visit to his Prophet, and then for Egypt, let God register his safekeeping, and double his glory, triumph and happiness.

§ The accoutrements of peace. Here a qadi's turban is surrounded by a man of the pen or writer's implements such as ink, books, a quill and knife for sharpening it, paper and paper container etc. (Marsigli, I, frontispiece.)

NOTES

Books and articles are cited in these notes only by author or publication and, where necessary, an abbreviated title. Full title and details are listed under the author or publication's name in the Bibliography.

Throughout the notes, numbers in square brackets refer to the page numbers of Ḥamad al-Jāsir's edition of *al-Baraq* of which this work forms the translation.

Translations of the Holy Quran are taken from Marmaduke Pickthall's edition, *The Glorious Koran* (London, 1930).

CHAPTERS 1–10

1. I have retained the use of the title 'His Excellency' on this occasion but have dropped it on most others since its continual use tends to restrict the flow of the story.

2. A Bosnian by origin, known as Lālā Muṣṭafā Pasha from his appointment as *lālā* or tutor to the future sultan, Selīm II, who was to protect him against numerous intrigues by hostile viziers. He had been appointed *sirdār* of the expedition to Yemen by the grand vizier, Sokollu Meḥmed Pasha, but had been replaced by Sinān Pasha, the new governor-general of Egypt, his mortal enemy from past intrigues at the Porte. Sinān was thought to have brought about the change through his own prevarication over providing Muṣṭafā with the necessary troops and supplies as well as his charge that Muṣṭafā had conspired to declare the independence of Egypt in the name of the son of Qansawh al-Ghawrī, the famous sultan of Mamluk Egypt (c.846–922/c.1441–1516) to whose daughter he was married. On the other hand, al-Nahrawālī has argued that there was widespread resistance in the Egyptian army to joining the expedition and that Muṣṭafā Pasha had taken the constructive steps of first attempting a diplomatic solution with Muṭahhar, the leader of the rebellion, and then of dispatching forthwith to Yemen the new governor-general, 'Uthmān Pasha, with strong reinforcements. At the time of Sinān's expedition Selīm II was the new sultan in Istanbul. (Sālim, 239–41; *EI*, VII, 720–1; al-Nahrawālī, 198–206; and Ṣāliḥiyyah, 57–8.)

3. Lit. a standard or flag, giving its name to a district administered by a *sanjak* bey. In Egypt and Yemen a *sanjak* did not necessarily carry a territorial connotation.

4. The *kushshāf* were tax collectors, the *mutafarriqah* a corps of elite, founded in 1554, comprising both cavalry and infantry; and the *būlukyāt* were squadrons of cavalry attached to the infantry of Janissaries. (Winter, 9; and Redhouse, 409.)

5. The journeys in 1815 from Medina to Yanbu' and from Mecca to Medina, described by John Lewis Burckhardt, include most of the places mentioned by the author. (Burckhardt, 401–9.)

6. The foundation of the Sharifate of Mecca in the fourth/tenth century reflected the relative independence of Western Arabia from the rest of the Islamic world from a religious and

political point of view. The Sharifate had taken an early opportunity to show fealty to the Ottoman sultan after his capture of Cairo in 923/1517, and under Muḥammad Abū Numayy and his son Ḥasan from 1524 to 1601 enjoyed a period of peace and stability, largely due to their astute diplomacy. Muḥammad Abū Numayy did not die until 1584 in Nejd at the age of eighty when Ḥasan, at the age of fifty-nine, formally succeeded him. (*EI*, VI, 148 and 150; and de Gaury, 132.) It is clear, however, that Ḥasan was undertaking duties on behalf of his father, the Grand Sharīf, during Sinān's visits to the Hijāz, and in this capacity I have often referred to him as the Sharīf Ḥasan, while occasionally referring to his father as the revered Grand Sharīf. Other members of the Sherifian family mentioned here would have belonged to the same Hasanite dynasty and display the cooperation shown by the family to help the Ottomans regain the Yemeni province.

7. The lesser pilgrimage which can be performed at any time except during the pilgrimage season (i.e. 8, 9 and 10 Dhū al-Ḥijjah). In it a number of the ceremonies of the full pilgrimage are omitted.

8. The circumambulation of the Ka'ba and a ritual course involving running which are among the rites of the pilgrimage at Mecca.

9. The display of gold-plated copper helmets and chamfrons, swords and other weapons, as well as the tents and tent material at the Military Museum in Istanbul illustrates the magnificence of which such an expedition would have been capable.

10. Whereas the analysis of the troops from Egypt, Syria and elsewhere directed by Ottoman *mühimme*, or important documents, to take part in the expeditionary force would indicate a total of some 5,500 men, the author of the analysis is satisfied that such a number was not reached and that al-Nahrawālī's figure, presumably based upon an eye-witness estimate, is the most accurate available. To these perhaps should be added troops offered by the Sharifate in Mecca, and, of course, those on foot. (al-Ṣāliḥiyyah, 43–4.)

11. The *aghas* were regimental commanders and the *jāwīshiyyah* or *chavūs* an elite corps of pursuivants, founded in 1524 and often used on sensitive missions. (Winter, 9.) The *levend* were privateers who joined the Ottoman navy with their ships when their services were needed. (nalcik, I, xlviii.) In Yemen they clearly acted as irregular mercenaries, often far from the sea.

12. Ottoman provinces, or capital of provinces. Karamān is to the north of the Taurus mountains and Mar'ash to the east. Āmid was the capital of Diyār Bakr in the upper basin of the Euphrates.

13. Governor-General of Egypt 956/1549; and Grand Vizier 968/1561 until his death in 972/1565. He was famous for his corpulence and his wit. (*EI*, I, 398.)

14. All such items are on display at the Military Museum in Istanbul.

15. Sarsenet, a silk tissue often shot with gold or silver thread and used for presentations. From the tenth/sixteenth century, it was the favourite fabric in Istanbul. (Öz, 72–3.)

16. The standard unit was the Ottoman sultan's gold dinar which was subdivided into *'uthmānī*, the number of which varied from province to province; in 1561 in Yemen, because of an increase in the copper content in what was nominally a silver coin, the number of *'uthmānī* had increased to 1,000. (Stookey, 137.)

17. Experts in *fiqh* or jurisprudence.

18. We have here a figurative allusion to the furious battles that were to rage over these two strongholds in the Zaydī heartland, north-west of Ṣan'ā'.

19. Senior ranking officer.

20. A busy Red Sea port which in the tenth/sixteenth century had frequently changed hands between the Sharifate of Mecca, the Turks and the Zaydī leadership. Visiting the port in 909/1503 Ludovico di Varthema found forty-five vessels from different countries. (*EI*, II, 515–18.)

21. This is the first mention, in the author's account of the campaign, of the rebel Zaydī

leader in Yemen, Muṭahhar (908–80/1503–72), the eldest son of the former Imam Sharaf al-Dīn whom the new Ottoman sultan, in his fury, had directed Sinān to 'punish and eradicate'. (Ṣāliḥiyyah, 57–8.) The Zaydī had existed in the north of Yemen, based in Ṣa'dah, since the third/ninth century, and professed a form of Shi'ism close to the Sunnī. They were often referred to as *al-madhhab al-khāmis* or the fifth school of orthodox Islam. (For a general survey of Zaydī history and an account of its founder in Yemen, see Serjeant, 'The Zaydis', and Eagle, respectively.) In the tenth/sixteenth century, the Imam Sharaf al-Dīn and his son had achieved a high degree of Zaydī control over most of highland Yemen; but it was only in 954/1548, in the face of the relentless Ottoman advance, that Muṭahhar had been accepted as Zaydī leader, despite his congenital lameness and lack of religious qualification, which precluded him from the imamship as such. Peace terms, reached with the Turks in 969/1552, granted him an Ottoman *sanjak* with limited authority over districts north-west of Ṣan'ā'. However, in 973/1566, he had come out in rebellion against the Turks and reduced Ottoman authority to an enclave surrounding Zabīd in the Tihāmah. (*EI*, VII, 61–2.) By now Muṭahhar was a veteran of sixty-eight years, with long experience in the use of guerrilla tactics against the Turks, in exploiting his mountainous terrain to the full and in harrying their supply lines; and with such methods he could make up for any inferiority in the weapons, discipline and training of open battle. However, he was vulnerable in two important respects, of which the Turks were to take full advantage: disunity among his family commanders and the implacable opposition of the Ismā'īlī community also present in Yemen.

22. Ṣabyā and Abū 'Arīsh were important religious settlements about twenty miles inland from Jīzān, enjoying long periods of quasi-independence. In the early twentieth century, Ṣabyā became the capital of Sayyid Muḥammad al-Idrīsī who accepted British help in fighting the Ottomans in the First World War in return for recognition as an independent ruler.

23. Born in Egypt in 933/1526/7, the son of a Mamluk and former governor-general of Yemen, Özdemir Pasha, he had been associated with Muṣṭafā Pasha in his bitter rivalry in Cairo with Sinān Pasha before travelling to Yemen. Owing to their mutual dislike the two failed to cooperate in Yemen as the author later makes clear ([238] below). The fact that Sinān held command of the Egyptian forces whereas 'Uthmān retained command of the Ottoman forces in Yemen made the situation explosive. Like his father he had held command on the other side of the Red Sea. His love of display and fine horsemanship reflected his Mamluk origin. Muṣṭafā Pasha had equipped 'Uthmān Pasha generously for the Yemeni campaign with 3,000 soldiers and seventeen ships. He had landed in the Zabīd port of al-Buq'ah and entered Ta'izz at the end of Rajab 976/19 January 1569. (*EI*, VIII, 183–4: Sālim, 243; and al-Nahrawālī, 207.)

24. Ḥasan Pasha had arrived as governor-general of the western and northern area of Yemen in Ṣafar 975/September 1567 to find that Zabīd, alone of his charge, remained outside rebel control. He had devoted his energies to extortion and tyranny and refused to send help to the Turkish garrison in Ta'izz.

25. A strategic island opposite the Yemeni harbour of al-Ṣalīf, south of Jīzān. Early in the century, the island had been fortified at intervals by Mamluk and Portuguese, with the latter's fleet, under the redoubtable Governor of India, Afonso de Albuquerque, spending three months there in 919/1513, before sailing to India. (Albuquerque, I, 28.)

26. The citadel, named al-Qāhiriyyah in the text and now known as al-Qāhirah, enjoys a position of great dramatic quality and strategic value on a northern spur of Mt Ṣabir. Muḥammad b. Shams al-Dīn, Muṭahhar's commander in the south, had displayed a degree of recklessness in joining his supporters in the citadel from which he had escaped only with great difficulty. (Yaḥyā b. Ḥusayn, 732–3.)

27. In Islamic belief there were seven tiers in heaven and seven in earth. There would have been special tents for the army's special needs and the commander's own tents may have been multi-coloured and lined with silk and satin. The scale and splendour of such an encampment is illustrated by exhibits and miniature drawings in the Military Museum in Istanbul.

28. Map 2 illustrates the positions of the leading commanders and forts at the time of the

forthcoming battle on 13 Dhū al-Qa'dah 976/29 April 1569. The Zaydī chronicler, Yaḥyā b. Ḥusayn, records how Muṭahhar had dispatched considerable reinforcements under his sons, Luṭf Allāh, Ḥafiẓ Allāh and al-Hādī, to assist his nephew, Muḥammad b. Shams al-Dīn, in his fight against the newly arrived Turkish governor-general, although it is probable that they had been dispatched once Ṣan'ā' had fallen, to take advantage of the anarchic situation following the retreat of the Turks. Local tribal leaders had advised Muḥammad to move from Mt al-Aghbar to more defensive positions; and Muṭahhar had written with orders for him to move to the strong fortress of al-Ta'kar above Dhu Jiblah to the north, but to no effect. The battle there resulted in considerable losses of men and equipment as well as morale. (Yaḥyā b. Ḥusayn, 732–4; and Blackburn, 'Collapse', 160–1.) In contrast, a modern historian has described the engagement as small, significant only as the first in a succession of retreats to the north by the Zaydī commander Muḥammad b. Shams al-Dīn, after he had been seduced into fighting with the Turks on level ground against all advice from his uncle, Muṭahhar. (Sālim, 248.)

29. This line contains resonances of Sūrah XI, 43.

30. Sūrah III, 159.

31. Mamluk, and brought up in Egypt.

32. Sūrah C, I.

33. We are here introduced to the Zaydī commanders whom Muṭahhar had appointed in the south. See n. 28 above. 'Alī b. Shuway' was, by origin, a sharīf from the Jawf who had been appointed *sanjak* by the Turks but had reneged and joined the rebellion. At one stage he was described as Muṭahhar's vizier. Ḥusayn was twin brother to Muḥammad b. Shams al-Dīn whose death nine months later made the latter long for peace. (Yaḥyā b. Ḥusayn, 739–40; and Blackburn, 'Collapse', 166, n. 185.)

34. Āṣāf b. Barkhyā was vizier to the biblical Solomon and was known for his wisdom and knowledge of magic. He always had access to Solomon who allowed him to use his talismanic ring, thereby transferring the throne of Bilqīs from Sheba to Jerusalem in the twinkling of an eye! (*EI*, I, 686.)

35. Support in Yemen, under the Sulayhid dynasty, for the Fatimid Ismā'īlī mission in Egypt had first been declared from the district of Ḥarāz in the fifth/eleventh century. However, by 596/1132 the Sulayhids had indicated their support for the Ṭayyibī *da'wah* or mission on behalf of the hidden Imam al-Ṭayyib, independent of the Fatimids. The first holders of the office of chief *dā'ī* or missionary of the Ṭayyibī sect were members of the Ḥamidī branch of the Banū Hamdān but for more than three centuries until 946/1539 the office had been held by the Banū Anf and the traditional stronghold of the Ṭayyibī *da'wah* had remained in Ḥarāz. (For the history of this schism and the doctrine and organisation of the *da'wah*, see Daftari, 277–80, 285–9 and 291–9.) In Yemen the movement had then been fragmented and the Banū Anf family virtually annihilated by Muṭahhar; and indeed, on the fall of Ṣan'ā' to Imam Sharaf al-Dīn in 923/1517, all Isma'ilis had been expelled save those who renounced their faith and were enrolled in the imam's army, branded on the forearm like slaves by his young son, Muṭahhar, with the words 'Muṭahhar, son of the Commander of the Faithful'. In contrast, the sect had been able to maintain generally peaceful relations with the successive dynasties that had previously ruled in the highlands. Against this background it is not surprising that the Ismā'īlī had usually sided with the Turks; however, the exactions of the governor-general, Riḍwān Pasha, in 972/1564, including the abolition of traditional tax exemptions, had alienated the community for the reasons graphically explained by the Dā'ī Ṣalāḥ (see para. 1 of [231] below). (Daftari, 303; and al-Nahrawālī, 165, 168–70.)

36. See n. 41 below.

37. The Dā'ī 'Abdullāh al-Hamdānī was related to the Dā'ī Muḥammad b. Ismā'īl (for the son, see Blackburn, 'Collapse', 160, n. 163; for the brother see Yaḥyā b. Ḥusayn, 728) who had been appointed deputy for military matters after the death in Zabīd in 946/1539 of the twenty-third chief missionary, Muḥammad b. Ḥasan, who was the last to lead the undivided Ṭayyibī

of Yemen and India. The Indian Bohra, Shaikh Yūsuf b. Sulaymān, then became the twenty-fourth chief dā'ī, with responsibility for religious matters. Shaikh Yūsuf returned to Yemen, where he had studied, soon after his appointment and died there in 974/1567 after which, due to the relentless hostility of Muṭahhar towards the Isma'ilis, the headquarters of the Ṭayyibī *da'wah* was transferred to Gujerat. The Dā'ī Muḥammad and his two sons were among the *sanjak* commanders in Ṣan'ā' when it capitulated to Muṭahhar in Ṣafar 975/August 1567. The Dā'ī Muḥammad was to die in 979/1572. (Blackburn, 'Collapse', 160, n. 163; Yaḥyā b. Ḥusayn, 726, 728 and 736; Daftari, 291 and 303; and al-Nahrawālī 169.) It is arguable that, without the Dā'ī 'Abdullāh's help and advice, Sinān's campaign could not have succeeded.

38. Translated from the poem by the pre-Islamic poet, Imra'u l-Qays. (Blunt, 6.)

39. A varying weight of 100 *raṭl*, or pounds.

40. Sūrah XXVI, 227.

41. In all probability the Ja'farites came from al-Ja'fariyyah, currently part of the fertile *qaḍā'* or district of Raymah in the highlands east of Bayt al-Faqīh, from which it would have been easy for the shaikh to dispatch the dā'ī to Zabīd. (al-Waysī, 57–8; and al-Maqḥafī, 123.) Later in his work (see [407] and [408] below), the author describes how the minister instructed two of his commanders to travel to Mocha and Zabīd by the Li'sān route from the highlands north-west of Ṣan'ā', with the clear implication that this was the most secure route at a time when renewed rebellion had broken out further south. It may be that the Dā'ī 'Abdullāh had threaded his way through what was left of the Ismā'īlī heartlands down the Wadi Sihām to Li'sān, a long plain north of Mt Bura' where the wadi flows into the Tihāmah.

42. A commander, 'Abdullāh al-Ja'farī, was listed among commanders taken prisoner by Muṭahhar at the fall of Ṣan'ā'. (Yaḥyā b. Ḥusayn, 726.)

43. It is worth mentioning that the Zaydī chronicler, Yaḥyā b. Ḥusayn, confirms Sinān's generous treatment of Ṣalāḥ and his party; for he refused to countenance 'Uthmān' Pasha's request to kill them despite the minister's promise of a secure pass. (Yaḥyā b. Ḥusayn, 734.) Such treatment would encourage reliance upon Turkish promises! (Sālim, 249.) And, in view of the vital support Sinān was to receive from the Isma'ilis, for strategic as well as diplomatic reasons, it would have been folly to alienate them.

44. These words reflect the importance the sultan, Sulaymān al-Qanūnī, the law-maker (926–74/1520–66), attached to Aden on religious and strategic grounds. The Ottomans had, of course, long been aware that Aden was a great entrepôt, not only for the Indian trade, but of the commerce with the cities of the East African littoral and the Hadramawt. It was immensely strong, enjoying the advantage of an excellent harbour, and was itself the southern terminus of caravan routes leading into Yemen. (Serjeant, *The Portuguese*, 7.) A report to the Ottoman authorities in Cairo in 933/1525, by the enterprising sea captain Salmān Rayyis, had opened their eyes to the revenues to be gained from seizing Aden, a port without equal in India, with an annual revenue of 2,000 *sulṭānī* (the *sulṭānī* was equivalent to a Venetian ducat throughout the sixteenth century). (Lesure, 157 and n. 34.) Aden had been captured by the Turks, in circumstances of great treachery, in 945/1538, and its loss to 'Alī b. Shuway', one of Muṭahhar's most powerful commanders, in 975/1567 (a-Nahrawālī, 80–1 and 191), would have had important strategic and financial implications for the Turks. It is interesting to note that, according to Ottoman statistics, by 1600 the revenue from the port of Mocha was about five times larger than that from Aden. (nalcik, 335–6.)

45. An ancient town 20 miles inland of Mocha.

46. A famous pre-Islamic, prolonged tribal war.

47. The words used by the author are *shafālīt al-jibāl*. *Shafālīt* (*s. shaflūt*) were mountain tribesmen who had taken the sultan's pay and served the troops. (Serjeant, *San'ā'*, 71b, n. 27.)

48. Sūrah XXI, 22.

CHAPTERS 11–18

1. The command of the expedition against the Knights of St John in Malta was divided between Muṣṭafā Pasha in charge of the army and Pialī Pasha in charge of the navy, but both were subject to interference from Draghūd Pasha and another famous corsair with vast experience of fighting the Knights in the Mediterranean, whom the sultan, Sulaymān, had given a watching brief over the campaign. Both Muṣṭafā and Pialī were jealous of Draghūd. Muṣṭafā Pasha was fifth vizier, a veteran of campaigns in Rhodes, Hungary and Persia and seventy-five years old. Draghūd Pasha had been active as a corsair in Mediterranean waters off Italy and North Africa for twenty years and was then governor-general of Tripoli. He was eighty years of age and was extremely popular in Istanbul and elsewhere. The argument really centred on the siege of St Elmo, the fort to the north of the passage to Grand Harbour which had been invested by the two commanders before Draghūd arrived on the scene, a strategy to which Draghūd objected, thinking that it would have been better to attack the island from the north. In the event, Draghūd was fatally wounded in an intensified assault on the fortress. The siege was raised after a campaign of three months on 15 Ṣafar 973/11 September 1565 with a loss of 20,000 men on the Turkish side. The failure of the siege before Vienna in 936/1529 counted less to the Turks than that at Malta. (For an account of the personalities involved and the campaign itself see Hammer, VI, 103–6; Bridge, 170–88; and Bradford, 228.)

2. Sūrah XXXIII, 37.

3. The *īwān* would have been part of the minister's tented pavilion, probably in the form of an arch-like enclosure, open to the outside. (Lane, *s.v.*)

4. A *mühimme* from Istanbul indicates that directions were given for some 400 such documents to be dispatched with the expedition. (Ṣāliḥiyyah, 30–1.)

5. Better known as Sokollu Meḥmed Pasha (c.910/11–986/7/c.1505–79). A Bosnian, he was grand vizier under three different sultans from 972–87/1565–79. He had become the future Sultan Selīm's son-in-law in 969/1561/2 and in Istanbul had charge of the unsuccessful operations in Malta (see n. 1 above). (*EI*, IX, 706–11.)

6. The author attempts to explain the pasha's extortionate behaviour in Zabīd, although his own view of the business becomes fairly clear. It is said that Ḥasan Pasha, who was Armenian (Yaḥyā b. Ḥusayn, 729) had served previously in Arabia, in which case al-Nahrawālī would have known him personally. (For a summary of the little that is known about him see Blackburn, 'Collapse', 161 and n. 169.) In any event, he was to be of great assistance to Sinān Pasha during his campaign and Sinān cannot have regretted placing his confidence in him.

7. Sūrah XXVI, 227.

8. Behrām Pasha was to arrive in Zabīd, with 600 troops in poor condition and without arms, at the beginning of Dhū al-Ḥijjah 977/7 May 1570 to take over as governor-general. He was the son of Muṣṭafā Qarah Shāhīn Pasha who had been governor-general in Yemen, 963–74/1556–60.

9. The last stopping place before Mecca where Sinān Pasha had received back his runaway slaves. (al-Nahrawālī, 217.)

10. *Shayb* could well be the new type of luxury material with gold and silver thread called *shahbenek* which was introduced into Istanbul in the sixteenth century along with *serāser* and *zerbāf*. (Öz, 55.) Both these latter materials are mentioned by the author.

11. As the son of a Mamluk, 'Uthmān Pasha would have offered what display he could and had perhaps returned with rather more troops than Sinān had intended! The author tells us later that he left Yemen with 300 of his original army. (al-Nahrawālī, 393.) This account may not do justice to the opposition levelled against him by Sinān Pasha in Yemen and the grand vizier, Meḥmed Sokollu, in Istanbul. Elsewhere we are told that only by making his way across the mountains, virtually by himself, was he able to escape Sinān's clutches; moreover, he had

told Yemeni leaders, nervous as to which Turkish side to support, that he was required in Istanbul by the sultan in his personal rather than military capacity. In Istanbul it was Lālā Muṣṭafā Pasha, the expedition's former *sirdār*, who succeeded in obtaining the sultan's favour for him against the wishes of his grand vizier. (Hammer, VI, 189–90.)

12. Mamluk sultan of Egypt (872–901/1468–96) under whom the Mamluk state enjoyed a long period of political stability and cultural revival. Senior visitors often stayed in the school. (*EI*, IV, 462–3.)

13. Named after the military base for which its ridge-like, strategic site was well suited.

14. This will be the pass through which the present road crosses between the 'gullies torn by torrents' with 'steep red earthen sides' described by the botanist Hugh Scott in *In the High Yemen* (100). Carsten Niebuhr, leader of the eighteenth-century expedition to Yemen, also writes of how in a 'violent storm' there 'torrents, rushing upon such occasions from the hills, produce the gullies'. (Niebuhr, I, 350–1.) From the pass one can look up westwards to the nearby fortress of al-Ta'kar which Sinān was soon to put under siege. (al-Nahrawālī, 266–7.)

15. This route runs to the east of that by Naqīl Aḥmar, by the flanks of Wadi Suḥbān. (al-Waysī, 42 and map facing 26.)

16. On maps and in other accounts, this well-known wadi is called Maytam. Its source is to the north and east of al-Ta'kar. (Hamdānī, 133, n. 4.) It flows in a wide arc into Wadi Tiban which flows southwards to Lahej and the sea. It would have represented a considerable diversion. The author states at this point: 'Maytham, I think from the root w-th-m, i.e. to pound or break. They talk of a Maytham boot as it is heavy in tread and strikes the ground.'

17. Goa had been established as the Portuguese capital in the East as long ago as 1510, and at this juncture the viceroy was Dom Luiz de Athaide (1568–71) whose portrait is among those hanging in the Archaeological Museum and Portrait Gallery in Old Goa. The Zaydī chronicler Yaḥyā b. Ḥusayn makes no mention of Qāsim b. Shuway''s arrangements with the Portuguese; and the only reference I can find to a Portuguese presence near Aden at this time is the dispatch there of two ships and three galleons by the viceroy under the command of Pedro Lopes Rabello and Giles de Goes. (Danvers, I, 545.) It is likely, however, that the ships mentioned by the author came from the Portuguese colony of Hurmūz. The Portuguese did make regular visits to the area and in c.954/1547 a small Portuguese force had been sent there in answer to an appeal for help by a neighbouring Arab chieftain who had seized the fortress from the Turks. The captain had fled in ignominious circumstances after spending only one night in Aden and, by the time a larger Portuguese force arrived, the Turks had retaken the fortress. (Serjeant, *The Portuguese*, 107–9; Whiteway, 316–17.)

18. The scene is illustrated in Rumūzī's *Futūḥ-i-Yemen* and forms the frontispiece to Serjeant's *The Portuguese*.

19. This image is used on a number of occasions by the author and reappears in Marmaduke Pickthall's novel *Said the Fisherman* (229 and n. 311).

20. The name given to a dim star that rides over the sixth of the Plough. (Tibbets, 111 and 134; and Lane, *s.v.*)

21. Towards the end of 972/May–July 1565, this Ṣafar Bey had come to Aden with ten ships bringing long-awaited supplies and ordnance to the garrison in an effort to curb Portuguese interference with Indian merchantmen trading at Aden and the Red Sea. Later in the year he died there of an unidentified sickness. (Serjeant, *The Portuguese*, 110–11; and Blackburn, 'Collapse', 164, n. 180.)

22. 851–914/1447–1508. Abū Bakr was born in Tarīm, the son of 'Abd al-Rahmān al-Saqqāf, known as 'Aydarūs. He spent his last twenty years in Aden and was famed for his piety and hospitality. He had been initiated into Sufism and was considered the patron saint of Aden. His mosque and mausoleum are in Aden crater. (See *EI*, I, 781, for further details.)

23. The highest mountain in Aden, to the west of the crater. Captain Haines, who conquered

Aden in 1839, wrote of an old Turkish fort of rubble masonry, heavily plastered and containing a circular cistern, which may have been the fort in question. (Norris and Penney, 17–19.)

24. The Zaydī chronicler Yaḥyā b. Ḥusayn makes no mention of the treachery but states that his killing infringed the truce granted to him! (Yaḥyā b. Ḥusayn, 735.)

25. Oarsmen were in great demand for galleys, especially for the Mediterranean.

26. Sūrah XVII, 81.

27. Murād Pasha, governor-general of the northern area of Yemen in the divided province, had been murdered in ignominious circumstances in Muḥarram 975/July 1567, soon after the outbreak of the rebellion, at al-Maḍraḥ not far from Wadi Khubān (DOS map, Yemen Arab Republic, 1444D3, 463664 and 6362) which flows into the Wadi Banā near Damt. He had been murdered by the grandson of the shaikh hanged in 945/1538 by the Ottoman expeditionary commander, Sulaymān Pasha, along with the Governor of Aden, on his way to fight the Portuguese in India. Murād's head had then been dispatched to Muṭahhar. (al-Nahrawālī, 174–82.)

28. The mountain east of Mecca where pilgrims gather on the second day of the pilgrimage (9 Dhū al-Ḥijjah) to hear the sermon which is an indispensable part of the celebrations.

29. Sūrah LXIX, 13.

30. The three days, after the Feast of the Sacrifice, *'Īd al-Aḍḥā*, i.e. 11–13 Dhū al-Ḥijjah, called by the Prophet Muḥammad 'days of eating, drinking and sensual pleasure'. (Lane, *s.v.*)

31. On a First World War map at 4420 13 46, south of Mt Suḥbān, a shrine is marked *merzed* near wells, and a market by *Turbat al-Ashūr* which could well be Masjid al-Qā'ah from the directions given in the author's account. The road taken by the Turks would then have continued east and north towards Wadi Maytam. (GS map, *South West Arabia*, Sheet 1; al-Waysī, 45.)

32. One of the followers from Medina who granted him refuge after the Hijrah.

33. The extract more or less follows the text given in the French translation, *Les Prairies d'Or*, V, 266–7, of the work *Murūj al-Dhahab* by Abū Ḥasan al-Mas'ūdī. Jābir b. 'Abdullāh had been kept waiting in Damascus for several days before being admitted to Mu'āwiyah who was then governor.

34. The Prophet's pool where people would drink on the Day of Judgment.

35. al-Mas'ūdī simply states that Jābir had been reminded of what he had forgotten.

36. A battle against the Meccans in 31/624/5 in which Muḥammad and the Muslims were worsted near the hill of Uḥud outside Medina.

37. 224/5–310/839–923. Polymath, famous as the supreme, universal historian and Quran commentator of the first three centuries of Islam. (*EI*, X, 11–15.)

38. Another example of Zaydī error in being persuaded to fight in open country, against all advice from Muṭahhar.

39. The words translated are *rand* and *shīḥ*; and I am grateful to Professor Rex Smith for the comprehensive note which follows:

rand (Persian): *Laurus nobilis* (L.) sweet bay, victor's laurel, a sweet-smelling desert tree/shrub. (Maḥmūd Muṣṭafā al-Dimyāṭī, *Mu'jam asmā' al-nabātāt al-wāridah fī Tāj al-'Arūs li-l-Zabīdī*, Cairo, 1965, p. 64; Bernhard Lewin ed., *The Book of Plants of Abū Ḥanīfa al-Dīnawarī*, Uppsala and Wiesbaden, 1953, Vocab., p. 37.)

shīḥ: *Artemisia judaica* (L.) Judaea wormwood coastal plant, used for making brooms, with a bitter taste but sweet-smelling; used as fodder for horses and livestock. (Dimyāṭī, 85; and Lewin, 41.)

40. The word used is *nafṭ* which could well refer to something like Greek fire since there are many allusions to fire and firebrands being hurled. The exact composition of such material would vary according to the gunners and those responsible. Basically, it was composed of a mixture of saltpetre, pounded sulphur, pitch, unrefined ammoniacal salt, resin and turpentine

and was packed into thin pots that would break easily. They could be hurled manually over twenty or thirty yards, or be fired by cannon or other device. The word used for weaponry is *zurdakhānah* or armoury. (For further information see Ayalon, 24–5; and Bradford, 101–2.)

41. This is the first mention of the *ḍarbuzān* which is normally compared with the culverin or falconet-type cannon. (Ayalon, 127.) It may have weighed between 85 and 100 pounds and have fired lead balls of 14–17 ounces. It may also have been larger and of varying sizes, with shot of 300 dirhem, and 1 or 2 okkas (0.96, 1.28 and 2.57 kg). These would compare with early sixteenth-century English demi-culverins, minions and falcons with balls of 5, 3½, and 2½ pounds respectively. (*EI*, 1, 1062–3; and Carman, 44.) But that stated, *ḍarbuzān* were often much larger still, as the author clearly indicates; indeed, on [263] he mentions three *ḍarbuzān* from the large cannon; and, in the gardens of the Military Museum in Istanbul, there are two mighty cannon from the time of Sultan Meḥmed al-Fātiḥ (1451–81), weighing 11 and 15 tons and labelled *ḍarbuzēn*.

42. The *zand* of pebbles is evocative of the device used at the siege of Malta four years previously which was filled with combustible material such as Greek fire (see n. 40 above) and snorted and belched before it burst, firing material and bullets at its target. (Bradford, 102.)

43. Sūrah II, 249.

44. A river in Paradise.

45. al-Ta'kar was a strong and ancient fortress overlooking Dhū Jiblah from the south. It was famous in Sulayhid times and used both as treasury and summer palace by Queen Arwa. The queen died in 532/1137/8 at the age of eighty-eight after reigning for thirty-one years. She is buried in a handsome tomb in the mosque she constructed at Dhū Jiblah. (Kay, 50 and 267.)

46. Sūrah XXXVII, 173.

47. A fort near Dhū Sufāl and within easy distance of al-Ta'kar. (G. R. Smith, 138.)

48. Lit. destroyed by hammers.

49. Captain of the Guard.

CHAPTERS 19–29

1. Khadid was an ancient fort dating from pre-Islamic times when it contained a magnificent palace, on Mt Khadid (3,000 metres), north-west of Ibb. (Kay, 246.) Mt Ḥubaysh (2,390 metres) is to its north-north-east. Both are in Ḥubaysh district within Ibb province.

2. Formerly an important centre, with a celebrated mosque allegedly founded by one of the Prophet's companions, Mu'ādh b. Jabal, and containing a stone pillar in its court, named after him. (Serjeant, *San'ā'*, 19.)

3. Sūrah XCIX.

4. The text gives Hirrān rather than al-Shamāḥī; however, since Hirrān is near Dhamār in the transmontane plain north of the Samārah pass, and since Yaḥyā b. Ḥusayn refers to Sinān's battle with Muḥammad b. Shams al-Dīn and Muṭahhar's sons at al-Shamāḥī, I have substituted al-Shamāḥī which, together with other sites mentioned by the author here, is on the Ba'dān mountain range. It was from al-Shamāḥī that the Zaydī leaders fled in such ignominious circumstances. We are told that Muṭahhar received his nephew, Muḥammad b. Shams al-Dīn, without a word of criticism for his flight or for acting against his orders. (Yaḥyā b. Ḥusayn, 735.)

5. Ibb lies on the ancient caravan route from Aden to Ṣan'ā' at the edge of the Ba'dān mountain range in an agricultural area blessed with reliable rainfall from April to September. Its whitewashed houses, set against green fields, were compared in the early 1920s by the traveller, Ameen Rihani, to a 'heap of pearl shells, fringed with moss'. (Rihani, 53.)

6. Al-Simāk probably refers to Arcturus, *al-simāk al-rāmiḥ*, the one with a lance, a bright red star of the first magnitude which marks east-north-east in the star compass of navigators in the Indian Ocean. Al-Naṣrān refers to 'the two eagles' of Altair and Vega, separated by the Milky Way. Altair was a marker for the east in the star compass of the Indian Ocean. (Varisco, 100–2.)

7. Sūrah LXIX, 23.

8. 'Āshūrā' is the name given to the voluntary fast day for Sunnī Muslims of the tenth day of the month of Muḥarram; for Shi'ites it signifies the great day of mourning on the anniversary of Ḥusayn's martyrdom at Kerbela in 60/679/80.

9. 'Call to the good, or to the good life' is made, with the call to prayer, by the muezzin. (For an interesting analysis, see Cragg, 140–5.)

10. A fine stretch of *saj'* or rhymed prose, common in Arabic, in which the author often indulges, especially to describe a battle scene. It is impossible to do justice to the alliteration and imagery, the puns and double-meanings, and to the sheer pace of the passage. The editor, the late Ḥamad al-Jāsir, in his preface to the work, points out that the use of *saj'* allowed the author to show off his linguistic skill and ability in Arabic; and such passages would ring in the ears of the Turks for whom it was intended. Many of them would have had only a slight knowledge of the language, their understanding of which went little beyond the Holy Quran. (al-Nahrawālī, Preface, 9–10.)

11. The Ottomans had soon regarded Yemen as a rich country which would provide steady revenue from taxes on spices coming from India; and by Muṣṭafā Qarah Pasha's time as governor-general (963–7/1556–60) such hopes had been well rewarded. Indeed, from the time of Özdemir Pasha as governor-general (956–62/1549–54), spices acquired from tax revenues were being sold in Egypt at a profit for the Ottoman state, a practice which Muṣṭafā Qarah's successor, Maḥmūd Pasha, organised on an annual basis. Governors-general, moreover, could have high financial expectations of their postings in Yemen, and Riḍwān Pasha is said to have spent 50,000 gold pieces in bribes for the post. He is also reported to have been exempted taxation on the spices he shipped through Jiddah in 972/1565 for sale on the open market in Egypt which he had acquired in Yemen in lieu of salary, following a tradition which began for senior officers such as *sanjaks* as early as 967/1560. (Blackburn, 'Collapse', 131–2, n. 47 and 49.) The figures given by the author illustrate the vast drop in revenue caused by the rebellion; and it is worth noting that in 1008/1599/1600, there was still a deficit of over 160,000 gold pieces. (nalchik, 85.)

12. Lines by the poet Bashshār b. Burd (c.95–c.167/c.714–c.784), and translated by Beeston (66, 6). Bashshār's career spanned the late Ummayad and early Abbasid periods. He was a master of panegyric and the erotic elegy and his barbed satires were much feared. He was charged with heresy, imprisoned and beaten to the point of death, and his body thrown into the Tigris. (*EAL*, I, 138–9.)

13. Ḥabb fortress still presents a spectacular sight as one approaches from the west along the flank of the Ba'dān range. It dated from pre-Islamic times and was regarded as one of the four strongest fortresses in Yemen; true to its reputation, its conquest presented the Turks with a formidable task. It had been owned by 'Alī b. al-Naẓẓārī, a wealthy man with connections with the Indian trade, who surrendered it, in circumstances of great treachery, to the governor-general, Maḥmūd Pasha, in 969/1562 after a siege lasting eight months. It was now occupied by 'Alī b. Sharaf al-Dīn, Muṭahhar's brother. (Kay, 18; and al-Nahrawālī, 130–2.) There is a description and plan of the fortress in Farah (39 and 41), in which we are told that the store chamber was carved out of the rock, with fourteen openings at the top, wide enough for a slender Yemeni to enter, and a storage capacity of several tons of grain. One of the cisterns measured 54 metres in length and 14 metres at the widest end.

14. Describing Wadi Sahūl, Hugh Scott wrote of 'this fertile vale' being 'framed in grand mountain scenery, especially on the right and the front', with 'rocky hillocks, rising from the broad cultivated valley-floor'. (Scott, 105–6.)

15. The text has Samār but the pass is known by the name of Samārah. Niebuhr, ill with fever, remembers little of his journey but Scott gives some atmospheric effect to his account of this dramatic passage at 3,000 metres leading to 'an abrupt descent of some hundreds of feet to the plateau of Yarīm'. (Scott, 109–10.) The fort is still in use and its clear-cut sandstone features are a familiar sight on the skyline.

16. Niebuhr's view of the town was less favourable, partly no doubt because of the death and burial there of his colleague, the naturalist Pehr Forsskål, in July 1763; and, although he was there more or less at the same time of year, the rains north of the Samārah pass had failed and there was a plague of locusts! He mentions that Yarīm was a seat of government, lodged in a castle on a rock. (Niebuhr, I, 356–60.)

17. This account is endorsed by John Jourdain who in 1609 added that it was 'populous and unwalled', on a fertile plain with abundant well-water drawn from outside the town. He noted that it held a garrison of about 200 soldiers. (Jourdain, 87.) It was famed for its horses and was an important Zaydī religious centre, with an extensive teaching mosque. (*EI*, II, 218.)

18. The exact route Sinān took northwards from Dhamār is not absolutely certain but in all probability it would have been via Zirājah, and not via Ma'bar (the route taken by the present main road). The route would have presented great difficulty but the fact that it normally took six stages, with Dhirā' al-Kalb halfway between the two, should not be forgotten. The exact whereabouts of the latter are not certain but Dhirā' (DOS map 1444A2 335478), north of Zirājah, the main town in al-Ḥadā' district, must be a strong candidate. It cannot have been Zirājah itself (Brouwer, 68 n. 1) because of its proximity to Dhamār. The route via Zirājah was taken by John Jourdain during his visit in 1018/1609, forty years later, as it was in 1177/1763 by Niebuhr who refers to the road being 'very rugged' and 'marshy and ill-cultivated towards Suradge'. In Captain Playfair's map of 1859 the main route north passes through 'Serajeh'. By 1917, it existed as 'an alternative and somewhat shorter track ... but it goes over very mountainous country; impassable for wheeled traffic but practicable for pack animals'. 'Nusail Zirajah' is listed on the route, 13 miles north of Zirājah. (Jourdain, 86–8 and n. 1 on 81; Niebuhr, I, 363; Playfair, facing xii; and *Yemen Handbook*, 145.) We have a further reference to this route being the main route when, in 1036/1626/7, a raid was made against the Turkish garrison in al-Dhirā' which guarded the 'Yemen road to Ṣan'ā'', causing the garrison commander to flee to Dhamār. (Yaḥyā b. Ḥusayn, 822.)

19. Of which the author was 'Abdullāh Muḥammad al-Ḥimyarī. See the Bibliography.

20. By far the best reference for these paragraphs concerning Ṣan'ā' is Serjeant's *San'ā'* which contains a comprehensive body of information about the city. G. R. Smith's article therein covering the city's early and medieval history, for example, contains the story of the appeal to the Persian emperor, Kisrā, (51b); and at 122–3 there is further information concerning the palace of Ghumdān and the fate of the false prophet al-Aswad al-'Ansī. We even obtain corroboration concerning the concentration of summer rainfall! (14).

21. Muḥammad b. Isḥāq (85–151/704/5–768/9) produced a *sīrah* or biography of the Prophet without rival, translated with notes by Alfred Guillaume. See the Bibliography.

22. In all likelihood this fortress is the one on the top of M. Ḥaḍūr, 18 kilometres west of Ṣan'ā' and, at over 3,600 metres, the highest mountain in Arabia. (al-Maqḥafī, 180.) It would have been the ideal place from which to harry troops and transport on their way to Thulā and Kawkabān, as the Turks already knew to their cost. Muḥammad b. Shams al-Dīn had used it as his base against Riḍwān Pasha in the early days of the rebellion. (Blackburn, 'Collapse', 145.)

23. An impregnable stronghold north-east of Ṣan'ā'. Earlier it had been in the hands of the Banū Anf, for long the leading family of the Ismā'īlī in Yemen. More recently, Muṭahhar's brother, 'Alī, had owned it but he had been dispatched to Ḥabb. Muṭahhar then gave it to his own son, Luṭfallāh, who remained there after both Sinān's expedition and Muṭahhar's death. (Yaḥyā b. Ḥusayn, 565, 763 and 745.)

24. The Ottomans were always short of oarsmen for their galleys. Ḥasan Pasha's raid into

this Zaydī area east of Ṣan'ā' for provisions and men cannot have endeared him to the local population!

25. Sūrah CI, 10 and 11 and Sūrah LXIX, 8.

26. The name given to the beast, generally depicted as a winged creature of exceptional fleetness, on which the Prophet is said to have ridden during his night-journey, accompanied by Jibrīl, from Mecca to Jerusalem and back. In later legend the beast developed into a flying steed and was associated with the Prophet's ascent to heaven, originally undertaken by ladder. (*EI*, I, 1310–11.) Muslims refer to the Wall of Burāq rather than the Wailing Wall.

27. Rather a gloomy village which the Austrian scholar Eduard Glaser described as 'a collection of black houses and huts' when he passed there in November 1883. (Werdecker, 30.)

28. Sinān may have thought that it would be possible to take Kawkabān by an assault from below, and the conquest of Shibām and the two bastions of al-'Āriḍah and Lubākhah would have been a first step towards such an end. Al-Nahrawālī makes such capture seem conclusive but elsewhere we are told that no sooner had Sinān's troops chased Shibām's fleeing inhabitants up to al-'Āriḍah, than they were attacked by Muṭahhar's men who had climbed up by another path. It is probable, however, that this simply reflects one episode in the fighting but it would be very difficult to maintain possession of the town without having charge of Kawkabān above. Continual skirmishing developed between the two sides after Sinān had moved his camp to the plain of Jawshān between Kawkabān and Thulā which was to remain his main base for nine months. (Yaḥyā b. Ḥusayn, 737–8.) The author betrays his lack of first-hand acquaintance with the town when he wrongly states that it was on the top of a mountain and four stages from the Ḥaḍramawt. (For more information see *EI*, IX, 425.)

29. See n. 19 above.

30. The word used here is *al-sabā*, the eastern wind. (Varisco, 116.)

31. His uncle may indeed have been the Dā'ī Muḥammad b. Ismā'īl but on another occasion the author was mistaken in referring to another Dā'ī 'Abdullāh as the nephew of the Dā'ī Muḥammad, when in fact he was his son. (Blackburn, 'Collapse', 135, n. 62.)

32. Called Jawshān. (Yaḥyā b. Ḥusayn, 736.) See n. 28 above.

33. Sinān will no doubt have been advised before this council of war concerning the best strategy to be adopted; and the fact that the *dā'ī* immediately afterwards left for his area to collect troops with a view to a joint attack on Kawkabān indicates that he had a central role in such a strategy. Indeed, as we shall see, Ḥasan Pasha was to be instructed to go and look for him since the Turks realised that, without his help, they could make no further headway. The *dā'ī* would no doubt have supported, indeed argued for, a strategy that concentrated on prising Muḥammad b. Shams al-Dīn and his fortress town of Kawkabān from Muṭahhar's influence. The Turks had made separate arrangements before with Muḥammad's father who, because of his frequent hostility to Muṭahhar, was seen as a more malleable target. The strategy was in the end to prove successful, but success was for long elusive and came only at great cost to the Turks.

34. A village nestling within the skirts of the Ḍula' mountain range between Kawkabān and Thulā, and not far distant from Sinān's base at Jawshān.

CHAPTERS 30–38

1. It is clear that, from his first arrival in Muṭahhar's heartlands, Sinān was subjected to guerrilla warfare on an unexpected scale; and his impatience for the Dā'ī 'Abdullāh's return should be seen in this light. For the *dā'ī* had exceeded the twenty days given for his commission only by a week or so when Ḥasan Pasha was dispatched, with a considerable force including the respected commander Maḥmūd Bey and the elite *mutafarriqah*, on 5 Rabī' al-Thānī/17 Sep-

tember to bring him back. Maḥmūd Bey was a mamluk and had taken part in the battle of al-Aghbar and the recent skirmishes at Ḥababah. (al-Nahrawālī, 223 and 295–6.)

2. The reported loss of the Janissaries described in this chapter must have disturbed Sinān badly. The Janissaries, like senior staff in the sultan's palaces and the Ottoman civil service, were recruited through the *devshirme*, the term used for the periodic levy of Christian children in countries under Ottoman rule. Of the seven corps comprising the Ottoman garrison in Egypt, the Janissaries were the largest and most important unit. They were an elite infantry corps and guarded Cairo and the citadel. By this time they would all have been carrying the arquebus, albeit with a longer barrel than that used in Europe. Reportedly, 2,000 Janissaries from Egypt and 500 from Syria had been directed to join the expedition. (Winter, 9; *EI*, I, 1061; Ṣāliḥiyyah, 44; and Serjeant, *San'ā'*, 71.)

3. A ancient town on a dramatic mountain-top site, with evidence of pre-Islamic occupation and some outstanding structures from successive ruling dynasties, including water tanks reputedly constructed by the Ayyubid leader, Ṭughtakīn, in the late sixth/twelfth century. The town had long been associated with the Imam Sharaf al-Dīn who had retired there with his immediate family and his favourite son, Shams al-Dīn, in 952/1546, remaining there until 960/1553; and to that period should be attributed the Great Mosque and teaching college which he founded. The gravestones of leading members of his family are further witness to the importance attached to the town. (See C. K. Smith, 33–50; and Yaḥyā b. Ḥusayn, 696 and 713.) The author returns to the subject of the ditch/chasm as the siege progresses. Kawkabān became an obsession with Sinān, as he saw its capture as the political key to the campaign. At this stage Yemeni morale was clearly high and Sinān's presence at its foot was signalled from Kawkabān to Thulā by cannon and fires, to be followed by an attack on his camp at Jawshān. Sarcastic references to Muṭahhar cannot disguise the irritation felt by the Turks at their failure to seduce the Zaydī into battle in the open field where they would be at a disadvantage against the disciplined and better-armed Ottoman troops.

4. After abandoning Ṣan'ā', Muṭahhar had fled to Thulā which he had made his base and where his father, the Imam Sharaf al-Dīn, had lived from 923–33/1517–28. Thulā is an ancient town built of stone of a glowing amber like that of Kawkabān, some 8 kilometres to the south. The town clusters to the east of the mountain top of 2,960 metres, holding its citadel called Ḥuṣn al-Ghurāb (Citadel of Crows), an impregnable site furnished with some nineteen stores for grain and a number of cisterns carved out of the stone. In 1873 Glaser was only able to climb to the citadel when assisted by local climbers and strong rope! The cannon, muskets and other weapons held there by Muṭahhar would have rendered it impossible to take by storm, whereas the rampart walls of the town below, dating apparently from Muṭahhar's time, would not have afforded that much protection, but there is no sign that Sinān launched a concerted attack against it; nor did he put it under siege. The town contains a number of ancient mosques, the oldest dating to the sixth/eleventh century, and a *madrasah* or teaching mosque named after the Imam Sharaf al-Dīn in which Muṭahhar is buried. The tomb within the qubbah supports a slab with fine calligraphy forming his sarcophagus. The cupola above is decorated with stucco work of exquisite design reminiscent of Iranian work. (*EI*, X, 449; and Golvin and Fromont, variatim, esp. 46–7.)

5. In other words, wonders never cease!

6. *Rumāh* or shooters, possibly with arrows rather than muskets. (Serjeant, *The Portuguese*, 109 and 171.) On balance, given the fact that Muṭahhar certainly possessed muskets, it is probable that they were used in an attack of this scale on the Turkish base. Yaḥyā b. Ḥusayn gives a very similar account of the engagement, adding that, again, the guns had sounded from Kawkabān and that the command in the area was divided between Muḥammad b. Shams al-Dīn and Muṭahhar, the latter having commissioned Farḥān to carry out the attack from Thulā. (Yaḥyā b. Ḥusayn, 738.)

7. Elsewhere, we are led to understand that Muṭahhar had ordered his son not to descend to the foot of the mountain; moreover, the engagement had ended in losses on both sides.

(Yaḥyā b. Ḥusayn, 738–9.) This chapter illustrates the venom and prejudice the author can display against Muṭahhar and the way he exaggerates what was probably a minor engagement into a major battle at a time when Sinān was in fact hard pressed to resist Muṭahhar's guerrilla attacks during the absence of the Dā'ī 'Abdullāh and Ḥasan Pasha. Al-Hādī had been, of course, one of Muṭahhar's valued lieutenants who had fought at al-Aghbar.

8. By mid-Dhū al-Ḥijjah 975/ mid-June 1568, Ta'izz, Aden, Mocha and Mawza' had all fallen to 'Alī b. Shuway' who had emerged for a time as Muṭahhar's principal commander in the south. However, the Zaydī met strong resistance as they approached Zabīd and 'Alī had been ordered by Muṭahhar to consolidate his position at Ḥays. From there he could have contained the Turks at Zabīd and forced their departure from the country through severing their lines of supply and communication. Instead, however, he advanced on Zabīd and, against the odds, was defeated near the town by Ḥasan Pasha. He was lucky to escape with his life. (Blackburn, 'Collapse', 167–8.)

9. These verses have been cited above [270], in a typical passage wherein the author displays his knowledge of Arabic poetry through the mouth of his protagonist.

10. Sūrah CIV, 4–7.

11. Sūrah IV, 78.

12. Sūrah XXX, 2–3. By Romans, Byzantines were meant.

13. These fortresses were of great strategic value and guarded the entrance to Wadi al-Ahjir (the Bāb al-Ahjir), the headwaters of Wadi Surdud, which leads westwards via Shamāt to al-Ṭawīlah. The Turks would have needed to secure this route in their efforts to climb the escarpment to Kawkabān from the south. The attacks on both 'Arūs and Sinān's camp, described in this chapter, are mentioned by Yaḥyā b. Ḥusayn, 739. The fortresses lie within one and a half miles of each other. According to written information provided by Nicholas Hall, Keeper of Artillery for the Royal Armouries at Fort Nelson, the range of a sound long gun of culverin type, with good powder, shot and crew, would have been unlikely at this time to have exceeded a mile and a half.

14. The irritation felt by the Turks at Muṭahhar's well-controlled harassment of the supply lines etc. is almost palpable.

15. A practice to be compared with that of the Kikuyu women in Kenya who traditionally carried heavy loads on their backs attached to thongs on their foreheads; and Berber women in the High Atlas still carry such heavy loads on their backs.

16. The word used for horse is *ziyam*, a horse belonging to Jābir b. Ḥunaynī. (Ibn Manẓūr, *s.v.*)

17. The word used is *'arabāt*, wagons, drawn by horses, oxen or mules, for carrying cannon, both large or small. Camels were used for drawing lighter types of gun, especially over difficult terrain. (*EI*, I, 1062.) Note the appearance of *'ajalāt al-ḍarbunzāt* or gun carriages at [317] below.

18. This is in many respects a sad chapter for Sinān, enlightened towards the end by the victory at Wadi Khubān, south-east of Dhamār. On this occasion the minister was unsuccessful in two attempts to take Bayt 'Izz, an important stronghold on Mt Ḍula', west of Kawkabān. It is likely that the minister's first attempt was up Wadi Ghazwān which has its source just west of the stronghold. Glaser was able to visit the ruins of Bayt 'Izz which he noted had been 'entirely destroyed by the Turks'. (Werdecker, 35.) From Yaḥyā b. Ḥusayn, we learn that the Zaydī were able to block the pass up the Wadi 'Arwān during the minister's second attempt after Ḥasan Pasha had returned to the area with the *dā'ī*. Wadi 'Arwān flows down the escarpment much further west in Banū Khayyāt country towards al-Ṭawīlah. From other references in the Zaydī historian, it would seem that Ḥasan Pasha was very far from having things his own way as he sought a passage up the escarpment to Mt Ḍula' but he must have established that this pass up Wadi 'Arwān was less likely to be blocked, as being further from Kawkabān itself. (Yaḥyā b. Ḥusayn, 736–7 and 739.) But this second attempt anticipates the story somewhat, to

be resumed after the diversion concerning the intervening movements of the *dāʿī* and Ḥasan Pasha who had gone in search of him!

19. Sūrah LXXVII, 32.

20. Sūrah XX, 2.

21. See n. 27 of Chapters 11–18 above. It has not proved possible to identify the castle of Durām (vocalisation conjectural).

22. There is a discrepancy in the date of the *dāʿī*'s departure for al-Ḥaymah. Here the author states that he left for al-Luʾluʾah on 6 Rabīʿ al-Awwal/19 August and was in Ānis by 11 Rabīʿ al-Awwal/24 August whereas on [294] he states that he left after the capture of Shibām on 11 Rabīʿ al-Awwal/24 August. The minister must have reached al-Munaqqab, the beginning of the *dāʿī*'s territory in Hamdān, on his initial journey from Ṣanʿāʾ on 6 Rabīʿ al-Awwal/19 August. The difference in dates is quite significant.

23. After raising his standard on Masār in 429/1037/8, in support of the Fatimids in Egypt, ʿAlī b. Muḥammad al-Sulayḥī had ascended and seized the fortress on Mt Ḥaḍūr, and then the fortress of Yanāʿ, on its lower slopes. (Kay, 251.)

24. The *dāʿī* has now moved north of the Ḥarāz mountains to the Banū Ismāʿīl country, north of Masār and south of Sāriʿ, which now falls more or less between the Wadi Surdud and the main road from al-Ḥudaydah to Ṣanʿāʾ, and, with Manākhah, forms a sub-district within the *qaḍāʾ* of Ḥarāz. Neither the two mountains, nor the two strongholds have been identified. It is possible that Ṭufayl is in the Ḥijāz. (Hamdānī, 334.)

25. Six of the eight tribes are listed in al-Maqḥafī (the exceptions being the Banū al-ʿAwādī and the Banū al-Daḥādiḥah) as representing *ʿuzlahs* or sub-sub-districts in the Sāriʿ area of the sub-district of Banū Saʿd, in the province of al-Maḥwīt. (al-Maqḥafī, 27, 348, 568, 702, 122 and 558.) (The last is named Majādil in the text.) The well-known market of Sūq al-Khamīs Banī Saʿd straddles the main al-Ḥudaydah/Ṣanʿāʾ road, south of al-Maḥwīt. (For information concerning Sāriʿ, an area now famous for tobacco, see al-Hamdānī, 110.) Apparently Sāriʿ was famous for the nimble donkey that scampered across it, to which there is an allusion in the Arabic text describing the *dāʿī*'s hasty progress.

26. Tays is the old name for Mt Banū Ḥabash, west of Kawkabān. (Hamdānī, 110; and al-Maqḥafī, 95.) Qarn al-Masjid (DOS map, 1543 D1 439895) is in the sub-district of Banū Saʿd.

27. The twelve zodiacal constellations were known as the *burūj* or *abrāj* (sing. *burj*). (Varisco, 85.)

28. The text indicates that these four fortresses were in Wadi al-Ḥaymah, the broad area some 37 kilometres from Ṣanʿāʾ, comprising al-Ḥaymah al-Dākhiliyyah and al-Ḥaymah al-Khārijiyyah. The former was formerly part of Ḥaḍūr, with one of its *ʿuzlahs* being Banū al-Aḥbūb, the second on the list. (al-Maqḥafī, 204–5.) al-Maṣnaʿah, the first on the list, is probably also in the area of Ḥaḍūr. (G. R. Smith, 180.) The Banū Suwayd appear as an *ʿuzlah* in Ḍawrān Ānis, to the east of al-Ḥaymah al-Khārijiyyah, which could be a strong possibility for the third fortress since the *dāʿī* is said to have gone there [324]. The fourth has not been identified.

29. The fortress of Barāsh al-Bāqir is 6 kilometres to the south of al-Ṭawīlah. (al-Waysī, 64.) The two Jalids are within the vicinity. Sinān decided that Barāsh had to be destroyed because of its strategic position *vis-à-vis* the approach to Kawkabān (see [347–8] below).

CHAPTERS 39–44

1. After the two previous diversionary chapters, the narrative resumes with the attempts by the Turks to climb the Ḍulaʿ massif escarpment and set siege to Kawkabān during which it is clear that Ḥasan Pasha and the Dāʿī ʿAbdullāh were in serious difficulty. Muṭahhar had so far succeeded in his intention, more or less, to dictate the field and type of battle the Turks were

to fight, and to frustrate their attempts to ascend the mountain massif where Kawkabān and so many of his strongholds were placed. To these his forces, often small in number, would retreat once they had succeeded in harrying the Turks. Hit-and-run tactics and ambushes in narrow mountain passes in harsh terrain did serious damage to Turkish morale and supplies but were termed defeats by the author and his contemporaries who sympathised with the Turkish aim to fight in set battle. Moreover, the Yemeni took every advantage of the mountainous terrain which they naturally knew well and where the Turkish cavalry was of no value. These tactics were to continue even after the Turks had climbed the escarpment when Sinān faced the additional task, from diminishing military numbers, of guarding those laying siege to Kawkabān and those from his own base below at Jawshān who took their daily turn in coming to their assistance. (Sālim, 258–64.)

2. Muḥammad b. Raḍī al-Dīn was the Imam Sharaf al-Dīn's grandson and another of Muṭahhar's nephews. We are told elsewhere that he was killed in a second engagement lasting three days between Ḥasan Pasha and Muṭahhar's commanders, 'Alī b. al-Shuway' and Muḥammad b. Shams al-Dīn, at a place called Ṣan'ān which must be the same place as the Ḍay'ān mentioned here. Muḥammad b. Raḍī al-Dīn's body was carried to al-Ṭawīlah where he was buried next to the stronghold well. (Yaḥyā b. Ḥusayn, 737.)

3. The date presents a real difficulty since it post-dates action that followed. Moreover, we may remember that the minister had already directed the Ismā'īlī leader and Ḥasan Pasha to take part in a two-pronged attack on Bayt 'Izz, supposedly on the night of 14 Jumādā al-Ūlā/25 October (i.e. in Islamic reckoning, the evening of 24 October) which had proved unsuccessful, largely because the other two commanders had not taken part. And the minister had returned despondent to his camp, to be heartened by the victory at Wadi Khubān which had taken place on 27 Rabī' al-Thānī/9 October (al-Nahrawālī, 319 and 322). Later we are told that the minister had sent two waves of reinforcements to Ḥasan Pasha on 8 and 9 Jumādā al-Ūlā/19 and 20 October, and that the escarpment was successfully climbed, and Bayt 'Izz taken on 16 Jumādā al-Ūlā/27 October (al-Nahrawālī, 334 and 340). At present there is no way of correcting these dates with certainty but we can infer that the minister's failed attempt on Bayt 'Izz took place long before 14 Jumādā al-Ūlā/25 October and that the engagement under discussion took place earlier in Jumādā al-Ūlā/October. It appears that it took time before coordination was restored between the three commanders after the return of the *dā'ī* and Ḥasan Pasha.

4. Sūrah XCIII, 2.

5. The Turks belonged to the Ḥanafī school of Islam.

6. Sūrah LXI, 4.

7. Mamluks were often given nicknames. (Goodwin, 42.)

8. This battle appears to have allowed the Turks to make the concerted and successful ascent of the escarpment described in the next chapter, as is corroborated in the account of Yaḥyā b. Ḥusayn, with the important difference that the latter states that it was the capture of the stronghold of Shamāt that allowed their ascent. Al-Nahrawālī places that capture rather later in his account but indicates that the artillery was carried up the escarpment behind Shamāt fortress for use against Kawkabān. The defeat caused the Zaydī commanders to scatter to various fortresses and the ascent of the Turkish cannon made Muḥammad b. Shams al-Dīn release Turkish prisoners held in Kawkabān who had been in Ṣan'ā' when it fell to Muṭahhar; for he was already losing his nerve and inclined towards a separate peace treaty with the Turks.

9. The chapter discloses how, at long last, Sinān's forces were able to climb the escarpment and set siege to Kawkabān. It is not certain as to which the Qillah route in fact was but it is probable that it was one of the routes in Banū Khayyāt country behind Shamāt, possibly that of Wadi Ghazwān leading into Wadi 'Arāwir, within reach of the stronghold of Ḥajar al-Rakānīn. Sinān Pasha was left to raise the sultan's standard over Bayt 'Izz which must have to some extent atoned for his two previous failures to take the stronghold. Again, however, the narrative makes clear the important role of the *dā'ī* in the endeavour. It had taken the Turks two months from their entry to Ṣan'ā' to put Kawkabān under siege from a site opposite the

north of the town, facing the main gate of Bāb al-Ḥadīd. Whatever the boost to his morale, however, Sinān would have had a fair idea beforehand of the strength of the town's fortifications, and of the vast natural chasm to be crossed by any wishing to take it by storm. Moreover, Kawkabān was defended by heavy cannon and other weapons which would have made it very difficult for Sinān to station his own cannon and *ḍarbuzān* within the 330 yards necessary for their point-blank or accurate firing range. Al-Nahrawālī indicates in the chapter heading that the town had already been hit by fire, and elsewhere we read that its northern part was damaged during the campaign. But the strength of its own fire, together perhaps with lack of ammunition on the part of the Turks, must go some length towards explaining why the stronghold could not have been blasted out of existence as was the case, for example, with that at St Elmo in Malta, four years previously. At St Elmo, at one stage, the Turks had used 6–7,000 cannon balls! (Sālim, 370; information from Royal Armouries, Fort Nelson; Yaḥyā b. Ḥusayn, 739; and Bridge, 180.)

10. These appear to be two separate indivduals. It may be that the āghā was the *dāʿī*'s uncle, who was among those rescued from al-ʿĀriḍah, see [293] above.

11. Sūrah C, 2.

12. The normal practice was for the lighter *ḍarbuzān* or culverin to be used to split the stonework after which the heavy cannon could bring down the structure. (*EI*, I, 1061.)

13. There is a pun here on Sinān's name which means spear head.

14. Information is given here about the chasm, Turkish attempts to bridge which were to be frustrated in the future.

15. Yemen was famous for such stones. In 1606, the English traveller John Jourdain noted that 'many blud stones, agatts and catts eyes' were to be found in a mountain near Dhamār. (Jourdain, 87.)

16. The modern road between Shibām and al-Ṭawīlah virtually circles this grim stronghold guarding the route westward. A battle had been fought over Shamāt in 956/1549/50 between the Turkish governor-general Özdemir and Muṭahhar in which over 100 Turks had allegedly been slain. (Yaḥyā b. Ḥusayn, 705; Wilson, 205.) Shamāt was of great strategic value to both sides.

17. We are told that Muḥammad b. Shams al-Dīn and his twin brother, al-Ḥusayn, were responsible for releasing the prisoners. (Yaḥyā b. Ḥusayn, 737.)

18. Of these Yaḥyā b. Ḥusayn lists Maḥmūd Bey (as Nāẓir Bey), Shāh ʿAlī Bey, Qizilbash Meḥmed Bey and Qarah Kawz, with a fifth, Commander Yūsuf. Elsewhere, all but Ḥusayn Bey are among those listed as captured by Muṭahhar when Ṣanʿā' capitulated. The same historian adds that Shāh ʿAlī had been *sanjak* commander of Ṣaʿdah, and that the commanders interned in Ṣanʿā' had been incarcerated in Kawkabān only after they had been discovered conspiring with the Turks in the Tihāmah. (Yaḥyā b. Ḥusayn, 737; and Blackburn, 'Collapse', 160, n. 163.)

19. Qizilbash. Literally 'red-head' reflecting the red cap worn by Turcoman soldiers and applied to those with Shiʿite tendencies. (nalcik, xlviii.)

20. That is, difficulties do not endure.

21. Abū al-Ṭayyib Aḥmad al-Juʿfī (303–54/915–65) usually known as al-Mutanabbī, he who professes to be a prophet, the widely travelled and famous panegyrist, is perhaps best known for his work over nine years as an official poet to the Amīr Sayf al-Dawlah at Aleppo. His philosophy tended towards the stoic and pessimistic but his poetry was extremely influential throughout the Arab-speaking world. (*EI*, VII, 769–72.)

22. This last phrase has resonances of the Quran, Sūrah LXXXV, 5.

23. A high mountain in Ḥarāz, 2,940 metres in height, near which the Sulayhid leader, ʿAlī b. Muḥammad, first came out in support of the Fatimid *daʿwah*, in 429/1038.

24. Āṣāf b. Barakhyā was minister to Solomon and regarded as a model, with easy access to the king. (See Chapters 1–10, n. 34.)

25. The spelling of the first fort is conjectural. It is possible that al-ʿAqabah refers to a stronghold on the long mountain range facing the al-Bawn district, in which case the Banū ʿAmrān may refer to the old town of that name, north-east of Thulā guarding the road to the north. (Yaḥyā b. Ḥusayn, 548.) These four forts may all have held strategic value for communication with the north of the country.

26. These twelve fortresses were situated in the south of the country, the majority of them north of the Samārah pass. Shakhab is a lofty stronghold on Mt ʿUmmār in Nadirah district, just west of Damt district. (al-Maqḥafī, 347.) The author, in enumerating these strongholds to the west, north and south of Ṣanʿāʾ, is clearly attempting to do justice to Sinān and his commanders' success in winning over parts of the country before the renewed revolt broke out in Ramaḍān 977/March 1570.

27. The conjectured spelling of *Qarāwul* seems corrupt. It may refer to *Qaraghul*, the Turkish word for patrol; or it may even refer to *Kara-Ulus* or Kurds (nalcik, 33) from Diyār Bakr who were among those in Sinān's army. (See [213] above.)

28. Another reference to the damage done to Kawkabān.

29. It is possible that this Abū Dāwūd whose father was called al-Hādī was the grandson of Muṭahhar. Al-Hādī b. Muṭahhar had been killed in a previous engagement (see [312] above).

30. The incident is in fact described on [176]. Aḥmad Qizilbash had left for Ṣanʿāʾ with 400 loads of grain and 100 horsemen when they were all killed on 9 Dhū al-Ḥijjah/17 June 1567. It is also described by Yaḥyā b. Ḥusayn (726–7), and by Blackburn ('Collapse', 154–5).

31. We are here reminded of the hopes placed on Muḥammad b. Shams al-Dīn by the Turks in view of his father's and his own past cooperation with them.

32. We have confirmation of al-Ḥusayn's death in Shaʿbān/January fromYaḥyā b. Ḥusayn, who states that it was the death of this twin brother that made him wish for peace. (Yaḥyā b. Ḥusayn, 739–40.)

33. *Zarbāf* from the Turkish *zerbāf* or cloth of gold or gold velvet brocade. (Oz, 73.)

CHAPTERS 45–50

1. These three chapters (45–47) show the extent to which Muṭahhar had succeeded in forcing the Turks to defend themselves against the sort of guerrilla warfare with which we have already become familiar. Muṭahhar's withdrawals, after 'hit-and-run raids', are called defeats; his propaganda as to Turkish weakness and his alleged exaggeration of small victories are resented; and his call for help to the tribes in the far north and east are vilified. The author loses no opportunity to display his knowledge of pre-Islamic and classical poetry as counterpoint to the sonorous phrases with which he describes the battle scenes in his *sajʿ* or rhyming prose. The effect in Arabic is a great deal more dramatic than when translated into English! By now the actual siege of Kawkabān is well into its fourth month, and we are told there are clear signs of Muḥammad b. Shams al-Dīn, Muṭahhar's nephew in Kawkabān, wishing to sue for peace.

2. In Rajab 974/January/February 1567, Ṣaʿdah had fallen to Muṭahhar's forces in the first of the series of engagements that ousted the Turks from most of Yemen. Since then this important, though isolated, northern Ottoman fortress and its adjacent territories had been governed by the two chieftains responsible for its capture. (Blackburn, 'Collapse', 144–5.)

3. The sixth-century poet, Ziyād Muʿāwiyah al-Nābighah al-Dhubyānī. A pre-Islamic poet famous for his panegyrics upon the Lakhmid and Ghassanid kings, he can be regarded as the first great court poet in Arabic literature. Ḥimyar, Judhām and Bakr b. Wāʾil were three great tribal federations of Arabia. The last was northern Kindah and occupied the area of Riyadh and al-Kharj in what is now Saudi Arabia. (*EI*, I, 962–4.)

4. There are references to drums, kettledrums and pipes here and on [369] and [374].

These instruments added to the cacophony of the campaign. The great drum, some 3 feet high and carried on horseback into battle, was beaten at both ends, the top with a great stick and the bottom with a small stick at every small or passing note. It could be played with great skill and gravity, and to agreeable effect. The kettledrums were played in pairs and the treble pipe or hautboy played continuously. Without the guidance of the great drum the sound could be discordant. A pasha of ministerial rank such as Sinān, with three tails, would have in his entourage such a drum as well as two pairs of kettledrums and seven pipes. (Goodwin, 51; Marsigli, II, Plate XVIII and 54–5.) The ancient Mehter band, containing all these and more instruments, plays regularly at the Military Museum in Istanbul.

5. We understand from elsewhere that the first to come from Ṣa‘dah was Sayyid Aḥmad b. al-Ḥusayn al-Mu’ayyidī. (Yaḥyā b. Ḥusayn, 740.)

6. The Janissaries would have been most suited to the task. They were tough and experienced. As cadets they would have been subject to years of hardship and later would have helped with bridge-building and other public works. Sinān Pasha developed a hold over the Janissaries and could inflame them with victorious zeal. (Goodwin, 41, 85 and 153.) Circassian mamluks were organised separately as one of the seven corps of the Egyptian army. Mamluks were also in the service of high-ranking officers and dignitaries from those of the rank of minister and governor-general like Sinān downwards. (Winter, 9–11.)

7. Sūrah VI, 121.

8. The minister's obsession with Kawkabān again emerges here.

9. Sūrah XXXV, 27.

10. I have taken this fort to be that of Ḥaḍūr al-Shaykh, 3,350 metres high on the massif west of Thulā, commanding the road to the north. There are excellent views southwards along the massif to Kawkabān and, of course, eastwards to Thulā. This Ḥaḍūr seems more appropriate than the mountain west of Ṣan‘ā’ by the same name. It would have been a site of great strategic value. Interestingly, Muṭahhar's father, the Imam Sharaf al-Dīn, was born there in 877/1473. (Blackburn, 'Ottoman Penetration', 65, n. 6.)

11. Sūrah XX, 2.

12. The battle with its important casualties on either side is mentioned by Yaḥyā b. Ḥusayn (740), after which he claims Muṭahhar wrote to the tribes. (See n. 13 below.) ‘Izz al-Dīn is described as one of Sharaf al-Dīn's sons 'of some political standing' who had been equally opposed to the Turks and Muṭahhar! When in charge at Ṣa‘dah before the rebellion he had been of considerable trouble to the Turks and had been captured by Özdemir Bey while moving south to retake Ṣan‘ā’ from them. He had died in Yanbu‘, in 954/1547/early 1548, on the way to Istanbul where the new governor-general, Muṣṭafā al-Nashshār, had directed he be sent as hostage. (Blackburn, 'Ottoman Penetration', 86, n. 73.)

13. It is at this stage that Muṭahhar employed the second prong of his campaign against the Turks by intensive propaganda throughout the country against their rule. This campaign which the author now describes was very successful and caused the country to come out in renewed rebellion at a time when Sinān was preoccupied in his camp at Jawshān with the siege of Kawkabān. There is little doubt that Sinān was forced in these circumstances to agree peace with Muṭahhar in what were essentially humiliating circumstances, as indeed al-Nahrawālī makes clear. (Sālim, 263–4.) In fact, the historian Sālim quotes al-Nahrawālī's words acknowledging his own recognition of Muṭahhar's success (see Sālim, 272; and al-Nahrawālī, 384, lines 1–3 and 385) when he describes the reaction of the tribes to Muṭahhar's letter.

14. The *kharaj* or land tax had been one of the principal sources of friction before the rebellion. The author, earlier in his work [167], describes how Wadi al-Sirr, east of Ṣan‘ā’, had such tax increased eightfold by Riḍwān Pasha. But Muṭahhar's suggested remission for three years would have been a rash move bordering on the desperate; and one questions whether he would have honoured it. The *kharaj* was far and away the major source of revenue in Yemen for the Turks. For 1599/1600, it was projected at 200,000 gold pieces as 50 per cent of the

budget, with income from port dues at 29 per cent. (There was a deficit of over 161,000 gold pieces!) The percentage for *kharaj* for Yemen was higher than elsewhere in the empire, as indeed was that for the custom dues which came largely from the Indian transit trade. (nalcik, 85.) We are told that Sinān had doubled the *kharaj* to 200,000 gold pieces. (Serjeant, *San'ā'*, 72.)

15. De Sacy points out that there would not have been an eclipse on this date. There would, however, have been one a month before on 14 Ramaḍān/20 February; and this date fits the context better. (de Sacy, 491, [i].)

16. Lit. women of the *Ashrāf* or descendants of the Prophet, a group held in high esteem throughout the Arab world. In Yemen such descent was one of the prerequisites for election to the Imamate. In all probability, the *Ashrāf* would have been exempt from tax.

17. The word translated 'noble' is *aḥāmīs*, denoting those whose mothers came from the Prophet's tribe of Quraysh.

18. The story has often been told, with some variations. The author omits to mention the famous seer from Jadīs, Zarqa' al-Yamāmah, whose reported sight of the approaching army was discounted. (*EI*, X, 359–60.) It is possible that the author, in describing the story of Jadīs and Ṭasm at such length, is revealing his own sympathy for the allegory's relevance for Turkish oppression in Yemen.

19. Historian of Mecca (775–832/1373–1429), ideally suited through his family connections and upbringing. He was appointed Mālikī judge in Mecca from 807/1405, with brief interruptions, until four years before his death. (Details of his life and works are given in *EI*, II, 828–9.)

20. Sūrah XXXV, 43.

21. Lines of the poet al-Mutannabī. Translated by Arberry (81, 29 and 30).

22. Sūrah XCIX, 7–8.

23. Sanḥān and Ḥaḍūr are respectively south-east and west of Ṣan'ā'. Sanḥān, a *nāḥiyah* of Ṣan'ā' district, is described by al-Waysī (77–8). Ḥaḍūr gives its name to the highest mountain in Arabia, also known as Jabal Nabī Shu'ayb, and is in the Banū Maṭar sub-district. (al-Waysī, 76.)

24. We have seen how Qaṭrān was removed from the stronghold of Bayt al-Khawlān on the top of Jabal Ḥaḍūr. See [287–8] above. He then crossed to Jabal Lawz in the *nāḥiyah* of Khawlān, east of Ṣan'ā', from which he harried the Turks in Ṣan'ā' and elsewhere. We are told that Qaṭrān al-Samāḥī and 'Alī b. Nushayr reacted most effectively to Muṭahhar's request to incite the tribes to renewed rebellion, especially along the route through Ḥaddā to Dhamār. (Yaḥyā b. Ḥusayn, 740–1.)

25. The building is known as the Qaṣr al-Silāḥ, or the Citadel.

26. I am indebted to Professor Serjeant for much of this translation of what is gramatically a very tight passage. (Serjeant, *San'ā'*, 70–1.)

CHAPTERS 51–55

1. Everything must have seemed to be conspiring against the minister. Not only had Muṭahhar dictated the field and type of warfare; but now Sinān was seriously short of the troops and funds required to meet the renewed rebellion that had broken out after Muṭahhar's propaganda campaign. The figures the author gives here for Sinān's position over funding and troops illustrate the seriousness of his position. They are consistent with his earlier statement that there were between three and four thousand horsemen in Sinān's cavalcade passing through Mecca. That figure takes no account of infantry such as the Janissaries. (See [212] and n. 10.)

Later he claims that the minister had only some 1,200 with him at his base camp at Jawshān on the plain below Kawkabān. (See [368].)

2. It is curious to read that it was Muḥammad b. Shams al-Dīn's mother who had released the commanders in Kawkabān. One imagines a medieval chatelaine with the keys at her waist! Earlier he had said that Muḥammad had done so. (See [345] and n. 17.)

3. The word used is *al-Turk* which clearly here, and elsewhere in this account of Sinān's campaign, means Turks in contrast to the Mamluks who are separately specified. Earlier in the century, and for that matter in al-Nahrawālī, *al-Turk* refers to the Mamluks whereas Turks are called *al-Rūmī*, i.e. from Anatolia. (Serjeant, *The Portuguese*, 48, n. 7.)

4. Sūrah II, 195.

5. The word used here is *yalb*, body protection from camel skin. (Ibn Manẓūr, *s.v.*)

6. It is interesting to see the prominent role played by Sinān's mamluks. The custom of recruiting boys and young men from the Caucasus as military slaves, or mamluks, and training them as soldiers in households geared to the purpose appears not only to have survived but to have flourished in Ottoman Egypt, long after the fall of the Mamluk state in 1517. By the time of the French invasion in 1798, Egypt's military elite was dominated by Caucasian, and notably Georgian, mamluks. (Hathaway, 108.)

7. This quotation appears on [327]. See also [327], n. 27.

8. The Fatimids. Qarāqūsh was a eunuch who was appointed vizier by the last Fatimid sultan, al-ʿĀḍid (555–67/1160–71). After the fall of the Fatimid dynasty to Saladin, he was given the task of constructing the citadel in Cairo and other buildings. He later held a number of important posts in Cairo, including that of regent. Contemporary historians bestowed the highest praise upon him but his name became notorious as a byword for stupidity, in large measure due to a number of absurd and severe judgments for which he was responsible. (*EI*, IV, 613–14.)

9. The commanders of the pilgrimage had to protect the caravans against the bedu who often attacked and pillaged them; moreover, they had to negotiate with and induce the bedu to cooperate with the caravans rather than endanger them. The mamluks' experience and background had convinced the Ottomans that Circassian commanders were natural and even preferable commanders for such an office. (Winter, 15.)

10. See [280]–[281] and n. 13.

11. Al-Shawāfī is a large *nāḥiyah* or sub-district, north-west of Ibb. (al-Maqḥafī, 367.)

12. See Chapters 11–18, n. 27.

13. The references to coffee houses in this and the next paragraph are exciting and in all probability represent the first such references to coffee houses in Yemen, although there is a reference to coffee being offered to the two Portuguese Jesuits in 1590, some twenty years later. We are told that the drinking of coffee as a social habit was first introduced to Istanbulin c.1555 by two Syrians although the practice had long been associated with Sufi orders in their worship. By the 1600s the Turks preferred to drink their coffee in coffee houses rather than at home. However, by the early 1500s coffee's use had no longer been restricted to Sufi orders in Yemen and was increasingly consumed in the Ḥijāz and Egypt. But outside the home, it was first associated with taverns and places of a rather disreputable nature. It would seem that here in Dhū Jiblah and Ibb, while such places may have been grouped together, the coffee houses were separate establishments. The inference is that they were well established and not a very recent development. In a disapproving account of the louche atmosphere of contemporary Cairene coffee houses, we are told by a late sixteenth-century traveller that they were filled with 'dissolute persons' and 'veteran soldiers, aged officers' (*chausan* and *muteferriqas*). (Hattox, 72–91 and 113–14.) Perhaps the sort of people well used to such coffee houses in Yemen!? Hattox does not appear to have noticed this reference; and al-Nahrawālī is among those he cites as showing no interest in the controversy surrounding its earlier, increased usage in Mecca. (Hattox, 30 and

n. 3.) We have a reference by Sir Henry Middleton in 1611 to poppy growing some 16 miles south of al-Makhādir on the road from Naqīl Samārah (presumably near Ibb) from which opium was made (which he claimed not to be good). A further 16 miles in a plain on the way to Ta'izz a coffee house is mentioned where his party rested. One wonders if opium was provided in these places of entertainment? (Kerr, 382–3.)

14. See above [232] and [233] and n. 44 and [249]–[253] and ns 17–25.

15. In a sense this was a case of carrying coals to Newcastle; for we know that there was a supply of sulphur near Dhamār from Mt Kibrīt and that gunpowder was made from it. (Serjeant, *San'ā'*, 73b and n. 39.)

16. The word used for intimate is *mubāṭin*. I was told by the then head of the civil service in the Yemen Arab Republic, Ḥusayn al-Muqbilī, that, when he was an official visitor among the bedu in the east of the country, the word was applied to someone honoured by being allowed to sleep with an unmarried daughter of the house, but without sexual congress! He had been honoured with the privilege.

17. In [399] above we were told that there were some 300 troops laying Ḥabb under siege before the arrival of Khiḍr Bey with the heavy guns. Barways Bey had gone to Dhamār with some fifty men. Elsewhere, we are told that the entire Turkish force of 800 was massacred in the forthcoming battle. (Yaḥyā b. Ḥusayn, 740.)

18. Riḍwān is the angel at the gate of Paradise, and Mālik that of hell.

19. The minister had put a good face on the defeat and reiterated his preoccupation with Kawkabān. By now he was desperate for peace terms.

20. Sūrah XXVI, 227.

21. Li'sān is the long plain just south of the Wadi Sihām before it passes north of Mt Bura' into the Tihāmah. After the Dā'ī 'Abdullāh's successful campaign through Ḥarāz the journey westwards from Jawshān would have been more secure.

22. See [281] above for the first mention of this commander. Muṣṭafā al-Nashshār had established the official pilgrimage for Yemen, with its own commander and *maḥmil* (ceremonial, camel-borne Islamic litter). The Grand Sharīf would meet the pilgrimage at Barkat al-Mājin, just outside Mecca; later the commander would stand with its own banner, drum and horn at the *waqfah* by Mt 'Arafāt. (al-Nahrawālī, 121–2.)

23. Radā' was an important town under the Tahirid dynasty (858–923/1454–1517).

24. Not to be confused with the Ṣafar Bey mentioned in [251], n. 21.

25. Presumably, an earlier detachment than the 600 who had arrived with Behrām Bey. (See [433] below.)

26. I am not sure whether these colours refer to the skin colour of the troops or the flags carried by the cavalry and the Janissaries. (Goodwin, 71–2.) I suspect the former.

27. See references to this ditch or chasm in [303] and n. 3, [342] and n. 14, and [343].

28. This sentiment seems misplaced in view of the earlier lament over the Turks' failure to take Malta. (See [239] and n. 1.)

29. No mention is made here of any shortage of gunpowder, in marked contrast to the Turkish position expressed in [418] below. Moreover, the author laments the fact that the Zaydī had supplies of gunpowder. (See [435] and n. 13 below.)

30. Sūrah XXXIX, 3.

31. Shams al-Dīn b. Sharaf al-Dīn. (See n. 33 below.)

32. Sūrah XLII, 23.

33. His father, Shams al-Dīn b. Sharaf al-Dīn, had become an active Turkish protégé during his rivalry with his brother, Muṭahhar, and an important, if not decisive, factor in the Turkish campaign against Muṭahhar. We are told by Yaḥyā b. Ḥusayn that, at the request of the new governor-general, Muṣṭafā al-Nashshār, Shams al-Dīn had sent his son to meet him in Bayt al-

Faqīh. Muḥammad had so disliked what he saw and heard in the Tihāmah that he advised his father to seek peace with his brother, Muṭahhar. During a subsequent and extensive friendly tour with him, Shams al-Dīn died at Barāsh in Ṣafar 963/December 1555, and was carried to Kawkabān for burial. There was no suggestion of foul play but news of his death was hidden from his father. (Yaḥyā b. Ḥusayn, 715–16.)

34. Lit. someone who beats *al-naqārah*, a Pharsee term for drum. (de Sacy, 498, [o]).

35. *al-Jāmi' al-saḥīḥ*, usually referred to as *saḥīḥ*, forms, together with the *saḥīḥ al-Bukhārī*, the most reliable collection of Prophetic traditions of all time, according to the consensus of Sunnī Muslim scholars. Muslim b. Hajjāj (c.206–61/821–75) travelled widely in search of such traditions and collected just over 3,000 distinct ones. (*EI*, VII, 691–2.)

36. This was play-acting on a grand scale and amusingly reported by the author. The importance of the agreement can be inferred from the dire position facing the Turks which was outlined in [418] above.

37. In view of Muḥammad b. Shams al-Dīn's letter having been dated 12 Dhū al-Qa'dah/ 18 April (see [422] above), the date for this letter cannot be correct. The minister's later letter incorporating the peace treaty was dated 10 Dhū al-Ḥijjah/16 May (see [426] below). The correct date was probably later in Dhū al-Qa'dah/April.

38. *al-'alīqah bi 'ishrīn muḥallaqan*. This translation is suggested by Professor Osman Sid Ahmed. An alternative translation might be twenty bales of forage; or indeed de Sacy's translation, meaning that every bale of forage cost 20 *muḥallaq*, a unit of currency. (de Sacy, 434, [o]).

39. Sūrah V, 95.

40. Sūrah XVI, 91.

41. Sūrah XXXVIII, 27.

42. The pre-Islamic name for Medina.

43. Kurj was the province of Georgia in Western Caucasia. The former governor-general of Yemen, Muṣṭafā Lālā Pasha, was to fight a successful campaign there in 986/1578. (*EI*, VII, 72.) By Daylum is meant the highlands of Gilan. (*EI*, II, 189–94.)

44. It should be noted that, in Sinān's agreement with Muṭahhar, he specifically excluded al-Ṭawīlah, presumably because of its strategic importance. (See [430] and [431] below.) In the previous agreement with the Turks Muṭahhar had to yield al-Ṭawīlah. (Yaḥyā b. Ḥusayn, 708.)

CHAPTERS 56–60

1. In 972/1564, Riḍwān Pasha, governor-general of the highland province, one of the two provinces into which Yemen had been divided, had increased the tax in Wadi al-Sirr, east of Ṣan'ā', and had imposed tax on the Ismā'īlī community, until then exempt. This grievance had been exploited by Muṭahhar and became the pretext for his rebellion. (al Nahrawālī, 166–7.)

2. This probably refers to the Muṣṭafā Rumūzī who composed the *Futūḥ-i-Yemen*, a versified chronicle of the campaign with 104 coloured illustrations, in the possession of the manuscripts library of the University of Istanbul which at the time of writing is closed to the public. One of the illustrations appears as Plate 101 in Serjeant, *San'ā'*, and shows the incident, described on [391], when the prisoners try to break out of jail in Ṣan'ā' to join Muṭahhar's general, Qaṭrān.

3. This would apply to the weekly sermon, delivered on Friday; and also to those given on ceremonial occasions such as 'Īd al-Fītr.

4. By al-Ẓāhir is meant the whole region east of an imaginary line drawn between Ṣan'ā' and Ṣa'dah, perhaps even stretching across further to the west. (G. R. Smith, 217.) Al-Ṭawīlah

had been important to the Turks throughout their occupation (see Chapters 51–55, n. 44 above). This strategic area would allow the Turks control over the routes to the west and the north.

5. Al-Nahrawālī's dates for this exchange of letters are a bit awry since Muṭahhar's letter (see [429] above) post-dates Sinān's reply (20 Dhū al-Ḥijjah/26 May and 15 Dhū al-Ḥijjah/ 21 May). See n. 6 below.

6. No date is mentioned here for Sinān's return to Ṣan'ā'. Yaḥyā b. Ḥusayn, whose dates for this campaign in the north at least are earlier, has Sinān leaving Jawshān by Dhū al-Qa'dah/ April/May, and then, after a period in al-Munaqqab, moving to Ṣan'ā' on 17 Dhū al-Ḥijjah/ 23 May. (Yaḥyā b. Ḥusayn, 742.) According to al-Nahrawālī, the truce with Muḥammad was confirmed only on 10 Dhū al-Ḥijjah/16 May. Yaḥyā b. Ḥusayn, however, states that Muṭahhar visited Kawkabān, before his own truce and after Sinān had left Jawshān for al-Munaqqab, and that Muḥammad told Sinān that truce could be concluded with Muṭahhar only when, as agreed, he had moved to Ṣan'ā'. (Yaḥyā b. Ḥusayn, 742.) A reasonable inference, therefore, is that, once truce with Muḥammad was concluded, the siege was raised and Sinān moved to al-Munaqqab, say, in al-Nahrawālī's time-frame, after 10 Dhū al-Ḥijjah/16 May, on about 14 Dhū al-Ḥijjah/20 May.

7. For comment on Behrām see n. 19 below.

8. Two provinces of the Ottoman empire. Wān, to the north of Diyār Bakr, is on the Armenian plateau, on the eastern shore of Lake Wān and gives its name to a province including Mosul of which the governor-general would be a pasha with two horsetails, like Yemen. It was often a bone of contention between Persia and Turkey. The Circassian Iskandar Pasha was made governor-general there in 955/1548.

9. See [345] above.

10. Resonances of the Quran. Sūrah XXXIII, 10. When eyes grew wild and 'hearts reached to the throats'.

11. The pass leading northwards to Ibb and the Ba'dān district. Behrām's movements are corroborated b Yaḥyā b. Ḥusayn who adds that the tribesmen who attacked him in al-Qā'idah came from the Ḥujariyyah district to the south of Ta'izz. (Yaḥyā b. Ḥusayn, 742.) Presumably there must have been other tribesmen with whom to muster in the passes to Ba'dān and Ibb.

12. A further sign of how desperate the situation was for the Turks as they negotiated truce with Muḥammad b. Shams al-Dīn and Muṭahhar.

13. Either there were Zaydī on Naqīl Samārah, leading southwards towards Ibb and the Ba'dān district, or this is a mistake for Naqīl Aḥmar.

14. In this scenario the army must have crossed Naqīl Samārah and then continued southwards across Naqīl Aḥmar. They would then have escorted Behrām northwards and eastwards across to Ḥabb stronghold. Alternatively, Behrām was already at the foot of the Samārah and they simply went with him across Ba'dān to Ḥabb.

15. An allusion to the *ḥadīth* contained in the *Kitāb al-Sunan*, by Abū Dāwūd al-Sijistānī, one of the six canonical books of Tradition accepted by Sunnis. (al-Sijistānī, III, 373–4.)

16. The stronghold had been owned by Commander 'Alī al-Naẓẓārī who had been under siege for eight months by the then governor-general, Maḥmūd Pasha. With one of the Ismā'īlī Da'is acting as innocent intermediary, 'Alī had surrendered the stronghold to Maḥmūd on the understanding that he would be granted property elsewhere in its stead. He had descended with his followers on 24 Rajab 969/13 March 1562, to be summarily executed on the orders of Maḥmūd Pasha who then confiscated the stronghold. (al-Nahrawālī, 131–2.)

17. Professor Osman Sid Ahmed informs me that he was told by a Yemeni friend that this episode involving an unfortunate cat was repeated in Aden in the 1960s!

18. In this series of puns the words, with their double meanings, all emphasise the extreme height and inaccessibility of Ḥabb stronghold.

19. According to another source, more favourable to Behrām Pasha, Behrām had arrived in Buq'ah, the port near Zabīd, where he had established a Ḥanafī imam in the Great Mosque in place of the Shāfi'ī, until then in place. He had left al-Mawza' for Ta'izz on 1 Muḥarram 978/5 June 1570 with his 'army, equipment and artillery'. After a great victory over the Zaydī, he had collected reinforcements from Sinān at al-Ta'kar and put the rebels to flight. He had been inspired by God to have the arsenal in al-Ḥabb blown up and had put the stronghold under siege on 17 Rabī' al-Thānī/18 September. 'Ali's death within had been suppressed for ten days, after which the stronghold surrendered on 6 Rajab 978/4 December 1570. Behrām had then reached Dhamār on 15 Sha'bān 978/12 January 1571 where Sinān handed over the government of the country. The author then describes how the commander at al-Ḥabb had rebelled and contacted Muṭahhar but had been killed by the Turks. Behrām was to remain in Yemen for another five years. (de Sacy, 'Livre des Voeux', 512–21.)

20. Sūrah XI, 41.

21. Stuff appertaining to the kings of Persia, of brocade, or red and gold embroidered. (Serjeant, *Islamic Textiles*, 295.)

22. Sūrah CIV, 5 and 6.

23. I.e. the full pilgrimage and the lesser pilgrimage (the *'umrah*).

24. The Ottomans devised their legitimacy from the Abbasids before them and were of the Ḥanafī rite.

25. al-Ḥudaybiyyah is a village on the edge of the *Ḥaram* or sacred territory of Mecca. It was the site of an important ten-year treaty between the Prophet and the Meccans in 6/628. (*EI*, III, 539.)

26. We are told that Sayyid Ḥasan began his rule as Grand Sharīf in 973/1566 (see *EI*, VI, 150), although his father, Abū Numayy, did not die until 1584 in Nejd at the age of eighty when Ḥasan, at the age of fifty-nine, formally succeeded him. (de Gaury, 132.) Ḥasan had for many years helped his father and it is clear from this account that, by the time of Sinān Pasha's appearance in Mecca, his father, who was then about sixty-six years of age, had retired from public life. It would appear that Abū Numayy was still accorded the title of Grand Sharīf. (For more information see de Gaury, 128–32.) No mention is made here of the letter that apparently Sinān had requested the Grand Sharīf to write to the Ottoman authorities confirming his military successes in Yemen. He was reluctant to write such a letter in view of Sinān's bad behaviour when passing through Mecca on the way to Yemen. When received by the Qadi Ḥusayn in the name of the reigning sharīf, Sinān had reportedly had his horses trample over some rare and costly Chinese porcelain presented to him as a gift. Only after considerable hesitation did the Grand Sharīf (or his son, Sharīf Ḥasan) write the letter for which he was allegedly awarded half the custom dues of Mecca. Sinān was known for his harsh and uncouth behaviour. (Faroqhi, 156–7.) The incident may well have taken place over a banquet prepared in his honour where signs of Sinān's pique are glimpsed. (See [213]–[214] above.)

27. The mountain to the north-east of Mecca where the Prophet received the first verses of the Quran through the angel, Jibrīl, his constant counsellor and helper. Muḥammad is said to have spent a month each year in a cave there in religious devotion. (*EI*, II, 362–3.)

28. *Ma'mūniyyah*, a crisp pastry made with ghee and sugar and sprinkled with cinnamon, is still to be found in the countryside in north Syria. Concerning *rashīdiyyah*, I could find no certain information. It may be a sweet dish, originating in Ḥarūn al-Rashīd's time in Baghdad, perhaps containing dates. *Kilāj* is a sweet pastry made with starch wafers, filled with clotted cream, cheese etc., and flavoured with rose water. A kind of mille-feuille, it is in widespread use in the Arab world and Turkey. For much of this information concerning these dishes I am grateful to the Fakhr al-Dīn restaurant in Piccadilly, London. Original recipes for *lawzīnaj, faludhāj, muhallabiyyah* and *sikbāj* are to found in Professor Arberry's translation, *A Baghdad Cookery-Book*, 14, 26 and 50. *Muhallabiyah* now, of course, normally refers to the ubiquitous cornflower blancmange.

29. Mt Thawr, about an hour and a half's walking distance south of Mecca, is a lofty mountain on the summit of which is the cave where Muḥammad and Abū Bakr took refuge. (Burckhardt, 176.)

30. A reference to the famous long poem by the Egyptian Ṣūfī shaikh and poet, of Berber origin, Sharaf al-Dīn al-Busīrī (608–c.694/1212–94). The poem is an encomium on the Prophet Muḥammad that is held in veneration and often learnt by heart. Its verses are sometimes used as talismans. al-Burdah was the cloak worn by the Prophet which he had handed as a gift to the poet, Ka'b b. Zuhayr after reciting his ode, *Banāt Su'ād*. (*EAL* I, 163.)

31. In Burckhardt's day the apparently large mosque was a ruin. Professor Osman indicates that there is now a modern mosque on the site.

32. A term applied to Basra and Kufa.

33. A place roughly halfway between Minā and 'Arafāt where the pilgrims may spend the night between 9 and 10 Dhū al-Ḥijjah and where pebbles are collected for the stoning. Hanafis follow the Prophet's example in overnighting there. They attend a discourse in the mosque and shed copious tears. The next day they set off before sunrise and climb up through the valley of Muḥassir to Minā. (*EI* II, VII, 825; and Burton II, 201, n. 1.)

34. Sūrah II, 198.

35. A very ancient mosque, of solid structure, surrounded by a high wall within which there was a public fountain. The mosque had a colonnade with a triple row of columns on its western side. (Burckhardt, 278.)

36. Lit. *Jamrat al-'Aqabah*. The *jamrah* is used at each reference to a stoning and is applied to the place of stoning as well as to the stones. (Burton, II, 203, n. 3.) In the following paragraph al-Nahrawālī gives details of the stonings later carried out by Sinān Pasha which are more or less in accordance with the rules described by Burton as applicable to members of the Ḥanafī school. (Burton, II, 222, n. 1.)

37. The Hanafis shave only one-quarter of the head. The remainder is shaved after their visit to 'Umrah. (Burckhardt, 97.)

38. A side valley between Minā and Mecca. (Burckhardt, 59.)

39. One and a half miles from Mecca, according to Burckhardt, it is also called al-'Umrah, since the *iḥrām* is often assumed there for the lesser pilgrimage. Burckhardt speaks of its small chapel, with a small row of columns, on the road to Wadi Fāṭimah. He also gives further details of the pilgrimage. (Burckhardt, 97 and 176.)

40. I.e. one-thirtieth, as the Quran is divided into thirty parts.

41. Just beyond al-Ma'lāh, on the way to Minā.

42. The ancient name for the Bāb al-Wadā', in the southern corner, through which the pilgrim passes in taking final leave of the Ḥaram. After completion of the *'umrah* or lesser pilgrimage, Sinān left to visit the Prophet's grave in Medina and went on to Egypt.

BIBLIOGRAPHY

Encyclopaedia of Arabic Literature (*EAL*), 2 vols (London, 1998)

Encyclopaedia of Islam (*EI*), new edn (Leiden, 1960–)

Director of Overseas Survey (DOS) maps, UK Govt, *Yemen Arab Republic* 1:50,000 [YAR 50] 1979–90

Geographical section, General Staff (GS), UK maps, *South West Arabia* 1:253,440 GSGS c.1916

Albuquerque, Afonso de, *The Commentaries*, trans. from Portuguese, 4 vols (New York, 1970)

Arab Bureau, *Handbook of Yemen* (Cairo, 1917)

Arberry, A. J., *A Baghdad Cookery Book*, trans. from Arabic (London, 1939)

— *Poems of al-Mutannabī*, trans. from Arabic (Cambridge, 1967)

Ayalon, D., *Gunpowder and Firearms in the Mamluk Kingdom* (London, 1956)

Beeston, A. F. L., *Selection from the Poetry of Bashshār* (Cambridge, 1977)

Blackburn, J. R., 'The Collapse of Ottoman Authority in Yemen 968/1560–976/1568', *Die Welt des Islam, n.s.* 19 (1979)

— 'The Ottoman Penetration of Yemen: An Annotated Translation of Özdemür Bey's Fethnâme for the Conquest of Ṣan'ā'', *Archivum Ottomanicum* 6 (1980)

Blunt, Wilfrid Scawen, *The Seven Golden Odes of Pagan Arabia*, trans. from Arabic (London, 1903)

Bradford, Ernle, *The Great Siege* (London, 1974)

Bridge, A., *Suleiman the Magnificent* (London, 1983)

Brouwer, C. G., *Cowha and Cash: The Dutch East India Company in Yemen, 1614–1655* (Amsterdam, 1988)

Burckhardt, John Lewis, *Travels in Arabia* (London, 1829)

Burton, Richard F., *Personal Narrative of a Pilgrimage to al-Madinah and Mecca*, mem. edn, 2 vols (London, 1893)

Carman, W. Y., *History of Firearms from Earliest Times to 1914* (London, 1955)

Cragg, K., *The Call of the Minaret* (Oxford, 1956)

Daftari, Farhad,*The Isma'ilis: Their History and Doctrines* (Cambridge, 1990)

Danvers, F. C., *The Portuguese in India* (London, 1894)

Eagle, A. B. D. R., 'al-Hādī Yaḥyā b. al-Ḥusayn b. al-Qāsim', *New Arabian Studies* 2 (1994)

Farah, Caesar, 'Yemen Fortification and the Second Ottoman Conquest', *Proceedings of the Seminar for Arabian Studies* 20 (1990)

Faroqhi, Suraiya, *Pilgrims and Sultans* (London, 1994)

Gaury, Gerald de, *Rulers of Mecca* (London, 1951)

Golvin, Lucien and Marie Christine Fromont, *Thula Architecture et Urbanisme d'une cité du haute montagne en république arabe du Yémen* (Paris, 1984)

Goodwin, Godfrey, *The Janissaries* (London, 1997)

Guillaume, Alfred (ed. and trans.), *The Life of Muhammad* (Oxford, 1955)

Hamdānī, al-Ḥasan al-, *Sifat jazīrat al-ʻarab*, ed. M. A. al-Ḥawālī (Riyadh, 1974)

Hammer, J. de, *Histoire de l'Empire Ottoman*, 16 vols (Istanbul, 1999)

Hathaway, Jane, 'Mamluk Households', in T. Philip and U. Haarmann (eds), *The Mamluks in Egyptian Politics and Society* (Cambridge, 1988)

Hattox, Ralph S., *Coffee and Coffeehouses* (Seattle and London, 1988)

Ḥimyarī, 'Abdullāh Muḥammad al-, *al-Rawḍ al-muʻṭār fī khabar al-aqṭār* (Beirut, 1984)

Ḥusayn, Yaḥyā Ibn, *Ghāyat al-amānī fī akhbār al-yamānī*, vol. II, ed. Dr S. A. Āshūr (Cairo, 1968)

nalcik, Halil, *An Economic and Social History of the Ottoman Empire*, vol. I (Cambridge, 1999)

Jourdain, John, *The Journal of John Jourdain 1608–1617*, Hakluyt 2 s., ed. William Foster (Cambridge, 1895)

Kay, H. C., *Yaman* (London, 1892)

Kerr, Robert, 'English East India Company' in *A General History and Collection of Voyages and Travels*, Vol. VIII (Edinburgh, 1813)

Lane, E. W., *Arabic English Lexicon* (London, 1863)

Lesure, M., 'Un document ottoman de 1525 sur L'Inde Portugaise et les pays de la Mère Rouge', *Mare Luso-Indicum* III (1976)

Manẓūr Ibn, *Lisān al-'Arab*, 15 vols (Beirut, 1955)

Maqḥafī, Ibrāhīm Aḥmad al-, *Muʻjam al-buldān wa al-qabā'il al-yamaniyyah* (Ṣan'ā', 1988)

Marsigli, L. F., *Stato Militare dell' Imperio Ottamanno*, 2 vols (The Hague, 1732)

Nahrawālī, Quṭb al-Dīn Muḥammad b. Aḥmad al-, *al-Barq al-yamānī fī al-fatḥ al-'uthmānī*, ed. Ḥamad al-Jāsir (Riyadh, 1967)

Niebuhr, Carsten, *Travels through Arabia*, trans. Robert Heron, 2 vols, (Edinburgh, 1792)

Norris, H. T., with F. W. Penney 'The Historical Development of Aden's Defences' *Geographical Journal* 121, 1 (1955)

Öz, Tahsīn, *Turkish Textiles and Velvets* (Ankara, 1950)

Pickthall, Marmaduke, *Said the Fisherman* (London, 1986)

Playfair, R. L., *A History of Arabia Felix or Yemen* (Farnborough, 1970)

Redhouse, J. W., *Turkish and English Lexicon* (Constantinople, 1890)

Rihani, Ameen, *Arabian Peak and Desert: Travels in Al-Yaman* (London, 1930)

Roque, Jean de la, 'Sir H. Middleton's Journey from Mokha to Sanaa', in *Voyage to Arabia*, trans. from French (London, 1732)

Sacy, A. J. Silvestre de, 'La Foudre du Yemen', *Notices et Extraits des Manuscripts de la Biblioteque Nationale* 4 (Paris, 1788)

— 'Le Livre des voeux accomplis ou Histoire du government de Behram', *Notices et Extraits des Manuscripts de la Bibliothèque Nationale* 4 (Paris, 1788)

Ṣaliḥiyyah, M. I., 'New Documents for Sinān Pasha Expedition to Yemen', *Annals of the Faculty of Arts, Kuwait University* 8 (1986–87)

Scott, Hugh, *In the High Yemen* (London, 1942)

Serjeant, R. B. *Material for a History of Islamic Textiles up to the Mongol Conquest Vols IX–XVI*, reprinted from *Ars Islamica* (1951)

— 'The Zaydis', in A. J. Arberry (ed.), *Religion in the Middle East: Three Religions in Concord and Conflict*, vol. 2 (Cambridge, 1969)

— *The Portuguese off the South Arabian Coast* (Beirut, 1974)

Serjeant, R. B. and R. Lewcock (eds), *San'ā': An Arabian Islamic City* (London, 1983)

Sijistānī, Abū Dāwūd al-, *Mukhtaṣar sunan Abī Dāwūd*, ed. A. M. Shākir and M. H. al-Faqī, 8 vols (Beirut, 1980)

Smith, C.K., 'Kawkabān: Some of its History', *Arabian Studies* 6 (1982)

Smith, G. R., *The Ayyubids and Early Rasulids in the Yemen* (London, 1978)

Stookey, R. W., *Yemen* (Colorado, 1978)

Tibbetts, G. R., *Arab Navigation in the Indian Ocean before the Coming of the Portuguese* (London, 1971)

Varisco, Daniel Martin, *Medieval Agriculture and Islamic Science* (Seattle and London, 1994)

Waysī, Ḥusayn b. 'Alī al-, *al-Yaman al-kubrā* (Cairo, 1962)

Werdecker J., 'A Contribution to the Geography and Cartography of North-West Yemen', *Bulletin de la Société Royale de Géographie d'Égypte* 20 (1939)

Whiteway, R. S., *The Rise of Portuguese Power in India* (London, 1899)

Wilson, G. M. 'Some Important Snap Matchlock Guns', *Canadian Journal of Arms Collecting* 26, 1 (1988)

Wilson, Robert T. O., *Gazetteer of Historical North-West Yemen* (New York, 1989)

Winter, Michael, 'Ottoman Egypt 1525–1609', in Michael Daly (ed.), *The Cambridge History of Egypt*, vol. II (Cambridge, 1998)

INDEX

'Abd al-Qaddūs Sayyid, 164, 166–7
'Abd al-Raḥmān b. Sayyidī 'Alī, Efendī, 16
'Abdī Bey, 152, 154, 174
'Abdul Bey, Commander, 174
'Abdullāh, brother of 'Abd al-Qaddūs, 166
'Abdullāh al-Hamdānī, Āghā, 103
'Abdullāh b. 'Umar, 47
'Abdullāh al-Hamdānī, Dā'ī Shaikh, 9, 27–8, 55–6, 72, 73, 74, 76, 77, 92, 93–4, 97, 98, 102, 103
'Ābir b. Iram b. Sām b. Nūḥ, 132
Abṭaḥ, 187, 191
Abū Bakr al-Ja'farī, Shaikh, 28
Abū al-Dardā', 62
Abū Dāwūd b. al-Hādī, 113–14
Abū al-Fatḥ al-Yu'amarī, 47
Abū al-Naṣr, 59
Abū Numayy, Muḥammad Sayyid and Grand Sharīf of Mecca, 12, 186
Abū Sa'īd, 47
Abū Yūsuf, Imam, 47
Aden, 30, 31, 41, 42, 43, 44, 45
al-Aghbar, Mount, 6, 22, 23, 24, 26, 31, 146
Aḥmad Bey (Jitr Qīl, *sanjak* of Radā'), 101, 174
Aḥmad Bey (Kūjuk), 36–7, 136, 147–8, 150–2
Aḥmad Bey Qizilbash, 107, 115
Aḥmad al-Ṣawbāshī, 144, 145, 151–2, 154, 178
'Alī, name of two orderlies, 33
'Alī Bey, 17, 183
'Alī Bey, Shāh (Shaikh 'Alī Bey), Commander, 107, 151–4, 172
'Alī b. Abī Ṭālib, 62
'Alī b. al-Ḥusayn, 176–7
'Alī Jāwīsh, 45
'Alī b. Nushayr, 135–8, 141–6, 152
'Alī b. Sharaf al-Dīn, 63, 146, 150, 152, 154, 155, 175, 176, 178, 179, 180
'Alī b. Shuway', 24, 30, 58, 60, 82, 97, 102, 103, 104, 115, 117, 177
'Alī Jiblī Likalk, 163
'Alī Pasha, 18
al-'Alīq, 46
'Alī Ṣawbāshī, 178
'Amrān, 170
al-'Aqabah, place of stoning, 190
al-'Aqabah, stronghold, 112
'Arafāt, 46, 184, 188, 189; well of, 186
'Arār b. 'Ajil b. 'Arār al Numawī, Sayyid, 39, 183, 185
al-'Āriḍah, fort, 71–2
Ānis, mountain, 93
Arayshah, stronghold, 113
al-'Arūs, stronghold, 84, 167
Āsāf, vizier to Solomon, 26, 111
al-Ashraf Qāyitbey, Sultan, school, 39, 184–5
al-Aswad al-'Ansī, 67
al-Aswad b. 'Ufār, King of Jadīs, 133–4
al-'Attar, stronghold, 96
al-'Aydarūs, Sayyid, 45

Ba'dān district, 63, 64, 136, 146, 147, 148, 150, 154, 155, 175
Ba'dān, Mount, 57–60, 64
Badr, 16
al-Bahhāl, Sayyid, 89, 116
Baḥrānah, 53–5
Bakr al-'Aydarūs, Shaikh, 43
Bakr b. Wā'il, 119
Bālī Āghā, 150
Banū al-A'ḍab tribe, 96
Banū al-Aḥbūb tribe, 96
Banū al-'Amrān, 112
Banū al-'Awādī tribe, 94
Banū al-Azraq tribe, 94
Banū Ḥubaysh, 150
Banū Ismā'īl, 93
Banū Muḥammad tribe, 94
Banū Qawī tribe, 111
Banū al-Shadīd tribe, 94
Banū Shaqā'iq tribe, 96
Banū Sūdān tribe, 96

Banū Suwayd tribe, 96
Banū 'Ummār, sub-district of, 113
Banū Walīd tribe, 94
Barāsh, stronghold, 109
Barwayz Bey, Commander, 63, 149–50, 151, 152, 154, 174
al-Basakrī, 37
Bayt 'Izz, 88, 89, 104, 167
Behrām Pasha, 6, 38, 172, 173, 174, 175, 176–80, 181
Burckhardt, John Lewis, 4
Burāq, the Prophet Muḥammad's steed, 70
Burton, Sir Richard, 11

Da'lah stronghold, 112
al-Daḥādiḥah tribe, 94
Damt stronghold, 113
Dāthawayh al-Abnāwī, 67
al-Dawrān stronghold, 65
Ḍay'ān, wadi, 97
al-Dayba', Yemeni scholar, 3
Dayr Rijum, village, 96
Dhamār, 63, 64–5, 66, 136, 137, 149, 150, 152, 154, 155, 176, 177
Dhirā' al-Kalb, 66, 115, 136, 137, 138
Dhū Marmar, 69
Draghūd Pasha, 35
Ḍula', Mount, 102
Durām castle, 88, 91–2

Fakhr al-Dīn Muṭahhar, 162, 169
Fanad, stronghold, 64
Farḥān, General, 81–2
Faris, Nabih, 1
Fayrūz al-Daylamī, 67

Goa, 41
Gujerat, 3

Ḥabābah village, 73
Ḥabb al-'Arūs, 84–7
Ḥabb, stronghold, 63–4, 136, 146–7, 148, 149, 155, 170–1, 175, 176–80,
Ḥadda, 184
al-Hādī b. Shams al-Dīn, 115, 159
al-Hādī b. Muṭahhar, Commander, 24, 82–3
al-Ḥaḍūr, district, 137
al-Ḥaḍūr, fort, 93, 128
al-Ḥā'iṭ, village, 74
Ḥajar al-Rakānīn, fort, 104
Ḥamad al-Jāsir, 3–4, 11
Ḥamād b. Khabīr (al-Zaynī), Commander, 79, 80, 81, 183
Hamdān al-Ḥarāz, 93
Hamdān, 71
Ḥamzah, Commander, 17, 19, 23
Ḥarāz, district of, 110, 111
al-Ḥasan al-Hamdānī, 1
Ḥasan b. Abī Numayy, Sayyid, Sharīf of Mecca, 12, 16, 17, 18, 39, 182, 183, 184, 185
Ḥasan Pasha, Governor-General of Yemen, 9, 21, 28, 37, 38, 39, 59, 69–70, 72, 76–8, 82, 89, 90, 92, 93, 96–7, 97–101, 103, 104, 105, 106, 142, 159, 160, 163, 171, 174, 175, 183
Ḥasan, an interpreter, 163
al-Ḥaymah, district, 93, 111
al-Ḥazwarah, 191
Ḥidād Banī Qawī, stronghold, 111
Ḥirā', 187
Ḥisān b. Tuba', 134
Hubaynī, stronghold, 97
al-Ḥubaysh, Mount, 55, 56
Ḥudaybiyyah, 185
Ḥusayn Āghā, 22
Ḥusayn al-Mālikī, Sayyid Qadi and Shaikh al-Islam, 16, 17, 39, 184, 185, 187
Ḥusayn b. Abū Bakr al-Ḥusaynī, Qadi, 182
Ḥusayn b. Shams al-Dīn, 24, 115
Ḥusayn Bey, 108
Ḥusayn, Commander, Sīnan Pasha's nephew, appointed governor of Aden, 44–5
Ḥusayn, Sayyid (Sharīf), 16, 17, 39, 183, 184
al-Ḥusayniyyah, 39
Huzaylah, daughter of Māzin, 132

Ibb, 57, 58, 63, 148, 150
Ibn Fatḥūn, 47
Ibrāhīm Bey, 183
Ibrāhīm ibn al-Ṣabāḥ, 71
Idrīs the one-eyed, 54
'Imlūq, King of Ṭasm, 132–4
Iskandar Pasha the Circassian, Governor-General of Egypt, 142, 153, 172

al-Ja'āfirah tribe, 94
Jabal al-Raḥmah, 189
Jābir b. 'Abdullāh al-Anṣārī, 46, 47, 89
Jābir b. 'Āmir, minister to Muḥammad b. Shams al-Dīn, 89
Jadīs tribe, 132–4
al-Jālid, fortress, 96
Janad, garrison, 55

Janissaries, 10, 14, 77
Jawf, district, 118, 122
Jawshān, camp at, 9
Jiblah, 52, 53, 63, 112, 136, 148, 150
Jiddah, 30, 182, 184
Jīzān, 4, 20, 21, 38, 112

Kadūk Farhād, 51–2
al-Kāhil, fortress, 96
Kamāl al-Dīn Abū al-Faḍl b. Abī ʿAlī, Khwājā, 18, 185
Kamarān, island, 21
Kawkabān, stronghold, 4, 6, 9, 10, 11, 19, 71, 72, 73, 76, 77, 78, 80, 84, 85, 87, 88, 89, 92, 96, 102, 103, 104, 105–8, 109, 113, 114, 116, 123, 124, 126, 136, 142, 143, 150, 152, 155, 157–9, 160, 163, 166
Kawkabān, Mount, 97, 99, 103, 104
Kaylān Bey, 183
Khabt Kulayyah, 16
Khadid fort, 9, 55–7
Khawlān, 68–9
al-Khayf, mosque, 190
Khayr al-Dīn (Qūrt Öghlū), 30, 41, 42, 43, 44, 136, 180; alias Khiḍr Bey, Admiral, 146, 148–50, 151
Khiḍr Bey, 139
Kisrā, 66
Kulābī Bey, Commander, 155–7

Lawth b. Iram b. Sām b. Nūḥ, 132
al-Lawz, Mount, 139, 140, 141, 143, 144, 145
Liʿsān, 152, 153
al-Lubākhah, fort, 71–2
al-Lu'lu'ah, village, 93
Luṭfallāh b. Muṭahhar, 24, 54, 55, 56, 58, 60, 69, 82–3

Madal, village, 91
Maḍraḥ, sub-district of, 113
al-Mafjar, 18
Maḥmūd Bey, nephew to Muṣṭafā Pasha (Qarah Shāhīn), 107, 183
Maḥmūd Bey al-Kurdī, Commander, 17, 63, 73–4, 77, 96, 100, 103, 146, 147, 148, 150, 151
Maḥmūd Pasha, former Governor-General of Yemen, 177, 188
Maḥmūd, Commander (Kūlah), 17, 23–4, 170, 174
al-Majādīn tribe, 94
Mājin, pool, 16–17
al-Maʿlāh, 39, 189
Malkān, 39
Malta, 34–5
Māmāy, Commander (*kāshif*), 17, 31, 41, 42, 43, 44, 68–9, 137, 183, 186
Māshiq, husband to Huzaylah, 132
Masjid al-Qāʿah, 46, 48
al-Maṣnaʿah stronghold, 96
Masrūq b. Abraha, 66
Mawzaʿ, town in Tihāmah, 30
Maytam, 40–1, 46, 48
Mecca, 1, 3, 4, 10, 12, 15, 16, 17, 18, 38, 39, 45, 165, 182, 184, 185, 186, 188, 190
Medina, 1, 4, 39, 191
Meḥmed Pasha, Grand Vizier in Istanbul, 2, 36
al-Mikhraf, 103
Minā, 190
al-Miqrānah, fortress, 113
Mocha, 30, 31, 152, 153, 154, 182
Muʿadʿid, fortress, 112
Muʿāwiyah, 47
al-Mudawwarah, stronghold, 64
al-Muftaraq, 185
Muḥammad b. ʿIzz al-Dīn, 129
Muḥammad b. al-Hasān al-ʿAyyānī, Sayyid, 158–9, 162–3, 168, 169
Muḥammad b. Isḥāq, 66
Muḥammad b. Raḍī al-Dīn, 97, 98
Muḥammad b. Saʿīd al-Madallī, 91, 92
Muḥammad b. Shams al-Dīn, 6, 9, 58, 60, 71, 78, 89, 97, 102, 103, 104, 107, 108, 115, 116, 143, 156–7, 158–9, 160–7, 168, 170, 171
Muḥammad b. Sharaf al-Dīn, 156–7
Muḥammad b. Yūnis, 185
Muḥammad, the Prophet, 9, 67, 130–1, 187–8
Muḥṣab, 190
Muḥyī al-Dīn Efendī b. Ḥājī Ḥasan Zādah, 184
Muḥyī al-Dīn Muḥammad b. Khiḍr Shāh b. Muḥammad b. Ḥājī Ḥasan Efendī, 189
al-Munaqqab, stronghold, 70, 73, 92
Muntaṣir al-Muraysī, Shaikh, 91, 92
Murād Bey, secretary, 188
Murād Pasha, 2, 46, 91, 107, 108, 113, 115, 148
Muṣṭafā al-Nashshār, 129
Muṣṭafā Bey, 15
Muṣṭafā Bey al-Rumūzī, 3, 170
Muṣṭafā Bey b. Ayyār Pasha, 81, 183

Muṣṭafā Lālā Pasha, 2, 15
Muṣṭafā Pasha (Qarah Shāhīn), 38, 61, 107, 172, 181
Muṣṭafā Pasha b. Isfindiār, 35
Muṭahhar b. Sharaf al-Dīn, Zaydī leader in Yemen, 2, 6, 9, 11, 12, 20, 24, 26–30, 31, 32, 41–2, 45, 55, 56, 58, 62, 64, 65, 66, 67, 68, 70, 74, 78–9, 80, 81, 82–3, 84, 85, 86, 87, 89, 91, 95, 96, 97, 103, 104, 108, 109, 113, 114, 116, 118–19, 120, 122, 123, 125, 126, 127, 128, 130–2, 134–5, 137, 138, 140, 145, 146, 148, 164, 167–71, 180
al-Mutanabbī, Abū al-Ṭayyib, 110, 121, 135–6
Muzdalifah, 189

Nābighah al-Dhubyānī, 119
al-Nādirah, 113
Nahād, stronghold, 111
Najmī Muḥammad Bey, 15
Namirah, mosque, 189
Naqīl Aḥmar, 40, 45, 48, 172, 173, 174, 175
Naqīl Samārah, 152, 154, 155, 174
Nāṣir b. al-Ḥusayn, Sayyid, 116, 117
Naṣr, lieutenant of horse, 80
al-Naẓẓārī, 63
Nūr al-Dīn ʻAlī b. Durrāj b. Hujjār al-Ḥasanī, Sayyid, 16
al-Nuzaylī, Shaikh ʻAbd al-Qādir, 95

Özdemir Pasha, 162

Qabḍān, fortress, 112
al-Qāhirah, citadel to Taʻizz, 4–6, 21, 22, 26–9, 31, 34, 40, 56, 71, 74, 146, 152, 154
Qā'id Muḥammad b. ʻAqabah, 20
al-Qāʻidah, 39, 40, 41, 44, 54, 172
Qarah Kawz Bey, 108, 141–2, 143–5, 151, 152, 154
Qarāqūsh, Fatimid governor of Egypt, 147
Qarn al-Masjid fortress, 94
Qāsim, captain of guard at Bayt ʻIzz, 89
Qāsim al-Bawṣnawī, Commander, *sanjak* of Jiddah, 18, 184, 186
Qāsim b. Shuwayʻ, 30, 41, 42, 43, 44, 45
Qaṭrān, 67–8, 135, 137–8, 140–1, 142, 143, 144, 145, 146, 152
Qaylah, fortress of, 113
Qayt Āghā, Commander, 81
al-Qillah, route, 103
Qizilbash Meḥmed Bey, 107
al-Qufl, fortress, 113
al-Qunfidhah, 182
Qūrt Öghlū Sinān Bey, 41, 148–50
Quṭb al-Dīn al-Nahrawālī, 3–4, 9, 10

Rābigh, 16
Radāʻ, district, 113, 152, 155, 177
Rājid, fortress, 113
Rawman, stronghold, 111
Raymān, fortress, 113
Riḍwān Pasha b. Muṣṭafā Pasha, 169, 189
Riyāḥ b. Murrah al-Ṭasmī, 134
al-Riyyaʻ, 185

Sabīl al-Jawkhī, spring, 16, 189, 191
Ṣabyā, 21
Saʻd b. Ḥibnah, 47
Ṣaʻdah, stronghold, 118, 122, 170, 180
al-Saʻdiyyah, 20, 39
al-Ṣafā, 185
Ṣafar Bey, Admiral, 43, 151–3
Ṣafar Bey, Captain, 151–3
Sahl Bāqir, 96
Saladin, 1
al-Ṣalāḥ, Dāʻī, Commander, 26–9, 74
Salāmah b. al-Khabīr, Commander, 17
al-Sallam, pool, 186
Sallāq Aḥmad, Commander, 183, 186
Samārah, 64–5
Ṣanʻā', 27, 31, 40, 45, 63, 64, 65, 66, 67, 68, 70, 107, 136, 137, 138, 139–41, 143, 144, 145, 158, 164, 166, 167, 171, 175, 176
Sānah, fortress, 113
Sanḥān, district of, 137, 143
al-Sarrāj, a headman, 20
Sayf b. Dhī Yazan, 66
Selīm b. Sulaymān (Selīm II), 2, 189, 67
Shabakah, valley, 57
al-Shabīkah, 185
Shakhab, fortress, 113
al-Shamāḥī, Mount, 60, 63
Shamāt stronghold, 105, 106, 155–7, 167
Shams al-Dīn al-Saʻūdī, Qadi Muḥammad, 160–3
Shams al-Dīn b. Sharaf al-Dīn, 6, 115
Shamsān fort, 43
al-Shāqah, 184
Sharaf al-Dīn Abū al-Qāsim b. Qarqamāsh, 182–4
Sharaf al-Dīn, Imam, 2, 9, 129
al-Shawāfī, 148, 150
Shem, son of Noah, 66
Shibām al-Yuʻfir (Shibām Ḥarāz), 110

Shibām, castle and town, 11, 70–2, 91
Shukr, Captain, 43
Sinān Pasha, Minister and Commander-in-Chief in Yemen, 1, 2–3, 4, 6, 9, 10, 12, 15, 16, 17, 18, 20, 21, 22, 23, 24, 25, 26, 28, 29, 30, 36, 38, 39, 41, 51, 52, 53, 54, 56, 57, 58, 59, 61, 63, 64, 65, 66, 67, 68, 69, 70–1, 71–2, 73, 74–5, 76, 77, 78, 80, 82, 83, 84, 85, 86, 87, 88, 89, 90, 91, 92, 94, 95, 96, 99, 103, 104, 105, 106, 107, 108, 110, 111, 113, 114, 116, 117, 120, 121, 122, 123, 124, 125, 126, 127, 128, 129, 135, 136, 138, 139, 141, 142, 143, 144, 145, 146, 148, 149, 151, 152, 153, 154, 155–6, 157, 158, 159, 160, 161, 163, 164, 165, 169, 171, 172, 173, 174–5, 176, 177, 178, 180, 181–91
Siwwān, Mount, 102
Suḥbān, sub-district of, 113
Sulaymān, Sultan, 3, 34–5, 93, 166, 187, 189
Sūq al-Qifāf, 94

Ta'īzz, 21, 22, 23, 29, 31, 33, 38, 39, 40, 44, 55, 77, 136, 146, 147–8, 149, 152, 154, 172
al-Ta'kar, fort, 49, 52, 53–4, 136, 148, 149, 152, 154
Ṭabarī, 47
al-Tan'īm, 190, 191
Taqī al-Dīn al-Fāsī al-Mālikī, Sayyid, 134
Ṭasm, tribe, 132–3
al-Ṭawīlah, 167, 170
al-Ṭawīlah, district, 109
Tays, Mount, 94, 95, 109, 155, 167
Ṭayy', 134
Thawr, Mount, 187, 188
Thulā district, 4, 19, 68, 85
Thulā, Mount, 65, 66, 68, 72, 75, 76, 78, 79, 82, 83, 85, 87, 88, 92, 102, 103, 108, 109, 114, 116, 119, 120, 121, 123, 125, 126, 130, 145, 152, 171
Thunaynah, fortress, 112
Turbah, route, 103
Turk Māmāy, 139–41
Turyādah village, 101–2

'Umar b. Yazīd, 47
'Udayn, 112
Usfān, 16
'Uthmān b. 'Abdullāh b. Yazīd b. Ḥārithah, 47
'Uthmān Pasha, Governor-General of Yemen, 21, 24, 25, 32, 33, 34, 36, 37, 38, 39, 142
'Ufayrah, daughter of 'Ufār al-Jadīsī, 133–4
Urayq Ḥasan Bey, 107–8

Wadi Bawn, 74
Wadi al-Ḥaymah, 96
Wadi Khubān, 46, 88, 91, 92
Wadi Maytam, 46, 49
Wadi Sahūl, 64
Wadi al-Sirr, 69
Wadi Suḥbān, 40, 45, 48
Wadi Yarīm, 65
Wahriz, 66–7
Waṣāb, sub-district of, 112, 113

Yaḥyā b. Ḥusayn, Yemeni chronicler, 9
Yaḥyā, a member of the *jāwīshiyyah*, 139
Yamāmah, district, 132
Yanā', 93
Yanbu', coastal town, 16, 39, 129
Yāqūt al-Ḥibshī, 163
Yarīm, district of, 113, 154, 155
Yathrib, 165

Zabīd, 4, 21, 28, 36–8, 44, 82, 152, 153, 171, 172
al-Ẓafir, stronghold, 84
al-Ẓāhir, district, 170
Zayd b. Arqam, 47
Zayn al-Dīn al Jazayrī al-Ḥanbalī, Qadi, 147
Ẓifrān, fortress, 112